The Progressive Rock Files

Jerry Lucky

All rights reserved under article two of the Berne Copyright Convention (1971). No part of this book may be reproduced or transmitted in any form or by any means, electronic or mechanical, including photocopying, recording, or by any information storage and retrieval system without permission in writing from the publisher.
We acknowledge the financial support of the Government of Canada through the Book Publishing Industry Development Program for our publishing activities.
Published by Collector's Guide Publishing Inc., Box 62034, Burlington, Ontario, Canada, L7R 4K2
Printed and bound in Canada by Webcom Ltd of Toronto
The Progressive Rock Files/ Jerry Lucky
ISBN 1-896522-70-X (2nd Edition 2000)
ISBN 1-896522-10-6 (1st Edition 1998)
Cover Art - Robert Godwin
Back cover poster courtesy Vernon Fitch - The Pink Floyd Archives

The Progressive Rock Files

by
Jerry Lucky

Updated Edition 2000

Dedication

...to my wife Sue who tolerated my time at the computer, to my daughter Rachel who had her musical tastes challenged while playing in my office ... and to all the friends I've come to know around the world who also share a love of progressive rock music.

Acknowledgements

There are so many people who need to be thanked. Since 1983, when the idea for this book first came about, I've met a lot of great people who've each helped in their own way to completing this edition. While it's impossible to remember everyone there are some key people who were there at the very beginning...Angel Romero, for his synopsis of Spanish bands, Ronnie Larkins for the information supplied through his fanzine **Exposure**, Sergio Antonio Lucindo for what he was able to supply on South American bands. Also a big thank you goes out to Francis Grosse and Bernard Gueffier and their excellent work, **La Discographie Du Rock Francais.**

It would not have been possible to put together the band listing without the help of Stephen Roberts at ZNR, Greg Walker at Syn-phonic, as well as Archie Patterson at Eurock. Their catalogues provided in many cases the initial comments of many of the bands in the A - Z listing. Those initial listings and musical descriptions were greatly enhanced with the help of Peter Thelen and the gang at **Expose**, John Collinge at **Progression** and Tierry Sportouche at **Acid Dragon**. These publications and others were invaluable.

Many of the quotes used come from personal interviews conducted with: Marillion, Genesis (Tony Banks), The Enid (Stephen Stewart), Tamarisk, Pendragon, Pallas, IQ (Pete Nichols & Martin Orford), Twelfth Night, Jethro Tull (Ian Anderson), Terraced Garden (Carl Tafle), Supertramp, Crack The Sky (John Palumbo), Kansas (Phil Ehart), Saga, Klaatu, FM, Cano, Northstar, Asia (John Wetton), Bill Bruford, Keith Goodwin, Eddy Offord and many others.

And last but not least my gratitude to all the gang at CG Publishing for their vision and assistance in getting my labour of love published. In particular thanks to Ric Connors for accepting my phone call and Robert Godwin who painstakingly went through the manuscript offering many insightful suggestions. To them and to the journalists, fans and anyone else who ever wrote about progressive rock or in any way provided me with some bit of information, THANK YOU.

Introduction

It's doubtful you would ever find a book that spoke disparagingly about reggae music or jazz. It's highly unlikely that you would find someone writing negatively about folk or even pop music. In fact you might even be hard pressed to find anyone who would take shots at punk rock or alternative these days. No, for the most part you can go up and down the list of music genres from ambient to zydeco and have difficulty finding a negative word about virtually any. That is until you come to progressive rock.

The mere mention of the phrase "I like progressive rock" music is likely to bring cries of derision, howls of laughter, verbal abuse and more than likely, all of the above. The 1995 edition of **The All Music Guide to Rock** says *"Devotees of progressive rock have to fend off more vilification than fans of almost any other rock genre."* It's strange that a form of musical composition can provoke such an unwarranted response. I've never been able to understand why, but it does.

My own discovery of progressive rock music occurred in the late sixties. I have never been a "hippie", nor have I particularly been taken with much of the "hippie" ethic. I was raised in a more practical environment and thought they should all go out and get a job, which in the end they did. But I did come from a musical family, and it was the music that eventually caught my attention. My upbringing included a valuable spiritual element as well, so I was immediately attracted to much of the philosophical nature of progressive rock lyrics. The local university FM radio station began playing some rather exciting things like Pink Floyd, King Crimson and Black Sabbath all of which sounded very different to my ears. At the time I was listening to The Beatles, Jimi Hendrix, The Doors, The Monkees, Paul Revere and The Raiders, nothing very progressive, but the new things I was hearing on the FM radio really caught my attention. When I started working at the local radio station in late 1970, I remember sitting waiting to go on-air one night and being quite taken with the cover of Pink Floyd's **Atom Heart Mother**. Sometime before I had purchased **Ummagumma** on the strength of the Pink Floyd name and it's unusual cover. In 1973 at the age of 19, while sifting through LPs at a small record shop one day I remember being impressed with the cover artwork of **Yessongs**. I hadn't heard the band but again was really taken with the cover and bought it. Strangely enough I didn't listen to the music for some months. I lent it out to a close friend a few months later who remarked what a fantastic record it was, so I quickly put it on and was amazed at what I heard. I remember being held spellbound as I listened to every note, the dynamics, the changing nature of the songs, the keyboards orchestrated symphonic sound and mostly the power behind songs like "Starship Trooper". I quickly went on a Yes buying spree, looking for anything by the band. Another friend said if you like Yes, try listening to Genesis but at the time my own listening skills were still developing and after Yes I found Genesis too sparse, too acoustic and perhaps too folksy. It wasn't until a year later while on holidays in another record shop I heard some rather interesting keyboard work and the line in the song went; "Selling England by the pound..." I rushed to the clerk to ask what was playing. "Genesis" she responded, and I wondered what I'd missed all along. It was clearly me and not the music. And so it went with many bands and different styles.

This book is very much the personal journey I have taken to discover and come to appreciate symphonic progressive rock music. From 1979 through to 1984 I was hosting a progressive rock radio program and each week I would expose many new artists to listeners. The program included as much biographical material on each band as I could find.

Unfortunately, in so many cases there was virtually nothing. Around 1982 I got fed-up and decided that since there was no book about progressive rock available, I should write one. That was the start of this volume. After over a decade there are only a few books written about progressive rock music. In fact other than my own, only two books, **Rocking The Classics** by Edward Macon and **The Music's All That Matters: A History of Progressive Rock** by Paul Stump have been published devoted exclusively to progressive rock. Some good books have been written about specific bands or artists like Yes and Genesis. Some of these books contain valuable personal history or a good sense of musical development in the early years of prog. Other general music books usually only contain a passing mention of the genre, if anything at all. Few claim to write about what it is, why it is and include a comprehensive listing of the bands with descriptive notes. That is what I've attempted to do here.

I also hope to show how progressive rock music has never really gone away or disappeared. Nor is it a form of musical composition that can be classified as a seventies thing. In fact since the late sixties it's always been with us in some form or other. It might rightfully be referred to as something from the seventies only because that's the period where it fully matured into a genre.

While the previous (3rd) edition focused on providing an expanded A-Z listing of bands, this 4th edition has been radically changed to give more of a sense of history and timeline to progressive rock. In fact the front half of the book has more than doubled in size. It still doesn't mention every band who ever played progressive rock, although there are many famous and many obscure bands mentioned. I have selectively gone through the years picking up on ideas, people, bands, events or albums that in some cases may have made a significant impact or for some reason may have gone unnoticed. In virtually every case you'll be able to find the bands described in the A-Z listing. My objective has been to de-mystify, analyse, define, categorise, and celebrate a wonderfully inventive and yet much maligned rock genre. Along the way we'll also make some attempt to put into perspective the criticism that has been levelled at progressive rock music.

This volume contains even more quotations than previous editions and that's done, as before, for a purpose. It seemed that since so many have voiced (in the printed word) their opinions for or against progressive rock, those words should be read by others. I've chosen this method as well as included a bibliography of the material I've used for research. It is my hope the quotations will help to set the proper context and attitude of the performer, writer or critic.

This 4th edition of **The Progressive Rock Files** has been extensively rewritten in an effort to satisfy two groups of fans. One, the aficionado who may know a lot of the history and many of the recordings listed, and two, the newcomer who may have only recently discovered progressive rock. The genre's seasoned veteran may discover bits of information they missed along the way or perhaps a band that they've neglected. The newcomer may enjoy reading about the music's past and how it came into being and most certainly will enjoy the comprehensive listing to aid in their recording quest.

File #1 deals with the history of prog. As I go year by year, I've stopped to insert short bios of some famous and some not-so-famous bands, as well as additional analyses to the events of the day. For example I discuss what musical influences were most influential to prog or why Asia missed the mark in terms of progressive rock. It's impossible to list every single LP or CD released each year, but what I've tried to do is give a relatively comprehensive overview of the year, touching on some of the interesting prog moments and reactions. I've also attempted to give more of a global picture, indicating events and releases in countries other than just Britain or the United States. While I believe that progressive rock music is a distinctly British genre, it has influenced musicians around the world. Their musical input should not be omitted.

File #2 tackles the thorny question of defining what progressive rock is. Like all forms of music, progressive rock has its fans and followers. As a matter of fact when taken into the global context progressive rock has quite a large following. Why else would you be able to find complete web sites on the Internet devoted to bands like Gentle Giant. Yet many have taken it upon themselves in crusade-like fashion to ridicule and criticise this particular form of music. The point of this book is to demonstrate that progressive rock music is a definable form of music, much the same way rap, country, folk or reggae are. I suggest by the definition detailed in the pages that follow, musicians can set out to create progressive rock music the same way a composer would sit down intentionally to write any kind of musical form. The composer creates within certain parameters that help define and preserve the form. This is something very different from labelling someone a progressive artist, and this must be borne in mind throughout. There are obviously progressive artists in all forms of music, but they don't all create progressive rock.

File #3 takes on the critics and their myopic attacks. It's obvious most critics didn't understand what progressive rock was all about. Few of them even tried. I have collected critical articles and fan responses over the years and in this file take a close look at what was said, how valid the criticism was and more than anything show how off the mark many of the critics comments were.

File #4 sums up where progressive rock has been, and where it is today with some helpful addresses. We talk about where to find out about progressive rock in the printed word and on the Internet. Finally this file summarises the state of progressive rock with an eye to it's future.

File #5 is in many ways a book unto itself containing an A - Z listing of over 1400 progressive rock bands. This fourth edition also includes a relatively complete but selective discography. The rationale for the bands included or the bands missing is outlined in the introduction to that section so there is no need to go through it here.

Like any book of this nature it will fail miserably to satisfy some, who will feel parts of the text are pointless or even wrong. I have strived to make a point by defining once and for all what progressive rock is and demonstrate that point by incorporating loads of quotes, history and examples. Too many individuals in progressive rock circles seem to spend an inordinate amount of time arguing about what is or isn't progressive rock, so it's always seemed to me that in order to get past that, we need a more precise definition and to that end, I feel I have done that. If we can get beyond this point perhaps we can then begin simply enjoying the music, regardless of the category it falls into.

8   Jerry Lucky

CONTENTS

FILE #1 - The History   10

FILE #2 - The Definition   120

FILE #3 - The Critics   134

FILE #4 - Progressive Rock Today   151

FILE #5 - The A-Z Listing   164

FILE #1 - The History

"Well, that first era from about the very, very late sixties-early seventies, people like Argent, ELP, Genesis, Colosseum, Yes whatever...changed the whole face of popular music - of rock music. One day somebody'll say it in print - it won't be me, but some journalist will suddenly work out that the whole face of rock music changed with that particular era."

Keith Goodwin - Progressive Rock Publicity Agent interviewed 1983

It Started In The Underground

In the beginning, before there was anything remotely resembling progressive rock there existed the "underground" scene and it's music was psychedelic. This radical departure from the pop norm had it's British roots in London of late 1965. With the times came the official underground band, namely Pink Floyd. While this version of the band bears little resemblance to the mega-stars they were to become, they, more than any other band, epitomised the times. A period of loosening musical boundaries, implementing the use of new musical instruments and incorporating trend-setting light shows all adding a new dimension to their live performances. In this underground world of musical exploration, it was Syd Barrett, who began experimenting with his guitar. Barrett later went on to become the genre's first acid casualty, but before that happened his sonic ramblings, along with the work of others came to form progressive rock's forerunner, psychedelic rock.

Every Sunday, London's Marquee Club became the location of "The Spontaneous Underground". The first of these impromptu club-within-a-club gigs was in February of 1966. These were unusual events in that nothing was advertised, the musicians and audience just showed up to see what might happen. The first known Pink Floyd appearance was March 13th, 1966. After this relatively quiet start where Pink Floyd had the opportunity to make a name for themselves before small but dedicated audiences, things really started happening as they moved to the UFO Club which had just opened in Tottenham Court Road. The move came in December 1966. The UFO Club more than any other venue became the heart of the underground music scene in London. It was an after-hours, non-alcohol club that stayed open all night. Each night the club would be filled with an almost equal number of males and females, some tripping, some dancing but most sitting and listening attentively to the performers. The clubs intimacy allowed the audience to remain very close to the musicians and this closeness proved to be a pivotal developmental point. In attendance at UFO happenings it would not be unusual to find various jazz performers, especially ones more on the fringe of their craft. Soon the element of jazz improvisation, began finding it's way into the music of performers at the UFO Club. Improvisation would play an important part in the early psychedelic rock style. However, in a few short years this improvisation would give way to a completely structured style of composition. Musicians began listening to everything from folk artists to 20th century composers like Stockhausen and incorporating many of these diverse elements into their music.

It was out of the underground, this period of total experimentation, that barriers began to fall away, not the least of which were musical barriers. The end result was that by the end of 1966 the era of psychedelic music was in full swing. Out of this younger generation's desire to stretch out in all directions, there sprang up a form of music that went beyond simply repeating what had gone before. This music strived to be different. But as Derek Jewell in his essay **Pomp and Circumstance** points out, really for music this was not new; *"In the past, both jazz and mainstream popular music had temporarily grown tired of the limitations imposed by simple instrumental combinations. This had led, among other achievements, to George Gershwin's-Rhapsody In Blue, Duke Ellington's series of jazz suites, Mile's Davis' involvement with orchestrator Gil Evans and the experimental dissonance's of Stan Kenton as well as to complex orchestral arrangements for records by Frank Sinatra and virtually every other leading popular singer."*

Time To Break Out

Now it was rock's turn to experiment, and break down some barriers. The early underground bands like Pink Floyd were all for trying new things, not only in terms of lifestyle, but in musical style. As pointed out by David Downing in his book **Future Rock** *"They didn't synthesise styles as the Byrds had done with the Beatles and Dylan - they pioneered new music from a marriage between existing styles and the mania prevailing around them. In 1966 and 1967 these groups (underground groups) were all outrageously different, as much from each other as from the established mainstreams."*

In America psychedelia had taken over. It's estimated there were upwards of 1000 psychedelic bands in the San Francisco area alone. It was around this time we also began to see the first rock music festivals, namely the Fantasy Faire and Magic Mountain Music Festival in the bay area and two weeks later The Monterey Pop Festival. Local bay area radio station KMPX changed it's format and noted disc jockey Tom Donahue became one of the first DJs to begin playing what was then called underground music.

Meanwhile, London's principle underground newspaper The International Times, always having financial difficulties, had just been raided by the police and virtually every piece of paper on site was taken into custody. Clearly it was time for drastic action so they decided to throw a huge psychedelic fund-raising event. It would take place on April 29th at Alexandra Palace. The event was called "The 14 Hour Technicolor Dream" and performing would be many of Britain's most popular psychedelic bands including Pink Floyd, The Crazy World of Arthur Brown, Alex Harvey, Alexis Korner, The Pretty Things and The Soft Machine. Pink Floyd took to the stage just before dawn as the sky was beginning to turn pink and performed to 10,000 people who, I'm sure remember the event to this day. Fortunately the event was captured on film by legendary film-maker Peter Whitehead in his documentary "Tonight Let's All Make Love In London". Whitehead paid Pink Floyd (who were yet to sign a recording contract with EMI) £60 to provide the soundtrack to his film.

For many this event proved to be the peak of London's psychedelic period and the resulting popularity brought Pink Floyd to the attention of EMI producer Norman Smith who produced their single "See Emily Play" in June of that year.

IT

14 Hour Technicolor Dream

**Pink Floyd
Arthur Brown
Alexis Korner
Pretty Things
Soft Machine**

Peter Whitehead

The Beatles And Psychedelic Rock

**1967
Pink Floyd**

Beatles

**Paul
McCartney
John Lennon**

August 1967 saw the release of Pink Floyd's first album, **Piper At The Gates Of Dawn**. It perhaps is no coincidence that they were recording their material at EMI Studios next door to the Beatles who were working on **Sgt. Pepper's Lonely Hearts Club Band**. I say no coincidence because it was this age of experimentation that led to the Beatles producing the album some say started the whole progressive rock movement. But this is not an entirely accurate observation. While it is true that in April 1967 during the recording of **Sgt. Pepper**, Paul McCartney and John Lennon attended "The 14 Hour Technicolor Dream" at which Pink Floyd performed, there is very little concrete evidence of this style in anything other than a psychedelic-pop format that appears on that landmark disc. There is no question that **Sgt. Pepper** had a profound impact on the music world but it would clearly be overstating the mark to say it was the first progressive rock album. To get a little closer to finding that album we might be better off going just down the hallway at EMI studios to hear Pink Floyd's **Piper At The Gates Of Dawn**.

David Downing in **Future Rock** went on to comment about Pink Floyd's second album, **Saucerful Of Secrets**; "It shared much more with Beethoven's pastoral than it did with the latest chart smash, or indeed with the more academic music of the avant-garde. Beethoven though, in his attempt to evoke the countryside, had the whole orchestra to play with. The Floyd had just four of them." What was perhaps the most revolutionary aspect of their performances was the length of the songs. Record buyers were still anticipating short snappy pop tunes and were therefore shocked as Pink Floyd could play for 45 minutes and perform only four or five songs. Pink Floyd's musical approach seemed best summed up in a **Melody Maker** headline from December 1967 that screamed - "HITS? THE FLOYD COULDN'T CARE LESS."

There is no question of the influence The Beatles had on the music world after the release of each of their albums. Perhaps if they are to be credited with anything here, it was their ability to break down traditional musical barriers. Or if not break them down certainly create an acceptability for new ways of recording and producing music. While The Beatles never worked in a progressive rock format they clearly made it easier for others to do so and thereby follow in the steps of bands like Pink Floyd. Nicholas Schaffner in his book **Saucerful Of Secrets** quotes long time Floyd associate Miles, who was friends with both The Beatles and Pink Floyd as saying *"In my discussions with* him, McCartney had always been convinced that there would be a new synthesis of electronic music and studio techniques and rock 'n' roll. He didn't see the Beatles as being quite the vehicle for that. But the Pink Floyd, he thought, were the very stuff that we'd been talking about." Clearly The Beatles were a pop band that dabbled (seriously perhaps) in the world of psychedelic music, but Pink Floyd were a psychedelic band that made no bones about their musical direction.

The First Progressive Rock Album

There has been much speculation about what might truly be called the first progressive rock release. If we are to find that album we must, as best we can, place ourselves back in time. To a time where the British press first coined the phrase progressive rock and initially applied it to some very specific bands. As explained more fully later in this work, the term progressive rock has come to mean something very different than was originally intended.

While Pink Floyd created and stimulated a whole rock genre that would come to be known as space-rock, their contribution to progressive rock has never been in question. Even though in the strict sense of musical definition their music bore only a passing resemblance to what we now hear as progressive rock. That responsibility falls more correctly to The Moody Blues, with their release **Days Of Future Passed** in November of 1967. This release contained many of progressive rock's trademark elements; longer songs, changing tempos, Mellotron, use of symphonic orchestra, cosmic or philosophical lyrics, etc.. The album set the tone for what was to come in terms of symphonic scope and dynamic rock blended into one, rightly labelled the first progressive rock release.

The Moody Blues had released an album before this. They even had a significant hit single with "Go Now". Unfortunately for them, but perhaps fortunately for us, they split up and in a reforming effort convinced the record label to let them record with a small symphony. Coincidentally, the record label was trying to show off it's new stereo capability and this seemed like the right project to do it with. Little did they realise the impact the album would have on future generations. What made this music possible was the addition of Justin Hayward and John Lodge into the Moodies. Their presence cemented the direction the band would take. **Days Of Future Passed** even left it's mark on the charts with "Knights in White Satin" and "Tuesday Afternoon". The Moody Blues more than made up for originally breaking up after the first album.

Jerry Lucky

Jefferson Airplane

Cream

1968

Dylan
Beatles

Pink Floyd

Procul Harum

Keith Emerson

The Nice

PP Arnold

Brian Davison
Lee Jackson

As 1968 dawned, "mono" was being phased out in favour of the more popular "stereo" and almost 5000 new LPs were being released each year with this new recording concept. Rock was beginning to have such an impact that noted media critic Ralph Nader was going around the United States claiming it was producing a nation with impaired hearing. While Jefferson Airplane made the cover of **Life** magazine, the eight to eleven year olds were in the grip of bubblegum music from bands such as The 1910 Fruitgum Company and Ohio Express. British blues band Cream played their farewell gig at the Royal Albert Hall and the Moog Synthesiser made it's debut via Walter Carlos' **Switched on Bach**.

By the spring of 1968 the underground music scene was going through more changes. This was partly the result of the music that had already developed and partly the result of the number of art school students who were becoming interested in music as a form of expression. The underground was rapidly coming to a close, and so was the era of pure psychedelic music. However, the underground over it's short life had swallowed up the influences from the non-rock fields such as folk, jazz and of course classical. No musical form had synthesised so many other genres before. In addition as Downing states: *"Dylan and others had changed the accepted scope of lyrical content. The Beatles, Pink Floyd and others had revolutionised the potential use of studio techniques."*

At least three LPs were recorded in 1968 that contributed to the development of progressive rock. Pink Floyd released their second album in June entitled **A Saucerful Of Secrets**. Procol Harum released their second album called **Shine On Brightly** in December, but perhaps most significantly Keith Emerson who was in a band called The Nice released **Thoughts Of Emerlist Davjack** in March.

The Nice had been together since 1967, having started out as little more than a backing group for P.P. Arnold playing a mixture of British soul and R&B. Originally starting out as a four piece, Davy O'List soon departed leaving the trio of Emerson on keyboards, Brian Davison on drums and Lee Jackson on bass and vocals. The Nice became popular not only because of superb musicianship but also for their diverse selection of material, which could include everything from Dylan songs to Leonard Bernstein's "America" from **West Side Story**. They were a major event everywhere they toured in Europe, packing the halls. Unfortunately their penchant for attracting publicity led to them burning an American flag during a performance at The Royal Albert Hall, which didn't endear them to the U.S. press.

While the first release from The Nice was by no means astounding it brought the keyboard style of Keith Emerson to the fore. His on-stage antics generated a tremendous amount of press. This propelled he and the band into the spotlight. As to Pink Floyd's second release, Syd Barrett had left, and they began to compose the longer, spacier material that would be developed over the next few albums. Procol Harum, much like The Moody Blues had a previous album and had achieved quite a substantial hit with "A Whiter Shade of Pale", yet this second release began taking them into much the same direction as The Moody Blues albeit with a somewhat more sombre tone. Procol Harum's release featured the 18 minute centrepiece "In Held Twas in I", and Gary Brooker's almost narrative approach to the lyrics of Keith Reid seemed the perfect match to create visions of wonder.

Progressive Rock is Born

As the "Summer of Love", slowly slipped away, so too did psychedelia. It was during the period that existed after the demise of the underground and psychedelic rock, that the style of progressive rock we know today came into being. Specifically it occurred with the November '67 release of The Moody Blues' **Days Of Future Passed**. The underground music scene had simply run out of steam, partly because of it's attachment to a certain lifestyle, fashion statement, drugs, and more than anything because of a lack of direction. Progressive rock claimed music was it's strength, and it continued to develop as more bands appeared. Downing says, *"As the Underground community that had nurtured the Floyd dissolved, many a band followed the Floyd into experimentation. Underground music became 'progressive music'. The focus was now no longer the interaction between a lifestyle and its musical expression; it was on the music itself. "ART" crept into the arena as the other justifications slipped away. The frontiers were no longer outer space, the true self, or the values of western civilisation - they were the verse-chorus structure and 4/4 time"* There was no doubt about it; rock 'n roll was growing-up and it's true what Hibbard and Kaleialoha state in their book **The Role Of Rock** that *"rock no longer was a form communicating common ideas in a common musical code. Instead of moulding their thoughts to fit the demands of rock forms, some composers now began to manipulate the form to more suitably express their conceptualisations."*

The one event that dictated there was no turning back, was King Crimson's release of **In The Court Of The Crimson King** in October of 1969. While The Moody Blues had introduced an almost ethereal sound, King Crimson, which had just formed in January 1969, created a dense and moody environment dominated by minor notes and minor chords. King Crimson certainly played with the symphonic arrangement but it was clearly a modern jazz influence that propelled the music, sweepingly grand and majestic at one moment only to descend into a discordant climax followed by a pastoral flute. King Crimson rode the gamut of musical emotion and fans loved it. There was always something sinister about their sound. Even during the most serene passages you are left with the feeling that something dark and foreboding was just around the musical corner.

WHAT PETE TOWNSHEND THINKS ABOUT KING CRIMSON...

An uncanny masterpiece. An uncanny masterpiece. Title? Song titles? You might know more than I, but I've got the ace card cos I've the album weeks before release to review no less. What depths one has to stoop to to hear new albums before everyone else. How marvellous is the feeling when I walk in a room and say, "you haven't heard it? More's the pity!" Cos I've heard it and its fucking incredible.

But its also over careful, cautiously rampant guitar solos scream all over you but never miss a note. Silent drums drum and a million bloody mellotrons whine and soar like sirens down a canyon. Endless, or at least seemingly endless passages through extemporised classic non-effervessant secret-keeping become boring. Drums click and sniff, mellotrons breathe, unidentifiable woodwind multiplies, a voice reminiscent of a Zombie sings. Its time consuming and expensive but somehow, even if you don't get into their complex musical fantasies and indulgences you have to stand and straighten your back when out of all that comes THE COURT OF A CINSONGKRIM. ("The Ultimation" says Plum) Bob the roadie comes round, he is already a fan of KING CRIMSON and is extra eager to listen. He doesn't leave his seat until the album is finished, then, after having hung around for about two hours decides to leave. I know when he's had enough.

You must have gathered its good. Undeniably. But in some ways too good too soon if thats possible. You will only know what I'm getting at when you hear it for yourself, its akin to being a ritual it really isn't. The ritual is future worship. The adulation of unneccesary perfection. I hear it, and I know it had to cost at least ten thousand pounds to make. If they chucked out as much as I think they did in order to embrace the remainder it could have cost twenty thousand. I can't tell if its worth it.

A friend listening to the album from a room below says, "Is that a new WHO album?" Deeply I'm ashamed that it isn't, but I'm also glad somehow. That kind of intensity is music not Rock.

Twenty first century schizoid man is everything multitracked a billion times, and when you listen you get a billion times the impact. Has to be the heaviest riff that has been middle frequencied onto that black vinyl disc since Mahlers' 8th.

An American chick comes round with a friend and tells me, "They're all real musicians." I don't know where to look. I was never more aware of any other single fact.

Oh well.   YINGYANGYINGYANGYINGYANGYINGYANGYINGYANGYINGYANGYINGYANGMYGGGGGGGENERATION.
OOH and by the way, THUNDERCLAP NEWMAN. Same to you.

King Crimson

Robert Fripp

Pete Giles
Ian McDonald
Greg Lake

Justin Hayward
Graeme Edge

Rolling Stones

The roots of King Crimson start pre-1969 with the light-weight, pop effort Giles, Giles & Fripp. After failing to get any gigs what-so-ever, and receiving dismal response from anyone who heard them, Pete Giles left. Around the end of 1968 Pete's brother Mike and Robert Fripp conceived of King Crimson and added Ian McDonald on reeds and Greg Lake on bass and vocals and thus was KC born. Interestingly while they were honing their chops in various London clubs and cafés, one evening Justin Hayward and Graeme Edge of The Moody Blues came by to listen and briefly considered signing them to their newly formed Threshold label. The smaller gigs started happening but in July of 1969 King Crimson secured a spot on the Rolling Stones free concert in Hyde Park, playing before an estimated 650,000 people. Their use of Mellotrons and classical influences electrified the crowd.

The Doors

Jefferson Airplane

Grateful Dead

A whole new genre of music had come into being, the psychedelic era had petered out, and progressive rock picked up where it left off, especially in Britain. In America the psychedelic era lasted somewhat longer particularly in the San Francisco area. In the United States this particular music scene was fuelled by a much stronger political climate that impacted on the nation's youth. Political movements of all kinds sprang up overnight to "ban the bomb" or "get out of Viet Nam". The West Coast drug-induced music scene was generally more tortured and many of the bands that sprang out of the scene reflected this feeling. The psychedelic music of the West Coast tended to have more in common with boogie music and jamming. While the songs were long, they were arranged in a simple manner. Bands like The Doors, Jefferson Airplane, The Grateful Dead and dozens of others never developed into a progressive rock style but went in other directions instead. This was not the case in Britain. There, the drug-induced psychedelic scene was more whimsical, almost ethereal giving rise to music that was less vehement. In many respects the genre was more musically driven and therefore more open to other influences. There was no "political message" to dwell on, it was more a matter of artistic endeavour. This was combined with a much stronger "classical" influence coming from the whole European historical tradition. Once you add the elements of folk, jazz and even a little R&B you begin to understand why progressive rock is distinctly a British or European form of musical composition.

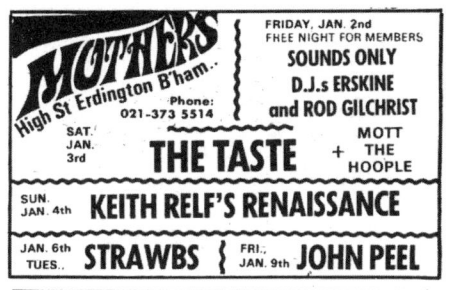

One of the bands that epitomised this blending of musical styles, yet managed to create music that retained each style's distinctiveness was Renaissance. The first incarnation of this band was started by ex-Yardbirds guitarist Keith Relf and drummer Jim McCarty. They recruited Relf's sister Jane and ex-Nashville Teens keyboardist John Hawken. The music they created was an astonishing departure from the music of the Yardbirds. They relied less on their R&B past and incorporated those other musical influences in a 1969 release simply called **Renaissance**. It was groundbreaking at the time however both Relf and McCarty were unhappy with the response and after releasing a second album called **Illusion** only in England, they left, leaving the rest of the band to form around bassist Jon Camp and new keyboardist John Tout. The addition of Annie Haslim in the 1971 line-up established Renaissance as one of progressive rock's most melodic and ambitious acts.

Renaissance

Yardbirds
Keith Relf
Jim McCarty

Nashville Teens

Annie Haslim

More Than A Lifestyle

It's virtually impossible to pinpoint the exact time that music suddenly became more important and fashion less so. As a result there is a divergence of opinion on the matter. For example drummer Bill Bruford was very close to the changes that were occurring in rock in the late sixties. Time spent in Yes, Genesis, King Crimson and UK has provided him with a special observation post. What's interesting to note is that from Bruford's point of view, there was, at least initially, still some connection between lifestyle and music. *"The pop scene in England was working class, it's a working class phenomenon. Then all these rich kids from universities, people like me, thought it would be rather fun to join this kind of thing and add some new ideas to it, and these were kids who could play a little better and who had maybe heard of Stravinsky and who maybe got fancy ideas about art school. There was a whole art school tradition. I think the term "art-rock" (i.e. progressive*

Bill Bruford

Yes
Genesis
King Crimson
UK

rock - see later definitions) is actually an import from England in the sense that those middle class art school kids had fancy ideas about dressing up and putting on stage shows and turning the whole thing out of the jeans and sweatshirts kind of working class thing."

Bill Bruford

A point worth noting, is Bruford's light-hearted outlook on this whole genre of music. An approach that goes against most, if not all, critics. They seemed to have assumed, that this new form of rock took itself too seriously. That obviously wasn't the case. Generally speaking the Art Colleges, Music Schools and Universities in England had far more of an influence on the British musician. America had no counterpart of such impact.

Barclay James Harvest

John Lees

Wooly Wolstenholme

Les Holroyd

Mel Pritchard

John Peel

Robert Godfrey

The Enid

1969

Yes

> 31st JANUARY, at 8 p.m.
> **BARCLAY JAMES HARVEST**
> S.U. CARDS PLEASE
> UNIVERSITY COLLEGE, GOWER STREET, W.C.1

Barclay James Harvest were your typical art school band. They were actually formed by John Lees and Wooly Wolstenholme in late 1966. Both had been in a band called The Blueskeepers and both had attended Oldham Art School and both were anxious to do more than play the blues based music they'd been doing until then. With the addition of Les Holroyd and Mel Pritchard they turned pro in 1967 and all lived together in a farmhouse. Their first chart success came with the 1967 release "Early Morning" which was given considerable air-play by John Peel. That exposure led to a signing with EMI's new in-house progressive label Harvest. They were one of the first bands signed and spent the balance of 1969 writing, rehearsing and playing live the material that would form their first LP released in 1970. Just after the release of **Barclay James Harvest** they undertook a UK tour using an orchestra of musicians from the New Symphonia conducted by Royal Academy of Music graduate Robert John Godfrey. The tour was a financial disaster but many said it helped legitimise the use of orchestra and rock. BJH were soon back in the studio recording their second LP **Once Again**. Robert John Godfrey continued to work with them for a time and eventually went on to form The Enid in 1975, but that's getting ahead of ourselves.

There was one other band that released an album in 1969. The album wasn't that great, it was their first, but the fact it came out was important because of who made it. The band was Yes, and this first release was assembled after a year of playing together and two tours of England. It contained, in rudimentary form, the beginnings of what would become the distinctive Yes sound: the up-front and trebly bass guitar from Chris Squire, the textured drumming from Bill Bruford, the swirling keyboards of Tony Kaye and the multi-part harmonies fronted by the tenor range of Jon Anderson. Anderson quoted in Tim Morse's book **Yes Stories** says, *"At that time, there was an internal decision that we wouldn't specifically try for singles. There were enough people doing that. We wanted to formulate some style of music, and package it as an album. That gives you a better chance of staying around."* The self titled album didn't do well commercially and disappeared quickly, but Yes would go on to chart a whole new course in the world of progressive rock music.

By the end of 1969, a couple of years had passed, since the underground first reared it's experimental head. Dylan was going back to the country, and the Beatles were beginning to forsake the studio wizardry they'd tried so hard to achieve. As Downing refers to it, the Beatles were, *"trying to get back to the fondly remembered MYTH of spontaneous rock and roll."* Progressive rock bands were springing up in all shapes and sizes. Bands with names like Cressida and Beggar's Opera were busy creating their first LP's. A popular pop band known as The Zombies metamorphosed into Argent named after keyboard player Rod Argent who proved to be as proficient at the keyboard as Keith Emerson. Argent would create a series of interesting prog flavoured releases through the early to mid seventies. Vincent Crane and Carl Palmer, who'd both spent time in the Crazy World Of Arthur Brown, added guitarist Johnny Mandala and formed their own outfit called Atomic Rooster. Crane had written Brown's hit "Fire" in 1968 and took his keyboard dominated style in a slightly different direction with this early prog trio. Palmer left within the year and was replaced by Rick Parnell on drums. The band peaked in 1971 with two hit singles "Tomorrow Night" and "Devil's Answer". Approaching the music from a completely different angle was Amazing Blondel, who after a pedestrian rock-oriented first release went in a very medieval acoustic direction predating the work of Gryphon by some three years. But it was Pink Floyd who once again were at the forefront of not only using the studio to its fullest capacity, but now intent on taking "studio quality" into the live arena. It is no small coincidence that technology was able to propel music forward. With the development of electronic music synthesisers bands were able to stay a manageable size and still reproduce music on the scale of a full orchestra. The Moody Blues forsook working with a full orchestra in 1968 and instead relied solely on the Mellotron to duplicate the string and flute sounds for their release **In Search Of The Lost Chord.**

22 Jerry Lucky

The Mellotron

Beatles

Paul McCartney

**Genesis
Moody Blues
King Crimson**

If there is one instrument that set progressive rock bands apart from the rest it would be the Mellotron. The keyboard's first mass exposure came from The Beatles in "Strawberry Fields Forever" when Paul McCartney used it to provide the plaintive flute sounds at the beginning and other sounds throughout the piece. This was the Mellotron's first hit single. The instrument had been around since about 1963 and had been in use with the BBC very early on. The Mark II version was in use from 1964 to 1967 and this was the version used by many early progressive rock bands like Genesis, The Moody Blues and King Crimson.

In simple terms the Mellotron was an analogue sampling keyboard. Internally were 35 strips of pre-recorded tape activated by pressure sensitive keys. Each piece of tape contained either flute, strings or choir sounds. When you pressed the keys you activated the tape to run over playback heads, so you were actually hearing real strings, flute or choir. You were even able to create a certain dynamic by how hard you pressed the keys. The unique feature of the Mellotron was that each piece of tape contained an independent attack of the note. If you were playing the strings each time you pressed the note "c" the tape would start sounding as if the bow had just been struck to the strings of the violin. The catch was that the piece of tape could only be about six feet long which meant that the note or chord you were playing could only last about 10 seconds, before soft springs would pull the tape back to the beginning. This required special compositional attention in order to ensure you didn't run out of choir sounds at the wrong moment. Mellotron chords had to be written to last no longer than the 10 seconds before changing chords.

While some disliked the keyboard's sound, Tony Kaye once described it's sound as five cats "yowling" at night, there were many including Robert Webb leader of the band England who maintained that the sound of the Mellotron was actually more pleasing than the continuous drone of synthesiser string machines. Webb maintained that while the Mellotron may have been troublesome to play and maintain, it replicated sounds in a manner the ear was more comfortable with, containing changes in pitch and tone. For prog keyboardist Tomas Johnson of Anglagard, it goes even deeper. His decision to incorporate twin Mellotrons was based on both sound and feel; *"You feel the Mellotron's motor turning through the keys, and it connects you to the instrument. It feels alive, as though it has a life of it's own."*

In total only about 2500 Mellotrons were ever produced, making them almost collector's items today. Interestingly in the nineties not only progressive rock bands were reviving the Mellotron sound but so were pop bands like Oasis, Blur, Radiohead and many others who were tired of the clinical sound of digital synthesisers. The Mellotron 300 came on the scene by 1968 and became a staple instrument for many bands working in the progressive rock environment in the late sixties.

1969 will always be remembered as the year of Woodstock, where over 500,000 music fans showed up for three days of peaceful music and fun. The music business was beginning to sit up and take notice as in the case of Columbia Records, rock music now accounted for 60% of it's recording output, up from 15% a scant five years before. As the sixties came to an end, an entire generation suddenly found itself growing up and facing a future of children, settling down and bills. It was as if Woodstock was one last fling.

A Musical Foundation

With the beginnings of a new decade, the 1970s, progressive rock's musical foundation had been solidly laid. Many writers maintain it was predominantly a seventies style. While I disagree, it's true what **The All Music Guide to Rock** says; *"progressive rock was one of the defining styles of seventies rock and responsible for some of rocks most ambitious - and pretentious - efforts."* The seventies were the springboard for the genre. Hundreds of bands came into existence and many just as quickly faded away after one or two releases. But from the roots planted in the late sixties we can begin to see what structures would fuse the influences together. In France rock music took hold in late 1969 and one of the first progressive rock groups to emerge was Alice.

They would be the inspiration for a host of French bands a couple of years later.

Robert Fripp

King Crimson

Yes

Peter Banks

Steve Howe

In March of 1970 Robert Fripp was asked to join Yes. He declined indicating he was still defining his style and as a result could only function as a leader. King Crimson would go on to release their second LP **In The Wake Of Poseidon** in May, while Yes went into the studio to record their second album **Time And A Word** eventually released in August. For reasons lost in time, the band grew unhappy with guitarist Peter Banks and he was let go. As a result the mix on the album has the guitar down low or in some cases eliminated entirely. To perform on the road and promote the release Yes brought in Steve Howe to replace Banks. Another year of playing and touring had been added to the band's history and the confidence showed in the material. Still, **Time And A Word** made little more impact on the charts than their first release and disappeared quickly.

Van Der Graaf Generator

Peter Hamill

Robert Fripp may have declined the invitation to join Yes, but he did agree to do guest guitar work on some early Van Der Graaf Generator albums, namely **H To He** and **Pawn Hearts**. Van Der Graaf had been around for some time having originally formed in 1967 at Manchester University. With no recording contract in sight they split in 1968, only to come back together to work on **The Least We Can Do Is Wave To Each Other**, which was originally intended to be founder Peter Hammill's solo effort. They managed to stay together through most of 1969, but split again while rehearsing for **H To He**. Things were patched up, sort of and they released **H To He** and carried on for a while longer, putting out what many consider their progressive rock masterpiece **Pawn Hearts**. While they were critically well received, their following never went beyond loyal cult status.

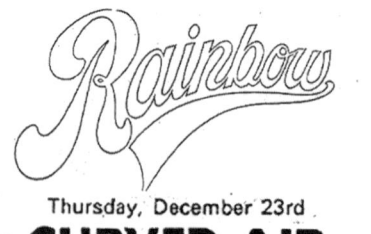

Curved Air

Sonja Kristina

Darryl Way

Francis Monkman

Such was not the case for Curved Air. They were launched into being during the winter of 1970, with all elements carefully packaged to capitalise on all the prevailing hot trends. They had a female vocalist in Sonja Kristina, classically trained musicians like Darryl Way and Francis Monkman, and of course the ever popular violin and synthesisers. All of this would have been for naught if it wasn't for the fact that Curved Air was able to write and arrange some very fine music. With a sizeable promotional budget behind them Curved Air made quite a splash and the resulting

Curved Air

pressures caused Way to leave in 1972 making room for seventeen year old teen prodigy Eddie Jobson to step in and fill his shoes.

Eddie Jobson

The Classical Influence

Of all the musical influences...which ones stood out? Certainly folk music had its input, considering the English heritage. The folk influence allowed for the softer side of prog to develop in the use of acoustic instruments such as guitar, flutes and even older instruments such as recorders. Jazz was able to impart to progressive rock a certain rhythmic quality which surfaced in prog's syncopated rhythmic patterns. But when all the options had been considered it was classical music that proved to be the most prominent. Not so much in terms of actual existing compositions but in it's arrangement and compositional approach. In many respects progressive rock is a blending of the classicism of the eighteenth century and the romanticism of the nineteenth century. The classicist composers of the 1700s tended to avoid emotionalism, they sought to create a perfect orderly piece of music based on elements such as beauty, reason and structure. The romantics of the 1800s on the other hand were more interested in the expression of emotion sparked by the inspiration of the individual. They in many ways revolted against established rules in an effort to express themselves. The

1900s were taken up with composers struggling with stronger elements of rhythm and harmony. It's not too much of a stretch to see rock 'n roll as the logical popular outgrowth of the romantic movement, given that much of rock is based on spontaneous expression of the individual. Rock places a high degree of value on spontaneity and the emotional baring of the soul. Progressive rock on the other hand grew out of a desire to create music with more structure, and while it didn't avoid emotionalism, it placed that emotionalism within a more arranged musical composition. Progressive rock took elements of classicism and romanticism to achieve a form of music that allowed it's composers to express their inner feelings, but do it in a manner of composition that contained a greater musical depth and where the music itself contained expression and was not just a carrier for the lyrics.

This new breed of progressive rock musician came face-to-face with the classics in terms of composition, structure, and style. Whereas many of the traditional pop and rock band members may have had little or no knowledge of reading or writing music, these individuals studied it. They studied it's history, knew not only the fundamentals but in many cases the subtleties. Armed with this knowledge they inevitably began to use it in the writing of rock music. So quite naturally this new breed of musician, the music or art school student, many classically trained, came to the fore. This included musicians like Keith Emerson, Francis Monkman, Rick Wakeman and many others.

Rick Wakeman

Keith Emerson

Francis Monkman

Curved Air

Referring to Monkman, Chris Charlesworth writing in **Melody Maker** proclaimed; *"One of the better things to have come out of the current leaning towards progressive rock music is the arrival of the intelligent, articulate rock musician."* Monkman who spent his early years learning the classical traditions in a London music school, found his way into the band Curved Air, and was never averse to sharing his thoughts on the music of the day. *"Monkman finds the state of the contemporary music scene exciting, it's getting a little bit corny to say so but he believes that many of the barriers, erected in prejudice are gradually tumbling. 'To a musician there are no barriers-or at least there shouldn't be, despite where his preferences lie. I think that the younger people discovering classical music are much more open minded than the classical ones discovering rock.'"*

Deep Purple

Jon Lord

Another individual who brought years of classical training to the world of rock was Deep Purple's keyboardist Jon Lord. **Keyboard** magazine said Lord tried transplanting familiar orchestral themes into extended introductions and chamber quartet interludes in various Deep Purple tunes, but fuelled by the heady experiments being undertaken in English rock during the late sixties, he went a step further and composed a concerto for rock band and symphony orchestra, presenting it in London's Royal Albert Hall with Malcolm Arnold conducting the Royal Philharmonic Orchestra on September 24, 1969 and again at the Hollywood Bowl a year later. Similarly grand projects, like **The Gemini Suite** and a film score for "The Last Rebel" flowed from Lord's pen during this period. Lord's love of classical and rock continued well into the seventies as he continually strived for the magic mix of rock and symphonic instruments.

Yet another of the bands that came to prominence using the classics was Renaissance. **Melody Maker** made these observations: *"Renaissance's main asset is the ability to be able to mix classics and rock in such a way that they seem made for one another, not as just a rock band with a couple of Bach rip offs."* The band's pianist Jon Tout explained: *"We've added a little more punch to the songs we play than the old band had. Even the classical bridges between the movements."* Lead vocalist Terry Crow went on to add; *"We use classics as a definite part of the song, rather than doing a jazzy piece of Bach."*

Perhaps the band that exhibited the greatest use of classical influences of the early progressive rock bands was The Nice, helmed by Keith Emerson. Their LPs and live performances were peppered with classics. Many times the band performed with large symphonies in an attempt to bridge the gap that exists between the two forms. When The Nice split up and Emerson Lake & Palmer formed it was only natural that this experimentation continue, albeit on a slightly different tack. **Keyboard** magazine made these observations, *"When the first ELP album came out in 1970, it stood out from the crowd of guitar oriented heavy metal bands like Led Zeppelin, Cream and Deep Purple that were dominating the airwaves at the time. Along with a level of aggression that appealed to a rock audience, it had such beautiful tunes as Greg Lake's, 'Lucky Man' which became a number one single and gave millions of listeners their first ever taste of lead synthesisers."*

Renaissance

Jon Tout

Terry Crow

The Nice

Keith Emerson

ELP

Led Zeppelin

Cream

Deep Purple

Greg Lake

JOHN MARTIN, DEREK BLOCK
WITH TONY STRATTON-SMITH PRESENT

THE NICE
IN CONCERT

TUESDAY, JAN. 27th 7.30	TUESDAY, FEB. 3rd 7.45
COLSTON HALL BRISTOL	FREE TRADE HALL MANCHESTER
THURSDAY, JAN 29th 7.30	WEDNESDAY, FEB. 4th 7.45
CITY HALL SHEFFIELD	PHILHARMONIC LIVERPOOL
SUNDAY, FEB. 1st 6.00, 8.30	FRIDAY, FEB. 6th 7.45
EMPIRE THEATRE SUNDERLAND	WINTER GARDENS BOURNEMOUTH
MONDAY, FEB. 2nd 7.30	SATURDAY, FEB. 7th 6.15, 9.00
CIVIC HALL WOLVERHAMPTON	FESTIVAL HALL LONDON

in association with Harold Davison

At Sunderland and Festival Hall special guests **"YES"**

Emerson Lake & Palmer Come Together

King Crimson

The Nice
Greg Lake

Robert Fripp

Keith Emerson

Atomic Rooster

Carl Palmer
Jimi Hendrix

ELP

Isle Of Wight

Moody Blues

The Who

Jethro Tull

Jimi Hendrix

ELP

In late 1969 King Crimson was supporting The Nice on an American tour playing four nights at the San Francisco Fillmore. Emerson, upon discovering similar musical tastes, ran the idea of forming a group by Greg Lake who at the time was lead vocalist and bass player with King Crimson. There was even some suggestion that Robert Fripp would join this new group but as the story goes Keith Emerson vetoed that idea because he was not keen to work with a guitarist. In any case, seemingly at the peak of their commercial success The Nice broke up in March of 1970, and Emerson renewed acquaintances with Lake and both started to look for a drummer. They later added Atomic Rooster drummer Carl Palmer whose own efforts to join up with Jimi Hendrix and Mitch Mitchell fell through. Together they formed one of the first progressive rock supergroups, Emerson Lake & Palmer. They officially came together in June of 1970 and played their first "unofficial" gig August 23rd at the Guild Hall in Plymouth. It was their second appearance before 600,000 screaming fans at the Isle of Wight festival August 29th 1970, that really got them the exposure they wanted. They performed "Pictures at an Exhibition" on a bill that included performances by such performers as The Moody Blues, The Who, Jethro Tull, Jimi Hendrix and many others. From the very beginning of their career ELP established themselves as a technically skilled band not afraid to tour. Their first highly anticipated LP released in November of 1970 didn't disappoint their fans either, containing the classic "Lucky Man" which would actually do quite well on the charts. The album showcased their highly developed musical skills combined with more than average showmanship, a balance of harmony and dissonance, acoustics and electronics. When asked to describe ELP, Emerson said:

"If you're looking for a description of what ELP is about, It's progressive rock with a lot of regard for the past."

Emerson Lake & Palmer always considered themselves first and foremost a live band, and their initial recording efforts reflected this. The feeling within the band was that the records should reflect the live sound. Musically, while they came from blues and R&B backgrounds, they decided to forego those roots and instead focus on the European musical influence but approach it with a jazz mentality. A unique approach that fit well with the experimental mood of the early seventies.

Another band that made it's mark during the Isle Of Wight Festival in 1970 was Hawkwind. The band weren't on the bill but they performed just the same, outside the festival fence and what's more they played for free. As a matter of fact they had already built up a cult following by playing just about anywhere for free. By festival time they'd gained quite a reputation, not only for their spacey-underground style of music but also for some well covered drug busts. Musically Hawkwind was led by Dave Brock and Nik Turner and from the very start specialised in long spacey, improvisational jams, a mix of psychedelic and acid-rock. From their beginnings as a loose "collection of freaks" the band quickly began putting their interest in science fiction to music and developed a series of sci-fi themed musical masterpieces. With LP titles such as **In Search Of Space, Space Ritual,** and **Warrior On The Edge Of Time**, they clearly positioned themselves as space-rock aficionados. But while Hawkwind were more on the fringe of the symphonic progressive scene, they performed many times on the same bill with many who were an integral part of it, including Genesis and Pink Floyd. Over the years, the band maintained a revolving door of personnel changes, but even into the nineties the vision of Hawkwind has been kept alive by Dave Brock.

Gentle Giant

King Crimson

Yes

It was around this time that the Shulmans, Derek and Ray decided to put together a more adventurous outfit. Based in Portsmouth they had gone through the late sixties known as Simon Dupree and The Big Sound and even had a hit single called "Kites". However the fact that none of them was actually named Simon Dupree and a growing dissatisfaction with playing music they were not keen on, caused the group to split. By 1970 they'd come together with Kerry Minnear who came to the band with a Royal Academy degree in composition and blues guitarist Gary Green and formed Gentle Giant. They had heard King Crimson and Yes and were fascinated by that whole sound. Their first LP was released in late 1970 and didn't do very well. Their second release **Acquiring The Taste** saw them solidify their unique sound and start to get noticed. The music Gentle Giant created was again very different even for the seventies. The music contained very complicated contrapuntal arrangements, dissonant instrumental voicings and incorporated complicated vocal arrangements and unusual medieval instruments. Non-the-less they won themselves a listening audience and would go on play a major role in shaping a whole sub-genre of future progressive rock bands.

The Beginnings of Genesis

Genesis

Peter Gabriel

Bands like Genesis came into their own during the seventies. Their first rather pop oriented release **From Genesis To Revelation** went virtually nowhere in late 1969. But as a result of the negative reaction to the band, whenever Peter Gabriel wasn't trying to line up gigs for them, they closeted themselves up in a cottage where rehearsing took on new meaning. They'd be up at 10am and rehearse and fine tune material for ten or eleven hours. Out of this dedication to perfection came **Trespass**, with their trademark song "The Knife". It was October of 1970. The band had been performing live, so each of the songs on the recording had been worked through in a live setting. This undoubtedly helped the group shape the material, finding out what worked and what didn't.

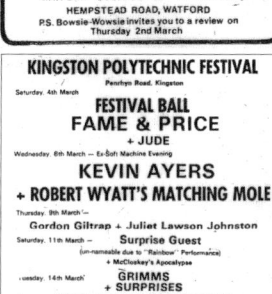

Armando Gallo's book **Genesis: I Know What I Like** goes into great detail regarding the intensity the band put themselves through to make an album like **Trespass**. It contained the hallmarks of the few progressive rock LPs that had been released to that date and would influence forever what would come after it. The material contained all the elements of colour, warmth, intricate chord changes, electric and acoustic dynamics and of course fairytale-ish lyrics. By the end of it's first year of release **Trespass** sold approximately 6000 copies world-wide. A vast improvement over the paltry 600 - 700 sold of their first LP.

Typically Genesis were not really into any of their contemporaries. As recounted in **Genesis: Peter Gabriel, Phil Collins and Beyond**, Tony Banks says; *"I think also that at that time (the beginning) when we were starting off, we didn't like most of the music of that particular era. There were a few people we liked. But we'd been influenced much more by some earlier groups - The Beatles and The Kinks and The Animals - and there some people influenced us. Bubblegum music and the blues music were the two main things happening then, and neither particularly appealed to us. Perhaps the only group which did appeal to us and which was current at that time would have been King Crimson."* It's all summed up neatly by Bank's; *"In a sense we were just trying to find different things to do by ourselves because we didn't find what other people were doing that interesting. And we found we could get away on stage with doing a kind of complicated music. We found we were slowly building up an audience."*

The pressures of recording and touring began to take their toll and original members, Anthony Phillips and John Mayhew left to be replaced with Steve Hackett and Phil Collins. Collins had been in a group called Flaming Youth and during this time his favourite group was Yes. In a strange twist of fate, Collins was at the Marquee club when 'he heard that Bill Bruford was going to be leaving Yes. He was able to talk to Jon

Genesis

Peter Gabriel
Phil Collins
Tony Banks
Beatles
Kinks
Animals
King Crimson

Anthony Phillips
Steve Hackett
Bill Bruford
Yes

Jon Anderson

Phil Collins

Steve Hackett

Peter Gabriel

Anderson who suggested he set up an audition. Later that same evening however he ran into old-friend Tony Stratton-Smith. Collins had seen an ad Stratton-Smith had placed about one of his Charisma groups and inquired who it was. When he heard it was Genesis who were looking for a new drummer, he was intrigued because he'd heard of the band, and thought they were going to go places. Collins was told he'd have to come and audition here as well. In the end Collins never did call Anderson, and the rest as they say is history. Steve Hackett had been looking for a band who were interested in creating music that went beyond the mainstream, and had placed an ad in **Melody Maker** stating this. The ad was seen by Peter Gabriel who called him up. Instead of the traditional audition Hackett invited the band to his house and listen to his work. They liked what they heard and he was asked to join. It was this line-up that would go on to create **Nursery Cryme** released in November 1971.

Tony Banks

Phil Collins

Steve Hackett

By this time, the playing had improved immensely. Tony Bank's had mastered tricky instruments like the Mellotron, Phil Collins delivered a much harder drumming style and Steve Hackett's desire to do as much sonically as possible with the guitar brought the band to the next level of accomplishment. All of the growing maturity was fronted by an ever more flamboyant Peter Gabriel whose bizarre costumes and song introductions only fuelled the band's stage persona. Tony Banks commented to **Trouser Press**: *"Peter put a fox's head on during that song ("The Musical Box") to get his picture on the front page of Melody Maker. There was no other justification for it. We then realised how effective a song like that could be from a publicity angle, but everything else we did was totally integrated. Every light, costume or whatever was thought out very carefully to go with the music."* **Nursery Cryme** was a major step forward for the band in many respects. Phil Collins' drumming style was able to provide a very solid and mature rhythmic element while Steve Hackett's experimental guitar tone qualities added to the groups adventurous musical spirit.

Genesis

Interestingly, by early 1972 Genesis, who were still not at all well known outside of London, found themselves on the record charts with **Nursery Cryme** reaching the number 4 spot in Italy. As Armando Gallo says: *"The Italians had never really identified with the twelve-bar syndrome of rock-n-roll, and young fans and musicians who had grown up within Italy's strong classical and operatic traditions suddenly responded en masse to the English progressive scene, forming a large cult audience."*

In many ways Genesis, more than many progressive rock bands was responsible for influencing the budding Italian progressive scene. And that influence continued to grow with each new release. Genesis matured musically to a point where their material would become the benchmark by which many of the neo-progressive rock bands of the early eighties would be measured. In fact many of them would see their own development as having been achieved when they could perform "Supper's Ready" and sound exactly like Genesis.

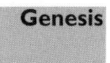

A New Musical Philosophy

In amongst the new instruments being used and the new influences being incorporated, came new ways of thinking. Genesis abandoned the loose jamming in favour of ensemble playing. Tony Banks comments; *"Everybody else sounded boring. You had a lot of people doing these extended guitar solos and with the exception of the very best they were very boring. The bass and the drums...they were only meant to keep the guitars going. That type of playing never really interested us."*

In Downing's assessment, *"The British group that seems most to deserve the dubious tag of progressive is Yes...Keyboards and vocal harmonies have remained central elements in their music, as it changed from reworking other people's songs to writing and perform-*

Rick Wakeman

ing extended suites of their own. The arrival of classically trained Rick Wakeman gave them an even wider scope. Their best period containing Fragile, Close To The Edge and Tales From Topographic Oceans saw the creation of music of great sophistication. Variations in mood, tone, time and volume...all held together by melodic hook phrases or verses over an extended composition."

David Cousins

Strawbs

Rick Wakeman who came to music with full music schooling had spent a number of years doing session work before joining forces with David Cousins of The Strawbs to forge a new sound. At the time The Strawbs was still very clearly a folk band and it was Cousins and Wakeman who felt they could chart new territory by introducing a more electric element to folk music as well as write material that drew on other influences. Their idea was to create the first true folk-rock band. To this end Wakeman's influence can clearly be heard on their 1971 release **From The Witchwood**. Wakeman remained with The Strawbs for a few years and on his last tour with them, they played in support of Yes, where

Chris Squire

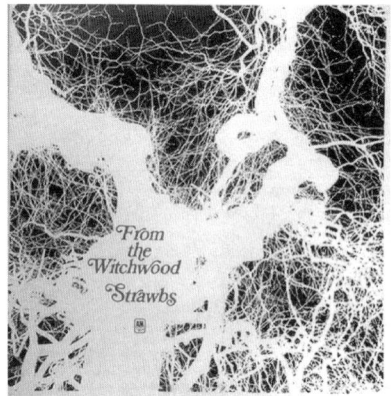

Chris Squire had the opportunity to see Wakeman's style in action. "After the tour, Wakeman decided he'd had enough of bands and was going to concentrate on session work. Shortly thereafter he received a middle-of-the-night phone call from Chris Squire to come and join Yes. Wakeman originally declined. A few days later Yes manager Brian Lane encouraged Wakeman to simply come by during rehearsals and see how it felt. After a day in the studio putting together some initial tracks for what was to become

Steve Howe

Fragile, Wakeman gave Steve Howe a ride home and suggested he'd pick him up for rehearsals the next day. The next day turned into the next day and before long Wakeman was firmly part of Yes. For Wakeman it was the chance of a lifetime to create and participate in the creation of music that went beyond the pop norms.

Yes

The sound that Yes created certainly bore little resemblance to what was happening musically around them and Wakeman was very vocal about the direction Yes were exploring, *"I think they are heading into what I can only describe as orchestrated-rock (i.e. progressive rock). You've had the heavy bands such as Cream and The Who, now we are trying to move one stage further into orchestral rock. I think we have the same excitement that heavy rock generated, but what Yes are doing is a hell of a lot more complicated and musically refined. Every bar is thought out when the song is formulated. Once the thing is together you can play it as you feel it, but there is a solid backbone and arrangement to work from."*

Cream

The Who

Yes : Their Music Had Feeling

Wakeman expresses two key elements that have come to epitomise the music of Yes: complicated arrangements and feeling. Yes might be criticised for any number of things, but lack of depth or feeling, certainly not.

Rick Wakeman

There is no question that one of the key aspects of Yes that attracts fans is the complicated style of the music. Given the nature of their compositional technique, the musical result should come as no surprise. Each member would come to the sessions with their own specific instrument and input. Each having been influenced by their own musical background and current listening habits. And while this may not be far off from what most bands do, it was what they were listening to as well as the manner in which it all came together that truly made the music different.

Yes

If you listen carefully and take each tune apart, you find that you actually have a very simple song. However it's with the arrangement that the traditional Yes-nature of the material begins to take shape. Katherine Charleton in **Rock Music Styles: A History** notes: *"The high level of musicianship of each member of Yes is obvious in their recording of 'Roundabout,' both in the way the individual instruments are played and in the careful way they play as a group without getting in each other's way. The arrangement is quite complex and played with the sensitivity one would expect of classical musicians."* Their arranging style was very complicated. That's what made it a Yes song. In the very early days, they listed influences such as The Nice, and Vanilla Fudge as well as The Fifth Dimension. While many casual observers drew the obvious comparisons to the classics with their music, the band also incorporated a slight jazz influence into their writing and arranging.

The Nice

Vanilla Fudge

Fifth Dimension

King Crimson

Just as their second album, **Time And A Word** was released, they heard a copy of King Crimson's **In The Wake Of Poseidon** at which point Bill Bruford sensed a dramatic difference in musical style. Not only was there a feeling that King Crimson had "got it right" so to speak,

Bill Bruford

King Crimson

Yes

Eddie Offord

Tony Kaye

Peter Banks

Rick Wakeman

Jon Anderson

but if you listen you'll hear the dramatic difference, in that Yes are very much a "major key group" while King Crimson were just the opposite, a "minor key group". Yes were a decidedly harmonious band producing music that stretched the traditional boundaries of the pop music world at the time.

Having heard the King Crimson LP combined with the touring and constant rounds of composition through 1969 and 1970, Yes finally achieved what for them was the musical crowning glory. **The Yes Album** truly represented what the band stood for musically. It sounded big, with grand, elaborately arranged compositions that were sweeping in scope and relying less on external input than drawing on each members highly developed musical skills. This third album which produced such classics as "Starship Trooper" and "Yours is no Disgrace" in no question benefited from the arrival of producer Eddie Offord. These mini epics clocked in at over nine minutes providing the band the opportunity to create music of a panoramic nature. The commercial success of The Yes Album put the band in a position to tour America as an opening act for the first time in 1971.

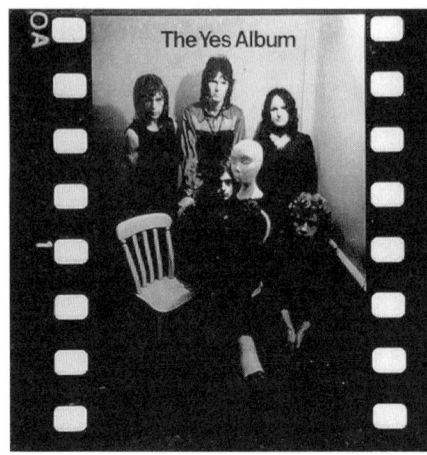

It was shortly after the release of **The Yes Album** that the rift developed between the band and keyboardist Tony Kaye. They were forging onward incorporating newly discovered ideas into their music as quickly as time would allow. Peter Banks had been officially replaced by Steve Howe for this album and he was in synch with the band, now incorporating many different styles and guitar sounds into their repertoire. Howe was able to take Yes to a higher musical level. The band wanted Kaye to look at incorporating the new Moog Synthesisers and Mellotrons to provide a more classically inspired sound to their already majestic music. Kaye, objected and finally left the band providing a hole to be filled by Rick Wakeman who would propel the band to it's next level of success.

The sound of Yes not only hinged on the up-front bass playing of Chris Squire, the searing guitar work of Steve Howe, and the unusually high vocal range of Jon Anderson, but certainly the keyboard work of Wakeman who in many ways set up the progressive rock keyboard ethic. He established the principle of elaborate embellishment, the effect being to soften the rhythm section's thrust and place it within a cathedral-like electronic ambience. David Aldridge writing in **Keyboard** magazine said it best; *"If rock and roll blew the doors open for electric* guitars, then progressive rock parted the cathedral gates for keyboardists."

Guitarist Steve Howe had his input as well; *"I'm fond of the "Yours Is No Disgrace" solo on the original album, particularly because it was a breakthrough to be able to start working like that, over-dubbing guitar parts, mixing parts...constructing a piece of music. I'd been wanting to do it for years, but until I joined Yes, I didn't have the facilities."*

It's interesting to hear the variety of influences on their first three albums. If you listen closely to some of those tunes, you'll hear snatches of "The Big Country" theme, and the television series "Bonanza" coming through. Yes were able to combine talent with the latest technology to come up with a sound that is as unique today as it was then. When it came to progressive rock, Yes seemed to be the yardstick others were measured by.

The New Record Labels

This new music didn't escaped the scrutinising ears of record company executives as many companies set up progressive in-house labels all through the early seventies. In England there were names such as Harvest, Dawn, Vertigo and Deram. In the case of the latter most notably made famous by signing The Moody Blues, who within a few short years launched their own label, Threshold.

Without question one of the most influential labels of the late sixties and early seventies and well into the eighties was Tony Stratton-Smith's Charisma Records. In the early days of prog, the Charisma label was home to such notable bands as The Nice, Genesis, and Van Der Graaf Generator. Charisma was eventually purchased by Virgin Records in the mid eighties.

On the continent names such as Italy's Cramps Records, Numero Uno, Germany's Brain, Bellaphon, Spiegelei, and France's Crypto began releasing progressive rock material. In his book **The History Of Rock**, author Tony Russell said it best, *"A super league had come into being; hit singles were irrelevant and promoting the album was the order of the day."* Jon Anderson, lead vocalist with Yes summed it up in 1971; *"In the next five years the music will grow into more of an art form than it is at the moment. Rock is popular now of course, but a lot of it won't be as lasting as we might think. We are beginning to think in terms of whole sides of albums and not just tracks, and making music with more depth. We're not trying to get into classical music, but get what classical music does to you. Rock music of today will become the classic electric music of tomorrow."*

Lofty ideas to say the least. Perhaps only time will tell whether in fact Anderson was right. However he wasn't the only one thinking along those lines. His comments came in 1971, while over a decade later, in 1983 publicist Keith Goodwin, who had been the publicity agent for such bands as Yes and Emerson Lake & Palmer, was still fighting the progressive rock cause. During an interview Goodwin said: *"The first wave of bands like Yes, I believe wrote things that should, by my reckoning, attain the same status as certain classical pieces, whereby they can be played by the Boston Philharmonic one night and the Strasbourg Philharmonic the next. I'd like to hear another band take hold of say Tales From Topographic Oceans and perform it as a piece - whether by a 60 piece orchestra or as a five piece band. It can be done, it should be done, but unfortunately, it's not being done. Maybe it'll be another twenty years before all this happens"* Actually it didn't take twenty years, as David Palmer has recorded a wonderful series of albums through the late 1980s and into the 1990s with the London Symphony performing the music of Jethro Tull, Genesis, Pink Floyd and Yes. In each case he managed to persuade members of each band to contribute to the work. The end result clearly shows the strength of the music these bands created. It truly stands the test of time and translation to a symphonic environment much better than just a "classical" reworking of pop material. This music is clearly head and shoulders above a "Mantovani plays the pops" type album, revealing a depth of musical composition that proved to be one of progressive rock music's strengths.

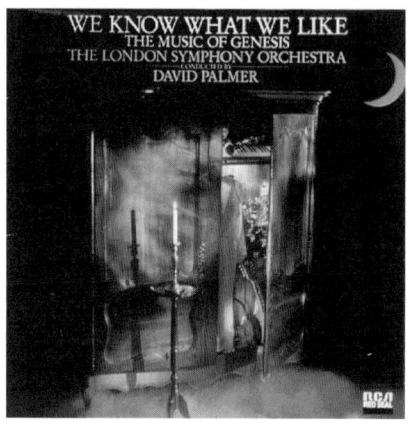

A Common Thread Of Musical Depth

The element of musical depth is definitely something that needs more explanation. For that let's take a look at Curved Air's, Francis Monkman, who back in 1971 felt that the original need for rock music, particularly it's accent on volume, could be traced back to the early 1800's. At that time the overall noise level was so much lower than it is now, that to listen to a large orchestra created a tremendous physical experience. For example Beethoven's Seventh in 1830 would have been played as loud as a rock band plays today.

This volume level increased in classical music up until the time of Stravinsky and Varese in the twenties and by this period jazz had achieved the position as the physical catalyst with musicians like Charlie Parker. However Monkman believes that jazz lost it's rhythmic feel so that by the fifties the public was ready for a music which placed the accent almost totally on physical stress. And rock was there for that purpose.

Many feel that as rock gradually became more intellectual in approach and content, the serious rock musician suddenly found him or herself faced with a dilemma: Should they be writing rock and roll and be content to fulfil just that role? Or should they make use of new musical thinking, the new approaches to tonality and modulation for example. Do you just keep playing that good old rock and roll or do you do something more with it?

Bill Bruford, has his own thoughts about some of the people who played in the early bands; *"None of the people were remotely jazz musicians in any of these bands. They were just better musicians, I think, and while King Crimson was a darker sounding group, much more prone to the minor key, Yes was all sunny and diatonic and a sort of vocal group. It's leader Jon Anderson was from a northern club atmosphere where it was entertainment - people had paid their two pounds and wanted nice entertainment, things were done for show - whereas King Crimson wasn't like that at all, but clearly doing what it wanted to do and creating much darker, much more aggressive textures. There was more playing."*

Bruford talked about switching bands. After all very few musicians can boast of being in so many progressive rock bands at one time or another; *"I wanted to go from the opposite of Yes, you see, and Crimson was as far away from Yes as I could get. Yes talked all the time, wouldn't play a note without a committee decision. We'd all sit around and decide whether the bass player would play F, and when we'd all agreed on that, we'd decide whether the next one would be a G and so on. We'd sit around and discuss this endlessly whereas Crimson didn't talk so much. It did play more...lots of things went unsaid."* Whether a band talked about it or not, the reality was progressive rock bands endeavoured to create music with more depth than the average pop song.

A Split In Musical Direction

As early as 1970 a split occurred in the progressive rock family tree. In simple terms the Yes, Genesis, ELP group became the "mainstream" while the other branch, many with roots in the Canterbury region of England came to be called the more "serious" group of musicians. Spearheaded by Soft Machine these bands included Caravan, Hatfield & The North, Egg, and National Health. In order to get to the roots of this branch we need to know about a band from the Canterbury region called The Wilde Flowers. While they never released a record during their existence they are important to the cause of progressive rock because of who floated through the band. This included members of Soft Machine and even

Bill Bruford

King Crimson

Jon Anderson

Yes

Genesis

ELP

Soft Machine

Caravan

Hatfield & The North

Egg

National Health

Wilde Flowers

Caravan

Robert Wyatt
Kevin Ayers
Mike Ratledge
Richard Sinclair

Caravan. These musicians, notably Robert Wyatt, Mike Ratledge, Kevin Ayers, Pye Hastings, Hugh Hopper, Richard Sinclair and others came from more of a non-pop musical background. It was Wyatt, Ratledge and Ayers who would go on to form Soft Machine.

To understand this side of progressive rock requires an understanding of just what was happening in Canterbury. Ian MacDonald who later would write **Revolution In The Head**, while editor of the **New Musical Express** in 1975 wrote about the goings-on at Simon Langton School in Canterbury: *"An exclusive, private establishment for the sons of local intellectuals and artists. Very free, emphatically geared to the uninhibited development of self-expression. A hot-bed to teenage avant-garderie."* Attending the school were many of the key players of the bands to come. In this idyllic world one of the primary sources of enjoyment came from going over to the 15 room mansion owned by Robert Wyatt's mother and listening to the latest new jazz albums from artists such as Mingus, Coleman, and Monk as well as contemporary composers such as Stockhausen.

Daevid Allen

Wilde Flowers

In early 1962 Wyatt, tired of school, ran off to Spain where he bumped into George Niedorf who taught him how to drum and introduced him to Daevid Allen. Also introduced to Wyatt at this time were psychedelic drugs. Shortly thereafter Wyatt returned to Canterbury and formed The Wilde Flowers. Their first live gig was at the Bear & Key Hotel where according to Hugh Hopper: *"We played Chuck Berry, Beatles and a few originals. Our first recording was a demo made at a private studio during early 1965."* Richard Sinclair left for college in the summer of 1965 and would later go on to form Caravan.

Soft Machine

UFO Club

14 Hour Technicolor Dream

Alan Holdsworth

Gong

UK

Asia

Taking their name from the William Burrough's novel, The Soft Machine actually had been around since August 1966 around the time of the third version of The Wilde Flowers. The Soft's line-up was forever changing and would eventually see over 15 different permutations. They had established themselves on the London Underground scene playing at the usual venues like UFO and The Roundhouse. They also performed with Pink Floyd at "The 14 Hour Technicolor Dream" in April of 1966 and made quite an impact. They had been working in a psychedelic style and began to incorporate free jazz and electronic composition. Later they began throwing in horns as well to an ever changing sound. The vocals were phased out by the third album and the band was left to create music based around the work of their organ player, Mike Ratledge. Over the years of their existence musicians came and went, including Alan Holdsworth and Kevin Ayers. Both would show up in a variety of other bands later in their careers. Holdsworth in Gong, UK and even Asia, while Ayers showed up in countless sessions and maintained quite a prolific solo career.

Steve Hillage

Another group from this side of the tree, that created a fantasy world of which to sing about was Gong, formed by ex-Soft Machine guitarist Daevid Allen in the early seventies. Gong initially employed the talents of Allen, Malherbe, Tritsch, Pyle, and recorded a couple of albums before a line-up change that would include Steve Hillage, Mike Howlett and Pierre Moerlen and others. Gong's musical style was not dissimilar to others on this side of progressive rock although they remained very squarely in the world of psychedelic music too. They took a more serious musical approach, peppered with jazz fusion and sometimes humorous lyrics.

Without question the most successful band from the Canterbury "school" is Caravan. Their history begins with The Wilde Flowers as well. While many of the other mainstream bands were accused of self-indulgence Caravan was seen to be a more sincere and even "light" progressive band. True to form, their material was jaunty, upbeat, and even somewhat humorous in tone all with the ever present jazzy feel. Their material came in both short and long songs, but even in the long material the tone is different from the symphonic bands of the time. And while Caravan did use the same instruments and even the occasional small string orchestra, their sound never seemed as large or some would say "pompous" as a Yes or Genesis.

Any discussion of this branch of the progressive rock family tree requires an understanding of the term "avant-garde". The dictionary says; avant-garde refers to those, especially in the arts who create or apply new or experimental techniques. And that is what was happening here. This term continually comes up when referring to bands of this nature. What personified them was their penchant for constantly playing rock and jazz with a heavy dose of 20th century classical composition. Or as in the case of Caravan and Gentle Giant creating a kind of busy music with even a baroque feel. The full expression of avant-garde is perhaps best heard in the outright experimentation of groups like Henry Cow, Material etc..

Speaking of experimentation, while in no way are they a Canterbury band Magma are mentioned here because their musical style is so distant from the mainstream they probably have more musically in common with this side of progressive music. They were a French band fronted by Christian Vander, who took progressive rock to a completely new level. Some say a new planet. Their albums wove an intricate science fiction story sung in a language created specifically for the tale. Chock full of chanting, dissonance and loud rock, this material was not for the timid. The band's stated influences include Bela Bartok, Stockhausen, Duke Ellington, blues-shouting all blended together to create a unique, adventurous form of music that was destined not to appeal to everyone. They, and bands that followed in their style came to form the Zeuhl sub-genre of progressive music.

Through out the seventies avant-garde progressive groups made significant advancements in their efforts to fuse various musical styles into a completely new form. They created music that was challenging to listen to, boasting elements of free jazz, improvisation, and a much more experimental direction based partially on a dissonant 20th century classical style of composition. For their efforts they won much critical acclaim and a sizeable following, especially in Europe. However unlike the more "mainstream" bands, if you wish to call them that, they never

Pierre Moerlen

Caravan

Wilde Flowers

Yes

Genesis

Gentle Giant

Henry Cow

Magma

1971

Pink Floyd
Yes
King Crimson

Jethro Tull
Moody Blues

Genesis

Procul Harum

Gentle Giant

Van Der Graaf Generator

Beggar's Opera

Focus

Supersister

Le Orme

Caravan

Strawbs

Barclay James Harvest

ELP

went beyond cult status as mass appeal alluded them.

The Growth In The Seventies

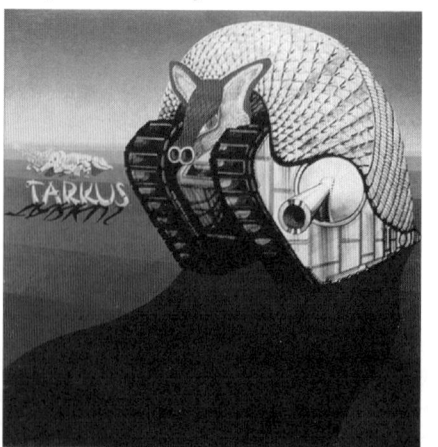

By 1971 the supergroups of progressive rock established themselves with musical releases which included: Pink Floyd - **Meddle**, Yes - **The Yes Album**, King Crimson - **Islands**, Jethro Tull - **Aqualung**, The Moody Blues - **Every Good Boy Deserves Favour**, Genesis - **Nursery Cryme** and Procol Harum's - **Broken Barricades**. In addition the year would also see the growth of groups such as Gentle Giant - **Acquiring The Taste**, Van Der Graaf Generator - **Pawn Hearts**, Beggar's Opera - **Waters of Change**, Focus - **Moving Waves**, Supersister - **To The Highest Bidder**, Le Orme - **Collage**, Caravan - **In the Land of the Grey and Pink**, The Strawbs - **From The Witchwood**, Curved Air -**The Second Album**, Barclay James Harvest - **Once Again** and many others. The year would end with the readers of **Melody Maker** voting Emerson Lake & Palmer as Best Band for 1971 with Pink Floyd in second place. ELP released two albums in 1971; **Tarkus** and **Pictures at an Exhibition**. The 20 minute multi-movement concept **Tarkus** was one of the first to focus on the progressive rock lyrical philosophy of "humanity" against "harsh-technology", while **Pictures...** was an adaptation of Mussorgsky's work in a rock setting recorded live in Newcastle in March of 1971. The album also featured their rousing encore "Nutrocker" which turned out to be a Top Ten single in both the U.S. and the U.K. **Tarkus** rose quickly to number 1 in the U.K. charts and wound up a U.S. Top Ten. All very adventurous for the time.

On the whole, the fragmentation of the rock audience was beginning to take shape as music itself became more fragmented. Almost overnight there sprang up dedicated followers of heavy metal, Southern rock, jazz rock, progressive rock, latin rock, glam rock and on and on. Unlike listening habits of the late sixties that were very tolerant of different styles, suddenly it was not overly fashionable to listen to much outside of your personally selected genre.

1972

Throughout 1972, underground FM radio stations playing album tracks started supplanting Top 40 AM stations playing singles. As a result, rock acts started to shift their focus from singles to albums. Glitter or glam rock acts such as David Bowie began to set the stage for the short lived disco and punk trends that would arise in the late seventies.

This was the year that progressive rock coalesced as a genre. The "supergroups" of Yes, Emerson Lake & Palmer, King Crimson, Genesis, et al, were well on their way, having defined their individual group sounds, each very different from the other. ELP released **Trilogy** which besides having some very strong songs such as the title cut and "The Endless Enigma", picked up on the idea of reworking a classical piece on each album, in this case Aaron Copeland's "Hoedown". This album did well on the charts as well, hitting the number 2 spot in the U.K. and number 5 in the U.S.

Yes started the year off with the January release of **Fragile**, containing their first major singles chart success in "Roundabout". Rick Wakeman had joined by this time, and this proved to be a very strong album with each member having the opportunity to demonstrate their talent on individual tracks, like "Mood For A Day" for Steve Howe, "Cans and Brahms" for Rick Wakeman, "The Fish" for Chris Squire, "Five Percent For Nothing" for Bill Bruford and "We Have Heaven" for Jon Anderson. The longer tracks such as "Heart Of The Sunrise" and "Long Distance Runaround" clearly displayed Yes' ability to seamlessly blend smaller song elements together to craft epic compositions. This album also marked the first of many successful collaborations with artist and designer Roger Dean who created the LP's wonderful fold-open jacket and booklet. The success of the single "Roundabout" had the band touring heavily, headlining for the first time.

Genesis meanwhile improved even further in their writing and studio skills with **Foxtrot,** containing songs like their popular live opener "Watcher Of The Skies" and the 24 minute epic, soon to be classic, "Suppers Ready". Italian fans gave the band their first number one by pushing **Foxtrot** to the top of the Italian album charts.

Genesis made a spectacular impact at the 1972 Reading Festival gar-

---

1972

David Bowie

ELP

King Crimson
Genesis

Rick Wakeman

Chris Squire
Bill Bruford

Jon Anderson

Roger Dean

Genesis

Genesis

nering rave reviews from virtually all the print media. **The Record Mirror**: *"The Knife and "The Return of the Giant Hogweed' were about the two best songs played all day and the standing ovation which Genesis received at the end of the set was more than well deserved."*, **Sounds**: *"Genesis, were clearly the stars of the show..."*, **New Musical Express**: *"...(Genesis) possibly played the best music of the night"*, **Melody Maker**: *"...But when Genesis came on stage, people stopped and listened. This band is really amazing...Genesis had done enough to steal the show."* The decision was made to take the band to America, however everyone agreed that a 45 minute supporting role would not do justice to their material. So in December Genesis made their first visit to the United States, to play a one-night, sold-out engagement, headlining at the New York Philharmonic Hall. Despite sound problems the one-off gig was a big success. Chris Welch wrote about the event in **Melody Maker** where he quoted Tony Stratton-Smith: *"It was a gamble coming here for one show, and the group can't believe how much New York loved them."* While the band may have appeared to conquer the "Big Apple", they were still very much a cult band in the rest of America. It would take a few more years for Genesis to become a household name.

Yes

Rick Wakeman

Bill Bruford

Robert Fripp

King Crimson

In September of 1972 Yes hit the record shelves again with the release of **Close to the Edge,** which featured the 19 minute title track showing them perfecting the classical sonata compositional structure in a rock setting. Of the track "And You And I" Rick Wakeman stated on the **Yesyears** video documentary that they incorporated all the elements that fans loved and critics hated to create an almost hymn like composition that was classic Yes. **Close to the Edge** turned out to be Bill Bruford's last Yes LP for a time. He'd decided to pursue his original love of jazz playing with Robert Fripp in the more unconventional King Crimson. Yes needed a drummer and they turned to Alan White. Just as they had done with Rick Wakeman, White came and fiddled-about during rehearsals. White's background was not jazz, it was solid rock and his playing style brought a renewed vigour to Yes' sound. After agreeing to join, he was informed he had three days to learn all the material before their first concert together in front of over 10,000 fans. White didn't let them down.

Jethro Tull

The early seventies were heady times for music. Bands began to spring up everywhere in England and the continent. Jethro Tull had actually been around since the late sixties but they started out playing basically R&B oriented material with a bit of a jazz influence None-the-less they had attracted quite a following. It wasn't until the release of **Aqualung** in 1971 that progressive rock fans really took note. **Thick As A Brick** followed in 1972 and showcased one continuous piece of music. It was critically panned but the fans loved it.

Camel

Pete Bardens
Van Morrison

Andy Latimer

Another band that came out of a similar R&B environment and formed in 1972 was Camel. At the heart of this band was Peter Bardens who had spent time with Them, Van Morrison's outfit and a few others before joining up with three guys in a band called Brew, they were Andy Latimer, Andy Ward and Doug Ferguson. Camel's style was very melodic with long instrumental excursions. Their first album wouldn't be released until 1973 but many more fine works would follow. Camel like many of the others mentioned have achieved the 'status-of-description', whereby new progressive rock artists' material is described as sounding like them. In later years Camel acquired Kit Watkins formerly of Happy The Man as keyboardist. Unfortunately the band would never achieve super-stardom like so many of their contemporaries. This wasn't because of a lack of musicianship or compositional skills, because their material stood up well against the others. Some have speculated that Camel's weak point was simply their nondescript nature. They had no individual out front like Ian Anderson or Peter Gabriel. In fact if Camel suffered from anything it was lack of image.

Peter Banks who had been let go as guitarist for Yes resurfaced with Flash, a band that bore more than a passing resemblance to a pared down Yes sound. Manfred Mann who'd had some pop success in the middle sixties, and had spent some time "jazzing" it up in Chapter Three came back to rock with a decided progressive edge with Manfred Mann's Earth Band. **Waterloo Lily** became the fourth release for Caravan, who'd seen some personnel shuffling as David Sinclair had left to work with Hatfield And The North, and was replaced by Steve Miller. This release saw a stronger jazz influence incorporated into their Canterburian style. Elsewhere the reincarnated version of Renaissance with Annie Haslam on vocals appeared and released their first album **Prolog,** and a host of Mellotron flavoured bands like Gracious, Beggar's Opera, and Jonesy had been in the studio putting together albums that added to the genre's foundation.

The Impact In Europe

Fiori Di Campo

Experience

Le Orme

Jumbo

PFM

King Crimson

Genesis

On the continent, two Italian bands, Fiori Di Campo and Experience joined together to form Banco Del Mutuo Soccorso or just Banco. In 1972 they released **Banco Del Mutuo Soccorso** and **Darwin** while the three piece Le Orme released their first **Uomo Di Pezza**. A couple of other Italian releases went on to become classics, namely Jumbo's **Vietato Ai Minordi Di 18 Anni?** and Il Balletto Di Bronzo's **Ys**.

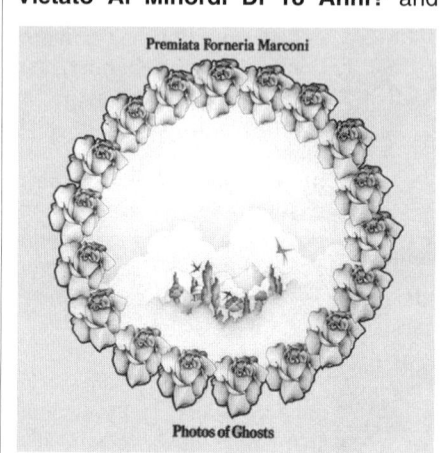

PFM released their first two LPs, which are considered classics of progressive rock, influenced by the leading bands of the day, namely King Crimson and Genesis and yet PFM don't sound anything like them. They were able to take the influences and distil them through their own musical culture and create music uniquely their own. But then the Italians were always a little ahead of the rest.

Premiata Forneria Marconi

Photos of Ghosts

The Turtles

Traffic

Mauro Pagani

Yes

Procul Harum

The members of PFM had been playing in various Italian beat bands during the mid to late sixties, one of them Quelli became quite successful doing cover tunes from groups like The Turtles and even Traffic. After some internal friction four members of Quelli, Franz Di Cioccio, Franco Mussida, Flavio Premoli and Giorgio Piazza formed PFM at the end of 1970 and took their name from a pastry shop in a town near Milano. Shortly after they formed they were joined by Mauro Pagani on violin. It was his appearance that seemed to gel the progressive rock elements together. By early 1971 they were on the road supporting bands such as Yes and Procol Harum. As always the road work prepared their musicianship for the writing and recording that was to come. The first LP, **Storia Di Uno Minuto** was released in January of 1972 while the second, **Per Un Amico** was released later in November of the same year. PFM were on their way to international recognition.

Ange

In France, Ange released **Caricatures** containing all the elements of their style in an early rudimentary form. They would set the stage for a flood of French progressive rock bands, just as what had happened in Italy.

Earth & Fire

Alquin

Focus

1972 also saw releases from Holland's Earth & Fire - **Song of the Marching Children** , Alquin - **Marks** and Focus - **Focus III**.

The Progressive Rock Files   47

Focus were one of the first continental progressive rock bands to get noticed in Britain and the United States. They came together as a trio consisting of Thijs van Leer on organ flute and vocals, Martin Dresden on bass and Hans Cleuver on drums in the middle of 1969. Guitarist Jan Akkerman was still with Brainbox but by November of 1969 he joined to make it a four piece. In 1971 they released **In and Out of Focus** and **Moving Waves** consisting of their uniquely classical and jazz influenced instrumental progressive rock style. Vocals were kept to a minimum. It was that second LP **Moving Waves** that contained their hit single "Hocus Pocus". It's unusual yodelling was heard on radio stations across North America. After some personnel changes the band released **Focus 3** in 1972 based around the core of van Leer and Akkerman along with Pierre van der Linden on drums and Bert Ruiter on bass. After three short, very successful British concert tours, they ended the year listed as **Melody Maker's** "Brightest Hope for 1972" and the **New Musical Express** "Best New Talent of 1972."

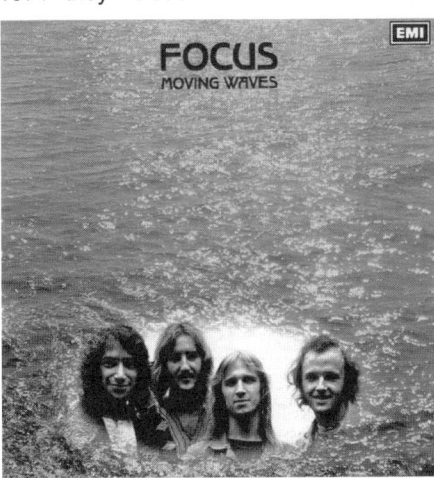

Many others released LPs including Germany's Grobschnitt - **Grobschnitt**, Triumvirat - **Mediterranean Tales**, Nektar - **Journey to the Centre of the Eye** and **Tab In The Ocean** . By this time Amon Duul II had released **Dance Of The Lemmings** and by 1972 were about to release **Carnival In Babylon** and **Wolf City**. Bands like Duul and the more electronic Kraftwerk and their offspring Neu as well as Tangerine Dream would give rise to the term "Kraut rock" coined by a Virgin Records publicist. Germany became a breeding ground for progressive

Hoelderlin

Novalis

Octopus

rock bands like Hoelderlin, Novalis, Octopus and others more on the jazz end like Kraan and Kin Ping Meh.

Hoelderlin came together in 1971 playing mostly folk music. Taking their name from German poet Friedrich Hoelderlin, their first LP 1972's **Hoelderlin's Traum** incorporated violin and Mellotron but was more of a symphonic folk effort with lots of acoustic guitars. Still it was a sign of things to come. The band was unhappy with the record company's efforts in promoting the LP and they parted company. The downside for the band was that it turned out to be two years before another label would sign them. The time was well spent performing live and refining their sound. The Hoelderlin that surfaced at the end of the two years had a very different, much more progressive rock oriented style.

1973 - Progressive Rock Takes Hold

Pink Floyd

Over the next few years progressive rock bands and record releases would appear at an ever quickening pace from all four corners of the globe. 1973 will forever be remembered as the year Pink Floyd released **Dark Side Of The Moon**, an album that would end up staying in the music charts for over seven hundred weeks! Longtime Floyd design associates Hipgnosis set new standards for LP packaging while Alan Parsons pushed studio production to new heights.

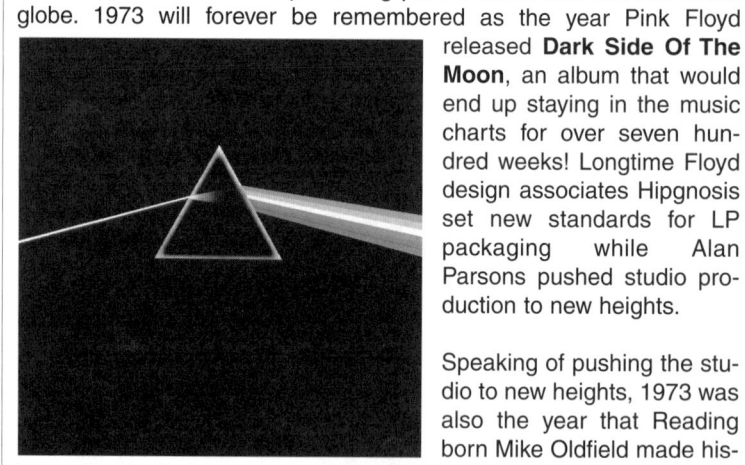

Mike Oldfield

Speaking of pushing the studio to new heights, 1973 was also the year that Reading born Mike Oldfield made history with his first release entitled **Tubular Bells**. Oldfield began his career playing folk music with his sister in his early teens. After putting his own band together to no success, he joined up with Kevin Ayers and The Whole World until they fell apart in 1971. During this period he had been working on an ambitious fifty minute demo tape but was finding no takers from any record companies. It wasn't until he crossed paths with Richard Branson that things came together. Branson was, at the time, owner of a highly successful chain of record stores. But he aspired to more. Upon hearing Oldfield's demo tape, he saw the perfect vehicle to launch his own record label. Branson arranged for Oldfield to spend all the time he needed in the studio, overdubbing each and every instrument to complete his epic composition.

In May of 1973 **Tubular Bells** became the first release for Branson's new label, Virgin Records. The critics were very kind and the public bought the LP in droves. **Tubular Bells** became a massive hit. In the United States sales were helped as a result of the composition being used in the movie soundtrack of The Exorcist. Oldfield would go on to write and record many more fine examples of progressive rock, while Virgin Records would become perhaps one of the most successful and respected progressive rock labels, home to some of the genre's most celebrated acts.

Mike Oldfield

Yes made valuable use of their extensive touring to produce the three LP set **Yessongs** featuring the most elaborate Roger Dean designed cover to date. The album effectively captured the band in the live element. Yes' keyboardist, Rick Wakeman released the first of a long line of solo efforts with **The Six Wives of Henry the VIII**.

Yes

Roger Dean

Rick Wakeman

In February ELP created their own record label, Manticore, a name taken from their mythological creature featured in **Tarkus**. This was also the year they put out their classic **Brain Salad Surgery** featuring an album cover designed by the as yet unknown H.R. Geiger. The album picked up on the theme attempted with **Tarkus**, "humanity" versus a "harsh-technological-society" well crafted in the 30 minute epic "Karn Evil 9". The album also featured "Jerusalem" and the chart topping "Still...You Turn Me On". A massive world tour ensued.

ELP

Genesis undertook their first British headline tour in March of '72. It was from this tour that their Manchester performance was taped for a radio program. Tony Stratton-Smith encouraged the band to release a live album, but put it out at a budget-price to provide the group with some much needed exposure. While at first the band was against the idea, feeling the sound quality of the recording was inferior, they eventually relented and **Genesis Live** hit the store shelves in the summer. While **Genesis Live** was selling, the band were in the studio working on their next recording and in the fall released **Selling England By The Pound**, which turned into quite a successful record giving the band their first chart success with "I Know What I Like" going to number twenty-one on the British charts. Genesis ended the year playing six successful nights at the prestigious Roxy Club in Los Angeles, further setting the stage for their conquest of America.

Genesis

Peter Bank's came out of Yes' shadow with the folding of his band Flash and assembled some great musicians to record **Two Sides Of Peter Banks**. The band Flash had been regarded as a carbon copy of one facet of the Yes sound. They recorded three LPs and while the first two had a distinct Yes flavour to them, by the time of the third the band had begun to forge their own sound. For the third LP Banks had recruited

Peter Banks

Flash

former Yes Keyboardist Tony Kaye. For his solo work Banks turned to quite a number of guests to help out including Steve Hackett and Phil Collins.

David Sinclair returned to Caravan at the same time his cousin Richard decided to leave. Their 1973 release **For Girls Who Grow Plump In The Night** showed the band at their symphonic best. The LP also featured extensive use of violin compliments of Geoff Richardson. His work would help define the band's sound in the next few years. This LP also featured guest Rupert Hine on keyboards.

On the continent the celebrated Italian one-shot band Semiramis released **Dedicato E Frazz**, while Banco put out their third **Io Sono Nato Libero** and Le Orme recorded **Felona & Serona**. One of the most highly thought of releases came from Museo Rosenbach called **Zarathustra**. Over the years this LP has taken on legendary status as perhaps one of the finest symphonic progressive rock recordings to come out of Italy. The band PFM were signed to the newly formed Emerson Lake & Palmer label Manticore and released an English version of their '72 LP now entitled **Photo's Of Ghosts**. The English lyrics were written by Pete Sinfield who chose not to translate the Italian directly but simply come up with completely new material. Many are critical of the English version but it's certain that releasing the material to a wider audience did a lot to raise the profile of progressive rock and more than that expose PFM to a much wider audience. France's Alice recorded **Arretez La Monde** and In Germany Eloy surfaced with an album entitled **Inside** creating a musical mixture of Pink Floyd and Tangerine Dream.

The 1973 edition of The Reading Rock Festival in August reflected the international flavour progressive rock was taking on. Over the festival's three days fans would see performances from Greenslade, Alquin, Tasavallan Presidentti, Magma, PFM, Ange and as a result of their stellar performance the previous year Genesis were headlining on Sunday. Ange lead vocalist and founding member Christian Decamps still considers this show to be one of the greatest performances the band ever did. They were slotted to perform following folk singer Leslie Duncan and before PFM (who by the way were being produced by Emerson Lake and Palmer in person). In any case they were allowed, like the other bands, forty five minutes for their set. According to Decamps the band had gone over time by about three minutes and were in the process of having power switched off. They were saved this embarrassment when the band's manager, John Claude Pognan literally jumped on the festival roadie before he was able to throw the switch. Unfortunately, the French journalists covering the festival were all busy eating while Ange performed and not a word of the band's performance appeared in the French papers. None-the-less they received a five-minute standing ovation from the crowd of 30,000 fans. New groups continued to appear with their own unique styles. Bands like Fruupp and Greenslade.

There aren't many progressive rock bands from Ireland. Formed by Vince McCusker in Belfast, Fruupp soon moved to London. The name Fruupp was actually the nick-name the group gave to the ghost of a young girl they claimed haunted the house where they rehearsed. In November of 1974 Chris Charlesworth wrote in **Melody Maker**: *"Fruupp are not the kind of band one expects to come from Ireland...Fruupp are in an ELP/Yes mould. They don't play rock and roll; instead their music comprises lengthy passages of semi-classical themes welded together into dramatic sounding pieces where the accent is on melody rather than rhythm."* Fruupp would eventually release four LPs all to high critical acclaim as did their live performances and yet their core of devoted fans never grew very large. The same is true of Greenslade.

Greenslade was the brainchild of Dave Greenslade and was put together in late 1972 with Tony Reeves, Dave Lawson and Andrew McCulloch. Greenslade and Reeves were former members of the more jazz oriented Colosseum. McCulloch had spent time in King Crimson and Fields, while Lawson played with Episode Six and Alan Bown, so all members had their fare share of jazz background and this showed in the tight arrangements and solid musicianship. Greenslade featured twin keyboard players and few vocals. In 1973 they released two LPs, their first self titled and **Bedside Manners Are Extra**. Both featured spectacular Roger Dean covers.

1974 – Progressive Rock's Acceptance

By 1974 a sign of progressive rock's acceptance was when **Melody Maker** ran it's annual amateur band contest with the winner receiving a recording contract, it was a prog band that won. The winner was a band called Druid who's material bore a striking resemblance to Yes in terms of arrangement, vocal style and bass playing. The critics were still doing what critics do, being critical. But the feelings about progressive rock could best be summed up by a comment once made by film mogul Louis B. Mayer; *"Everybody hated it, EXCEPT the public."*

The established bands were maturing. While Yes released their magnum opus **Tales From Topographic Oceans,** King Crimson released **Red** and **Starless And Bible Black** and then decided to call it a day, they wouldn't be heard from again until the early eighties. Strawbs put out the album many cite as their finest progressive rock achievement **Hero & Heroine**. Gentle Giant released **The Power And The Glory**, Gryphon put out **Midnight Mushrumps** and **Red Queen To Gryphon Three**, Renaissance **Turn Of The Cards,** Fruupp had two releases **Prince Of Heaven's Eyes** and **Seven Secrets**, and Greenslade released their third **Spyglass Guest**, Camel's second LP **Mirage** showed them maturing. Keyboardists Rick Wakeman and Jon Lord both did solo work, **Journey To The Centre Of The Earth** and **Windows** respectively.

Genesis began what turned out to be the torturous task of recording **The Lamb Lies Down on Broadway**. The project began innocently enough, but soon the scope of the material grew and became unmanageable for just one disc, so it became two. Peter Gabriel had insisted on writing the lyrics, but was also experiencing tremendous personal trials at home with the birth of his first daughter, so he was having trouble concentrating on writing. On top of that his commuting from London to Bath (Peter's home) meant that he was out of touch with the rest of the band much of the time. In the end the band were well behind schedule and were working virtually 24 hours a day to complete the recording on time. November saw the release of the troubled concept LP and the start of a massive 102 date tour to promote **The Lamb** that began in the United States. Little did fans realise the tension that existed within the group during this time and the impact certain events would have on the band's future.

Sidebar:

Druid

Yes
King Crimson

Strawbs

Gentle Giant
Gryphon
Renaissance
Fruup
Greenslade
Camel
Rick Wakeman
Jon Lord

Genesis

Peter Gabriel

For those who had wondered whatever became of The Nice after Keith Emerson left to form ELP, they got the answer when Refugee hit the record shelves. Following Emerson's departure, Lee Jackson sunk a "ton" of money into a band called Jackson Heights that went absolutely nowhere. In 1973 he'd run into Patrick Moraz and decided to put a band together to feature Moraz's keyboard work. Jackson enlisted ex-Nice drummer Brian Davison and the trio became Refugee. Their self titled and only release hit the record stores with a lot of publicity, good reviews and the start of some successful concerts. Fortunately or unfortunately depending on how one views these things, Yes had just lost Rick Wakeman and they were looking for a keyboard replacement and Moraz took the job. A classic case of history repeating itself for Jackson and Davison who were left without a keyboard player just like The Nice. Refugee folded shortly thereafter.

Tension of a different kind had been building in Yes through the latter part of 1973 as they recorded **Tales From Topographic Oceans**, an album that was as controversial then as it is today. It was this album that would lead to Rick Wakeman's departure. He simply felt they were moving into a musical territory where he had little to offer. This double record set was a massive undertaking even for Yes and it's four side-long songs proved to be just as massive an undertaking for listeners. In the end people either loved it or hated it, there was very little middle ground. The project was spearheaded by Jon Anderson and Steve Howe but in the end there was so much space that everyone was able to contribute a lot. Rick Wakeman quoted in **Yes Stories** says: *"I was due to start rehearsing with Yes for the American tour, when I decided to call management and tell them I was going to leave the band. Not more than a minute later, A&M Records in London called to tell me that my solo album, Journey To The Centre of the Earth, had just gone to number one in the charts. On top of it all it was my birthday! It was a strange mixed day."* Wakeman finished out the European portion of the tour and called it a day. Yes had started out the tour with the intention of playing all four sides of their new release, but after finding audiences having a hard time with so much new material, they shortened the new set and began including older songs as well. After the tour Yes were back in the studio and in November released **Relayer** with Patrick Moraz on keyboards. **Relayer** in it's own way was even more adventurous than **Tales...** . Moraz during his brief stint with Yes clearly left his mark in terms of injecting a strong avant-garde-fusion feel to portions of the LP's three pieces.

In Italy, Le Orme released what some cite as their best work **Contrapunti** and PFM released the English version of **L'isola Di Niente** which became the **World Became The World**. Once again the lyrics were rewritten by Pete Sinfield, only this would be the last time as the band insisted his lyrics become more a literal translation of the Italian ones. Since Sinfield didn't care for the political nature of the band's lyrics he chose not to work with them anymore. PFM also released two versions of live material from their Canadian and American tours.

The Nice

Keith Emerson

Patrick Moraz

Refugee

Yes

Rick Wakeman

Jon Anderson

Steve Howe

Le Orme

PFM

Pete Sinfield

Ekseption

Trace

Focus

Former Ekseption keyboardist Rick Van Der Linden's new band Trace also made quite a splash with their self titled release. Trace produced a very keyboard oriented sound that in many ways was a combination of what Ekseption had done and what Focus were doing. The classical influence was very strong not only in arrangements but in the band's willingness to perform classical covers much as Ekseption had done. Also from Holland, Focus released one of their most highly acclaimed LPs **Hamburger Concerto**, and Kayak released their first self titled LP, while Alquin put out **Nobody Can Wait Forever**.

Styx

American band Styx released **Man Of Miracles**. But Styx had actually been around in one form or another since 1964. The members had been playing in a variety of Chicago bands and finally connected as a unit to record their first LP in 1972. Their second and third releases were put out in 1973. Each of these releases leading up to **Man Of Miracles** contained long tracks with innovative use of the classics all-be-it in a somewhat rockier environment than most British progressive rock bands.

The English sound had filtered into many European countries and in Spain, 1974 was the year it seemed many bands decided to come out of the country's underground music scene. Given the political climate in Spain during the early seventies, music of an experimental nature (anything other than pop music) was discouraged. So while progressive rock LPs could be purchased, there were no venues for Spanish prog bands to perform. By the mid seventies however, the political climate was relaxing and these bands began to play at a variety of music festivals and the impact they created was significant. Spanish progressive rock, perhaps more than any other country has been musically influenced by it's folk and ethnic roots. So much so that bands will be described as having a Basque influence or a Flamenco influence. This has more to do with the fact that each province in Spain seems to impart it's own musical influences to it's bands. Having said that, bands throughout Spain took these cultural influences and borrowed from the well-established British, French and Italian progressive rock schools. Bands like Triana, Canarios, Fusioon, Granada, Atila, Itoiz, Mezquita and others were releasing vinyl. Elsewhere in Europe, Germany's Eloy released **Floating** still in their Pink Floyd phase, France's Ange released **La Cimetiere Des Arlequins**. All in all it was a strong year for progressive rock.

Triana
Canarios
Fusioon
Granada
Atila
Itoiz
Mezquita
Eloy
Ange
Pink Floyd

1975 - The Anglo-American Sound

By 1975 the United States was fully into the progressive rock scene with Styx's **Equinox** and a band from Topeka, Kansas called naturally enough Kansas. Kansas had spent the previous few years playing clubs and small halls. It was this incessant gigging that enabled them like many a prog band before to hone their playing abilities. Before their recording contract came about their main claim to fame was having opened for The Doors in New Orleans, one of Jim Morrison's last concerts. It was at the end of 1974 that Don Kirshner heard their demo tape and signed them to his label. Their first LP Kansas was released in 1974, while 1975 would see their Anglo-symphonic progressive rock sound perfected in **Song For America** and **Masque**. Fireballet's **A Night on Bald Mountain**, Crack The Sky, Happy The Man and Pavlov's Dog's **Pampered Menial** were just a few more American recordings starting to get noticed. On the more avant-garde side Frank Zappa was well on his way, doing for American progressive music what Soft Machine had done in England.

In Britain, Pink Floyd followed up **Dark Side**... with **Wish You Were Here** and Camel made headlines with their release of **The Snow Goose**. Many consider this album to be some of Camel's best work. The album was a musical interpretation of the book of the same name by Paul Gallico. As far as the band were concerned their music was a mirror-image of the book, however the author had other ideas. To make things worse, he hadn't been consulted on the use of the name or the ideas. A legal wrangle ensued which resulted in Decca records being forced to publish an apology for the fact that no formal permission had been sought. All the publicity didn't hurt and Camel would go on to win **Melody Maker's** "Brightest Hope" award for 1975. Strong LPs were produced by Gentle Giant - **Free Hand** and **A Giant Step**, Renaissance - **Scherherazade**, Strawbs - **Ghosts**, Jethro Tull - **Minstrel In a Gallery**, Barclay James Harvest - **Time Honoured Ghosts**, Curved Air - **Midnight Wire**, Caravan - **Cunning Stunts**, Gryphon - **Raindance**, and Greenslade - **Time and Tide**. Taking their cue from Rick Wakeman, each member of Yes took time to record solo efforts including Jon Anderson's **Olias Of Sunhillow**, Steve Howe's **Beginnings**, and Chris Squire's **Fish Out Of Water**.

A host of European bands were busy including Holland's Earth And Fire - **To the World of the Future**, Germany's Novalis, Grobschnitt - **Jumbo**, Eloy - **Power & the Passion**, Tea, Trace - **Birds**, Tritonus,

Styx
Kansas
The Doors
Fireballet
Happy The Man
Pavlov's Dog
Frank Zappa
Soft Machine
Pink Floyd
Camel
Gentle Giant
Renaissance
Strawbs
Jethro Tull
Barclay James Harvest
Curved Air
Caravan
Gryphon
Greenslade
Yes
Earth & Fire
Grobschnitt
Eloy

Triumvirat

Hoelderlin

Triumvirat - **Spartacus**, Harlis, Hoelderlin, Mirthrandir - **For You the Old Woman** and many others. Hoelderlin had secured a major label deal and had been in the studio with the results being **Hoelderlin** showing a re-focused rock sound. Musically the Mellotron was ever present, but so was the viola, and while the bands early folk roots were not forgotten they were definitely placed more in the background. This album would be the start of a very prolific release schedule as Hoelderlin would have a new release each year for the next five years.

Ange

From France, Ange were riding on the success of their latest LP **Au Dela Du Delire** which many consider their best. It turned out to be the last with the group's original line-up. Ange were the prototypical French band. They communicated to their home audience in poetic songs, stories, language and style that were uniquely French and well known to their audience. The band made their initial appearance as far back as March of 1970 and their first appearances got them a lot of media attention. Unfortunately pressure within the band caused a personnel change. Band leaders Francis and Christian DeCamps, joined by Jean-Michel Brezovar on Guitar, Gerard Jelsch on drums and Daniel Haas on bass became the band that would create their first LP **Caricatures** in late 1972. While the sound may have been somewhat rudimentary in comparison to their English contemporaries, their theatrical style and musical delivery was well on the way to defining French progressive rock. Other French bands, Atoll released **L'araignee Mal**, Tai Phong released their first self titled LP, and Carpe Diem released **En Regardant Passer Le Temps**. Canadian French band Morse Code put out **La March Des Hommes**.

Atoll

Tai Phong

Carpe Diem

Morse Code

Gabriel Calls It A Day

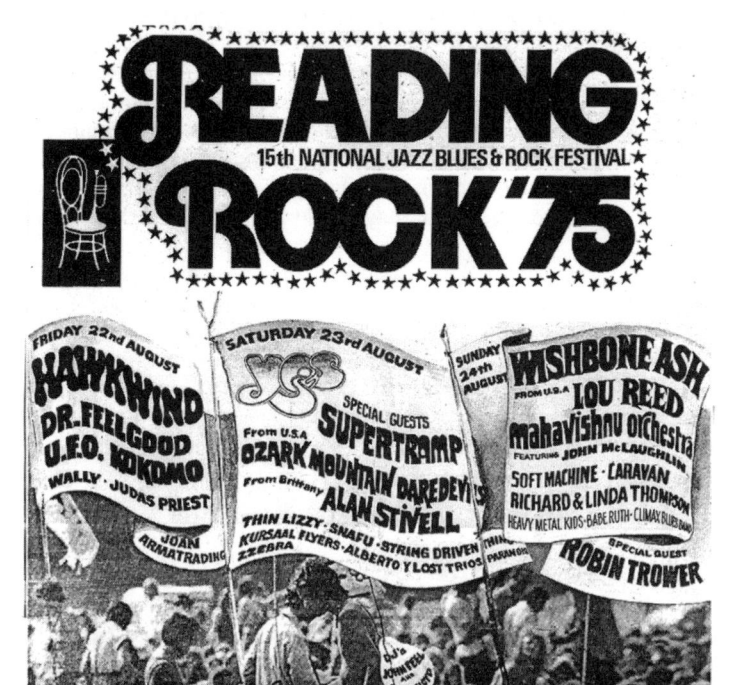

The massive tour to promote **The Lamb Lies Down on Broadway** had taken it's toll on Peter Gabriel. In November of 1975, fans of Genesis were dealt a blow with Peter Gabriel's announcement he was leaving the band after the completion of the tour to promote **The Lamb Lies Down On Broadway.** In an interview with **Exposure Magazine** Gabriel explained; *"I felt it (the group) was getting stale. I felt if I stayed, Genesis would get a lot more successful and I'd become the rock-star tied to the success that I had wanted in the beginning. Initially, we felt the band was there to express the music of the four of us and in the end, I felt that we were there to express this large machine of the band. I wanted to take some time off at home - make a baby and grow some cabbages."* Gabriel was tired of being in the spotlight. In addition cir-

Peter Gabriel

Genesis

Genesis

Peter Gabriel

cumstances in his personal life caused him to want to move in different directions than the band. At the time he needed to be able to spend more time at home with his family. The media were quick to jump on the news. They had always made the assumption that Gabriel WAS Genesis and that without him, the band would flounder. The rest of the group had at first tried to convince Gabriel to change his mind, but once over the shock, they realised their experience with **The Lamb** had prepared them to carry on. All they would have to do was find a new vocalist.

Steve Hackett

Brand X

Some of the tension for members of Genesis was released with the beginnings of solo efforts. In the fall of '75 Steve Hackett released his first solo recording, **Voyage of the Acolyte**. On the recording he had help from Mike Rutherford and Phil Collins. Phil in the meantime took up a position with the jazz-rock Brand X, giving him an outlet for his drumming. In time Collins seemed to appear guesting on dozens of recordings.

1976 - Stand Back It's The Enid

Gentle Giant

Van Der Graaf Generator

Strawbs
Caravan
Jethro Tull
Pulsar
Hoelderlin

1976 dawned with more releases from all the established bands like Gentle Giant's **Interview**, Van Der Graaf's **World Record**, The Strawbs' **Nomadness** and **Deep Cuts**, Rick Wakeman's **No Earthly Connection**, Caravan's **Blind Dog at St. Dunstans**, Jethro Tull's **Too Old to Rock and Roll**, and more new bands released material such as France's Pulsar **Pollen**, Germany's Hoelderlin with what some feel is their best effort **Clowns & Clouds** showing a return to a more orchestral sound, and England's The Enid. For a few months it looked like progressive rock was invincible. Who knew that punk rock was just around the corner.

The Enid

If there was ever a band to contrast the sound of punk, it would have to be The Enid. Attempting to describe the music of The Enid is difficult. It's perhaps the ultimate blending of orchestral arrangements in a rock setting. The instrumentation is typically rock, guitars drums and keyboards, but for most of their material that's where the comparison ends. The music created is majestic, panoramic, dynamic and definitely not rock. They were formed in 1974 by Robert John Godfrey, Stephen Stewart, and Francis Lickerish. Godfrey had done some orchestral arranging in the early days for Barclay James Harvest that would prove to be a means-to-an-end as far as The Enid was concerned.

January 1976 would see the release of their first LP **In The Region Of Summer Stars**. Chris Welch wrote in **Melody Maker**: *"The music is pretty, intelligent and mixes rock and classical elements with some fine keyboard work from Robert...the range of sounds they achieve is often dramatic and startling. It's music that needs plenty of concentration and a relaxed state to enjoy and savour."* While the album was independently released at first, The Enid were quickly signed to a world-wide deal with EMI International. This event would go on to be the source of aggravation for the band as they felt EMI didn't understand what the band was all about and wasn't in their estimation doing a very good job to promote them. According to the band, because of poor sales and little interest EMI had deleted the recordings from their inventory. The Enid attempted to get the masters back to release them independently, but when all efforts to acquire the masters for the first three LPs failed, the situation became quite acrimonious. It was finally sorted out and since that time The Enid have happily lived a life of independence from the music business, relying on their fans for support.

Progressive rock had a solid grip in Europe with releases from Ange **Par le Fils du Mandarin**, Banco **As In a Last Supper**, Eloy **Dawn**, Le Orme **Verita Nascoste**, Celest, Nektar **Recycled**, PFM **Chocolate Kings**, SFF **Symphonic Pictures**, Sensations Fix **Finest Finger**, Trace **The White Ladies**, Nova **Atlantis**, Tai Phong **Windows**, Eela Craig **One Nighter**, Harlis **Night Meets the Day**, and Octopus **The Boat of Thoughts** to name a few.

In America Kansas released **Leftoverture**, containing their hit song "Carry on Wayward Son" which put the band onto radio stations everywhere and just as quickly catapulted them onto the big arena rock circuit. Styx released **Crystal Ball** which turned out to be in the same style as the previous years **Equinox** and showed the band very adept at not only their brand of American progressive rock but also at crafting shorter radio-ready songs with good hooks. Fireballet went on to release their second LP entitled **Two Too**. Todd Rundgren's Utopia released **Faithful**, while two new comers released first LPs; Starcastle and Yezda Urfa.

Starcastle had been banging around clubs for a few years before making a tape of the song "Lady of the Lake" which through good fortune was aired on a radio station in the group's home town of Champaign, Illinois. The response from listeners was tremendous and this led to a club date in February of 1975 where Epic records saw them, and based on their perfor-

The Enid

Ange
Banco
Eloy
Le Orme
Nektar
PFM
SFF
Trace
Nova
Harlis
Octopus

Kansas

Styx

Tod Rundgren

Starcastle

Starcastle

Yes
Kansas

mance that night, signed them to a long term deal. Starcastle's first self-titled LP released in 1976 showed a sound based on an emphasis on music, multiple voicing, counterpoint and counter-melodies and yet much of their material is very accessible. Their style incorporated certain elements of Yes and Kansas. While it's become fashionable in some circles to be critical of the band it should be remembered that for the time Starcastle represented a solid example of Americanised-Anglo-progressive rock. They also gained fame in the amount of detail spent on their stage performance, as reported in **Walrus**: *"You've got to see and hear it to believe it - fantastic! The band brings along it's own lighting and other special effects including rotating mirrors and fireworks. the show was superb."* Starcastle would ultimately release three LPs of what can easily be called progressive rock before succumbing to the urge to go completely commercial.

Yezda Urfa

Gentle Giant

A commercial sound is something Yezda Urfa never came close to. The French magazine **Harmonie** said Yezda Urfa; *"is the most authentic progressive music that America has to offer. The record's (Sacred Baboon) elaborate instrumentation sets a new progressive genre. Impressive!"* The group formed in the fall of 1973 and managed to survive to the spring of 1981. It was always their intention to take the progressive rock genre to it's limit in terms of composition and instrumentation. In these goals most would agree they succeeded. Often they are compared with Gentle Giant, especially in terms of vocal arrangement and their unique instrumentation which not only included the usual bass, guitar, drums and keyboards but things like; vibes, recorder, marimba, cello, mandolin and flute. Some have also seen a Yes Influence in the vocal and rhythm styles. The name was actually arrived at while flipping through a dictionary one day. After changing a few letters to aid in pronunciation Yezda Urfa was born. The unusual aspect of the band is that they never went on any tours. In May of 1975 they released an independent demo LP called **Boris**, which contained some early versions of the songs that would appear on **Sacred Baboon**. During the summer of 1976 the band went into the studio to record **Sacred Baboon** which represented the band at it's most progressive stage. At one point they thought they had a deal with a small label but the whole thing fell apart and as a result the master tapes sat Idle for about 13 years. Until a man by the name of Peter Stoller, who had a copy of **Boris** brought the band to the attention of Greg Walker at Syn-Phonic records. Walker liked the band enough that in 1989 the LP was finally released on Vinyl.

Klaatu

Beatles

For a few months the music world was a-buzz with the release of an album by a band called Klaatu. The material was clearly head-and-shoulders above your regular pop fare and borrowed heavily from the world of progressive rock on compositions like "Calling Occupants", "Little Neutrino" and "Sub Rosa Subway". The sound quality and production of the release caused many to sit-up and take notice. Even more so when a newspaper journalist in the United States ran an article with the headline "Is Klaatu band The Beatles?" This rumour that, in fact Klaatu were The Beatles who had reformed under the pseudonym to release the album created an intense interest in the band.

Everyone went searching for clues, much as they had done for the Paul-is-dead hoax. Everyone "inside" the industry played the mystery for all it was worth and it certainly contributed to the success of the LP. It turned out the band were actually three talented Canadian session musicians, and while this took nothing away from the quality of the album, it undoubtedly was disappointing to some. The sudden fame was going to be difficult to follow-up.

Another Canadian band that made a big splash in 1976 was Rush with the release of **2112**. Rush had started out as pretty much a straight ahead hard rock band forming in 1969 with their first LP released in 1974. As a three piece their inspiration came from bands like Cream and even Led Zeppelin. A change in personnel for the second LP **Fly By Night** brought in lyricist and drummer Neil Peart, he along with bassist Geddy Lee and guitarist Alex Lifeson were about to become famous. Their third release **Caress of Steel** in 1975 contained their first concept piece, the side-long "Fountain of Lamneth". Unfortunately the album was completely passed over by almost everyone. With the assistance of Terry Brown, who'd been their remix engineer on the first album and producer from the second onward, Rush crafted **2112** with it's side-long title track. Conceptually and lyrically it was true-blue progressive rock, with the individual triumphing over an impersonal and technologically bound society. This LP more than **Caress of Steel**, exposed Rush to a prog audience and over the next few years they produced some exciting progressive rock releases.

While many in the media saw Gabriel's departure as a fatal blow, Genesis decided to carry on and immediately went into the studio to work on their next album. Given that the four remaining members, Banks, Rutherford, Hackett and Collins had actually written all the music for **The Lamb Lies Down on Broadway**, they were ready to tackle the next project. Two brilliant LPs followed in quick succession putting to rest the rumour that the heart and soul of the band had left with Gabriel. The harder edged **A Trick Of The Tail** released in February, showed them in fine form with the powerful "Dance On A Volcano" and "Los Endos". The troublesome task of finding a replacement singer was solved one day in the studio with Phil Collins doing the vocals on the harder-edged "Squonk". The group had always known Collins could handle the softer ballads, but with him being able to handle the harder songs, the problem of who should sing was decided. The band went on tour to promote the album with Collins on vocals and

Rush

Cream
Led Zeppelin

Peter Gabriel
Genesis

Phil Collins

Bill Bruford

Genesis

Steve Hackett

none other than Bill Bruford on drums. Genesis finished the tour and headed straight back into the studio to produce the more melodic and pastoral **Wind & Wuthering** in late 1976 to be released in January of 1977. This album demonstrated that their ability to craft fanciful material was still alive and well. In fact, Tony Banks has said that **Wind & Wuthering**, was one of the most non-commercial albums they'd done to date. It was also one of his favourites, perhaps in part because he wrote much of the material on it. Unfortunately **Wind & Wuthering** never got much of a fair hearing in the media as it was released at the height of the punk rock introduction. It was also a difficult time for Steve Hackett who'd received good response from his solo release and was looking for more space on the next Genesis release. While he contributed some fine material, he had more to give and started to feel discouraged. The seeds of dissent had been planted.

1977 - The Return of Wakeman

Yes

Rick Wakeman

Patrick Moraz

Yes who hadn't been heard from since **Relayer,** had spent a month rehearsing for the new album, but the band realised things were not meshing smoothly with their keyboard player. They dismissed Patrick Moraz and patched things up with Rick Wakeman. Wakeman for his part got over his dislike of the **Tales From Topographic Oceans** episode, came in as a session player to do the keyboard parts at the request of their mutual manager Brian Lane. Once he got into the new material he really liked where the band was going musically. Their 1977 release was **Going For The One,** featuring another twenty minute Yes epic "Awaken".

Klaatu

Klaatu were able to successfully follow up their first album with the epic **Hope**. A tale of a planet fighting for freedom which included full concept, story-line and symphony orchestra. Once again production values and musicianship were top-notch. Unfortunately this would be the last of their progressive work as they soon contented themselves trying for the next hit single and divesting themselves of the qualities that made them popular in the first place. Fellow Canadian's Rush continued in their sci-fi mode with **A Farewell To Kings** which contained their hit "Closer to the Heart."

Rush

Genesis

Genesis were on tour to promote **Wind & Wuthering.** The tour started in England and included a stop in Paris, Brazil, and the States before winding up back in England for three nights at the Earl's Court Exhibition Hall. The Paris dates were recorded and were released in October of 1977 as the double record set, **Second's Out**. Sadly for some, the final dates in England were the end of Steve Hackett's involvement with Genesis.

Procol Harum
Gentle Giant

Jethro Tull
Camel
Styx

Progressive rock releases were significant in 1977 with music from Procol Harum **Something Magic**, Gentle Giant **The Missing Piece**, Jethro Tull **Songs From The Wood**, Camel **Raindances**, Styx **The Grand Illusion** with the hit single "Come Sail Away" showing the group moving away from their more complicated efforts into a more pomp-mainstream sound, Caravan **Better By Far**, Kansas **Point of Know Return** with their biggest hit "Dust In The Wind" penned by Kerry Livgren, The Strawbs **Burning For You**, Ange **Ange Tome VI**, Kayak **Starlight Dancer**, Le Orme **Storia O Legganda**, Novalis **Brandung**, PFM **Jet Lag**, Gryphon **Treason**, Earth & Fire **Gate to Infinity**, Pulsar **Halloween**, SFF **Sunburst**, Sensations Fix **Boxes Paradise**, Starcastle **Fountains of Light**, Triumvirat **Pompeii**, Hoelderlin **Rare Birds**, Epidaurus **Earthly Paradise**, Finch **Galleons of Passion**, Utopia **Ra** and many, many others. Of particular interest was a band called England. It was the brainchild of Robert Webb whose penchant for Mellotron is clearly evident on their release entitled **Garden Shed**. England borrowed heavily from Yes, Genesis and King Crimson but synthesised the elements into a sound that was clearly it's own. France's Carpe Diem followed up their successful debut with **Cueille De Jour**. This five piece outfit produced a Canterbury influenced sound which emphasised melody more than any other musical component. Their mostly instrumental music represented some of the best French progressive rock of the late seventies.

There were three American groups; Quill, Babylon and Easter Island who produced material showing just how strong the Genesis influence was on American progressive rock groups of the time. Each of these bands from different parts of the country had clearly spent time listening to those early albums and incorporated various elements from playing technique to instrument sounds into their individual styles.

Babylon were from Florida and had developed quite a cult following playing the local pubs and University gigs. They released a well produced self-titled album in 1977 showing a highly inventive mixture of vocals with plenty of long instrumental passages.

Meanwhile in Kentucky, a band called Easter Island were crafting their own sound based on the same Genesis influences. Their LP called **Now and Then** was limited to a 300 copy run and as a result quickly became a collectors item. Easter Island showed influences from King Crimson and Yes.

Quill on the other hand were a trio from California that consisted of Keith Christian, Ken DeLoria and Jim Sides. After spending the usual years individually playing mindless cover tunes in lounges and clubs they decided in 1976 to join forces and begin performing music that was more dramatic and emotional, in other words, progressive rock. Their first LP was recorded in late 1976 and

Caravan
Kansas
Strawbs
Ange
Kayak
Le Orme
Novalis
PFM
SFF
Utopia

King Crimson
Yes

Carpe Diem

Quill
Babylon
Easter Island

Genesis

Quill

early 1977, it was called **Sursum Corda**, and was released in such a limited edition it immediately became a collectors item. The band would spend the next couple years fending off the popular music of the day and would eventually write a second LP but it was never recorded or released. They eventually split and took jobs within the music industry. It once again fell to Greg Walker at Syn-Phonic to release a CD of Quill's first release many years later.

ELP

Emerson Lake & Palmer released the ambitious double record set **Works** and then shortly after released a single LP of solo pieces entitled **Works Volume II**. This was followed up with an even more ambitious world tour. Three weeks of which included taking a full 67 piece orchestra with them to concerts throughout the United States and parts of Canada, including Montreal where the event was filmed and released as a live concert video. If Yes' **Tales From Topographic Oceans** tour started the critics talking, the ELP tour had them ranting about the excesses and overblown nature of progressive rock. The band even today are quick to point out that staging has always been an important part of dramatising the ELP musical experience. Nevertheless when one enterprising critic discovered it was an expensive Persian rug that Greg Lake stood on, that was all the critics needed to begin their critical assault of not only ELP but the entire genre. The origin of the rug, so the story goes actually has little to do with Lake and a lot to do with an over exuberant roadie. Earlier in the tour, Lake had received a shock during the tune-up while standing on a wet portion of the stage. When he asked to have it corrected and have something to insulate him from the floor, it was the roadie who went out and purchased the rug. All this unbeknownst to Lake. Still small picayune details such as the truth would only get in the way of a good story, so the critics ignored it and had a whale of a time pointing out the so-called "excesses" of progressive rock.

Yes

Greg Lake

marquee
90 Wardour St., W1 — 01-437 6603
OPEN EVERY NIGHT FROM 7.00 p.m. to 11.00 p.m.
REDUCED ADMISSION FOR STUDENTS AND MEMBERS

Thurs. 10th March (Adm. 60p)
NASTY POP
Plus Support & Ian Fleming

Fri. 11th March (Adm. 70p)
NOVA
Plus Support & Ian Fleming

Sat. 12th March
Free admission with this ad before 8 p.m.
HEARTBREAKER
Second Avenue & Ian Fleming

Sun. 13th March (Adm. 60p)
Free admission with this ad before 8 p.m.
LEE KOSMIN BAND
The Stukas and Nick Leigh

Mon. 14th March (Adm. 65p)
BACK TO FRONT
(Featuring Pete Brown)
A. J. Webber & Jerry Floyd

Tues., 15th March
See Panel Below

Wed. 16th March (Adm. 90p)
Special Welcome to...
MEAL TICKET
Plus Support & Jerry Floyd

Thurs., 17th March (Adm. 65p)
ILLUSION
(Ex- Renaissance)
Krician Kogcan & Ian Fleming

Hamburgers and other hot & cold snacks are available

1977 was probably the most prolific year for progressive rock bands during the seventies. Still because of the impact of punk rock and disco, for the first time in a few years, it wasn't progressive rock bands who were making the headlines. For a variety of reasons.

So What Happened?

Towards the end of the seventies, progressive rock began to run into trouble. Publicist Keith Goodwin feels a major reason for the near demise of this genre of music was the economic recession that began to take shape in 1976. Record buying had moved away from the 45 rpm single as the prime source of recorded entertainment. We were now living in an age of albums. Albums that were costing more and more each day it seemed. Goodwin may not be far off the mark on that score. Album sales had been declining slowly but surely and by 1979 disc and tape sales were down 6% in units and 11% in dollar volume. To compensate LP prices were steadily raised. In 1977 they went from $5.98 US to $6.98 US. By 1981 they were $8.98. As a measurement of successful sales the number of Gold and Platinum records was dropping steadily. In 1979 Platinum was down from 112 the previous year to only 42, while Gold declined from 193 to 112. The entire record business was in the doldrums and they blamed a large part of it on home taping.

It's also worth pointing out that the business side of the music industry could never really come to terms with progressive rock music. To put it another way - it was a hard sell. Unlike what they'd been used to, selling pre-packaged easily definable and easily listenable pop stars or for that matter easily categorised folk, jazz or rock artists, progressive rock proved to be an overwhelming challenge. It wasn't accessible enough to be played on radio so exposure was difficult. In the end it was easier to 'slag' it off than try to change the system, the way the music itself had changed. Progressive rock was not helped by the industry nor by the fact that there would always be a demand for material that pandered to a lower common denominator. The music industry has traditionally chosen the path of least resistance.

Another very important element was the backlash of punk to everything that stood for the establishment side of music. Suddenly, overnight if you had been in business for any length of time, you were considered a "boring old fart" or at the very least a "dinosaur." This along with the media's fascination on the extreme or the latest "fad-de-jour", and their own growing displeasure with a form of music they did not fully understand, nor in fact wanted to, it appeared to many that progressive rock slunk quietly into hibernation. Derek Jewel sums up his version of the "demise"; *"A new generation of Punk and New Wave bands began to undermine the supremacy of these artists during the late seventies, the epithet progressive became popular as a critical term of abuse in many music papers in Britain. But changing musical fashion should not blind anyone to progressive rock's achievements and durability. Genesis, The Who, Jethro Tull, ELO, Barclay James Harvest, Camel and even a version of Yes all played into the eighties. This is as remarkable in rock as was the progressive rock influence upon virtually every rock movement of substance thereafter. Of course they were pretentious at times. Of course they didn't always succeed in their aims. However the multitudes that attended concerts by Genesis or ELO or Bowie or Tull in the eighties - and bought their albums - bore testimony to the lasting virtues and popularity of these artists."*

Genesis
ELO
Barclay James Harvest
Jethro Tull

Yes

In discussing this period of the mid seventies and the rise of punk rock, Bob Doerschuck of **Keyboard** magazine wrote: *"Those qualities championed, even flaunted by the band (Yes) had fallen into disfavour. Yes was known for it's grandiose sound, it's long textured arrangements that moved through stately tempos like elephantine cloud banks in a breathless sky. Rock was stretching from youth to adolescence when Yes arrived on the scene, it was taking itself very seriously, experimenting with ambitious ideas and cloaking it's raw energy in flashy new fashion...Nowadays the climate has changed. Expectations have diminished. Rock bands are no longer expected to be pseudo-cosmic visionaries. Once again people want to dance to the raw beat, distractions from that fundamental imperative are considered superfluous and pretentious."*

Doerschuck sums up many of the attitudes we're dealing with, but he also brings up an interesting point, that of growth. Like anything, music should grow. It can't simply reflect new technology, it must incorporate the new with what has gone before to continually reflect what is happening in the present. It's important for artists to give credit where credit is due. One's influences are not something to be shunned or hidden, they are there to learn from. This attitude, more than many was being expressed by the first wave of progressive artists who searched and borrowed from others. Building on the shoulders of others is one of the keys to maturing.

The Music Business Learns To Adapt

Peter Frampton

Beatles

Something else that came out of the punk rock experience was the music industry's recognition that it had to become more involved in the process of creating popularity in order to sell records. After all, if you could create or determine fads and trends you would be in a much better position to capitalise on them. This had actually begun to take place in 1976 with the release of Peter Frampton's **Frampton Comes Alive**, which became the largest selling live rock album to that time, eventually selling over ten million copies. Frampton was interviewed in 1997 on the ABC television show **Turning Point** and related the tremendous pressure he experienced from the record company to follow one hit with another. Frampton's situation was the real turning point where record company executives began to focus more on marketing "success" than on marketing different musical styles. Some would argue that the business has always done this, citing The Beatles as an example. While this may be true to some extent it was never done with such disregard for the music itself. The music itself became important only to the degree it could be marketed and sold. With punk rock, a form of music that on the surface came into being to pull down the traditional establishment, the industry realised here was a genre they could easily mass produce. And so they did. Suddenly the business side became responsible for creating hundreds of bands claiming to be punk rock and when that was on the decline the business moved into New Wave, which again proved to be an easily duplicated genre.

This has come full circle as the industry closely guards what musical fad is allowed to be heard by the masses. If it's alternative rock they look for or create a lot of bands in that genre, if it's rap they find many rappers, and so on. What I mean by this is that the industry creates the environment in which all you hear is what they want you to hear. Rap for example has been trying since the early seventies to be heard on radio. It always had an urban street following that bought the records, but it wasn't until the industry got behind it and made sure that enough radio stations played it that the genre really took off. Today if you see the top charts you might be fooled into thinking that "everyone" is listening to "this" or "that" kind of music when really it's simply the industry creating the demand by allowing only the choice of purchasing a limited number of releases.

It is strange that the very target of the industry that punk rock rose up against, the idea that dinosaur bands were controlling what people were able to listen to, was the very thing that led to the demise of punk rock itself. The industry or business of making money got smarter. The art of creating music suffered.

There is yet another aspect that led to progressive rock's temporary hiatus, and that's dealt with by Ian MacDonald in his wonderful book **Revolution In The Head** a book that looks at the sociological side of The Beatles music and the sixties. MacDonald exposes a rather unpleasant side effect that technology itself has had to play in all this. He clearly describes how through the seventies and to the present day we have become virtual hostages to the technology we've created around us. This has not made us better but has more likely made us lazier, and nowhere near as passionate about the things around us; *"Pop music, too, has played a role in reinforcing the relaxation of goals and standards observable since the sixties. Aside from the inescapable fact that this relation was to various degrees willed by the majority, pop and it's shatteringly sensationalistic cousins rock and disco have been as much colonised by technology as any other area of modern life. It's once flexible human rhythms replaced by the mass-production regularity of the drum-machine, it's structures corporatised by the factory ethic of the sequencer, it's vitality digitised to death and buried in multi-layered sytheticism, pop is now little more than a soundtrack for physical jerks."*

In the context of our discussion here, MacDonald's comments have direct relevance. The one thing that distinguished progressive rock from it's pop or rock cousins, was it's desire to put the music first. In it's own way it tried to distance itself from the popular material of the day and be something more. For this it was certainly criticised, but more from a standpoint of a lack of understanding than from correct musical analyses. Progressive rock prided itself on it's musical virtuosity. An entire keyboard ethic was created based on being able to play two or three instruments at once in real time. Long solos required a great degree of instrumental dexterity. Where little skill existed at a band's outset, by the release of the second or third album the members had

Beatles

very likely matured in their ability to master the number of notes required. However as technology advanced, the skill level diminished as you could leave it up to the technology to do the work for you. The ability to play more while doing less impacted on even the musicianship of progressive rock. Devices like sequencers may have made it easier to play certain complicated parts but for some it took away the creativity that can be borne out of adversity. In the hands of a trained or experienced keyboardist sequencers became a bonus to add even more layers of complexity, but in so many others with little or no experience they had the effect of reducing the musical virtuosity to little more than arpegiated sequences. Sadly the net effect of much of the new technology was that the music began to sound the same and simpler in structure.

Third Time Lucky

As we moved through the late seventies and into the eighties, the business learned how to take hold of an artist and with a few bits of production technical wizardry perform miracles in the studio which would inevitably appeal to the lowest common denominators. This did nothing for the music, but it made money for the industry. And it was easy. Sadly, the development of all this technology has ensured to some degree anyway, that we may never see a band like The Beatles again, because what's been thrown out of the equation is development. Artists are no longer given time to develop and hone their material, instead they are thrust into the limelight with multiple hits off their first album as the business tries to make as much money as possible as quickly as possible only to discard the artist in the end. The fact that the artist may be burned out prematurely is not of their concern. It's true what's been said: *"Those who burn twice as bright...burn out twice as fast."*

The reality is, without development, there is a very good chance the material will be lacking in depth. You may find a catchy tune, a nice melody etc., but when it comes to staying power, there is precious little to fall back on. Progressive rock has always been on the fringe of all this, and that is one of the reasons it continues to this day. The very fact that it strives for something more lasting than instant pop status or commercial success ensures it will have neither, but will in all likelihood continue to exist by those who practice it.

There is a theory that I hold too called "third-album-success". Now, for the most part this theory applies typically to bands or artists who are signed to a traditional major label deal. The theory goes like this; the first album is quite strong because it contains material you've been working with for quite a while, the second release comes out just after you've been out on tour to promote the first and so it contains a few left over pieces from the beginnings and material you've quickly put together on the road so it's not as strong, with the third album you've had time to hone your playing and writing skills and have developed as a band. The third album tends to be strong, take for example bands like Genesis - **Foxtrot**, Yes - **The Yes Album**, Marillion - **Misplaced**

Childhood, and so on. Bear in mind this is just a theory and doesn't apply in every case. In the world of progressive rock many bands never make it past the first or second release. Add to this how the music environment has changed to so much independent production of music and you can see it's a very different music world than when Yes or Genesis were starting out.

If we are generous the punk rock era blossomed and died over the brief span of 1976 to 1978. Only two short years for a self-confessed musical style that thrived on it's lack of skill and professionalism. Unlike so many releases from bands in the punk and new wave era whose LP's found their way very quickly into the delete bins, it's important to note that much of the recorded material from that so called "golden era of progressive rock" is available on CD now and being purchased by a new group of fans interested in something a little more adventurous.

Punk rock, economic recession, a change in radio programming and more control exerted by the music business, these are undoubtedly just a few of the factors that have contributed to the lean years of the late seventies and early eighties. During this time the releases of progressive rock material came few and far between. Punk rock may have surfaced to put to death the industry's dinosaurs, but it failed miserably. Not one punk band lasted more than a few years, while progressive rock proved very resilient. Perhaps because it has always been based around music and not fashions, fads or trends.

1978 - In The Aftermath Of Punk

In truth all was not lost. 1978 saw releases from all the mainstream bands such as Renaissance **A Song For All Seasons**, Genesis **...and then there were three**, Gentle Giant **Giant For a Day**, Barclay James Harvest **Gone to Earth** and **Number 12**, Strawbs **Dead Lines**, Camel **Breathless**, and dozens of others. It's true that some of these releases were weak. Most progressive rock fans had long since given up hope on The Moody Blues and **Octave** didn't excite anyone terribly much. As far as Emerson Lake & Palmer's **Love Beach**, most tend to

Renaissance
Genesis
Gentle Giant
Barclay James Harvest
Strawbs
Camel

Moody Blues

ELP

Rush

Yes

Chris Squire

Jon Anderson

Genesis
Steve Hackett

Peter Gabriel

Phil Collins

Mike Rutherford

agree they were simply going through the motions. Two Canadian trio's recorded new LPs. Rush put of **Hemispheres** their seventh LP while FM released their second LP **Black Noise**, following up on an unusual direct-to-disc first release. This second release once again demonstrated their unusual sound which not only included keyboards and drums but the use of violin and mandolin in place of guitars. While Yes had come back strong with the previous years release of **Going For The One**, their 1978 release of **Tormato** showed them losing direction. As Chris Squire explained in Dan Hedges' **Yes: The Authorised Biography**: *"There was never any intention to do another Close To The Edge, or even a follow-up to the long "Awaken" . It's not easy to work on extended pieces. They need an incredible amount of foresight and arrangement, and the knowledge to encompass them so that they come off well."* Even Jon Anderson felt the project was a bit of a mess. Still, the band went on their successful "in the round" world tour, without a new album to promote. Fortunately Yes would return to producing epic scale music on future releases.

Elsewhere, Genesis had lost Steve Hackett during the final days of recording **Wind & Wuthering**. Hackett's first solo release **Voyage Of The Acolyte** had come out in 1975. Even at that time there was the feeling that Hackett was writing too much material to ever be included on a Genesis record. Hackett's reason's for leaving were somewhat different to Gabriel's as explained in **Exposure Magazine**; *"There came a point where there were so many ideas going on in Genesis, that it was impossible to get them down on one album. It was really a problem - there were just so many creative ideas going on - not least of all from myself and I found that the majority of my ideas, I was having to shelve. It wasn't diplomatically possible to produce solo albums at the same time as I was doing Genesis albums - it met with too much opposition. So therefore, I had a choice to make: Either I followed my own heart, or I kept watching my bank balance!"* His first solo effort was very well received and by the time of the recording of **Wind & Wuthering**, he was having a deep personal struggle whether to stay in Genesis or not. In the end he quietly, much to the dismay of the other band members, left. April 1978 would see the release of his second solo effort **Please Don't Touch**. Genesis, feeling they had survived the loss of Peter Gabriel saw no reason why they couldn't carry on as a three piece, and in 1978 released **...and Then There Were Three** showing a more keyboard driven sound and a much simpler writing style as Phil Collins became more actively involved in the compositional process. Another aspect that changed the sound of Genesis at this point was Mike Rutherford's feeling that their music hadn't contained much humour recently. In **Trouser Press** he said: *"We missed not having some humorous, lightweight moments, like "Match of the day" and "Pigeon," on Wind & Wuthering. So we said to ourselves, 'let's not make the songs quite so long. To get more variety on it.' I feel that set the mood of the album more than Steve's departure."* The album also contained "Follow You Follow Me" giving Genesis their first top ten hit. The change in writing style would make a further transition with their next release, **Duke,** where finding any real progressive rock moments on a Genesis record became harder and harder. There were other bright hopes, however. One group of note was UK.

The Supergroup UK

At the tail end of the seventies along came the band UK. **Record Review** said; *"A band with all the promise and potential in the world, UK was almost doomed from the beginning. Four world class musicians gathered in an attempt to set the standard in progressive music. For a short time they were brilliant."*

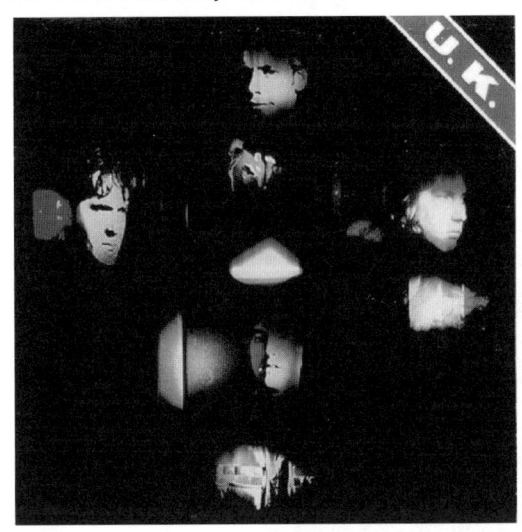

UK were brilliant. The "star" line-up for the first self-titled album released in 1978 was Bill Bruford, Eddie Jobson, Alan Holdsworth and John Wetton. Both Bruford and Holdsworth departed after the first LP and UK became a trio adding former Zappa drummer Terry Bozzio. Their use of textures and moods in the songs produced over a very short career, out-shone much of the other music released on vinyl at the time. This was a supergroup just as Asia was to become. Only with UK the music remained important. They created more than just some nice catchy songs or tunes. It seemed that success, if it came would be nice, but the band determined to soldier on despite the lack of radio airplay. The crowds loved them live, as witnessed by the fact their last LP was a live recording. The element of commerciality in the music of UK was addressed by Eddie Jobson, who without a doubt was one of the bands driving forces: *"Record companies won't sign you unless they think they have something commercial. In the early seventies the whole progressive thing was getting underway and commercial appeal wasn't one of the criteria for getting signed. Now the company wants to be sure they have something they can sell. Now it really doesn't matter how good you are, the company has to think they can get you on the radio."*

A good point, especially when you consider that the vast majority of record company people don't seem to understand what progressive rock is all about. They think of music in terms of unit sales. Now here's the problem; if for example you have people who are used to flogging vacuum cleaners (i.e. pop music) and along comes this blender (i.e. progressive rock) and they don't know HOW to sell it, because they don't know if it works because they don't know how it works. There may

UK

**Bill Bruford
Eddie Jobson**

John Wetton

Terry Bozzio

Asia

Eddie Jobson

**Curved Air
Roxy Music
Jethro Tull
UK**

very well be an audience out there, but these people wouldn't know it if they were standing in front of them in a group.

Jobson's history in progressive rock music is one to be admired, coming through the ranks of Curved Air, Roxy Music and even a stint in Jethro Tull. He came to UK for their first album and after that bands demise, released the excellent **The Green Album** with his own group of musicians called Zinc. What he learned in those early years was not lost in the eighties. It was certainly updated, changed all right, but the essence of the definition listed elsewhere still applies to the music he produces today. So what are Jobson's thoughts on this resurgence in progressive rock? *"I think it's great. I had predicted it years ago. I predicted it when we started UK, I was just a little ahead of my time... I would like to see this kind of music come around again and make things more musical. I think a lot of the pop tunes are quite musical. I would like to see things with a little more depth to them. There was nothing coming out of England for a long time but the last two years has been incredible."*

Happy The Man

Cathedral

**Genesis
King Crimson**

Two other interesting US bands that appeared around this time were Happy The Man and Cathedral. Cathedral released their only LP in 1978 called **Stained Glass Stories**. It has since gone on to almost legendary status featuring a style that some have described as a cross between early Genesis and King Crimson but in truth was more rooted in a Yes style than anything else. Their sound featured soaring guitars and plenty of Mellotron and other keyboards showcased in a musical style featuring complex melodies and polyrhythms. After the LP went nowhere they simply faded into obscurity.

Gentle Giant

Happy The Man had been around a little longer and have been described as one of the best U.S. symphonic-progressive rock bands of the mid seventies. They took their name from Goethe's book "Faust" where many phrases begin with the line..."Happy the man who..." Their first LP, on Arista Records a major label no less, was released in late 1977. The band was from Harrisonburg, Virginia and had formed in 1974 at the local University. Their sound was very Canterbury influenced featuring complex mostly instrumental compositions that managed to avoid the dissonant excesses of bands striving for complexity. Instead Happy The Man incorporated the melodic style of Yes along with the musical complexity of Gentle Giant. The 1978 release of

Crafty Hands showed them at their best, but was caught up in a musical period of the much simpler New Wave. Unfortunately it was after this release the band decided to split up. Kit Watkins would go on to fill the keyboard slot with Camel for a couple of years before launching a very successful independent solo career.

While we began to see fewer progressive rock releases each year the quality of many remained quite high. Ange's **Guet Apens**, Atoll's **Tertio** and Eloy's **Silent Cries Mighty Echoes** are just three examples, there were others from Machiavel, Rameses, and Novalis. In the late seventies the Spanish progressive rock scene kicked into high gear with many bands releasing LPs. Unfortunately in many cases they turned out to be one-shot releases. One of the few Spanish bands to stay together long enough to record more than one LP was Bloque. Their first self titled LP showed roots in the British prog school but still managed to showcase the bands ethnic folk roots.

American band Crack The Sky had two releases in 1978. Their **Safety In Numbers** was still a very good LP even though the band's driving force and original member John Palumbo chose to leave. Their second release for the year was **Live Sky** and showed the band in their element, a live setting performing their classic numbers like "Ice", "Hold On", "Surf City" and even a great version of the Beatles' "I Am The Walrus". Shortly after this release however the band broke up. Fortunately for Crack The Sky fans the band would continue to exist in various forms mostly as the result of John Palumbo's leadership. Palumbo has remarked that as hard as he has tried over the years to put Crack The Sky out of his life, it's something that refuses to go away. For fans of the band this has proven to be a good thing indeed.

1979 - The End Of A Decade

As we moved into 1979, many of the major bands released some fine work. Take for example Pink Floyd's **The Wall**, UK's **Danger Money**, Renaissance's **Azure D'or**, Camel's **I Can See Your House From Here**, and The Enid's **Touch Me**. In Canada, FM would release **Black Noise** and True Myth their self titled LP which according to all sources was the first Canadian and second international digital LP to ever be commercially released. The story of True Myth begins with classically trained Tom Treumuth. After many years playing covers in pubs, he met up with the other members who would form True Myth and it's then they decided to begin working on original material. Treumuth having been inspired by much of the British

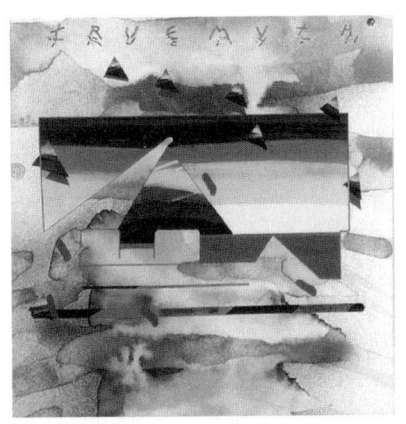

Camel

Ange
Atoll

Eloy
Machiavel
Rameses
Novalis

Bloque

Crack The Sky

Beatles

Pink Floyd
UK
Renaissance
Camel
The Enid
FM

True Myth

progressive rock he'd been listening to wanted to go in that direction. The long days of rehearsals paid off and the band was to go into the studios in early 1979 and there they would record each of the seven tracks 100% live with no overdubs.

Spanish band Bloque released their second offering **Hombre, Tierra Y Alma** with the biggest change from their first effort being the addition of a Mellotron giving the band a much more symphonic sound. Many rate this second release as one of the best Spanish prog releases of the time. In Italy, in spite of the rough political and economic climate Le Orme put out **Florian** while in Germany LPs were released by Hoelderlin **New Faces**, Grobschnitt **Merry Go Round**, Novalis **Flossenger**, SFF **Ticket To Everywhere**, Streetmark **Dry**, Rousseau **Flowers in Asphalt** and new-comers Anyone's Daughter **Adonis**.

While the established bands such as Hoelderlin were beginning to stream-line their sound making it more accessible, new bands like Anyone's Daughter were picking up where the others left off. The short history of Anyone's Daughter actually goes back to 1973 when Matthias Ulmer and Uwe Karpa, both about 15 years old formed the group named after the Deep Purple tune on **Fireball**. After spending the next few years gigging and putting tapes together they finally got some air-play on a local Stuttgart radio station around 1977. After finishing school, they rented a small country house where they began rehearsing in the garage. Turning professional in 1979 they released **Adonis** their first LP. Anyone's Daughter came together in a time where influences of the first progressive rock bands was still very clearly felt. Much of their early material was predominantly instrumental. Later they combined long instrumental passages with lyrics in English and German to create a sound uniquely their own. Uwe Karpa makes it clear: *"We are laying more stress on the music than on the words, because we regard ourselves more as musicians than as poets."* For them music was a communicative form of art, where borders are bound to be surpassed.

After the success of the In The Round tour, Yes retreated to Paris to start rehearsing for a new album. They chose Roy Thomas Baker to produce, but within weeks of putting demos together the recording was put on hold. The magic just wasn't there. Jon Anderson and Rick Wakeman chose to leave the group.

1980 - Progressive Rock in the Eighties

By 1980 if you heard anything about progressive rock music it was because you were a fan and you went looking for it. By this time the media had completely forgotten about it, and was doing everything in it's power to not recognise it ever existed. Some would have said prog was on life-support and yet as we look back on the year Yes released **Drama** to the shock and amazement of the media and fans. After losing both Wakeman and Anderson, Chris Squire had recruited Trevor Horn and Geoff Downes, more commonly known as the Buggles, who coincidentally were also handled by Yes manager Brian Lane. Unknown to most Yes fans at the time, was that Trevor had been a strong Yes fan himself since **The Yes Album** and the prospect of replacing Jon Anderson was giving his nerves a thorough going over. Eddie Offord was even brought in to produce the backing tracks. With it's stripped down eighties production values **Drama** went to number 1 in the UK charts and the tour was a surprising smash success. After the tour however Trevor Horn chose to step out of the limelight and return to record producing, leaving Yes without a vocalist.

Genesis released **Duke**, their first album in almost two years. Over that time, both Tony Banks and Mike Rutherford released solo albums, **A Curious Feeling** and **Smallcreep's Day**, neither of which achieved much commercial hearing. **Duke** showed Genesis moving even more in the prog-pop direction with Collin's influence now firmly planted. As a result of the year long tour for their previous album, Phil's marriage came apart and **Duke** was the first LP where he was able to devote 100% of his time to writing and recording. The song "Misunderstanding", a big hit in America, was written exclusively by Collins and shows his pop style even then, and "Turn It On Again" was another top ten hit for the band. Banks was quick to distance the band from a tune like "Misunderstanding" saying that while it was clearly a Genesis song, it was only a small part of the overall Genesis sound. To promote **Duke**, the band undertook a tour that included many smaller venues in an effort to get the band back to a closer relationship with the fans, and it worked.

Gentle Giant released their last LP **Civilian**. It was put together with the assistance of noted FM radio programming guru Lee Abrams. The style was still clearly Gentle Giant with their inventive vocal counterpoint but Abrams made his influence known in the streamlined sound of each song in an effort to gain radio airplay. Unfortunately they got none, the true fans were disappointed and the band decided to throw in the towel. Jethro Tull released **A**, one of the high points in their catalogue. The band had enlisted the talents of Eddie Jobson on keyboards and violin.

French band Asia Minor were one of the bright spots of the year with the release of their second LP entitled **Between Flesh and Divine**. Many would say musically speaking they were one of the best French progressive rock outfits of the late seventies. The band had actually been kicking around since 1974, where after a rather luke-warm reception to their first album Asia Minor went through some serious personnel changes. By mid-June 1975 they were still performing, only now the music was more "cosmic-rock". More changes would ensue and essentially the band ceased to exist at the end of 1978. Bassist Robert Klemper had kept in touch with drummer Lionel Beltrami and what Asia Minor had been up to. Lionel suggested he join and play bass and keyboards, which he did. The band now consisted of them and vocalist/guitarist Setrak Bakire and Eril Tekeli on flute and guitars. A period of intense writing and rehearsing led to the recording of **Between Flesh and Divine** in July of 1980. A deal for major distribu-

Genesis

Amge
Kansas
Styx

BJH
Eloy
Steve Hackett
Le Orme
FM

tion of the disc fell through and band decided to distribute the CD themselves.

By this time many of the progressive rock old guard were beginning to streamline their sound, much as Genesis had done. Groups like Ange **Vu D'un Chien**, Kansas **Audio Visions**, Styx **Paradise Theatre** and others released albums that disappointed their fans. In the process they may have picked up new followers but for the old fans, they would have to look to the newer bands to satisfy the prog craving. On the brighter side there were some good releases in the form of Barclay James Harvest's **Eyes of the Universe**, Eloy's **Colours**, Steve Hackett's **Defectors**, Le Orme's **Piccola Rapsodie Dell Ape**, FM's **Surveillance** and a self titled release from Anyone's Daughter.

1981

Asia

Steve Howe
Chris Squire
Jimmy Page

John Wetton
Carl Palmer

1981 - The Low-Point of ASIA

The lowest point for many progressive rock fans came at the beginning of 1981 with the arrival of Asia. With the departure of Trevor Horn, and the failure of the ill-fated XYZ project comprised of Chris Squire, Alan White and Jimmy Page, Steve Howe left and for all intents and purposes Yes ceased to exist. Asia had the potential makings of a great band in the tradition of British progressive rock. In it's initial form the band consisted of Steve Howe (Yes), Geoff Downes (Yes), John Wetton (Family, Roxy Music, etc.), and Carl Palmer (ELP). A true supergroup in every way. Wetton described the group's formation in one of Pete Frame's Family Trees: *"Towards the end of 1980, I started talking to Brian Lane about getting a band together - and there came a point when I decided to move everything...management, publishing, recording - from EG to Brian Lane. It really felt like the right time to make a positive move. So Brian and I went to L.A., found that Geffen*

Records were interested in our ideas, and when we got back to London he introduced me to Steve. That was in January 1981, when we began to get serious. We approached Carl, who I'd talked about getting together with during my UK days and then Geoff came down and started to rehearse with us. He was in the middle of the second Buggles album but quit them to come with us. That was it really...as soon as the four of us sat together in the same room, it looked like a band and felt like a band. We were ready to go!" On the surface this was seemingly a great band except for a couple of things.

An article in the **Los Angeles Times**, **Calendar Section**, by Michael Watts ran through some interesting history of the band, but to my mind brought up some of the problems we've been discussing here; *"Asia's music, which to my ears blandly updates the seventies progressive rock is even less trendy than last year's pirate costume and has met with disparaging reviews in both England and America. But despite the bad or scant publicity, Asia's success with the silent majority of record buyers may offer clues to the development of eighties rock...fundamentally Asia fills the gap in the market that manager Brian Lane was quick to exploit. 'It's art-rock with all the fat cut off'...Howe and Wetton emphasise America's enduring love affair with the right sounding British groups, 'I don't think we could get our foot in the door in America without there being something English about us,' Howe said over herbal tea, 'An English group makes it in America by sounding English. It's the European mixture of jazz, rock and the classics, and the different backgrounds which I don't think a musician gets in America.'"*

The point about blandly updating the seventies progressive rock is probably not far from the truth actually. The songs are shorter, contain fewer tempo changes, deal with different subject matter etc. For a person who truly enjoys the purist form of progressive rock, Asia won't cut it. The material is great for what it is, but there's something missing. Every time you expect to hear something new or different in their songs, the band flees to the safety of another chorus. But then Asia, it seems was always more concerned with writing songs rather than pieces of music. In fact, the style of Asia's writing is very traditional...verse, chorus, verse, chorus, middle eight, verse chorus. Great for the pop format but severely lacking for progressive rock fans.

It might be likened to giving a famous artist a complete set of paints and all he does is paint the canvas red. Some might call it art, but somehow you'd expect more. That's not to say that we should look at what's not there, as opposed to what really is there. It's simply more a recognition of the fact that the artists involved in Asia do seem to be holding back, or at the very least exerting a self imposed restriction, in the areas where each has excelled in the past. One wonders, if radio airplay were not such an important element in the business of making music, whether things might not be very different.

Lane's comment of 'trimming the fat' is interesting. It sounds very nice, but quite frankly if you've ever tried to trim the fat off a cut of meat, you will invariably have taken some of the muscle off with the fat. That certainly seems to be the case with Asia. In November '83 issue of **Keyboard Magazine**, Dominic Milano took the time to describe Asia this way; *"Driving polyrhythms, intricate keyboard lines, classically flavoured guitar antics and extremely long pieces that would never see the light of radio airplay have been forsaken. Oh, the influences were still audible, no mistake about that, but somehow the sum total was different. Asia plays what some might think of as corporate power rock. Their style bears more resemblance to that of Journey, Foreigner and Loverboy than it does to that of adventurous progressives like Peter Gabriel and King Crimson. Asia's hooks are strong, the textures thick and powerful. It's stuff hit singles are made of. Critics hate it, old fans are disappointed by it, but the kids are eating it up."*

Asia
Journey
Foreigner
Loverboy
Peter Gabriel
King Crimson

Actually I couldn't have said it better myself. Young people around the world bought Asia's first album, so did I. However unlike myself a lot of these kids were not disappointed by the band's self imposed limitations. Asia definitely was an assembly line band of the eighties, not unlike the Monkees or Duran Duran. Unlike many of the truly great progressive rock bands, Asia started to find itself in trouble with the release of their second LP. It, even more than the first, showed the lack of depth in the material. One of the new elements as pointed out in this article was that Downes brought the keyboards back into the rhythm section, where he felt they belonged. It was a gamble, but it didn't work. With the keyboards squashed between everything else, the wall of sound that emanated from the second album lost it's identity. Confronting this dilemma, Downes comments; *"Some of the mixes were too simple. But like I say, you gain on the swings and lose on the roundabouts. I think that you can really get selfish about the whole question. The important thing is that at the end of the day the whole thing sounds like a composite of parts rather than too many individual parts just jammed together. That was one of the main problems with Yes. There were too many producers. Too many people getting involved with wanting to hear what they wanted to hear rather than being happy with the group sound. The Drama album is an example of that. I remember when we mixed that album, there were actually five pairs of hands on the faders at any given time. That's not the way to do it. Group production is rarely a good thing. I think that you get too much featuring of things here and there and the whole thing sounds contrived. You*

Monkees

Duran Duran

have to learn to settle for a good overall sound."

If by saying certain albums or bands sound contrived, Downes is saying they are artificially intricate then it would seem that Asia are as much at fault as any of the progressive rock bands. A traditional pop song is one of the most contrived musical forms. If on the other hand he is simply saying they are contrived, that is to say planned out and laboured over, then what's the harm in being contrived? It must be stated, that to sit down and write for the purpose of filling a three minute time slot is without doubt the most contrived undertaking.

Talking about Yes, Howe went on to say in the **Los Angeles Times** article that they never had their **Dark Side Of The Moon**, referring to Yes missing that kind of huge break that comes from having an album purchased by millions and millions of fans. One can certainly argue about Yes not having their **Dark Side Of The Moon**. But being realistic, how many bands do. In fact Pink Floyd came about it quite unknowingly. There was in fact only one real single off the album **Dark Side Of The Moon**, and yet the LP was in the charts for more than a decade. One possible reason for this is that it was not written or recorded to please or pander any certain segment of the audience. This work, first and foremost set out to please the artists, who would then have the task of taking the concept and promoting it to an audience. Pink Floyd were very successful, because as artists they first set out to please themselves and in the process, their fans. They did not then and do not today bend over backwards to give the fans what they want, or what they think will make their fans happy. Now certainly, Pink Floyd want their fans to enjoy what they hear. But that involves their fans keeping up with the band. After all famous painters like Dali or Picasso didn't paint to please their followers they painted what they felt in their hearts. It's no different with The Floyd.

Now this appears to be different from Asia, who on the surface appeared to try very hard to come up with something that would be radio ready and please a very mainstream following. Given that Howe would return to Yes and continue to create adventurous progressive rock his comments regarding Yes never having had their **Dark Side Of The Moon**, may have been more intended as a temperamental dig at Yes the band or perhaps the music business rather than the music Yes created or the musical genre of progressive rock.

A Neo-Beginning!

Just when it seemed the light at the end of the tunnel was about to go out, a new and younger, revitalised wave of progressive rock musicians surfaced in late 1981, bearing testimony to the lasting values of this musical form. Sure the sound was a bit different...a little more bite, a little more eighties but it was very much influenced by what had gone before. Bands like Twelfth Night, Pallas, Marillion, IQ, Pendragon and dozens of others were again holding high the banner of progressive rock. Their attitude and musical style gave rise to the sub-genre term "neo-progressive" meaning new-progressive. Generally speaking neo-prog was mostly identified by it's edgier, song-driven style. The material could still be longish but it tended to be based around an adventurous song format. Typically the drumming was more present and somewhat more constant. While some inside the progressive rock community would later begin using this term in the pejorative sense there is no denying the life saving injection these bands performed on progressive rock. For one thing it made the media sit up and take notice, that this was a genre that had not, and was not going to go away.

Mike Oldfield
Streetmark

Rick Wakeman

Genesis

Not only that but some of the old guard, Mike Oldfield, Streetmark, Jane and many others suddenly found themselves in the New Age record bins. Even Rick Wakeman produced a New Age album of solo piano work entitled **Country Aires**, the first of many. Genesis released **Abacab** which displayed a major change in production and compositional style. Phil Collins who had worked with Hugh Padgham on his solo efforts, suggested he be brought in to make the band sound different. At the same time instead of writing material away from the studio and bringing it in to complete, now they had their own studio and could spend as much time in it as they wanted. This led to Genesis coming to the studio almost empty handed, jamming for a few days, and then selecting to work on or complete the bits that were working. It would mean typically shorter, simpler songs. While each album would continue to provide an epic or two, the new composing style meant these longer songs were structurally much simpler. This new style of composing was one that would serve the band well into the 1990s. On

Rush

the other hand Rush released what many consider to be their progressive rock best with the 1981 **Moving Pictures**. Incorporating a stronger synth presence the LP contained such popular songs as "Tom Sawyer", "Red Barchetta" and the instrumental "YYZ." Unfortunately, while Rush would continue to produce excellent material, much to the disappointment of many fans, they began moving away from more complicated pieces choosing instead to focus on shorter songs.

Robert Fripp
Adrian Belew

King Crimson

Robert Fripp got together with Adrian Belew and put together a completely different King Crimson and released **Discipline**. The name was the same, the music to most people's ears was still progressive, but it certainly wasn't symphonic progressive rock. Katherine Charlton points out: *"Their new work drew on some of the musical variety and richness of their past work, as well as incorporating touches of African polyrhythms. One of Fripp's greatest concerns was to avoid the tendency of reverting to older styles and creating, in his words, a 'dinosaur' sound."* In an effort to maintain a progressing musical style Fripp made it very clear to band members, that each of them should maintain some kind of musical independence from other members. This freedom was intended to spark the musical development to higher levels. Not unexpectedly, this King Crimson was harder, heavier and a lot more "out there" in terms of compositional style.

One of the first of the new wave of neo-progressive bands was Twelfth Night who released **Live At The Target** in February 1981 followed closely by Scotland's Pallas who's own independent live release **Arrive Alive** came out in June 1981. Both of these vinyl releases pre-date and were certainly as good or better than anything Marillion had produced to date. So it's interesting how and why the media took such a liking to Marillion.

Twelfth Night hailed from Reading and their beginnings go back to Reading University where Brian Devoil and Andy Revell met and decided to play music. Later Clive Mitten and Rick Battersby would join while Geoff Mann was responsible for painting the groups performing backdrops. Their first gig as Twelfth Night came in 1979 with their first recorded material on cassette in January of 1980. Even then Guitarist Andy Revell, in an **Afterglow** interview, found it difficult to describe their musical style; *"I think we are in the same market in which Genesis and Pink Floyd appears, but I think we are more contemporary, more aggressive than other bands."* Playing the usual pub and club venues the band were the first to carve out a following and the first to put out a vinyl release with **Live At The Target**. Originally performing only instrumental material they developed quite a sizeable following, however it was felt that in order to be in the same league as other bands gaining in prominence they would need a more theatric stage presence. Enter lead vocalist Geoff Mann, with whom Twelfth Night opened The Reading Festival in 1981. Their first studio LP **Fact And Fiction** came out in December of 1982 to positive fan response. Twelfth Night never seemed to get the breaks other bands did and had to fight hard for recognition and even their eventual signing to a major label never exposed them to a wider audience, unlike Marillion or Pallas.

Twelfth Night

Pallas

Geoff Mann

Genesis
Pink Floyd

Marillion

Scotland's Pallas, like Twelfth Night pre-dated Marillion to some degree, but in the end, had a much shorter life span. Pallas released their first live LP **Arrive Alive** in June of 1981. The group came into existence in 1976, known at that time as Rainbow. When Ritchie Blackmore left Deep Purple, and took the name for his band, they had to choose another and after an evening poking in the dictionary they selected Pallas. Playing everywhere for anyone who would have them, they honed their style which included the obligatory Genesis cover tunes. They saved their money, and were able to record the live material for the album **Arrive Alive**, which included fan favourite "Crown of Thorns" and the epic "The Ripper". The independently produced LP eventually sold 10,000 copies. In 1982 they decided to undertake a national tour, which helped their playing style and won them a sizeable following. They eventually signed what was to have been a "long-term" recording contract with EMI-Harvest in August of 1983, and were thought to be next in line for success.

1981 finished up with releases from The Moody Blues' **Long Distance Voyager**, Renaissance's **Camera Camera**, Camel's **Nude**, Rick Wakeman's **1984**, Barclay James Harvest's **Turn of the Tide**, Steve Hackett's **Cured**, Taurus' **Illusions of a Night**, FM's **City of Fear** and **Piktors Verwan** from Anyone's Daughter.

1982 - Marillion Step To The Front Of The Class

Without question, the band most responsible for the resurgence of progressive rock during the early eighties is Marillion. It was Marillion who struck terror in the hearts of music critics in Britain in 1982 by selling out two nights at the prestigious Hammersmith Odeon on the strength of releasing only one single. Marillion's roots go back to 1978 when then drummer Mick Pointer formed a four piece instrumental group called Silmarillion. Guitarist Steve Rothery came on board in 1979. They gigged around their home base of Aylesbury to less than enthusiastic response. Sometime late 1980 they decided to add a vocalist. Enter Fish. By this time they had dropped the "Sil" and were just known as Marillion. After a few weeks of rehearsals they performed their first vocal gig March 1981. It was around this time they sent out their first demo to promoters. It contained "He Knows You Know", "Garden Party", and "Charting The Single". Later in the year they hired Keith Goodwin to be their publicist. Goodwin had done his share to help progressive rock the first time around as the publicist for Yes and ELP among others. His experience allowed him to put the name Marillion in front of all the right people. They played live everywhere. Halls, pubs, clubs everywhere, and in the process fine tuned their music, their style, their stage show and most importantly their musicianship. Around the end of the year they were looking for a new keyboard player. They remembered seeing Mark Kelly performing with a band called Chemical Alice and he was asked to join. In January of 1982 they played their first Marquee date. By the fall of 1982 they proved to be the first of the neo-progressive bands to be signed to a major recording contract. It was with EMI, a company they remained with until 1996. A couple of singles were quickly released. They were voted "Best New Band of 1982" by **Sounds**. Things were going along very nicely as they released their first LP **Script For A Jester's Tear** in March of 1983.

Yes

ELP

Marillion

Musically, like so many of the neo-progressive rock bands, Marillion were a lot harder sounding. There was definitely more of an edge to their music, even in their lyrics. Interestingly, Marillion claimed no credit for being at the forefront of the genre's revival. They even went so far as to distance themselves from the usual influences. While they never denied being influenced by Pink Floyd, or Yes or even Genesis, they also listed such diverse and equally influential bands as The Doors, Rush, The Beatles and even ABC.

Genesis
Pink Floyd
Yes
Genesis

The Doors
Rush
Beatles

Carol Clerk in her book **Marillion in Words & Pictures** says, *"The fact that Marillion played long songs with often complex arrangements and*

Marillion

poetic language added fuel to the charges against them. Fish would retort that Marillion were aiming for musical value, that the subjects he dealt with in the lyrics, would not easily lend themselves to a three minute dance track, nor could they be covered thoroughly in that length of time." Certainly this was not only true of many of the neo-prog bands but was true of progressive rock music in general.

Bands quickly discovered that there were many who wanted to hear progressive rock. Fan dedication and loyalty, far from dying out was still very much alive and well in the eighties. Progressive rock fans, more than most, are serious about their music and why they like it. Martin Orford, keyboard player with the band IQ, talking to **Kerrang Magazine** came up with this assessment as to why; *"Their dedication is something that appears to be peculiar to progressive rock. They have this odd devotion and loyalty which is probably fuelled by the fact that most folk hate it. They get really into the lyrics and the music rather than the image side of things. In fact they worship the music more than the people who play it which is exactly how it should be."*

IQ

Solstice

Having been in attendance at the Marquee Club on a couple of occasions, I was fortunate to see IQ and Solstice on their first headlining gigs in September of 1983. I was struck by a number of images. Of course there were those in the club you'd expect to see...the ones wearing the neo-hippie garb, but there were also representatives of virtually every strata of education and livelihood. Blue-collar, white-collar, no collar. There were also many girls and women present. It was hard to miss the fans devotion with tables present to purchase the latest independent cassette, T-shirt, newsletter or other choice piece of memorabilia.

IQ came together after members shuffled in and out of a number of smaller outfits. Both Peter Nichols and Mike Holmes had been in a band called The Lens back in 1976. The band went through various personnel changes but survived to July of 1981, at which time Mike and keyboardist Martin Orford continued on as IQ. Later in May of 1982 Peter Nichols was asked to join as vocalist. Shortly after this their first cassette album, **Seven Stories Into Eight** was released. By this time the band had made the move to London. Their cassette release showed them not ashamed of displaying progressive rock roots. The cassette's complex time changes and shifting moods displayed their influences from Camel to Genesis

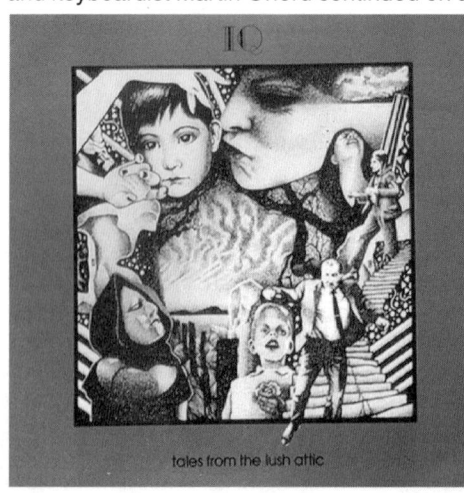

Camel
Genesis

tales from the lush attic

with the ever-present Mellotron. What followed was a lot of hard work writing, composing and working on the road including their first appearance at The Marquee in September of 1982. Major exposure came when they had the opportunity to open for The Enid on a number of dates. All this activity culminated on September 15 1983, with their first headlining appearance at The Marquee and the simultaneous release of their first vinyl LP, **Tales From The Lush Attic**. It was a smashing success and IQ were turning out to be a progressive rock force to be reckoned with and they would continue to be an influential act in the years to come. They went on to record a number of independent albums before vocalist Peter Nichols would exit the band. They eventually were signed to the Squawk label a division of Polygram. A couple more albums followed, and with each release the band, in an effort to achieve success found themselves straying from their roots creating music that was slightly more mainstream. That is until Nichols, rejoined. The 1993 release of **Ever**, showed IQ returning to their more progressive rock roots.

The balance of the significant releases in 1983 included Jethro Tull's **Beast and the Broadsword**, Camel's **The Single Factor**, Rick Wakeman's **Rock and Roll Prophet**, Eloy's **Planets**, and **Time to Turn**, Novalis' **Neumond**, Twelfth Night's **Fact & Fiction**, Anyone's Daughter's **In Blau**, and Quasar's **Fire In The Sky**.

1983 - The Progressive Comeback

The early eighties were heady days for progressive rock fans. Many of the neo-progressive bands had come together and the fire was ignited in countries around the world. By 1983 Marillion's **Script For A Jester's Tear**, Pallas' **Arrive Alive** and IQ's **Tales From The Lush Attic** had set the tone, but so had France's Nuance with **Il Est Une Legende** and La Rossa's **A Fury Of Glass**, Iskander's **Boheme** and Brazil's Bacamarte's highly regarded **Depois Do Fim**. Canada's Terraced Garden with it's King Crimson influence contained in uniquely shorter songs released **Melody and Menace**. Band leader and multi-instrumentalist Carl Tafel's compositions showcased all the progressive rock components from flute to Mellotron. Speaking of King Crimson, Robert Fripp and company released **3 Of a Perfect Pair** and once again decided to put the band in a holding pattern. Also out of the picture was Kansas. Steve Walsh, the group's primary songwriter had become unhappy with the group's more commercial direction, and decided to call it a day. The band had carried on for two more albums with assistance of John Elefante on vocals but without Walsh, Kansas lacked direction and broke up. Coming back after a brief time away was Caravan with two releases **The Album** and **Back to Front**. Genesis continued releasing more pop-oriented material with **Genesis** giving them hits like "Mama", "That's All" and "Illegal Alien". But aside from a few setbacks, the ground swell had started and nothing would stop it now. Other releases included Pink Floyd **The Final Cut**, Renaissance **Time Line**, Rick Wakeman **Cost of Living**, Barclay James Harvest **Ring of Changes**, The Enid **Something Wicked This Way Comes**,

Steve Hackett

Happy The Man

Eddie Jobson

Haze

Anyone's Daughter

Neue Sterne

Steve Hackett **Highly Strung**, Happy The Man **Better Late...**, Eddie Jobson **The Green Album**, Amber Route **Ghost Tracks**, Haze **The Cellar Tapes**, and of course the latest effort from Anyone's Daughter **Neue Sterne**. The fans began to spread the word through home-made fanzines featuring the latest news on the popular as well as obscure bands, a precursor to the internet in the 1990s.

Yes

Chris Squire

Trevor Rabin
Tony Kaye

Jon Anderson

Police
Genesis

One of the biggest surprises came in November of 1983 with the release of a new Yes LP entitled strangely enough **90125**. This Yes was strikingly different from the last version that released **Drama** in 1980. While Yes' sound in the seventies was based more on melody their sound in the eighties had come to be based more on rhythm. After **Drama** Yes had pretty much split and Chris Squire and Alan White started working on some projects which resulted in a unique single called "Run With The Fox". A catchy and upbeat piece of music that didn't get much airplay. Looking to get a band together they were joined by Trevor Rabin and eventually Tony Kaye from the first version of Yes. After most of the album had been written and recorded Chris played a couple cuts for Jon Anderson who expressed a desire to sing on the release. Up until now the band had intended to go by the name Cinema, but with Jon joining it seemed only natural they revert to the name Yes. The first single release was called "Owner Of A Lonely Heart". And it shot to number one on the radio charts. The 1983 version of Yes sounded very different from previous versions. Tony Kaye interviewed in **Keyboard** magazine: *"We knew that the album would have to be somewhat simple. So we kept it dimensionally sparse. We wanted it to be more modern sounding; we wanted to appeal to an audience that the Police or the new Genesis would appeal to."* Alan White speaking on the **Yesyears** video said: *"We spent eight months rehearsing all that material. A lot of the success of that album came from dedication to a new kind of sound."* Interestingly enough Trevor Rabin's work might not have turned in the same result if things had gone differently. Interviewed in Tim Morse's book **Yesstories**, Rabin said: *"What we did on 90125 based on the demos I had written was so different from Close To The Edge or Fragile. If I knew that it was going to turn into a Yes album I would have done things a bit differently; more from my orchestral point of view. But when I first met Chris and Alan we didn't even talk about that — I was a guitarist who wrote and sang."* To everyone's surprise the album was one of their most successful releases and was well received by critics and fans alike.

While Yes were changing their look and sound, there were plenty of new bands to fill the progressive rock void in 1983. Rick Wakeman interviewed in **The Revealing** spoke candidly about the change. While Wakeman liked what he heard on **90125**, even calling it as important an album as **Fragile**, he was quick to point out the hole it created; *"You see everyone said then that the music Yes did in the seventies was dead. What came along? The gap was filled by Marillion, perfectly thank you very much! Fish [Marillion's lead singer at the time] is a good friend of mine and he said to me 'This is crazy, Yes are our idols. If they're not gonna do that anymore, well, we're gonna carry on doing it' You should learn from these lessons."* Marillion and a host of other neo-progressive bands did indeed carry on creating progressive rock.

A sign of the impact the progressive rock resurgence was having in the music world was felt at Britain's biggest outdoor music gathering The Reading Festival which in 1983 featured no less than six prog bands. On stage Friday was Pendragon, Solstice, and Pallas. Saturday Marillion had the spotlight, while on Sunday Twelfth Night and The Enid performed. Over 20,000 fans were exposed to some of the country's finest progressive acts. The media had a field day and the progressive rock fans and fanzines thought they'd died and gone to heaven. It just kept getting better. By the end of the year cassettes or independently produced LPs were being sold at gigs by Trilogy, Gothique, Liaison, Mach One, Dagaband, Airbridge, Minas Tirith, Quasar, Tamarisk, and countless others in Britain alone. The media were writing articles both positive and negative which were showing up in all the British music papers. The spin-off benefit to all this was "exposure". Suddenly everyone seemed to realise that progressive rock was having a major come back.

1984 - Trouble In Pallas Land

As 1984 dawned all of the British neo-progressive rock bands released material. Marillion's second **Fugazi**, Pallas' **The Sentinel**, Pendragon's **Fly High Fall Far**, Twelfth Night's **Art and Illusion**, Solstice's **Silent Dance** and plenty of others including records from Haze **Ces't La Vie**, Craft, Mach One **Lost For Words**, BJH **Victims of Circumstance**, The Enid **The Spell**, and others. It was a big comeback year for prog. Canada's Terraced Garden released their second **Braille**, America's North Star released **Triskellion** on tape and many of the old guard were still there including material from Jethro Tull **Underwraps**, Camel **The Stationary Traveller**, Rick Wakeman **Silent Knight** and Steve Hackett **Till We Have Faces**.

After the signing of their recording contract, Pallas were whisked off to Atlanta Georgia, the unlikely location of Eddie Offord's recording studio to record **The Sentinel**. The former Yes and ELP producer had received tapes of the band and expressed interest in working with them. Graeme Murray; *"We'd always wanted to work with him after hearing the stuff he'd done with Yes and ELP."* Unfortunately all did not go as well as planned and after the record was released there was a

Wakeman

Marillion

Fish

Pendragon
Solstice

Pallas
The Enid

Trilogy

Minas Tirith
Quasar
Tamarisk

Twelfth Night

Haze
BJH

Jethro Tull

Camel

Camel

considerable amount dissension over the mixing that had taken place.

There were accusations that Offord had rushed and squeezed the mixing into five days to enable him to work on another "more important" project. Whatever the real story, the band made an about-face about the decision to use Offord. Murray was later quoted in Sounds 1985; *"We made mistakes like having Eddie Offord produce The Sentinel. We thought he had a really modern attitude but we now realise he didn't. We suffered for that. Now we feel that we've got to get across that we're not stuck in a formula rut."* In a later interview in **Exposure** magazine Murray and other band members claimed **Sounds** actually had misquoted them and Murray went on to add: *"We all thoroughly enjoyed working with Eddy and became very friendly with him. He taught us a huge amount. The atmosphere throughout the two months was superb. We've been misquoted in the UK press as saying that we didn't like Eddy's production. This is not so. Eddy is one of the best heavy rock producers."* Never-the-less someone was unhappy with the production because the LP was remixed shortly after release. To add insult to injury, the tour in support of the LP went very badly. The crowds just were not there. The band also began to feel lead vocalist Euan Lowson wasn't carrying his weight anymore and sacked him, hiring Alan Reed as his replacement. Unfortunately the article in the June 15th 1985 **Sounds** didn't help the band, as it had the band slagging everyone from Offord to Lowson to progressive rock in general.

1985 - The Neo-Prog Honeymoon Is Over

Pallas

1985 saw Pallas release an EP entitled **Sanctuary**. It showed them moving away from the type of songs that had made them popular in the first place. Gone were the epics...gone was any mention of Atlantis.

Pallas, having to some degree alienated their old fans were hunting for new ones with a more mainstream, hard rock sound. Elsewhere, this would be a watershed year for Marillion as they released what many feel was their finest release to that date, **Misplaced Childhood**. An album that brought both their musicianship, writing and performing skills together. Pendragon after experiencing some major delays with a record company that was having cash flow problems, released their first full length LP, **The Jewel**. IQ issued **The Wake**, after which lead vocalist Peter Nichols decided to call it a day. Speaking to **SI** magazine in November of 1991, Nichols explains his dilemma back in 1985; *"When I left, the internal relations within the band were rather bad. We didn't speak to each other. I don't know how it came to this... We were spending a lot of time together, lived in the same house together and finally it all became too much claustrophobic. We were going to search for our freedom outside the band. When I left, it wasn't actually what I wanted, but the situation was getting worse and worse instead of better. So I thought to myself: either I went on with something I didn't appreciate at all or I'd leave. In the following two years we didn't have much contact. During that period I did Niadem's Ghost. The idea lying behind this was to do something completely different from IQ. It wasn't IQ part 2, because then I wouldn't have had to leave IQ!'* His replacement was Paul Menel and a quasi-bootleg called **Nine In a Pound Is Here** was released. It turned out to be Paul's rehearsal sessions plus a hint at what some of the new material might sound like.

In France around this time Minimum Vital released their debut cassette entitled **Envol Triangles**. Brothers and co-founders Thierry and Jean-Luc Payssan had been in a band called Concept since about 1983. During the initial months of that band they wrote and performed a lot of material as they developed their sound and playing style. In 1984 the band won a rock contest and took advantage of the prize; some studio time that would eventually lead to their debut cassette.

While American band North Star released their second effort **Feel The Cold**, another U.S. band starting to get noticed was Djam Karet. They came together out of the ashes of a few Los Angeles bands in late 1984. The first gigs took place at various colleges and universities, primarily places that would let the band get away with playing a very unconventional and improvisational guitar dominated music. By the fall of 1985 the band brought out their first cassette release entitled **No Commercial Potential**. The one hour tape was totally improvised and recorded live in the studio with no overdubs and was distributed in underground prog circles in both the US and England. The band continued to perform in southern California until the summer of 1986 when they decided to spend some serious time developing the conceptual themes that kept recurring in their live performances. It was during this time, much like Genesis had done in the cottage, where Djam Karat's true musical identity was established. The fruit's of their labour, the music itself would come to life on **The Ritual Continues** CD release.

1986 - The Return Of Kansas

By 1986, while The Moody Blues and Genesis were floundering with mediocre progressive rock releases like **The Other Side of Life** and **Invisible Touch** respectively, Keith Emerson got back together with Greg Lake in hopes of reviving ELP. Carl Palmer was busy and so to keep the initials the same they enlisted Cozy Powell as a drummer for what they hoped would be ELP stage two. Unfortunately it lasted for only one album, but it was an album of superior music for the times. France's Nuance released a second recording called **Ami**, The Enid hit the shelves with **Salome**, while Twelfth Night recorded **X**. Of note was the formation of the band GTR around the writing and playing styles of notable prog guitarists Steve Howe and Steve Hackett. The band was put together with a desire to showcase their writing and playing styles and included Max Bacon as lead vocalist. Cover stories in all the guitar magazines and positive press led to an American tour but the band quickly fizzled. The new year started off really well for IQ with new vocalist Paul Menel as they signed a major label deal with Squawk a division of Polygram. The final transformation of Pallas had taken place with the release of **The Wedge**. It showed them no longer interested in producing the style of progressive rock that initially brought them attention from fans and media alike. Most felt this release was rather ordinary and Pallas quietly slipped into obscurity shortly thereafter.

Coming back into the picture was Kansas, reformed in 1986 with original members Steve Walsh, Rich Williams and Phil Ehart. Brought in to the group was ex-Dixie Dregs guitarist Steve Morse and bassist Billy Greer. Their LP **Power** showed Kansas still writing material in a shorter format, but now being a little more musically adventurous within that time constraint. Kansas were proving to be a progressive rock band that really rocked when they chose to.

1987 - A Worldwide Prog Momentum

In 1987 Trevor Rabin had clearly made his mark in the revamped Yes with the release of **Big Generator** an album that was arduous to make and lacked focus. Pink Floyd, after a somewhat stormy and litigious battle with former composer and bassist Roger Waters over who really owned the band's name released a solid eighties effort entitled **Momentary Lapse Of Reason** followed by one of their trademarked tours. The year also saw releases from Jethro Tull **Crest of a Knave**, French TV **After a Lengthy Silence**, Haze **Stout & Bottle**, Iskander **Mental Touch**, and Mr. Sirius **Barren Dream**. IQ's new deal had led to writing, rehearsals and the 1987 release of **Nomzamo**. Many were disappointed with **Nomzamo** as it seemed to be quite a bit more mainstream than their previous work. As discussed elsewhere it wasn't an effort on the part of the band to find a hit song, it's just the space they were in. Marillion did their best to follow up **Misplaced Childhood** with **Clutching At Straws** and many critics felt they succeeded. In the United States progressive rock fans were treated to the first release by Mastermind called simply **Volume I**. This powerhouse cassette was like ELP full bore on steroids. It rocked hard but there was no mistaking it's prog sensibilities. The interesting thing about Mastermind was they had no one playing keyboards. It was all skilfully programmed through Bill Berend's guitar synthesiser. So skilfully done, it put bands with keyboard players "on notice" so to speak. The drumming came courtesy of brother Richard. The two had played together since they were in their teens, and when they decided to do music more seriously it was only the two of them and usually one other person. A trio concept that has a rich history in progressive rock from ELP to Rush. Djam Karet's release **The Ritual Continues** received excellent reviews eventually selling upwards of 4000 copies with positive reviews in many mainstream magazines around the world including **Rolling Stone**, **Keyboard** and **Guitar Player**. Minimum Vital had spent the time since the release of their first cassette performing and in 1986 had met the people at Musea, the French progressive rock label. Musea listened to the cassette and were impressed enough to suggest the next step, an LP release. Thus the band released their first LP **Les Saisons Marines** recorded over the summer of 1987 in Bordeaux.

1988 - Yet Another Version Of Yes

The year 1988 might be considered a breathing space year. While there were a number of notable prog releases, few of them were spectacular. Rick Wakeman came back with **Suite Of The Gods** and **Zodiaque**, Kansas recorded a very satisfying concept album produced

Jerry Lucky

Eloy
Ra
Pulsar

Moody Blues
ELP

Robert Berry

Miriodor

Gentle Giant

The Enid

Rousseau

by Bob Ezrin entitled **Spirit Of Things,** and while it wasn't really very prog sounding, it did contain all the Ezrin production elements including choir and orchestration and huge sound. Also out that year were releases from Eloy **Ra**, Pulsar **Gorlitz**, It Bites **Once Around the World** and even The Moody Blues **Sur la Mer**. After the break up of Emerson Lake & Powell, Keith Emerson and Carl Palmer tried again to make a go of it with another band simply called 3 featuring Robert Berry on vocals. They released an LP called **To The Power Of Three** and while there were a couple of interesting tracks it was less than satisfying. Elsewhere, Canada's jazz oriented Miriodor released their first recording showing a slight Canterbury-ish, Gentle Giant influence, and Terraced Garden released their third called **Within**. The Enid's release of **The Seed and The Sower** proved to be the final work from messieurs. Godfrey and Stewart. Differences of direction had even set in within the Enid's household and the recording would be the last to include Stephen Stewart. German band Rousseau released their third LP **Square The Circle** and seemed to have developed a split personality. On the one hand there were some longer instrumental tracks with intricate compositional structures very reminiscent of Camel, and on the other hand the LP had a number of rather light-weight pop songs sandwiched in between the more adventurous material. It was symptomatic of the times as some bands struggled to find their musical way in the marketplace.

ABWH

I have tried to make the point that progressive rock has always been with us in some variation or other. This was brought home with the release of an album by Jon Anderson, Bill Bruford, Rick Wakeman and Steve Howe called **Anderson Bruford Wakeman and Howe** in 1989. While there was all the media attention being paid to the newer progressive rock bands, some of those who'd been around for a while continued making music the way they'd always done. In talking about the latest release from ABWH the reviewer in the radio trade publication The Gavin Report started out his review saying, *"Like it or not, orchestral rock will never die. Now it's a matter of who does it best and who merely releases laborious, meandering imitations. And yes, we've been through lots of Yes reincarnations, but to these sore ears, ABWH sounds like the best and most integral...I'll bet Steve Howe finally sleeps at night after recording this one."*

Wakeman

The previous ten years had seen tremendous technological development in musical instruments and keyboards specifically. A whole generation of keyboard players had grown up knowing more about programming sequencers than about physically playing. With ABWH there was a concerted effort to play more of the music in real time. Rick Wakeman interviewed in **Keyboard**: *"We wanted to have* the musicianship of the seventies and what we called proper writing utilising the technology of the eighties. We all felt very strongly that the eighties will probably be remembered, more than anything else, for it's surge of technology, which has been so powerful that musicianship has been sadly lacking." The band's effort with this release was to create in an environment, where music was the only rule that governed everything. Wakeman went on to say: *"If you write a piece of music that's eight minutes long, then it's eight minutes long. If you write a piece that's two-and-a-half minutes long, then it's two-and-a-half minutes long. If your piece needs four tempo changes for the mood you're trying to create, then you do them. Arista felt that the time was right for the return to the ideology of the seventies, of musicians producing music."* The band's underlying philosophy was that there were still people who wanted more in their music, a greater depth and tonal coloration. ABWH was able to provide the musical substance that was lacking in much of the music of the eighties.

Wakeman

Jethro Tull

Other releases from the old-guard included **Rock Island** from Jethro Tull and **Seasons End** from Marillion with their new vocalist Steve Hogarth. Fish had decided to call it a day and work on his own, feeling he had done everything he could do with Marillion. Quasar released their second recording entitled **The Loreli** this time with the addition of Tracy Hitchings on vocals. IQ released another mainstream release called **Are You Sitting Comfortably** which left their hard line fans feeling a bit uncomfortable, and there were a number of other bands making more waves. In the United States, Djam Karet had spent most of the previous year performing live and purchasing studio equipment to allow them greater control over their studio life. After nine months in the studio the band released **Reflections From The Firepool** in June of 1989 and would eventually sell over 6000 copies and gain glowing reviews. San Francisco, Bay area band Episode released a second independently produced cassette **Into the Epicentre**. Musically they'd been compared to Yes, Pink Floyd and Renaissance, primarily because of their female lead vocalist. The group had formed in 1984 playing throughout northern California. After various personnel coming and going, the band line stabilised and added Roe Tyler on vocals. Italy's Fancyfluid released their first self titled cassette release and would signal a major resurgence of progressive rock in Italy.

Fish

Marillion
Quasar
IQ

Djam Karet

Episode
Yes
Pink Floyd

In America the Syn-Phonic label came into being dedicated to releasing old and new progressive rock recordings. Their first two releases turned out to be a set of live recordings from the Florida band Babylon, who'd become cult classics back in 1977. The tapes were recorded in May of 1978 during some performances at The Empty Keg, a pub at the University of South

Babylon

1989

Florida. The two LP's, while not the greatest in sound quality managed to capture the sound of the band and more than that demonstrated to fans in 1989 that there was much they had not heard. Syn-phonic would go on to release many undiscovered "classics" and provide an opportunity for fans to rediscover lost recordings.

In fact 1989 can be considered the beginning of yet another wave of progressive rock. This resurgence proved to be slower than in 1983 because of the lack of mass media coverage, let alone support, but it would also benefit from the experience of the neo-progressive bands around at the time. This lack of media coverage proved beneficial in another way. It ensured that this time the progressive rock movement would not be seen as a fad. Instead the mass media ignoring prog has allowed the number of bands and the music to grow on it's own in a very underground fashion. The bands were also aided by the ease with which CD recordings could now be made and the worldwide network of independent progressive rock distributors.

Prog In The Nineties – Another Resurgence

1990

Minimum Vital

Halloween

Tiemko

Kalaban

1990 would continue in much the same manner as 1989...slow and careful with steady releases from the growing numbers of progressive rock bands around the world. In France, Minimum Vital, in an effort to improve on the disappointing sound of their previous vinyl LP went to CD, and released **Sarabandes**. Countrymen Halloween released an LP entitled **Laz** which showed them maturing greatly from their first but continuing to produce a dark and eerie prog style in keeping with everything their name implies. Halloween were actually one of the first French progressive rock bands to emerge in the late eighties. They had originally formed in 1983 and after going through a number of permutations, at one time being five members, then six and then down to three, it was the trio that would record their first release **Part One** in 1988 on the then recently formed Musea label. Halloween, along with Minimum Vital and Tiemko would lead a French progressive rock revival.

In the United States a band called Kalaban began making waves. The band had actually been together in one form or another since 1981 but it wasn't until 1985 that they had built up enough material to release a cassette entitled **Don't Panic**. As is usually the case with these things the cassette managed to find it's way into the hands of progressive rock fans in Japan, South America and even Spain. It finally landed on the desk of Gary Walker at Syn-Phonic who got in touch with the band and convinced them to re-record some of the material from the cassette and release it on vinyl in 1990. The CD version came out shortly thereafter. With an independent label deal and the promotion system in place the band were ready to carve out a niche for themselves.

Japanese symphonic progressive rock fans had much to cheer about with the second release from Mr. Sirius entitled **Dirge** featuring a uniquely Japanese blending of an early Enid style with heavy rock oriented symphonics. This second LP was a follow-up to their first **Barren Dream** and there are some who consider these the finest symphonic releases from Japan. They featured superb musicianship and the already mentioned influences along with hints of Gentle Giant and Genesis. Their forte was blending that orchestra sound within a rock structure. Former Marillion lead vocalist, Fish put out his first solo entitled **Vigil In A Wilderness Of Mirrors**.

After many years away, 1991 would see Procol Harum, whose last release was **Something Magic** in 1977, get back together and release **Prodigal Stranger**. Genesis continued their march to commercial acceptability with **We Can't Dance** which featured a harder edge and a couple of longer tunes like "Driving The Last Spike" and "Fading Lights" to satisfy the older fans. Jethro Tull released **Catfish Rising**, Camel **Dust and Dreams**, and Marillion **Holiday's In Eden**.

Steve Howe made an appearance with his solo effort entitled **Turbulence** but it was Yes who generated the most amount of media interest. It was no surprise that there were really two Yes bands since the release of **Anderson Bruford Wakeman and Howe** and **Big Generator** and since both were working on new releases, management suggested it might be interesting to put the two bands together and see what happened. The result was the album **Union** and a tour that tested even the most patient of band members. The album itself had no less than seven producers or co-producers and featured Yes music from both factions. While there were many good bits of music it was easy to pick out which Yes was playing what. The tour was another issue. Putting eight egos on one stage was destined to cause problems. Trevor Rabin looking back felt that this album would be seen as a black mark on Yes' career while Rick Wakeman insists on calling the album "onion" because every time he listens to it, it brings tears to his eyes.   Interviewed in **Keyboard Magazine**, Wakeman went on to explain: *"The first (demo) cassette I received from Arista went out the limo window after about fifteen minutes. The next one went out the hotel window. It's taken me a long time to calm down and be rational about it. In a nutshell, I am one hundred percent unhappy with every piece of keyboard work that's on that album."* Still the very fact this album came together was a good omen that Yes could and would continue to create music.

France's Asia Minor had tried to carry on since their second release in

Asia Minor

1980. Because so much time had transpired, various members playing together tried the name Interface and then Eurasia before reverting back to the original Asia Minor. They worked on new material, even recruited a new vocalist-keyboardist-guitarist by the name of Michel Rousseau and as late as 1991 were trying to get a third album together.

Ozric Tentacles

Pink Floyd Hawkwind Gong

There were a few other bands of note. One, was a British band called Ozric Tentacles who released an LP called **Strangeitude**. It's been said Ozric picked up where Pink Floyd left off. In fact as a group they sort of fell together around 1983 playing a keyboard and guitar dominated music that was influenced by not only Floyd but also Hawkwind and Gong. In many respects Ozric's style remains more solidly in the psychedelic realm but they maintain many fans from the progressive rock world as well.

Echolyn Narcissus

Another group of note was an American five piece band from Pennsylvania called Echolyn who released their first self titled release. Their history goes back to a band called Narcissus who primarily existed performing progressive rock cover tunes. The band consisted of Bret Kull, Ray Weston, Paul Ramsey and Tom Hyatt and with the addition of formally trained keyboardist Chris Buzby, Echolyn was formed. Their music was complicated yet accessible, structured yet easy to get into. They wrote about deeper, philosophical topics than most bands but the subject matter didn't deter a strong following from forming. A following that grew each time the band played live in a new community.

ELP

Emerson Lake & Palmer surprised everyone in 1992 by getting back in the studio to record and release **Black Moon**. The album had many of the hallmarks of ELP. There was the obligatory classical piece redone, the acoustic ballad and the concise drumming. But it was also a very different album and the die-hard fans noticed it right away. The songs were shorter and much more straight forward. In an interview with **Keyboard** magazine Keith Emerson explained their approach; *"We wanted to get the effect of a live performance. In fact, a lot of the recordings - most of them actually - were made in rehearsals, so you get that interplay that used to exist with ELP. The Hammond had to be brought back in too, because there's no way you can duplicate a Hammond organ and hide the fact that it's played live."* Still the simpler keyboard approach and much more commercial sound disappointed some fans who decided to look elsewhere for the obligatory symphonic fix. ELP spent most of the year on a world "Come Back" tour that included three nights at the Royal Albert Hall in London.

Anglagard

Sweden's progressive rock scene jumped into high gear with a trio of new bands all basing their sound back to the organs, flutes and Mellotrons of the seventies. Anglagard released their first CD **Hybris** which captured all that was good about the seventies sound with nineties production values. They had formed in 1991 with the specific idea of recapturing that early seventies sound and wasted no time going into the studio in mid 1992 to record the material they'd written. While fan response in their home town of Stockholm was small, interest was so high in the United States that the band was invited to perform at the inaugural Progfest 93.

Also from Sweden the heavier sounding Anekdoten borrowed from the darker King Crimson era and released a five song demo cassette. They had actually been together longer than Anglagard, forming in early 1990. Before that a few members who'd all desired to play progressive rock played primarily King Crimson covers throughout Sweden in a band called King Edward. In early 1991 the existing members of Anekdoten were approached by cellist Anna Sofi Dahlberg who was also interested in prog and asked if she could join. Her addition to the group brought about the name change and rehearsals ensued for this first release. The band spent most of 1992 rehearsing and playing live, refining their performing and writing style.

Anekdoten

King Crimson

Anglagard

Producing a somewhat darker audio landscape is a five-piece band called Landberk. Like their country-mates, they incorporate a strong seventies feel only in this case the influence on instrumentation and composition in their CD **Lonely Land** is Van Der Graaf Generator..

Landberk

Van Der Graaf Generator

Meanwhile in Japan a female trio called Arsnova who'd gone through a number of line-up changes since their formation in 1983 released their first CD **Fear and Anxiety** displaying an instrumental style very reminiscent of bands such as Craft, The Nice and ELP. American bands were hard at work too. Mastermind released **Volume II - Brainstorm**, Echolyn continued developing their complex writing style and vocal harmonies and produced their second release **Suffocating The Bloom**, and North Star resurfaced with **Power**. Another band, this one based in Washington DC, called themselves Cathedral, released their first CD called **Kingdom Of Ends.** They were the second US band to use the name but no relation to the first group. This version of Cathedral had formed in early 1991 and are considered one of the pioneers of the U.S. neo-progressive rock sound. Minimum Vital released their fourth effort entitled **La Source** which saw the brothers Thierry and Jean-Luc go in a more spiritual direction. The brothers had long made it a practice not to write lyrics in any one language but instead chose to create their own language based more on sound and flow. What they came up with was a mixture of French, Portuguese and their own sylabalising. For the tour to promote the CD the vocals proved

Arsnova

The Nice
ELP
Mastermind
Echolyn

North Star

Cathedral
Minimum Vital

Anekdoten

Everon
Episode
Kalaban

Asgard

Deus Ex Machina

Area

Solstice

nearly impossible to perform on stage so many of the songs were rearranged to be performed as instrumentals.

By 1993 the full impact of the resurgence which had started in 1989 could be felt world-wide, with progressive rock recordings of extremely high quality. Sweden's Anekdoten had spent many hours fine tuning their sound and released **Vemod** to enthusiastic response in Sweden and abroad. Germany's neo-prog band Everon released their first called **Paradoxes,** and Bay area band Episode put out their first CD **Starlight Tales**, while Kalaban having received good reviews with their first release put out their second CD entitled **Resistance Is Useless**. In Italy, neo-prog band Asgard released their fourth CD called **Imago Mundi**, while Deus Ex Machina released their first self titled release demonstrating their own unique musical style and a vocalist resembling Demitrious Stratos from the legendary Italian band Area.

England's Solstice, who everyone thought had broken up released their second album called **New Life**. In fact Solstice had stayed together since their 1984 release **Silent Dance** and had concentrated more on writing and playing live rather than recording. The one thing this accomplished was to build a solid fan support. The intervening ten years had seen considerable personnel changes, but the core of the band remained Andy Glass on guitars and Marc Elton on violin and keyboards. Their first LP was reissued on an independent label and the sales surprised everyone. So much so that the band decided perhaps it was time to record something new. The vocals were now handled by Heidi Kemp whose style tended to be stronger than Sandy Leigh's Jon Anderson style. The new album showed the band holding on to their original sound and quasi "hippy" ethic.

IQ

Def Leppard
Metallica

Following the release of IQ's **Are You Sitting Comfortably**, the record label Squawk began having financial difficulties. This eventually led them to drop IQ from the roster. Keyboardist Martin Orford commented about the situation on IQ's Internet mailing list: *"I don't entirely blame Squawk records because they always played fair by us, um, the problem that Squawk Records had was that they were a subsidiary of Q-prime which was the management company of, and still is the management company of Def Leppard and Metallica and bands like that, and although they had loads of money that they were prepared to put into IQ what they didn't have was distribution, mar-*

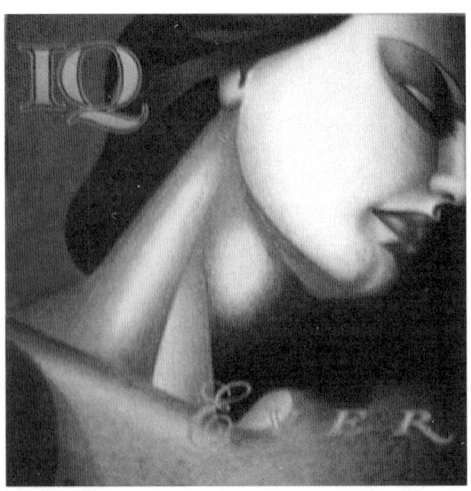

keting and the rest of it and they trusted that to the Phonogram organisation and Phonogram just weren't interested." Shortly after this, the label disappeared entirely. At the same time as the record deal fell apart bassist Tom Esua and vocalist Paul Menel, decided to quit, feeling the future of the band was in question. IQ recruited former Len's bassist Les "Ledge" Marshall to play bass with Peter Nichols coming in to guest on vocals. Shortly after this Marshal committed suicide which created a tremendous amount of anxiety and a deep feeling of loss for the remaining members. Peter Nichols recalled what happened in **SI** magazine: *"When Ledge died everything became unsettled, nobody knew what they wanted anymore. So it was decided to stop the band for a while to give everybody some time to get over the loss of a personal friend. In January [1991] everybody got together again. Mike called me and asked me if I would like to do some things with the band, and I said yes, sure! So in January we decided to go on with the band. Now that we'd lost Ledge all the differences of the past seemed very childish. Ledge's death made us realise that we had to maintain our friendship because it's very valuable."* The band members had actually begun looking for day-jobs, but Peter's desire to return interested and intrigued Orford. So day-jobs or not they set about recording their next album, returning to their initial sound and style. They released **Ever** showing them back in fine form.

The Glass Hammer Discovery

More and more bands continued to discover there was a market for progressive rock music. Bands such as the Chattanooga, Tennessee based Glass Hammer. Back in the late eighties Fred Schendel was playing in a country band called Murphy's Law, while Steve DeArque was in a group called Band Of Angels. Both bands were set to hit it big with large recording deals, however both individuals were really wishing they could play progressive rock. In the end both deals fell through and the two met in a record store introduced by a mutual friend who knew of their interest in progressive rock. At the time, the late eighties, they were unaware of the size of the prog market and so they did what they thought they had to, to make some money and that revolved around creating a tape of background music for people playing Dungeons and Dragons called **Alternity Tracks**. After that they decided to hit the same sci-fi community with a major effort, a full CD called **Journey Of The Dunedan**. The end result was a piece of music that contained sound effects, narration and some impressive progressive rock music. It eventually landed on the desk of Ken Golden at Laser's Edge who broke the band to the progressive rock community in 1993. When he purchased 500 copies of the **Journey** CD it surprised both Schendel and DeArque. As far as Schendel was concerned; *"We really felt we were the only ones trying to do progressive rock at the time [1993]. Of course, now we know that it's happening all over the place."*

Adding even more fuel to the resurgent "underground" of progressive rock has been the creation of progressive rock festivals. The granddaddy of them all is California's Progfest first held in 1993. The idea

**Anglagard
Citadel
Quill**

IQ

**Genesis
Jethro Tull
Kansas**

Yes

**Marillion
The Enid**

Pink Floyd

Landberk

Clepsydra

to hold such an event sprang from discussions held by three indie executives, namely; David Overstreet (Art Sublime), Gary Whitman (Citadel's Manager) and Greg Walker (Syn-Phonic). It was their idea to establish a network that would represent the many smaller independent American prog labels. This premiere event took place on Memorial day weekend and featured the American premiere of IQ and Sweden's Anglagard, along with Citadel and Quill from California. David Aldridge writing in **Keyboard** magazine said; *"For a die-hard audience, the first annual Progressive Rock and Arts Festival offered no shortage of Minimoog throbs, sweeping B-3 growls, and haunting Mellotron shimmers. Progressive-heads stampeded down the aisles for front row seats, proving that the music punk couldn't kill and disco couldn't comprehend is still alive and well."* The article spoke well of the fan's reaction to the music they loved. Quill had actually come out of a 15 year retirement to perform and they along with Citadel performed music in the classic progressive rock style while IQ showcased a more neo-progressive sound. But it was Anglagard's complex Mellotron laced seventies inspired set that stole the show.

While the music had changed significantly for Genesis they continued to release albums that sold tremendously well, as did Jethro Tull, Kansas, and Yes. In fact the 1994 **Talk** from Yes contained some of their best material of the nineties. More adventurous than the "Owner of a Lonely Heart" phase. Included on Talk was the classic Yes epic "Endless Dream" clocking in at over 15 minutes in length. Quoted in **Yes Stories** Jon Anderson said, *"I think it's exactly as good as anything we've done. The last third is a remarkable musical structure. I'm in heaven when I'm singing that like I am when I do "Close To The Edge" or "Awaken." It really works on a par with them. It's very modern, very hectic at the beginning, very wild."* The big news of 1994 was the amount of progressive rock coming from countries other than Britain. True, Marillion released their best work in many years, a concept CD entitled **Brave** and The Enid reformed with Robert Godfrey and a host of new, young musicians to record **Tripping The Light Fantastic**, Pink Floyd made an appearance with the release of **The Division Bell**, an album that sounded in many ways similar to **Wish You Were Here** in it's compositional style. IQ spin-off's Jadis released **Across The Water** to good reviews as well, but take a look elsewhere.

Sweden's Anglagard followed their first successful CD with the eagerly awaited **Epilog**. Fans were not disappointed. The trademark Anglagard sound of analogue synths and Mellotrons with guitar, flute and drums were all present in their usual complex and very seventies sounding style. Also from Sweden Landberk released their second **One Man Tells Another,** showing how much the band had matured over the two years since their first release. Switzerland's neo-prog Clepsydra released **More Grains Of Sand**, showing a strong Marillion influence.

In the United States, Iluvatar a five piece group based in Baltimore released their first self titled release, while the Washington based band Cathedral released their second CD entitled **There In The Shadows**. US band Magellan released **Impending Ascension** showing the band maturing in a style that strived to be complex and yet still remain accessible. Incorporating musical elements of Rush, Mastermind and Pendragon, Magellan made significant stylistic improvements with this release focusing on multi-part harmonies in a harder edged guitar style.

In France, the spirit of bands such as Ange and Mona Lisa was kept solidly alive with the release of Versailles' third **Le Tresor De Valliesres** displaying the typical hallmarks of the French symphonic sound. It had been four years since Halloween had put out any new music and with their 1994 release **Merlin** they came back with a new sound which incorporated female vocals and a variety of new instrumentation including a small string and horn section. In each decade, the legend of King Arthur has proven to be durable subject matter for progressive rock bands. In 1975 Rick Wakeman tackled the subject with his third solo release **The Myths and Legends of King Arthur and The Knights of The Round Table**. Then in 1981, the Dutch band Kayak released an album entitled simply **Merlin**. While these two LPs contained some great music, Halloween's nineties release came the closest to resembling an actual soundtrack for the mythic tale. Speaking of changing musical styles, Canada's Visible Wind released their third CD entitled **Emergence** showing more of a guitar oriented sound than previously. Yet another Canadian band Kaos Moon surfaced in the province of Quebec, long the leading province for Canadian progressive rock, with their first CD entitled **After The Storm**. Their music showed a hint of King Crimson mixed with Saga. While elsewhere the Japanese female trio called Arsnova put out a powerful second CD called **Transi**, which showed them still in an ELP mode only darker and even more intense and Germany's Everon recruited Grobschnitt drummer Eroc to produce their second CD called **Flood**.

Iluvatar

Cathedral

Magellan

Rush
Mastermind

Pendragon

Ange
Mona Lisa

Halloween

Wakeman

Kayak

Visible Wind

Kaos Moon

King Crimson

Saga

ELP

Grobschnitt

First Deus Ex Machina

Barrock

1994

Sebastian Hardie

**Episode
Kalaban
Echolyn
Anekdoten
Anglagard
Mastermind
Discipline
Iluvatar**

**Masque
Tangle Edge**

1995

ELP

Jethro Tull

Kansas

Two releases from Italy garnered rave reviews. First; Deus Ex Machina for their third release entitled **De Republica**, with critics calling it one of the best progressive rock releases of the nineties, and secondly Barrock and their release **Oxian**. Barrock's sound unlike many who strive for a polished seventies sound, was very modern, with no Mellotrons in sight. Instead this six piece band create a music that is firmly rooted in progressive rock with a strong classical influence and fronted by two female vocalists. As such the vocals don't predominate and there is lots of opportunity for the dynamic music to come to the fore.

Progfest '94 was pushed to a two day affair featuring eight bands and took place in November. Adding another day enabled organisers to include more opportunity for record buying and trading. The line-up included some international heavy-weights including the re-formation of Australia's Sebastian Hardie. The United States was represented by Episode, Kalaban and Echolyn, Sweden by Anekdoten and a return visit from Anglagard, and France's Halloween and Minimum Vital. On the East coast the first Progscape '94 was held in Baltimore, Maryland and despite a lower than expected attendance, everyone in the hall seemed to enjoy the featured bands which were Anekdoten, Mastermind, Discipline, Echolyn and Iluvatar. The idea of music festivals took on a decided International flavour with the first progfest Sweden featuring Roine Stolt, Masque, and Norway's Tangle Edge.

1995 - A Mixture of Old and New

Emerson Lake & Palmer's 1995 release of **In The Hot Seat** disappointed many, including, as it turned out, ELP. Far from being progressive rock it was clearly an attempt to take the ELP style and simply play accessible material. In terms of song writing the material failed to hold up under scrutiny. Again all the ELP elements were there but the new streamlined approach pioneered on their last album showed them going no further. They would spend some time on the road in support of Jethro Tull and trying to decide if they should carry on as a group. A sad state of affairs.

Kansas came back with a vengeance releasing **Freaks Of Nature**. They were ably assisted with new member, violinist David Ragsdale. His input into the material brought back a heightened progressive rock sensibility, and while the songs were not overly long they did contain elements of superior arrangement and structure. All in all their release was for fans the beginnings of a return to their earlier style and for newcomers plenty to hold their interest. After a decade away, King Crimson was back with a CD entitled **Thrak** which was followed by a virtually sold-out U.S. tour. Sound-wise they had picked up where they left off in the middle eighties, incorporating a few new technological gizmos to produce their trademarked guitar dominated dense sonic textures.

King Crimson

New releases would be heard from Jethro Tull - **Roots To Branches**, Marillion - **Afraid Of Sunlight**, and someone rummaging around in the back room at EMI found some unreleased tapes for what was to have been the second release from England. This came out under the name of **Last Of The Jubblies**. Brazilian band Apocalypse released their second **Perto Do Amanhecer** with a strong neo-progressive, Marillion influence. Also in the neo-prog vein is Italy's Fancyfluid who released their third CD entitled **The Sheltering Sea** showing a continuing progression in their abilities. New bands continue to emerge and old ones resurfaced if only on disc.

Jethro Tull

Marillion

Apocalypse
Marillion

Fancyfluid

Echolyn was signed by Sony and after spending three months in the recording studio they released **As The World**. There was some concern, that with the major label deal Echolyn's sound would be compromised but instead this release showed a more mature and every bit an uncompromising band. For Echolyn, the music remained central. Interviewed in **Expose** magazine keyboardist Chris Buzby commented about the albums composition: *"Well, there were two attitudes - one musical, and the other lyrical, and obviously, they combined to make an album. I think musically we went in and just tried to create something that worked as an album as a whole - there's a beginning, a middle and an end. We didn't write the album that way - every song took on it's own character, and at the end we pieced it together. I think what we were mainly after is trying to capture all the parts of Echolyn. You've got your very intense in-your-face kind of sections, you've got your delicate instrumental breaks, there's strings, there's flute, there's three part vocals, keyboards with drums, vocals with nothing - again it's just trying to capture all those elements."* The CD was released to rave reviews.

Echolyn

Meanwhile Mastermind released their third effort **Tragic Symphony**. Guitarist Bill Berends commented on their musical goal with this release in an Expose' interview: *"The primary aim was to not repeat our*

Mastermind

previous efforts. I wanted to do something a little more deliberate, paced. I also wanted to add some more dynamics to our live show so this album was a good place to do that...you can't do two hours of Brainstorm, it wears people out!" This release would mark the first time the band would record a piece without the use of electric guitar in an effort to bring about the musical dynamics Berends referred to.

Landberk
Anekdoten

King Crimson

Spock's Beard

Echolyn

Magellan

Saga

Swedish band Landberk released their second CD called **Unaffected** as did Anekdoten with **Nucleus**. Anekdoten's release saw them moving away from their King Crimson influences somewhat and refining their own compositional style while still incorporating many of the elements that made their first CD so popular. The new bands included Norway's White Willow's mysterious sounding, Mellotron led **Ignis Fatuus**, Leger De Main's harder edged **The Concept Of Our Reality** and Spock's Beard's quirky first CD entitled **The Light** in the same vein sound wise as Echolyn or Magellan featuring a very nineties sound and production quality all the while hanging on to a solid seventies symphonic style. The band was reminiscent of the best elements of Crack The Sky, with roaring guitar, stop-and-go tempo changes accompanied by melodic Beatle-ish vocals. All in all it was a stunning debut. Speaking of "stunning" Canada's Saga, caught many prog fans by surprise. After always being on the fringes of progressive rock they thrust themselves into the fray with not only a concept album but a "rock-opera" called **Generation 13**, which began winning over a whole new group of fans.

Rush
UK
Dixie Dregs

Dream Theatre

Ohio based band Leger De Main (a name which means "slight-of-hand") was another of the new American bands forging ahead with progressive rock with a harder edge. Formed by brothers Chris and Brett Rodler, the band came into being out of the ashes of their previous outfit Drama, which turned out to be their first attempt at creating progressive rock music. With a history of diverse musical influences the brothers listed Rush, UK, Dixie Dregs, Marillion and early Dream Theatre. In fact it was upon first hearing Marillion that Chris' musical future was shaped. In an interview at the bands website Chris explained: *"Probably the album that changed my musical direction most drastically was Marillion's Script For A Jester's Tear. I can still remember the day that I heard that album! From that day on I could only seem to listen to music like that."* Out of this desire Drama was formed with bassist friend Kevin Hultberg. The problem with Drama Chris' explained was it had too many rules about length of songs etc. So the brothers decided to strike out on their own. Chris Rodler, himself a big fan of the current burgeoning underground progressive scene explains: *"It always comes down to the music for us. If it is our band, then we can feel free to explore any musical idea that we choose If a song is four minutes long, then fine, if it ends up taking twenty minutes to get our ideas across then that is fine as well. Imagination and creativity are cornerstones of progressive rock and as such it is nice to exploit the options available to you."* Their album was released to positive reviews.

Progfest '95 again a two day event reflected the international scope of progressive rock in the nineties, and featured, Mexico's Cast, Japan's Arsnova, Italy's Deus Ex Machina, Scandinavia's White Willow, Hungary's Solaris, Sweden's Landberk, England's Pendragon and the American Spock's Beard. The success of this event has sparked others into action and now it's possible to hear progressive music at various events across the United States, Japan, Brazil and Sweden. Festivals like Progfest, Progscape, North Carolina Progday, San Francisco's East Bay Prog Day and others around the world have proven to be a valuable showcase for the bands to gain exposure not simply with fans but with the media.

After all the ego bashing during the Yes **Union** tour and the release of **Talk**, Trevor Rabin decided 12 years in one band was enough and announced he was leaving Yes. This left the door open to put together the original five members who recorded **Fragile** and **Close To The Edge**. This line-up released the much heralded **Keys To Ascension** in 1996, showing perhaps that you can go back...and move forward at the same time. The double CD included newly recorded live performances of such classics as "America" and one side of **Tales From Topographic Oceans**. But it also contained two new tracks: one a ten minute rocker and the other a seven part epic in the grand style of **Close To The Edge**. At the time of release plans were in the works for **Keys Volume II** which would contain over 45 minutes of new material.

Stalwarts Marillion, still in there, ended their long association with the EMI label by releasing a double live album called **Made Again**, while perennial underdogs, Pendragon released the very strong **Masquerade Overture**, and even Camel surfaced with **Harbour Of Tears**, a moody concept album about a small town on the Irish coast. Glass Hammer, hot off the success of their first, after finally finding the prog market put out **Perelandra** and Mastermind continued their onslaught with **Volume IV Until Eternity**. The departure of Echolyn bassist Tom Hyatt would end up being one of the determining factors leading to what many thought was the band's break-up. Not able to find a replacement, Chris Buzby would leave to form Finneus Gauge while the remaining members would carry on as Still. Echolyn far from being dead released a CD entitled **When The Sweet Turns Sour** containing a number of demo tracks and other material that was destined for the second Sony CD. While the two bands would continue in their own musical directions Echolyn guitarist and vocalist Brett Kull made it very clear that Echolyn would continue in some form. Quoted in **Progression** magazine #21 Kull stated: *"We're going to hire different musicians to give a different flavour to the new stuff. I'd love to be able to keep putting out Echolyn albums until I'm dead."* Although no firm plans for recording or touring were in the cards, the news was good for the legions of fans around the world.

1996 - And Then There Were Two

In 1996 the face of progressive rock changed yet again, with the announcement of Phil Collins departure from Genesis. The Internet

Genesis

was a-blaze with tears of joy and a few sad ones as well. There was the hope that Genesis would return to their roots just as Yes had done earlier in 1996. The indications from remaining members Mike Rutherford and Tony Banks were that the new Genesis would return to a darker, perhaps heavier sound. In the weeks that followed Collin's departure Genesis added Stiltskin vocalist Ray Wilson and two new drummers including Nick D'Virgillio of Spock's Beard. Their CD release **Calling All Stations** hit the record shelves in September of 1997.

Kansas

Styx

After what seemed like an eternity of playing small halls and smoky clubs, Kansas went back on the stadium circuit, opening for Styx. Fan response at the shows and on the internet was overwhelmingly positive. While Styx concentrated on mostly pre-**Cornerstone** material, Kansas included some songs off their latest release **Freaks of Nature**, which had by the middle of 1996 sold in excess of 80,000 units. Also on the tour front the unlikely pairing of Jethro Tull and opening act Emerson Lake & Palmer hit the road, playing across the United States. Again fan response was very positive, even though the ELP portion of the tour was limited to an hour and consisted of mostly older, shorter, familiar pieces. The Tull portion of the show was in support of their CD **Roots To Branches.**

Jethro Tull

ELP

Still
Miriodor

Porcupine Tree

Iluvatar

Braindance

Bacamarte

Minimum Vital

The progressive rock festivals continued in 1996 exposing new talent and established bands to fans everywhere. Progscape II happened in Baltimore featuring one of the first official outings for Echolyn spin-off band Still, Canadian band Miriodor, Porcupine Tree, Fourth Estate from Colorado, Glass Hammer, Iluvatar, New York prog-metal band Braindance, the fusion oriented Boud Deun and French symphonic band Eclat. Overall a well attended event with everyone singing the praises of the organisers. The most ambitious festival to date took place in Brazil at the first annual Rio Art Rock Festival with over 1200 fans in attendance. It featured Bacamarte, Sagrado, Solaris and Minimum Vital. While it was only a one day affair it had the trappings of a much larger event including a 27 meter stage, huge video screens and overwhelming sound system.

Revelation
Catweazle
Land's End
Ring Of Myth

1996 was a year with many new bands releasing great material. Bands such as Revelation, Rocket Scientists, Standarte, Catweazle, Providence, Relayer, Lands End, Ring of Myth, and so on. To see how much progressive rock has grown in the nineties, all you have to do is acquire one of the progressive rock catalogues listed from the suppliers elsewhere in this book to see that there are literally hundreds of new releases coming from countries around the world. Brazil and Argentina currently support three record labels and four or five progressive rock fanzines. And the re-releases of older material from the seventies onto CD has proliferated at an amazing rate. Labels such as France's Musea, Japan's Belle Antique, Brazil's Progressive Rock World-Wide and Italy's Mellow Records have provided us with re-releases of many of the genre's classics as well as many current releases. And labels such as Syn-Phonic, Laser's Edge, Cyclops, Kinesis, and Distributions Mezzo are just a few companies that provide us with an endless supply of new CD releases.

1997 ... And Beyond

One of the highlights of the year was the reformation of Italian progressive rock legends Le Orme and the release of **Il Fiume** which had many prog critics hailing it as some of their best work. In fact Le Orme wound up stealing the show at the 1997 Progfest event in Los Angeles. They performed along with England's Arena, Sweden's Sinkadus and The Flower Kings and perennial favourites Spock's Beard. The Flower Kings performed material from their 1997 double CD release **Stardust We Are**, showing there is plenty of creative life in the world of symphonic progressive rock.

The year closed with the release of two CDs from Yes. First, came **Keys To Ascension 2** featuring the last studio work done with Rick Wakeman, and was immediately followed by **Open Your Eyes** featuring long-time associate Billy Sherwood on guitar, keyboards and backing vocals. Sherwood replaced Rick Wakeman who was unable to remain with the band due to an assortment of management squabbles. The band immediately set out on a world tour with additional assistence from "newcomer" Igor Khoroshev on keyboards.

The December issue of Keyboard featured the magazine's picks for best albums of the year and while usually progressive rock is avoided, contributor Dan Barrett chose some of the years best prog releases for his top choices including ex-Echolyn, Finneus Gauge's **More Once More**, Spock's Beard's **Beware of Darkness** and new Italian band D.F.A's first CD **Lavori In Corso**, which he credited as possibly being his favourite release of the past three years.

Much to the chagrin of most critics, progressive rock music is not only alive and well in the nineties, it's thriving!

1997

Le Orme

Arena
Sinkadus
Flower Kings

Spock's Beard

Yes

Wakeman

Spock's Beard

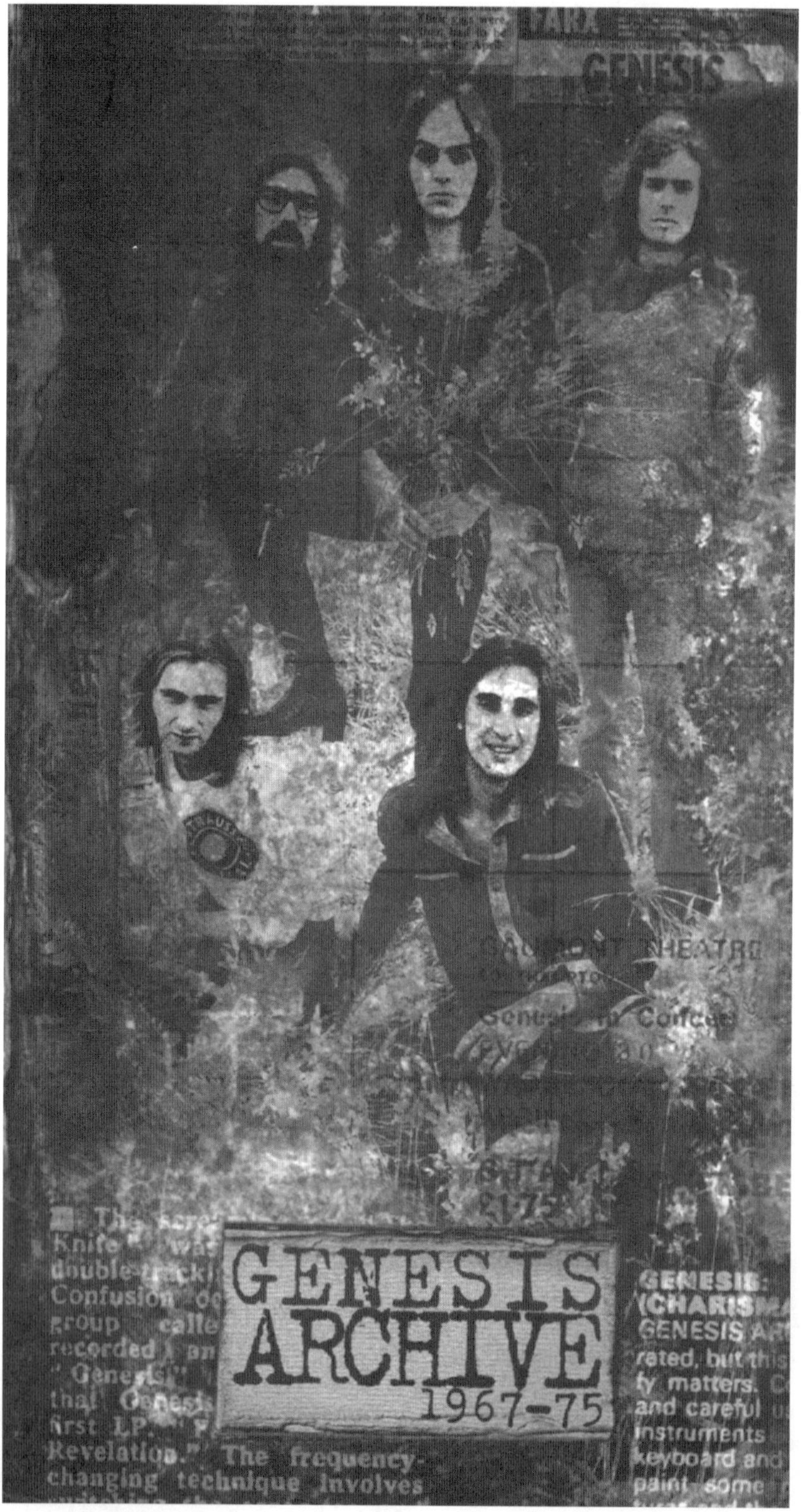
GENESIS
GENESIS ARCHIVE
1967–75

Proof of this was not only the volume but the quality of prog releases that hit CD players around the world. Canada's Visible Wind released their most symphonic album yet with **Narcissus Goes to The Moon**, full of organ, Mellotron and lush orchestration. In the United States, Discipline released **Unfolding Like Staircase**, and Djam Karet put out **The Devouring**. The remnants of Echolyn resurfaced going by the name of Still. Their CD entitled **Always Almost** featured a more-earthy guitar/grunge sound. Then later in the year changed their name to Always Almost and adjusted their musical style slightly again and released **God Pounds His Nails**. Spock's Beard set the prog world ablaze with **The Kindness of Strangers** and on the more dissonant and angular front 5uu's released **Crisis in Clay**. In other parts of the world, Present released **Certitudes** to widespread acclaim, The Enid released one of their most symphonic efforts yet with **White Goddess**, Minimum Vital – **Espirit d'Amor** and Porcupine Tree – **Coma Divine**.

	Visible Wind
	Discipline
	Echolyn
	Spock's Beard
	5uu
	The Enid
	Minimum Vital
	Porcupine Tree
	Cast

Of particular note on the prog festival front was Cast and Baja Prog. Cast have been around since 1978 and have released a total of 12 CDs since 1993. The line-up has been constant from the beginning with core members; Francisco Hernandez (guitar), Rodolfo Gonzalez (bass), and Alfonso Vidales (keyboards). In 1993 Dino Brassea joined on vocals along with Jose Caire on percussion. While all of the members have full time jobs or own their own businesses, they still make time, to create some of the best neo-progressive rock today. Their earlier music borrowed from mid period Genesis, but over the years the band has firmly established their own style. In many cases their music has become infinitely more complex than the original inspiration. Their first major exposure to the prog world was the third annual edition of Progfest in 1995 in Los Angeles. Since then they've performed in other parts of the U.S., Argentina, Canada and even Europe. In an effort to promote the progressive rock genre Cast took to staging a number of highly successful prog festivals in their home country of Mexico, called Baja Prog the first of which took place in 1997. These well run events have been nothing short of first-class affairs featuring international line-ups of some of the top prog bands of the day.

1997 also marked the coming of age of the Classic Rock Society based in England. This vibrant prog organization had actually formed in 1991 under the leadership of Martin Hudson as their promo information says, "out of sheer frustration". Their self-proclaimed mandate was to promote progressive rock to the world. In those early years their activities went largely unnoticed to much of the world, but at home the organization steadily built a following by pub-

Jerry Lucky

Camel
Fish
Jadis
Arena
Flower Kings

lishing a monthly magazine entitled *Wondrous Stories* and putting on a series of regular prog performances. By 1997 word of the Classic Rock Society had spread to fans around the world by way of the Internet. It was also the year of the first three day UK Spring Prog Fest featuring Camel, Fish, Jadis, Arena, Flower Kings, Enchant and a host of others. Suddenly the CRS was a prog-force to be contended with on the world front. As of this writing they hold title to producing the longest running monthly prog publication. No mean-feat given the difficult deadlines a task like this entails. Additionally the CRS holds an annual prog awards evening citing the 'best of the best' in this rather unrecognized musical genre. With honorary president Rick Wakeman the world of progressive rock in England seems to be in good hands.

And who would have thought Canada would ever see a progressive rock festival, but it happened in 1997 in Quebec City called Prog'est. Different yet again, it took place over four nights in this historic city and each night a local Canadian progressive rock act was teamed up with some of the bigger names in the prog world. Featured artists included Cast, Iluvatar, Flower Kings, Arena, and Visible Wind.

Cast
Iluvatar
Flower Kings
Arena
Visible Wind

1998 – Prog Festivals Come of Age

As 1998 dawned, the world of progressive rock continued to spread far and wide aided by an ever-growing Internet and maturing CD distribution network. Symphonic bands were springing up every month in South America, updating a long and proud history of melodic prog from that part of the world. While a number of world tours by Dream Theatre had inspired the unlikely blending progressive rock and heavy metal giving birth to prog-metal bands who were taking Europe by storm. The other sub-genres of space-rock, RIO and Zeuhl were also experiencing growth proving their was room for everyone.

Dream Theatre

RIO
Zeuhl

Ten Jinn
Iluvatar
Puppet Show
XII Alfonso
Minimum Vital
Edhels
Equinox
Salem
Crux De Hierro
Cast
Boud Deun
Soundscape
Alaska
Discipline
Crucible
A Peidi Nudi
Pallas

The second edition of Baja Prog 98 picked up where the first adventure left off. This time the cast of prog bands included the likes of Ten Jinn, Iluvatar, Puppet Show, XII Alfonso and Minimum Vital (France), Edhels (Monaco), Equinox (Panama), Salem (Canada), and from Mexico Cruz de Hierro and Cast. For the fourth year in a row prog fans crowded the outdoor fields at Storybook Farm to drink in the musical delights of Prog Day 98. Talent included Boud Deun, Soundscape, Alaska, Discipline and Crucible (United States), A Piedi Nudi (Italy), Cast (Mexico), Flower Kings and Par Lindh Project (Sweden). Overseas the 2nd Annual UK Progfest under the auspices of The Classic Rock Society took place in May featuring a distinctly British flavour with bands such as Mr. So & So, World Turtle/Haze, Primitive Instinct and The Enid. The International guests turned out to be Cast from Mexico.

The CRS was also instrumental in re-launching the career of Pallas. After a decade away from the prog spotlight Pallas recorded **Beat the Drum**, which was given high praise with a rating of 9-out-of-10 stars in Classic Rock magazine. Reviewer Nick Shilton said "**Beat the Drum** ranks up there with the likes of IQ's **Ever** as a truly momentous comeback." The band, having been one of the key 'neo-prog' bands of the early eighties had disappeared from sight following their 1986 release **The Wedge**. Having stayed in touch, trying off and on to work together Pallas finally received the stimulus needed while performing at a Dutch festival in 1995. Their new CD contained the best of both worlds with due homage paid to the classic prog style as well as more straight-ahead rock tunes. All in all many were glad to see Pallas back on the scene.

Bands like Nathan Mahl or fellow Canadians Mind Gallery were only now beginning to discover the power and scope of the world of progressive rock on the Internet. As with so many bands, the discovery of a whole world of potentially millions of fans was inspiration enough to move forward without looking to the established industry for assistance. Mind Gallery guitarist Gary Bourgeois quoted in The Georgia Straight explains: "The tools that are out now are orders of magnitude less expensive than in the heyday of the progressive rock era in the '70s, when the idea of million dollar recording budgets was common place. Moving stuff more and more onto the Web site means that you can produce something and then a week later post it as an MP3 file. It really changes the whole concept: now you're creating music and having it distributed worldwide instantaneously." The ability for bands to release independent CD's and promote their product to a market that's tuned in to the Internet has in no small measure helped spread the word.

Listed elsewhere in this book are a few websites to check out, but it's worth pointing out the fluid nature of the Internet. Given the high-labour involved with information rich sites, a site that is there today may be gone tomorrow because the person involved can no longer devote the time necessary to maintain the site. That being said, here are a few sites that are active as this is being written. Check out....ghostland.com, progressiveworld.net, and the Dutch progressive web site at dprp.vuurwerk.nl where you'll also see a listing for virtually every band with a website at their 'Links' page. Each of these sites has plenty of up-to-date news, upcoming releases, reviews and photos from the prog world. If you are into listening to prog on the net you'll want to visit sites such as Music Sojourn or the more comprehensive progradio.net which is really a prog radio mall featuring six different sites, each playing a slightly different style of prog. It's all as close as a mouse-click away.

Nathan Mahl
Mind Gallery

1998 saw many progressive rock CD releases. U.S releases of note included a band called IZZ who came out of the blue with a fine CD entitled **Sliver of a Sun** featuring a very dramatic, progressive rock track that even won a Billboard song writing award. There was also Puppet Show – **Traumatized**, Glass Hammer-**On to Evermore**, Shadow Gallery – **Tyranny**, A Triggering Myth – **Sins of our Saviors**, Djam Karet – **Still No Commercial Potential**, and upon the release of **The Stolen Bicycle**, prog-fusion favorites Boud Deun called it quits to pursue other ventures. New music coming out of the U.K. included Marillion – **Radiation**, Galahad – **Following Ghosts**, Camel – **Coming of Age**, Arena – **The Visitor** and the very fine first effort from

IZZ
Puppet Show
Glass Hammer
Shadow Gallery
Triggering Myth
Djam Karet
Boud Deun
Marillion
Galahad
Camel
Arena

Janson Edge

Par Lindh Project
Sinkadus
White Willow
Eloy
Flamborough Head
Mona Lisa
Flower Kings

Roine Stolt

Kaipa

Janison Edge entitled **For the Services of Mary Goode**. It was just the tip of the iceberg not counting all the European, Asian and South American releases. Sweden's Par Lindh Project released **Mundus Incompertus**, Sinkadus – **Cirkus**, White Willow – **Ex Tenebris**, Eloy's most proggy effort in a long time was the sequel **Ocean 2**, Ars Nova – **Book of the Dead**, Flamborough Head – **Unspoken Whisper**, Mona Lisa reformed with the band's lead vocalist backed by French proggers Versailles and released **De L'ombre A la Lumiere**.

The prolific Flowers Kings followed up the previous years double with yet another twin CD of excellent prog entitled **Flower Power** highlighted by the 60 minute cut "Garden of Dreams". When it comes to symphonic progressive rock of the nineties The Flower Kings have turned out to be one of the favourites. The music, whether it's a one-minute piece or a twenty-five minute epic is dynamic and dramatic, containing many moods and musical virtuosity. The roots of The Flower Kings and Roine Stolt go back to the Swedish band Kaipa where Stolt was guitarist. Kaipa, often compared to Camel produced three LPs of vintage although not earth-shattering progressive rock in the mid-to-late seventies. After Kaipa's demise, Stolt spent time as a solo artist/producer/and session player on the Swedish music scene. In late 1993 Stolt got together with drummer Jamie Salazar and percussionist Hasse Bruniusson to record **The Flower King**, an album that was to take him back to his progressive roots. Following its release he put a band together to rekindle the creative interplay he missed, working as a solo artist. Both Salazar and Bruniusson agreed to join the new group. They were quickly joined by Stolt's brother Michael (bass) and long time friend Tomas Bodin (keyboards). The group was asked to perform at a local prog-rock festival in Sweden and with only four hours of rehearsal the band worked well together on stage and the audience loved it. Thus The Flower Kings as a group was born.

UK

The year ended with the news that the long-awaited return of UK was not going to happen. It had been known for some time that original members Eddie Jobson and John Wetton had been working together to that end. Egos being what they are some said it was too much to hope for and sure enough after considerable time in the studio it was announced that Wetton would not be singing on the new material. Which begged the question what was going to come of all the work. Keyboardist Eddie Jobson indicated the split had been amicable and that while much of Wetton's bass and guitar parts would remain, he would be looking for a new vocalist. Unfortunately he also indicated the material would not be released under the UK name but would come out under the name "Legacy".

Legacy

1999 – A Year of Reflection

In 1999 prog continued to look both forward and backward in the best of senses. Whoever it was who said "you can't go back" wasn't referring to Deep Purple who back in 1970 got together with the Royal Philharmonic Orchestra and recorded a live album in Royal Albert Hall. Nearly 30 years later, this time with The London Symphony Orchestra, Deep Purple returned to The Royal Albert Hall to record anew. The band were also reported as saying they were in the studio recording what for them was going to be their "Sergeant Pepper" album.

Deep Purple

The year also started with the news that Greg Lake was 'officially' quitting Emerson, Lake and Palmer. After the lack-luster **In the Hot Seat** fans were excited to learn that the band was in the studio working towards a more authentic ELP recording. However the inevitable 'musical directions' issue reared its ugly head and problems developed. Ultimately Lake wanted more of the production credits and when that didn't happen, he decided enough was enough and he wanted out. The future of ELP remained unknown.

ELP

Spock's Beard created their most accessible recording yet, **Day For Night** but still were able to throw a ton of inventive symphonic prog chops into the mix. The band Spock's Beard was created in 1992 by brothers Neal and Al Morse. Al had a small home studio and they set out to create music they liked as opposed to what seemed popular. At the time Neal played keyboards and handled lead vocals while Al worked the guitars, cellos, other stringed instruments and backup vocals. From the very beginning their music consisted of many layers of musical textures, with both guitar and keyboards sharing the spotlight. Like others they began working in a prog style before realising the size of the prog underground that existed at the time. As the compositions progressed the brothers began to focus on the rhythm section and brought in long time friend Dave Meros on bass and vocals. Drumming chores were handled by Nick D'Virgilio who claims early Genesis as his favourites and who's done session work with Tears For Fears, appears on the Genesis **Calling All Stations** CD and most recently worked with Peter Gabriel. The final band member to join the fold was Ryo Okumoto an LA keyboardist who's worked with the likes of Phil Collins and Eric Clapton. He came on after the release of Spock's Beards first CD **The Light** released in 1995. In many ways **The Light** proved to be a ground breaking album, combining the epic scale compositions of the progressive rock genre with a strong pop/rock sensibility and it won rave reviews around the world.

Spock's Beard

Genesis
Peter Gabriel

Phil Collins
Eric Clapton

Nathan Mahl

Coming out of nowhere, Canada's Nathan Mahl released **Clever Use of Shadows** and appeared at the inaugural North East Art Rock Festival, taking everybody by surprise. The band was co-founded by Guy LeBlanc back in 1981and released a vinyl recording entitled **Parallel Eccentricities** in 1983. The band then lay dormant until the mid-nineties when LeBlanc decided to re-release the earlier vinyl on CD. Even then the band's musical direction was out of the mainstream blending elements of progressive rock and fusion in shorter compositions. In January 1999 Nathan Mahl released **Clever Use of Shadows** a far more adventurous symphonic prog recording and it was on the strength of this CD they were invited to perform at NearFest. The performance was breathtaking and caught everyone off guard. Reviews gave them high praise.

Alaska
Hand Farm
Mastermind
IQ
Ice Age
Crucible
Solaris
Spock's Beard

This first annual NearFest was in the words of Progression magazine an unqualified success. Just over 420 fans came to hear not only Nathan Mahl but a good cross section of prog including Alaska, Scott McGill's Hand Farm, Mastermind, IQ, Ice Age, Crucible, Solaris and Spock's Beard. Those in attendance were also treated to a guest lecture from none other than keyboard whiz Larry Fast. The initial success of the inaugural event caused the immediate announcement of the next year's event moving to larger facilities.

Magma
Porcupine Tree
Gong
Brand X
Rocket Scientists
Par Lindh
Arena
Quidam
Halloween
After Crying
Tempano
Iconoclasta
Cast
Crucible
Ten Jinn
Genesis

As far as prog festivals, the 1999 fifth-edition of Progfest was moved from Los Angeles, North to San Francisco and took on the more official name International Progressive Music Festival. The bands also took on a more avant-garde flair featuring Magma (France), Porcupine Tree, Gong, Brand X (England), Rocket Scientists (United States), Par Lindh (Sweden) and Bondage Fruit (Japan). The third annual Baja Prog 99 carried on a successful tradition with bands such as Arena (England), Quidam (Poland), Halloween (France), After Crying (Hungary), Tempano (Venezuela), Iconoclasta and Cast (Mexico) and Crucible and Ten Jinn from the United States.

After thirty years, rumors began to spread that Genesis may be calling it quits. The tour booked in support of their release **Calling all Stations** had not generated the response hoped for, particularly in the lucrative American markets. In fact the problem was that with the departure of Phil Collins the band was simply being ignored. Genesis have steadfastly 'ignored' the prog fan base that brought them to popularity choosing instead to become more of a pop band, now the fickle world of pop music was deserting them, moving on to the next popular musical flavour. Published reports quoted Tony Banks as saying, "There's no way we can reinvent ourselves to say we're new, young and fresh. It's a question of whether we want to keep on with that kind of thinking or if we want to stop." As of this writing no final announcement had been made, although all original members did reunite in the studio to re-record a new version of "Carpet Crawlers" for the record company's obligatory greatest hits CD entitled **Turn It On Again – The Hits**.

Genesis

It was no secret that many Yes fans were hugely disappointed with the 1997 release of **Open Your Eyes**. Steve Howe was quoted in Classic Rock magazine as saying "I was never sure about it. While we were working on it I was shouting, 'Surely you don't think Yes fans are gonna like this?'" Fact was they didn't and Yes knew it. That's why they were in Vancouver working on material that was more along the lines of what fans had come to expect. The new release entitled **The Ladder** was a lot more in keeping with the Yes formula of progressive rock. Howe went on to explain their dilemma to producer Bruce Fairbairn, "We told Bruce face-to-face that we're not looking for a pop hit. We'll write the way we used to…it has to be a more complex album…Yes needs to make wonderful music again." The end result, **The Ladder** was seen as a major improvement from **Open Your Eyes** but there were many fans who still felt Yes could do better.

Yes

Musical releases in 1999 were of the highest order. Dream Theatre created their most progressive effort yet with **Scenes from a Memory** a sequel to the track "Metropolis" off their **Images and Words** CD. Fish followed up **Sunsets on Empire** with **Raingods with Zippos**, Came released **Rajaz**, and Cast were busy as usual with three releases, **A Live Experience**, **Legacy** and a double CD of some of the material redone in Spanish. Italian proggers DFA returned with **Duty Free Area** and keyboardist Guy LeBlanc took time out of Nathan Mahl to record a solo entitled **Subversia**. Saga went back to the beginning and released **Full Circle**, which once again featured the 'bug creature' and contained three more 'chapter' songs that were so popular with fans of their early albums. Clive Nolan added to his already hectic schedule by getting together with Oliver Wakeman to record a concept CD based on the **Jabberwocky** tale. The album featured contributions from Peter Banks (ex Yes), Bob Catley (ex Magnum), Tony Fernandez (ex Strawbs), Peter Gee (Pendragon), Tracy Hitchings (Landmarq) and the voice of Rick Wakemen. And speaking of Rick Wakeman, never one to shy away from epic scale projects, he worked out a deal with the classical music

Dream Theatre

Fish
Came
DFA

Nathan Mahl
Saga

Rick Wakeman

Trevor Rabin
Justin Hayward

Easter Island
XII Alfonso
Finneus Gauge
Steve Hackett
El Reloj
Happy The Man
Il Balletto
Iluvatar
Ten Jinn
Porcupine Tree
Solaris

Greenslade

Gnidrolog

Kansas

Yes

label Angel to update and record **Return to the Centre of the Earth**. This time Wakeman would call on guests to help out including Trevor Rabin, Ozzy Osborne, Justin Hayward, Bonnie Tyler and the story was to be narrated by Patrick Stewart of Star Trek fame.

Other releases were simply too numerous to mention but highlights included: Easter Island – **Mother Sun**, XII Alfonso – **Odyssees**, Finneus Gauge – **One Inch of the Fall**, Steve Hackett – **Darktown**, El Reloj – **Hombre de Hoy**, Happy The Man – **Death's Crown**, Il Balletto di Bronzo – **Trys**, Locanda della Fate – **Homo Homini Lupus**, Iluvatar – **A Story Two Days Wide**, Ten Jinn – **On a Darkling Plain**, Porcupine Tree – **Stupid Dream**, Solaris – **Nostradamus** plus many others. All in all a stellar year for prog, and the beginnings of yet another new trend.

2000 – New Beginnings

The year 2000 turned into perhaps the busiest year yet for progressive rock music. The most startling thing was the number of bands from progressive rock's golden years that came to realization there was still a market for their music. This led to a number of reunions. Dave Greenslade reassembled Greenslade minus Dave Lawson. Early proggers Gnidrolog seeing the positive response to the re-release of their albums from the seventies decided to revive the group for more recordings. All members of Happy The Man, but Kit Watkins came together to perform at NEARFest 2000, and after a number of false starts Jurgen Fritz put the finishing touches on the new Triumvirat recording,

One of the strongest Kansas line-ups reassembled with Steve Walsh, Kerry Livgren, Robby Steinhardt, Dave Hope, Rich Williams and Billy Greer. All members were back in the studio with a new set of Livgren penned tunes recording an album entitled **Somewhere to Elsewhere**. The band had signed to Magna Carta records and this new release boasted a host of long epic songs hearkening back to the symphonic prog style the band came to be known for. Kansas then took off on their biggest tour in many years in support of Yes.

Speaking of Yes, mid-way through the year they would go through another one of their perennial line-up changes as Billy Sherwood announced he was leaving. After spending a number of years in the

band he chose to return to a solo career. Yes would continue with an almost classic lineup, Anderson, Squire, White, Howe, and Khoroshev.

After a number of interesting band permutations the members of Echolyn came together once more to record **Cowboy Poems Free**. This much heralded reunion was greeted with enthusiasm from prog fans all over the United States. The revised line-up included original members, Chris Buzby, Brett Kull, Paul Ramsey, Ray Weston and newcomer Jordon Perlson as the band's second drummer/percussionist. The music on the release shows a more varied style, incorporating much of the musical experimentation which had taken place during the members solo effort adventures of Still, Always Almost and Finneus Guage. There was a little more aggressive guitar in spots, a little more jazzy keyboard work, some less structured material all mixed with songs that were unmistakably Echolyn. Interestingly following their Sony experience Echolyn was reborn as a business entity, Echolyn Inc. with their own label, Velveteen records.

Echolyn

If there were four bands that represented the current state of progressive rock, I would say they are Spock's Beard, The Flower Kings, Dream Theatre and Marillion. Since the birth of rock'n'roll there have been 'supergroups'. So much so that the term has been sorely overused or misapplied. But if there were ever a time where the term truly made sense it would be with the band effort Transatlantic, comprised of Neil Morse from Spock's Beard, Roine Stolt from The Flower Kings, Mike Portnoy from Dream Theatre and Peter Trewavas from Marillion. Trying to conceptualize the results of this creative foursome in the studio left many unsure of what the results might be. The final recording was an uncompromising blend of some of the best symphonic progressive rock available. The CD was entitled **SMPT:e** and quickly became a favorite of many fans and critics alike.

Spock's Beard

Flower Kings
Dream Theatre
Marillion

On the Festival front, March dawned on Baja Prog 2000 and once again proved to be three days of spectacular progressive music from around the world. Bands included Halloween and Eclat (France), After Crying (Hungary), Jadis and Pallas (England), Five Fifteen (Finland), Nexus (Argentina) and Flower Kings and Isildurs Bane (Sweden). As usual the closing party was bigger and better than ever. The 2nd annual NEARFest was a smashing success having moved to a new larger 1000 seat facility the event sold out in record time. Bands included the reformed Happy The Man, Thinking Plague, North Star (United States), Il Balletto di Bronzo and DFA (Italy), Anekdoten and Par Lindh (Sweden), Nexus (Argentina) and the previously mentioned

Halloween
Eclat
After Crying
Jadis
Pallas
Five Fifteen
Nexus
Flower Kings
Isildur's Bane
Happy The Man
Thinking Plague
North Star
Il Balletto
DFA
Anekdoten
Par Lindh
Nexus

Jerry Lucky

Echolyn
Kopecky
Yoke Shire
Tiles
Nathan Mahl
Mary Newsletter
Landmarq

Kenso
Codice
Supersister
Mona Lisa
Tempus Fugit
Spock's Beard
Rocket Scientists
Camel

Transatlantic. As a special treat, as if one was needed, the Friday before the event featured the reformed Echolyn performing a special club date. ProgDay 2000 at Storybook Farm in North Carolina, while moving the event date a little later into the Fall still proved to be a highlight on the prog lovers musical calendar. Bands included Kopecky, Yoke Shire and Tiles (United States), Nathan Mahl (Canada), Mary Newsletter (Italy) and Landmarq (England). The granddaddy of all the prog festivals Progfest had run into some difficult times and even left Los Angeles for two years, it returned with a vengeance in the year 2000 once again under the direction of Gary Walker of Syn-Phonic records, David Overstreet and Alex Castro. The stellar line-up for Progfest 2000 in September included the multi-national Transatlantic, Banco (Italy), Kenso (Japan), Codice (Mexico), Supersister (Netherlands), Mona Lisa (France), and Tempus Fugit (Brazil). This year's festivities featured a pre-event evening performance by Spock's Beard and The Rocket Scientists at the famed Troubador club. And as if that weren't enough Camel announced they were launching their 2000 tour at roughly the same time and would be performing the evening before these festivities were to take place. As a note of interest, Guy LeBlanc, keyboardist and co-founder of Nathan Mahl having just completed their double CD epic entitled **Heretik**, was to be playing keyboards for the new Camel tour.

The festival concept had really proven to be the best vehicle to provide live exposure for progressive rock bands all around the world. And it seemed each year more festivals were springing up. For the year 2000 additional live prog festivals included events in Mexico City, Panama, Sweden, England and Germany.

Flower Kings
Everon
Equinox
Dixie Dregs
Mastermind
White Willow
Iona
Thieves' Kitchen
Metaphor
Jadis
Tempano
Soft Machine
Rocket Scientists
Glass Hammer
Forever Einstein

Musical releases for the year continued at a rapid pace. Here's a sample: The Flower Kings – **Space Revolver**, Everon – **Fantasma**, Equinox – **Spirit of Freedom**, Dixie Dregs – **California Screamin'**, Mastermind – **Angels of the Apocalypse**, White Willow – **Sacrament**, Iona – **Woven Cord**, Thieves' Kitchen – **Head**, Metaphor – **Starfooted**, Jadis – **Understand**, Tempano – **Childhood's End**, Soft Machine – **Noisette**, Rocket Scientists – **Oblivion Days**, Glass Hammer – **Chronometree**, Forever Einstein – **Down With Gravity** and that was just the beginning.

With so much going 'right', the question continues to come up in prog circles…"well now that the prog world has become so big, is there a chance it will become mainstream and get radio airplay?" I would suggest that doesn't seem to be part of prog's future. It's perhaps best summarized in a recent article in Canada's Georgia Straight music magazine, while interviewing Vancouver proggers Mind Gallery who quickly described prog as "The real Alternative music." Keyboardist Elio Bruno went on to say, "The record companies don't want to promote it, radio stations don't promote it…nobody promotes it, so how alternative can you get?" Fellow Canadian's Nathan Mahl in the liner notes of their

Nathan Mahl

Clever Use of Shadows say "While a lot has changed in the 15 years since Nathan Mahl was first born, the spirit of play and the passion for the music has remained the same. This is but one of the many reasons why our music will never be radio friendly. We do not seek to impress media-types and business people with a 'songwriting' skill of a clever hook and formulaic appeal. Instead we've found that real people tend to like what we do more than they hate it, so we go directly to them bypassing the 'industry' in body and spirit."

So there you have it: the state of progressive rock in the year 2000. Alive and well on its own terms. A true underground, alternative music, which thrives on the Internet for the distribution of music and information. With magazines such as Progression, Expose and Wondrous Stories to spread the word to perhaps millions of fans regularly and a fan base that faithfully supports an independent network of progressive rock festivals, prog labels and distributors. A fan base that grows continually as younger fans seek a more challenging musical genre and as older fans who've left return with the new-found knowledge that the music they loved when they were younger is alive and well. The Progressive Rock genre may never be like it was for a short time in the seventies but I would suggest it is already much bigger than it was then. Back then it was more of a localized phenomenon, whereas today it is truly a global musical genre. So the next time someone you know asks if you remember those "old" progressive rock "dinosaurs", give them a copy of this book and a few CDs from your collection to tune them in. They just may thank you for it.

FILE #2 - The Definition

"It's anyone's guess as to what prog rock is. The lines used to be defined fairly well, but these days, who can tell? People argue over whether Dream Theatre is progressive or metal and moan about various "progressive" giants having sold out. Everybody is hell-bent on musical classification that they've forgotten the most important thing: Is this good music? Basically it's up to you. Listen to everything and decide for yourself. Don't let others tell you what progressive rock is. Chances are nobody agrees anyway."

David Durst - 1993 - letter to *Keyboard* magazine

So, What Is Progressive Rock?

In spite of the preceding letter, it strikes me that unless we wish to continue wallowing in confusion we need to define precisely what progressive rock really is. The writer accurately makes the point that *"the lines used to be defined fairly well."* The term, coined by the British music press in the late sixties, was by the very early seventies solidly in use to describe bands such as Yes, Genesis, King Crimson, Moody Blues et al. One of the earliest known uses of the term "progressive rock" actually appears on the liner notes of the first Caravan LP released in 1968, where it states: *"Caravan belong to a new breed of progressive rock groups, freeing themselves from the restricting conventions of pop music by using unusual time signatures and sophisticated harmonies. Their arrangements involve variations of tempo and dynamics of almost symphonic complexity."* At that time if you used the term it was very clear the type of band or music you were trying to describe. However as bands continued to develop and incorporate ever more diverse musical elements and styles, the term came to be a "catch-all" phrase for any band who was working outside the Top-40 or pop norms of the day. This misuse of the term progressive rock has led to a lot of confusion, which is still with us today. How can we strip away the confusion? The first step is to define progressive rock, and that means setting aside our preconceived ideas or personal definitions.

To some degree the term progressive rock is a victim of the "relativism" that surrounds us. As indicated by the above letter many have come to feel that we can create our own definition regardless of what history or reality demonstrates. To this end we have come to confuse the adjective "progressive" and the noun "progressive rock." Even within the progressive rock community there is a tremendous amount of disagreement over what is or what isn't progressive rock. This is quite unusual and seems to be peculiar to this genre. Not only is there a constant questioning about whether this-or-that band qualifies, but you also have an incredible animosity in prog circles to other sub-genres like neo-prog. You would think fans could live in harmony with the overriding goal of spreading progressive rock to the world, but instead some have become no better than the critics who constantly deride prog through their lack of understanding or indifference. The progressive rock sense of community is at times very shallow.

A letter to **Keyboard** magazine in 1993 raised the question; *"What are the official criteria for labelling something progressive rock?"* It was a legitimate question and the letters in response were quick to come in and unfortunately in many cases added more to the confusion than anything else. Here's a sample;

> *"There are no official criteria for labelling something 'progressive'. You are the person who defines what is progressive music and what is not, and not one person will be able to prove that your opinion is incorrect."*
> from Robert Werntz

> *"The term progressive once applied to bands striving to go in artistic directions, such as Pink Floyd, Yes and Genesis. Nowadays the term is used by bands, mostly metal, who think they're intelligent or who have singers who think they're talented because they sing in an unintentionally self-parodying operatic style such as Iron Maiden or Queensryche."*

from Christopher X. Brodeur

There were other less cynical responses;

> "Basically it boils down to this: 1- Emphasis on shifting time signatures and unconventional chord progressions. 2- Classical influences ranging from Baroque to contemporary. 3- Varying degrees of disregard for limitations on duration and listenability imposed by marketing considerations. 4- Lyrics that embrace themes and images that range from fantasy to social commentary. 5- A fair amount of technical dexterity."
> from Sergio de Regules

> "Prog has something to do with not caring about marketability but being faithful to music as a challenging act. Play the best you can, play your heart out, play with passion."
> from John P.L. LaSanga

That's just a few of the letters, but you can quickly see the need for some clarification. Over the years the question has continually been posed: What is progressive rock?

Yes bassist Chris Squire interviewed in **Mojo** magazine had this to say: *"Progressive is the word that they use to define our kind of music. That's the term that stuck anyway."* In the same article Rick Wakeman expanded: *"Progressive is taking the rules and bending them, the only way you know. It's down to musicianship. Its down to brains to fingers, as opposed to brains to machines. Music will never be the same as it was back then. The seventies was the last era when the musicians were ahead of the technology."* When asked about historical appropriateness of progressive rock, Jon Anderson's response was that, *"Yes should always make music without having to time it - without that restriction"* From the old guard to the new. The same article asked that question of Legend's Debbie Chapman: *"Classical symphonic structure. You have a theme, you develop it, you bring it back at the end. I learned that at school."* World Turtle's Chris McMahon's response was somewhat more pragmatic: *"It's all a matter of when you stop. When you write a song you can get a verse, a chorus and a middle eight and stop there. With a prog song you just keep going."*

Of the many neo-progressive bands that came to the fore, Marillion more than any others paved the way in the early eighties, and while there will always be detractors - those who persist in making comparisons to Genesis - Marillion did what they do best. Tarin Elbert of **Music Express** magazine; *"One aspect of Marillion that is pretty straight forward, though, is their approach to their craft. They're not afraid to take risks when others would rather play it safe. They're eschewing current trends and delving into unbridled passion, back to an era dominated by grandiose cerebrally aimed songs and it's working for them."*

Says Marillion's former lead vocalist Fish speaking of the non-prog bands that were so prevalent in the mid eighties; *"Some people are tired of all the fashion bands which seem to be dominating the charts right now, they want to hear real music again. They want to listen and get into music - not just on the surface, but on a level where you're mentally stimulated."*

Still some have shunned the tag progressive rock as something they'd sooner have nothing to do with. In all honesty, it seemed that a few of the bands caught up in this genre weren't even aware of their involvement. It's not always a conscious decision made to start a progressive rock band, it's more of an internal, natural desire to compose outside of accepted musical boundaries. More of a reaction to what musicians see happening around them. That perhaps is the most important aspect of this genre. Unlike the claims of it's detractors, progressive rock could be considered one of the less contrived forms of music because while it has structure, it is never limited or defined in scope. It's structure and style is better interpreted as a response or reaction to so much of the formulaic pop music we hear. Yet, more than one critic has labelled progressive rock as contrived, however it can easily be argued that the MOST contrived form of music we have is the pop song. In contrast to progressive rock, pop music is created in a strict ABACAB structure, where A = verse, B = chorus, C = bridge, with the final composition clocking in at three to five minutes in length. Another element that distinguishes progressive rock is that it's full of musical surprises. The songs tend to be musically unpredictable. Regardless of the style, a pop song needs to be predictable. It's the predictability that breeds the familiarity the industry thrives on. Pop music is, and always has been, novelty-loving, faddish and ultimately disposable. One is hard-pressed to remember the top ten singles from six years ago. What was once a popular catchy tune fades from memory. To knowingly structure music along these parameters certainly tests the composer's timing skills but ultimately risks the final composition becoming a floggable commodity that puts chart success before artistic endeavour.

Coming To Terms With ... Terms

Part of coming to terms with a definition is dealing with what I call "the progress trap". Already alluded to elsewhere, it goes like this; "the artist didn't do anything new here." The thinking is that the artists are compelled to "progress" and create something very different from before, to satisfy the listener. We are consumed by the idea of "progress". The concept of "progress" is very much a product of this current century. For years musicians were quite content to work within set parameters making only minimal qualitative adjustments to composition, skill level, arrangements etc.. A comparison of Mozart's symphonies over the course of the composer's life display little "progress" as we define it today, but rather a tremendous amount of fine tuning and style development added to each of his compositions. Certainly Mozart's compositional skills progressed as did his desire to write something new. But the <u>pace</u> of progress in the 18th century versus the <u>pace</u> of progress in the 20th century is very different. The concept of "progress" as we know it today was not something Mozart was burdened with. Similarly I'm suggesting, with progressive rock music, "progress" is NOT the be-all-end-all. If the material is enjoyable to listen to, it shouldn't matter whether it sounds like the last album or not. Just because it hasn't "progressed" according to some jaded critics criteria, does not make it less appealing.

There is also the point of, what exactly constitutes something "new" these days? Is it noise? Is it more dissonance? Is it more angular guitar work? On the extreme end, there are some people who are of the opinion that in order for music to be called "progressive rock" it must be full of dissonance, musically angular, and not sound like anything that has gone before. These people tend to dismiss the more listenable or mainstream progressive rock material as somewhat inferior. Music that is difficult to listen too may qualify as progressive in the adjective sense but certainly not as progressive rock in the sense being defined here.

Much has been written over the years about how progressive rock "plundered the classics". The negative connotation of course is that somehow prog wasn't an entirely original genre of music but instead relied more on rehashing those other elements. In fact books and essays have been written detailing the musical segments or motifs that some have described as being lifted (i.e stolen) from classical music. This is a rather strange and isolated form of prejudice since all musical genres borrow from somewhere. Dylan borrowed much from the folk genre, The Beatles admittedly borrowed from Motown, The Byrds synthesised Dylan and The Beatles, the 1990s so called alternative crowd continues to borrow heavily from Pearl Jam and REM and on and on it goes. Martin Orford of IQ had this to say to detractors who were always making negative comparisons with other bands: *"The thing is I don't believe any music is strictly original anyway. I think you could trace practically everything back to something else that's gone before it."* The mere fact that elements of different genres are incorporated into one's music should not be considered a bad thing. Ultimately it's what one does with those influences. No one seems the least upset that so many of the "alternative" or "heavy-metal" bands sound alike. Why should it matter that certain progressive rock bands sound similar.

Yet, within the progressive rock community many are quick to be negatively judgmental using phrases such as "Yes-clones" or "neo-progressive" in the derogatory sense. Most bands at their inception are going to display some obvious influences. If given enough time to grow and mature these influences are usually assimilated into a style or sound that becomes unique. Take for example a band like Druid. Their first release on a casual listen bears a striking resemblance to Yes. On closer inspection however, while the vocalist is a high tenor as is Jon Anderson and the bass playing is similar in it's trebly sound there is a lot that is dissimilar to Yes. The drumming is not in the style of Bruford or White, the guitarist does not have the same technique as Howe nor the number of different guitar sounds, the lyrics and vocalisation are not at all like Yes, the organ sound bears more of Tony Banks style and there is far more Mellotron than Yes ever used. On top of all that the songs are not structured like Yes' material. So in the end the resemblance to Yes is a very superficial one. By the time of their second release, **Fluid**, the band had matured to where there is even less of a Yes influence. Had there been a third album there is no telling where they might have gone musically. These points apply to other bands such as Starcastle who have also been unfairly tagged as "Yes-clones" or Marillion as "Genesis-clones". Sounding like your favourite influences on your first album is hardly a crime. If the sound failed to grow in it's own direction that's another matter. The casual listener who unfairly labels bands in this way does a great disservice to the entire progressive rock community.

Taking a look at the other term, neo-progressive, much of the above applies. As we'll see in the definitions that follow, this term when used in a positive manner can lead fans of this contemporary form of progressive rock (and there are many) to follow the bands they enjoy. The creation of the term was never intended to be a harsh reprisal for, in the minds of some who use it, selling-out. On the contrary, neo-progressive rock is as much a part of the progressive rock community as any other aspect of the genre. It is not one to be maligned, and as a sub-genre shows as much diversity as progressive rock itself. Within the scope of neo-progressive rock groups you have the more complicated like IQ or Jadis to the more mainstream like Everon or Visible Wind. Furthermore any of these bands from time to time will come up with material that is as challenging as any outside of the neo-progressive rock fraternity. Rather than see this sub-genre as somehow inferior, it's better viewed as simply a different aspect of the total sound.

If you spend any time what-so-ever in the newsgroup "rec.music.progressive" you will invariably come across a thread where someone is trying to figure out what is or isn't progressive. These discussions usually go pillar-to-post talking about taste or opinion, and usually end up with the person challenging the accepted view of progressive rock calling it retro, retrogressive, sounding too seventies or some other disparaging remark. These individuals typically are looking for something far more "challenging" musically. Some are even looking for material that can't be identified as music. If you look carefully even some bands use their promotional material to distance themselves from what they call "reliving the seventies" as if that in and of itself was a bad thing. What's missing in virtually all these discussions is the "mooring" or "anchoring" of the discussion to what progressive rock really is. We have a lot of people talking about it, describing it, trying to personally define it but no two people seem to be coming at it from the same view point. The end result is that the discussion degenerates into idle chatter as no resolution is forthcoming or even possible. Furthermore these discussion groups tend to create more confusion than they solve.

As indicated in the Introduction, the definition of progressive rock outlined here is one where I've chosen to differentiate it from the adjective term 'progressive', which can rightly apply to musicians of any type. I've done this because of the tremendous confusion that exists regarding what-is and what-is-not considered progressive rock music. We're not talking about a progressive jazz artist, or a progressive classical composer, we're talking about musicians who create <u>progressive rock</u>. More to the point, in all my research I have yet to find such terms as progressive country, progressive reggae, or progressive anything except, progressive rock.

For the sake of clarity, I suggest the term progressive rock should be used to describe a specific style of rock created within certain perimeters, rather than used to describe music that just sounds different, strange, bizarre or difficult to listen to. It's a mistake to think that just because a certain form of music is not popular with the masses it somehow qualifies as progressive rock.

But The Songs Are So Long

The length of songs became a very important factor that separated the progressive from pop. Yet the length of the material is not the be-all-end-all in determining whether a band qualifies as progressive rock. Many bands in the late sixties and early seventies like Blind Faith, Cream, Iron Butterfly, The Doors, Jefferson Airplane et al created music of considerable length, but in no way should they be considered progressive rock. Much of it was a hold-over from the psychedelic era and had more in common with blues jamming.

It may be surprising to find out that in many cases the length of a prog song is arrived at, not by a contrived method (i.e. let's write a long song), but as in the case of much of the early Genesis material, a melding of musical thoughts, a grouping of musical ideas arranged to make some sense or musical order. Keyboardist Tony Banks explains; *"It's like books, I like long books. In some ways it's easier to get involved in long songs. It's more of a challenge to write a good short song. A song like "Supper's Ready" was a combination in many ways of lots of individual sections, some of which weren't even developed into songs. You might just take a verse from something and a chorus from something and just do them once. And then go into something else, or a bit you couldn't call anything, just an atmospheric piece and then go into something else. It's just a different way of constructing."* As Rick Wakeman said earlier if it feels like the song needs to be eight minutes to express the emotion desired, you write an eight minute piece.

In his comprehensive biography of Genesis, Armando Gallo explains how during the days before **Trespass** the group had decided they wanted to become a professional band, so they spent countless hours rehearsing and fine tuning their sound. Songs like "The Knife" came into being during this period. The songs evolved, with one section hanging around for a while before being joined with some other piece. Section upon section the songs would take shape. Tony Banks talked about the early days in **Trouser Press**: *"It's no coincidence that I feel the strongest tracks on those albums are "Stagnation," which was about eight or nine minutes, "Musical Box," which is about 10 minutes, and "Supper's Ready," 26 minutes. If you do it right you can tell a story within a song like that, and use the contrasts in the music."* Over the years things tend to change but when I interviewed him in the mid eighties, Banks said many of the bits Genesis use for their songs are still the same as in the old days, it's simply the manner in which these pieces are arranged today that makes their music sound different. Unlike the old days however, the manner in which Genesis arrive at their songs is very different. Certainly for the last few releases they have appeared in the studio with nothing. Then they start jamming. Out of countless hours of jamming they decide what will become songs or at least elements to be included in the few longish songs they still manage to squeeze on their releases.

It was similar for the band IQ. When asked about whether they prefer longer, epic pieces Mike Holmes replied: *"Personally I do, we're not going to do just longer epics but one or two I think are really good because they are something you can really get into and it's worthwhile sitting down for about half an hour and put an effort of getting into it or going to a gig and you can put on a lot more show with a long track, you can put a lot more story line into it as well."*

For a band like Twelfth Night, the term progressive rock had somewhat of a special meaning in that they really tried to move forward. They took the basis of the music rooted in the seventies, but incorporated modern technology and attempted to make a mix of musical styles that hadn't been done before. They described their music as punk-floyd. Yet there was almost a fear on the part of the early eighties wave of progressive rock bands to be branded with that label because of some of the things it's come to stand for. Clive Mitten from Twelfth Night explains; *"The thing is it's really a bad tag now, because to be labelled progressive today means you're ten years out of date."* It becomes a problem trying to come up with another more descriptive phrase to apply to the music. Drummer, Brian Devoil; *"There isn't a tag we use. It's slightly intelligent rock."* Clive again; *"We just write pieces of music that are three to twenty minutes long. The actual sound of it is such a mixture of styles. It's stuff to think about really."*

In the case of the band, The Enid, guitarist Stephen Stewart, also has some concerns over the term; *"I'm a bit worried about this word progressive. I think it's one of those words that takes on a whole new meaning. It stops meaning anything and becomes associated with something. So the actual word progressive which probably should describe all sorts of kinds of music, has been lumped on this particular style of music at the moment which is mainly to do with music that's incredibly derived from other specific bands like Yes, Genesis and those other bands. And it does seem to be a word that's describing a type of music as opposed to what the music's actually doing. So I don't think the term applies to us. But at the same time I'd hate to think of us as not being progressive. (Laugh)"* In fact Stewart is correct in his observation on the use of the word progressive, if you think of it in terms of a noun rather than an adjective. It originally was applied to bands like Yes and Genesis and is a word that's describing a type or style of music as opposed to what the music's actually doing.

Peter Munday once in a band called Tamarisk explains; *"It's good in the way the crowds know...who particularly want to hear our type of music...they'll know to come and see us...because of the word progressive. That's how it's working well for us. But the only bad point about it is that when you say progressive they automatically think, Yes or Genesis sound a-likes. That's the only harm it's doing."*

Another neo-progressive band Pendragon uses the term only for the convenience sake in the eyes of the public. Explains Peter Gee; *"We play a similar type of music to Marillion, Pallas and all the other bands. Therefore we fall into the same category and it's just a wide term used to express all the bands."*

At the outset of this section I mentioned how progressive rock became a "catch-all" category for just about any and everything that wasn't your regular pop fare. I'm not convinced this was a good thing but it's perhaps too late to turn back the clock. The "catch-all" approach certainly hasn't helped define the cause of progressive rock to music programmers, record labels or even the general public. For them progressive rock simply became this amorphous grouping of music that was by and large difficult to listen to. If there is a bright side to all of this, it's that what developed in the wake of this confusion over the term are many well-defined sub-genre labels. It's obvious we need to look more closely at the music we intend to label progressive rock.

What About All Those Labels ?

Perhaps the best place to start is to figure out what isn't rightfully called progressive rock. We'll explore terms such as 'art-rock', 'space-rock', 'pomp-rock', 'classical-rock' and even 'symphonic-rock', plus many others. The practice of labelling is usually considered a negative activity. We have learned in our "politically correct" culture that labelling is a bad thing. And I would agree if we're talking about labelling people negatively. That's not what this is about. The use of labels in a musical context is simply an aid to listening, discovery and definition.

It's worth pointing out that many critics in the United States for some reason felt more comfortable using the term "art-rock" rather than progressive rock. Why this came about is unclear, but Katherine Charleton in her book **Rock Music Styles: A History** points out: *"The growth of interest in theme albums and the establishment of FM radio stations playing longer works influenced some musicians in the late sixties to expand rock music in more artistic directions. Several new rock styles grew out of the music by these artistic rockers, most of whom were British, and the name given to this group of styles was art rock (the term progressive rock might be used, except that much jazz rock is also progressive rock)."* I think after reading the definitions below it will become easy to see that art rock and progressive rock may have some elements in common but that they are two distinct musical directions populated by bands with very different musical objectives. Given that progressive rock was born in Britain and that was the term used to describe the music, that's the term I feel is the right one. Let's take a closer look at some of these musical categories:

ART ROCK: (10CC, Roxy Music, Supertramp, etc.)
What perhaps typifies this music best is its need to be 'nice' with lots of major chords and bright harmonies. The music can be very structured and even adventurous, sometimes heavy, sometimes mellow, strong melodies, good hooks are an integral part of most of this material. Bands in this category can and have produced material falling into other categories as well. There may be moments of out-right progressive rock but with more of a pop influence and certainly a tendency towards shorter songs.

RIO-ROCK IN OPPOSITION: (Henry Cow, Art Bears, etc.)
Trying to define a sub-genre of progressive rock that defies description may seem like a dead end. This style, originally very politicised is one originated by ex-Henry Cow drummer Chris Cutler. The music is extremely challenging and can be difficult to listen to. It's an acquired taste. Bands like Art Zoyd and Univers Zero generally fall in this category.

SPACE ROCK: (Vangelis, Tangerine Dream, Hawkwind, etc.)
This is a term that goes back to the early days of Pink Floyd. Space-rock basically came to represent bands that used either guitar, organ or synthesiser breaks that extended themselves for extended periods using few tone changes. In some ways this might be called minimalist but only for certain segments of the songs in question. Usually long passages where little is happening other than mood or atmosphere being created. The need for lyrics is almost secondary, and if they existed at all it is usually for the purpose of setting up the narrative. Lyrics may revolve around some cosmic or science-fiction themes. I have intentionally included Electronic artists in this category.

ZEUHL: (Magma, Zao, Honeyelk, etc.)
A sub-genre of progressive rock created by the French band Magma that is really a unique and very challenging form of jazz fusion incorporating chanting, dissonance and loud rock. Stylistically there are elements of Bartok, Stockhausen, Duke Ellington, and blues shouting.

CANTERBURY: (Caravan, Gentle Giant, Soft Machine, etc.)
It was from this area of England that a whole sub-genre of progressive rock sprang and the music created now bears it's name. Typically this music is more intricate or complex, yet not without a sense of humour. A busy almost baroque style often wrapped in playing that resembles light-jazz.

CLASSICAL ROCK: (New Trolls, The Nice, The Enid, etc.)
The need for experimentation began to draw on many influences. One of the greatest sources had to be the classical composers. Contemporary rock bands might lift titles, bridges, bars, passages, in other words virtually everything in their quest to find the 'new'. No place was this more in evidence than in Italy. The material will also be very influenced by the classical style of arrangement and structure. The music tends to be composed of longer passages, containing dynamics, changes in time and tempo, lyrics usually referred to everything from romance to fantasy.

POMP ROCK: (Styx, Nightwing, Magnum, etc.)
Possibly an offshoot of the whole progressive rock idea. This music is characterised by two basic qualities...1) Numerous crescendos, possible changes in time and tempo, accompanied by relatively bombastic intros and extros, 2) The music tends to be relatively fast paced and heavier through out. LPs tend to sound at first listen basically like hard rock with a few ballads thrown in. Lyrics tend to be on the aggressive side. This sub-genre led directly to prog-metal bands like Dream Theatre.

SYMPHONIC ROCK: (Yes, Genesis, Emerson Lake & Palmer, etc.)
This is the category where we find most of what we have come to know as progressive rock bands. The aspect of orchestration is the most important characteristic. Songs will be longish, contain extended solos for emphasis, changes in time and tempo, and more than any other category highlighted by strong dynamics and changes in mood. Very much an album oriented classification, like classical-rock much was borrowed in terms of arrangement and structure. Lyrics involve many aspects, but typically more philosophical or fantasy oriented even in their telling of modern day subjects.

NEO-PROGRESSIVE ROCK: (Marillion, IQ, Cast, Iluvatar, etc.)
This style of progressive rock came into existence more or less in the early eighties and is generally based on a symphonic-rock style, although with more of an eighties or nineties edge. The music is still in the long and short format but typically is based on an adventurous song style with more constant drumming. Lyrically neo-Prog still dealt in philosophical matters but on a more down-to-earth, day-to-day level.

This book deals primarily with the last five of these categories. The first two, art-rock and space-rock are better left for some other in-depth work that will do justice to each. While the boundaries are somewhat amorphous, it is gratifying that after nearly a decade of research in this genre, more authors and critics have come to see a little more clearly the demarcation of art-rock bands like 10cc or Roxy Music and progressive rock bands like Yes or Genesis.

Just for clarification there are some other sub-genres that we should say something about. Categories like progressive folk or progressive metal speak for themselves. Electronic music or artists are included in the space-rock category. And there are two styles not fully discussed, namely RIO (Henry Cow) and Zeuhl (Magma). It's conceivable entire books can be written about any of these sub-genres however I've simply drawn the line based on my personal research efforts.

When you get right down to it, very few books written about rock contain definitions of the major categories, let alone something like a category for progressive rock. One of the few books to deal with this subject is **The Rolling Stone Encyclopaedia Of Rock And Roll** by Perelis and Romanowski. Their comprehensive and quite accurate definition reads;

"Generally, progressive denotes a form of rock music in which electric instruments and rock band formats are integrated with European classical motifs and orchestrations, typically forming extended, intricate, multi-sectional suites.

"The progressive rock movement began in Britain in the late sixties as an outgrowth of psychedelia's adventurism, and owes it's lyrics frequent use of cosmic themes to acid rock. But progressive rock is definitely a seventies genre, accenting a daunting instrumental virtuosity and grandiosity over earthly directness.

"One of the earliest and most influential progressive rock albums in an album oriented genre is King Crimson's In The Court Of The Crimson King, though that record pointed to the genres prior influences, Procol Harum and The Moody Blues (for their churchy/symphonic classicism) and Jimi Hendrix (for his cosmic highly distorted guitar style). "Progressive rock" bands of the European classical virtuoso class of widely varying quality and popularity include The Nice, King Crimson, Gentle Giant, Yes, Genesis, Emerson Lake & Palmer, Focus, Kansas and Van Der Graaf Generator.

"Progressive rock is sometimes also known as 'art-rock', though bands like Roxy Music, who rocked hard but made full, witty use of a self conscious ironic detachment that was less high minded than Yes, ELP et al, are also known as 'art rockers', which can cause some confusion.

"Ancillary to the British/European techno-flash movement was the whimsical jazz-rock-psychedelic fusion of Canterbury band Soft Machine, who begat a related school of more sedate, less grandiose chamber-oriented bands that were virtuosic in a more playfully jazzy manner—the Anglo/Gaelic, Gong (who later went the fusion route, Hatfield and The North and Caravan. This latter form of progressive rock has proven far less commercially successful than that of Yes, Genesis, ELP et al."

Now before we carry on, let's take a moment to talk about just a few other musical definitions to once again help clear the air. Skimming the surface of these other categories will assist in avoiding some confusion and hopefully prevent any form of elitist attitude from forming. Again the idea behind these classifications is simply to help come to a better understanding, perhaps a better appreciation for the work, and not simply to pigeon hole or restrict the performing artist. The idea behind defining these categories is only to make it simpler for all of us to know more about what we are listening to at any given moment. Therefore it is more than a simple exercise in vocabulary expansion.

POP: (I refer again to the **Rolling Stone Encyclopaedia**)
"Pop is the melodic side of rock - the legacy of show tunes and popular songs of the pre-rock era. Pop's standards of what makes a well constructed song still

apply to much of rock, which strives for memorable tunes and clear sentiments; the tension between pop virtues (such as sophisticated chord structures and unusual melodic twists) and incantatory, formulaic blues elements animanees much of the best rock, like that of the Beatles. Pop also connotes accessibility, disposability and other low culture values, which rockers have accepted or rejected with varying degrees of irony."

RHYTHM & BLUES: Known as R&B it's a euphemism for black pop music. It's given way to soul, funk, disco and other predominantly black styles. Linked the Big Band Jump Blues of the 1940's with early rock and roll.

SOUL: Merger of gospel charged singing, secular subjects, and funk rhythms, grew out of the fifties R&B, no clear division between late sixties soul and black pop that followed it.

BLUES: 12 bar song form, bent notes, blues attitude, arose after the American Civil War, influenced by music brought over by slaves, during the thirties the electrification of the blues started.

ELECTRONIC: Goes back to the thirties for it's first experiments. It stayed in laboratories till Walter Carlos while working with Bob Moog came out with an album entitled **Switched On Bach**. Germany has always been a hotbed for purely electronic musicians. The music is characterised by long atonal passages with white and pink noise accents along the way.

JAZZ: Depends on improvisation, reflects a long tradition of changing ideas of structure, freedom and swing, very respectful of tradition.

FOLK ROCK: Tends not to contain much folk, or much rock. Sets folk songs of the Hootenanny era to a rock beat, closer to pop than rock, strumming guitars, use of more sedate rhythm section as back up, lyrics tend to be 'folky' or topical or cause oriented. Not unusual when one considers that the early origins of folk revolved around spreading news or story telling of the day. Many bands have made their fortunes refining this sound best exemplified perhaps by the Byrds.

HEAVY METAL: Guitar oriented, heavily amplified, can be melodic but often sacrifices this quality for power, appealing primarily to a white adolescent male audience under the age of 25. The music often relies more on the projection of a certain stance than it tries to be musical. This music represents, like punk, a rebellious lifestyle to varying degrees.

PUNK ROCK: Raw, abrasive, basic and very fast, unfunky, musicians usually untrained, rebellious and hard core.

NEW WAVE: An out-dated term which at one point came to mean pop with punkish trappings, faster tempos, stripped down arrangements, alienated lyrics, hardly applies to music today.

ALTERNATIVE: Came to define bands like REM and their ilk, who were playing music to a younger (Generation X) crowd and not receiving any airplay. Strangely, as more of these bands became popular they no longer qualified as alternative but fell more in the pop mainstream. The music was typically angst laden and guitar driven.

A Comprehensive Progressive Rock Definition

Within a small, but growing musical world much is being written about what progressive rock might be. To some there is still an aversion to labelling themselves as progressive rock musicians because of the general perception that it only relates to the bands of the seventies. Others use the term progressive as an adjective and feel it should describe music that continues to progress or move forward. Some feel that certain Alternative bands are progressive because they're writing material that's out of the mainstream. Los Angeles Times music journalist Steve Hochman once wrote *"Prog-rock is aimed at the brain, while blues-based rock is aimed at, well, another much loved organ."* Clearly progressive rock has always tended to be more cerebral while mainstream rock more visceral. So where do we go with this.

One of the many new progressive rock record companies, Kinesis lists what I feel is an accurate and insightful philosophy on their Internet web site. It states: *"Progressive does not simply mean new or different. If it did, the term would be rendered meaningless, since it could not refer to the same music for any length of time. It is fashion that concerns itself with ever-changing superficialities, often going nowhere but in circles. Progressive was coined to represent a philosophical approach to rock. That philosophy embraces a nobler goal, the goal of any art form, to be able to express a greater range of emotions and ideas, with greater shades and nuances."* For the purposes of my work, I couldn't agree more. But let's pick it up from here. Having established the philosophy part of progressive rock, what about the actual elements of composition.

Just as a musician can create a piece of music that is clearly a reggae tune, or a madrigal so should another musician be able to, if motivated, create a progressive rock piece. The only thing that really changes are the criteria by which the music is constructed. Just as an individual knows what elements are involved to end-up with a country song or a rap tune, we need to clarify what elements are involved with the creation of progressive rock.

What follows are the criteria, by which we will be able to define or create progressive rock music:

Progressive Rock is music that incorporates:
Complex arrangements usually featuring intricate keyboard and guitar playing.
- Songs predominantly on the longish side, but structured, rarely improvised.
- A mixture of loud passages, soft passages, and musical crescendos to add to the dynamics of the arrangements.
- The use of a Mellotron or string synth to simulate an orchestra backing.
- The possible inclusion of live symphony orchestra backing.
- Extended instrumental solos, perhaps involving some improvisation.
- The inclusion of musical styles from other than a rock format.
- A blending of acoustic, electric and electronic instruments where each plays a vital role in translating the emotion of compositions which typically contain more than one mood.

- Multi-movement compositions that may or may not return to a musical theme. In some cases the end section may bear little resemblance to the first part of the song.
- Compositions created from unrelated parts, i.e. Genesis' 'Supper's Ready'.

It should be mentioned that while many progressive rock bands released singles, they came to prominence in an era that shunned radio singles, and as a result very few 'hit songs' came from these bands. It should also be pointed out that bands very easily bounced from one category to another. A band may have started out creating progressive rock music and then changed, or perhaps made only one or two progressive sounding albums, or they may have only recorded one song on an album that might fall into this category.

One of the better explanations of progressive rock can be found on the liner notes from the second Gentle Giant entitled **Acquiring The Taste**, where it states: *"It is our goal to expand the frontiers of contemporary popular music at the risk of being very unpopular. We have recorded each composition with one thought - that it should be unique, adventurous and fascinating. It has taken every shred of our combined musical and technical knowledge to achieve this. From the outset we have abandoned all preconceived thoughts on blatant commercialism. Instead we hope to give you something far more substantial and fulfilling. All you need do is sit back and acquire the taste."*

Two points made here are what we shall look at next....being unpopular and the difficulty many had in acquiring the taste.

FILE #3 - The Critics

"The whole notion of art rock triggers instinctive hostility from those who define rock in terms of the early-middle stages of it's morphology. Rock was born as a street rebellion against pretensions and hypocrisy-of fifties society. Thus the very idea of art rock strikes some as a cancer to be battled without quarter, and the present-day reversion to primitivism is in part a rejection of the fancier forms of progressive rock."

John Blackwell - 1976 - **Rolling Stone Illustrated History of Rock & Roll**

The Rebuttal

It would be an understatement to say that critics have been less than kind to progressive rock. Some who started out liking certain bands, like Alan Jones with his affection for early Pink Floyd, in later years crusaded heavily against the genre. Many others continue to be in a serious state of denial best summarised by Rob Chapman writing in the February 97 issue of **Mojo** magazine: *"We are still, it appears, participating in a collective catharsis to disguise the fact that, in the mid-seventies, pretty much everyone who wasn't a glam tart, a disco dolly, a dub warrior or a northern soully was listening to prog. Writers of a certain vintage still pen articles about how hideous the genre was and how they were listening to Donny Hathaway all along, while at the same time displaying a suspiciously sound knowledge of the collective works of Wishbone Ash or Rick Wakeman. Over-compensating, it's called."* It's true while music critics can be the first on the bandwagon for "new" things they are usually the first ones to begin slagging off that "new" thing. It has never been more true than for progressive rock.

According to an old and simple definition, *"Art has to be non-utilitarian, and worthy of contemplation for it's own sake."* By that definition it's very easy to see that music can indeed be art. The danger of using a word like "art" to describe music is that it opens you up to being labelled pretentious. Yet one of the elements of progressive rock music that distinguishes it from other forms of contemporary music is that it tries to be more than just songs. Like the classics that have survived these many years, progressive rock attempts to transcend the boundaries of the traditional rock and roll song structure.

For it's efforts in trying to attain these objectives, progressive rock has been verbally slagged off many times. So it might be good to get to the bottom of a few of the words used to disparage progressive rock. Words like, 'pretentious', 'contrived', 'self-indulgent', etc.. Armed with the Merriam-Webster Dictionary lets take a closer look.

Pretentious:
1) :making or possessing claims (as to excellence) :ostentatious [a pretentious literary style]
2) :making demands on one's ability or means :ambitious [too pretentious an undertaking]

Contrived:
1) :plan, devise
2) :frame, make
3) :to bring about with difficulty

Self-indulgent: (Self=to ones self)
1) :to give free rein to,
2) :to yield to the desire of,
3) :to gratify one's taste or desire for,

You can see that by strict definition none of the verbiage is in fact that derogatory, given that each of these words or phrases can be used to describe any form of music from pop to classical. It is true however that many critics have used these words in a negative connotation when describing progressive rock. A good rule to keep in mind whenever reading negative reviews is that there is a good chance the reviewer doesn't like progressive rock and very probably doesn't know what he or she is talking about, other than telling you their likes and dislikes. More on this as we move along.

GROBSCHNITT

What The Critics Had To Say

Critics have generally been quick to dismiss progressive rock. As is too often the case they confuse being a "critic" with simply being "critical". Strangely many critics write about this music as "taking itself too seriously", as if this was somehow a bad thing. Fact is, if you are going to do something, you should do it well, and if that means you take it more seriously than another person, what's the big deal. I suggest that critics in general are prone to bad-mouthing things they don't understand. Perhaps because they don't understand progressive rock they are somewhat afraid of it. This being the case they find it easier to slag it off, than to come to a better understanding of it.

Take for example the writer of a column in the **Rolling Stone** known as **The Record** who said, *"A progressive rock revival threatens to be the first clear trend of 1983...This new wave of progressive music has sent a shudder of horror through critics (including many of the Record's staff) who thought they had nailed the coffin shut, but the bands already have played at the Venue, The Marquee and other important gigs."* Here is a classic case, a virtual admission of being afraid of the music. Why else the so called 'shudder of horror'. So why do some critics feel they must protect us from progressive rock?

Going back a few years, a review of a Yes concert appeared in one of the British papers. Author Willis Riley wrote in his column about the clinical and some-say overly complex, self-indulgent style of Yes music. In it he said; *"I'm not prepared to get involved too deeply in the self indulgent bit. Suffice to say that all musicians are guilty on this score. Musicians are performers: performers are entertainers: find me an entertainer who isn't on some sort of ego trip and I'll find you a guy who isn't working. But the clinical thing...that's where I make my stand. If by clinical people mean a studied approach to their music, then Yes are right in there. But where is the harm in striving for perfection? And surely the complexities inherent in the music give it greater depth, added interest and a durable lasting quality that enable the listener to go back to the same piece time and time again without encountering the smallest whiff of boredom."*

Riley obviously likes the band, but what's important to note is the rationale behind his written thoughts. It's fine for any writer to come up with slanderous remarks about something they may not like, but it must be admitted that the rationale for making these comments should have some basis other than using the opportunity to create verbal diarrhoea. If we look at the comments made above by these two writers, it's easy to see that the first 'journalist' was only writing to express his opinion, while journalist number two at least provided some backing to the argument. (i.e. his reference to striving for perfection). Some might say it's all semantics, but that brings us to the next point.

Why criticise an entire music genre? Honestly, so many bad things have been written about progressive rock that it would appear many rock journalists take it upon themselves to crusade against this music, trying to dissuade the public from liking it because if that should ever happen, who knows, next they may have to buy the records themselves. Steve Wilson of the band Porcupine Tree was interviewed in **Progression** on why the mainstream rock press has a tendency to trash progressive rock. Here's his response: *"I think the main thing is that many of the people in the music press and the media come from the punk and immediately post-punk era ... It has something to do with the fact that progressive music, for lots of journalists, is something slightly beyond their understanding. I don't mean that in a patronising way because, for example, a lot of classical and jazz is beyond my understanding. But I don't damn (classical and jazz) for that. Unfortunately, a lot of people in the music press tend to damn things they don't immediately understand. Progressive music, because it does tend to stretch genres and stretch barriers in that way, they have a problem with."*

Who Does Like It?

A strong case can be built showing that progressive rock has certain qualities which puts it on another level of appreciation as opposed to other popular forms of music. Most pop tunes can just be 'on', you don't have to actually listen to them. Try that with progressive rock and it gets really distracting. Progressive rock requires your attention, you have to make the effort to actually listen. On the other hand take heavy metal, which relies more on decibels and posing than anything to do with music appreciation. It's mostly attitude. But then there is a school of people who have grown up to feel that rock and roll needs to be rebellious or at the very least contrary. Again, it has a lot to do with attitude. This idea of what rock and roll is supposed to represent certainly does not apply to progressive rock. And this bothers a lot of critics.

The problem with the critics approach is that they seem convinced no one else likes this kind of music either. Yet a quick scan of the record shelves and you find that many of the top progressive rock bands still have comprehensive catalogues available. Critics might say, that's all fine and good, but we're only talking about a handful of bands, and we should really take a look at the number of progressive rock bands that don't have any of their albums still in print. What's interesting to note is that with the advent of CDs we now have more product available from the seventies than ever before. A few American and European companies have been steadily re-releasing the older material to old and new fans alike.

The element of quality can be brought up as a reason for the sales of certain bands like Yes and Genesis over these many years. While there is no discounting the quality of the bands that have survived, it just does not follow that the bands that have disappeared over the years did so as a result of a lack of quality. The element of quality takes on a pivotal role in the formulation of progressive rock music, and to assume that bands failed because quality was not evident makes the assumption that the public only buys based on quality. Any study of record sales clearly shows the public has NOT always been conscious of quality. The casual music shopper tends to buy what is popular, not necessarily what is of lasting quality.

The Music Comes First

The style and shape of progressive rock has as many permutations as there are bands. In the beginning Yes didn't sound like Jethro Tull who didn't sound like ELP who didn't sound like Genesis who didn't sound like King Crimson who didn't sound like anyone else! It wasn't until much later that bands began to formulate a sound that might be traced back to one of the original progressive rock groups. Even today the progressive rock genre contains a wide diversity of groups with their own distinctive sound. Over the years, many of the ideals have remained the same: the music comes first, depth of composition is important, dynamic volume, more attention to arrangement, along with the other points brought out in our earlier definition remain cornerstones of the genre. Nonetheless, criticism continues over the style of music few in the business seem to understand. On the fan side, things have always been different. For example these letters from Melody Maker from the early seventies;

> "The in word when it comes to criticising people is pretentious. The music of Moody Blues, the old Tyrannosaurus Rex and ELP has been branded pretentious as has the showmanship of Move's Roy Wood and Elton. It seems uncool to make music which is in any way different from the superficial, grinding, riff ridden music to which we are accustomed or even to act in any way different from the cool down to earth boring musicians of today. Music is a form of entertainment. And the showmanship of Roy Wood and Elton John in presenting their music is all part of the entertainment. OK...if some people do want to be cool and down to earth, but if others want to create something different or paint their faces one shouldn't criticise them for having the guts to do so."
> - Pete Bone, Kidderminster. Sept. 11/71

> "Roy Hollingworth's final article in the State of Rock series is a shallow and unfair attack on some of the most worthwhile music of today. By that I mean serious rock. Yes - rock that can be listened to, not just for easy entertainment, but for the expression of more complex ideas and emotions. Groups like ELP, King Crimson and Pink Floyd are not strange esoteric monsters. They are great bands who have helped to bring rock to it's present day maturity."
> - Stephen Barnes, Bristol Oct. 23/71

> "After listening to the new Genesis album Foxtrot, we feel we must praise the magnificent depth of not only the music but also the lyrics of this incredible album. Genesis' Nursery Cryme took pride of place in our record collections but we have never heard more mastery than is to be found in the message conveyed by Foxtrot. A musical miracle is surely the only true description of this LP. Congratulations from two ecstatic and avid fans, to five young men who can only be described as geniuses in their own right."
> - Jenny and Dot, Billericay Oct. 28/72

Some Critics Liked It ... Others Hated It

Now certainly critics came from all corners. One who championed the cause of progressive rock was Chris Welch, who never failed to find something positive to say about a band regardless of how he felt about their style. Welch rarely strayed from the facts, and more than many writers, reflected the mood of the event in usually glowing terms.

This can't be said for Alan Jones, who seemed in the early seventies to take it upon himself to champion the cause of putting down this adventurous kind of music. Perhaps Alan Jones' legacy will be one of being the only critic to pan two very influential albums of his generation, namely Pink Floyd's, **Dark Side Of The Moon** and Supertramp's, **Crime Of The Century**! What's more, it wouldn't have been so bad had he simply come out and said he didn't like them. For Alan Jones not to like these two LP's is certainly his prerogative...he does not <u>have</u> to like them. But to say they were BAD albums is so far from the truth it's laughable.

Let's take a look at some of Jones' writing in regards to progressive rock and perhaps analyse it in a different light. Back to 1974 he wrote an article called 'Moodies-Floyd-A-Bore' which appeared in **Melody Maker**. Here he goes on to say; *"It all started with Pink Floyd. An admirable band to be sure. After Syd Barrett wandered into the other room, they faltered badly, but they didn't go down."* From this, we can assume that Jones' is not impressed with the post Barrett, Floyd. He continues; *"The trouble was, and is, that the post Barrett, Floyd have never had much to say about anything. They've produced some beautiful music and Roger Waters is always so concerned, but when it comes to actually confronting those concerns through his music all we are left with is the vacuum of Dark Side Of The Moon."*

A bold statement, but one that many would disagree with. It is certainly Jones' prerogative to not like the work of Roger Waters, but to call **Dark Side Of The Moon** a vacuum is tantamount to not even recognising what exists on vinyl. Any critic responding in this fashion seems more interested in seeing their own words in print. It's more akin to critiquing, not what's there, but what they'd like to see there. A critics role should be to constructively evaluate the musical composition as it stands, not question whether it should exist or not. Their role should be to determine how well the artist accomplished their musical objective, not to flippantly or callously dismiss their efforts simply because of taste.

He goes on; *"The Floyd weren't playing rock and roll, that was for sure, it wasn't jazz, it wasn't even the blues. It must therefore be a relatively new concept - yeah man, this was classical rock."* Jones' bias come even more to fore. He now begins to take issue with something he admits he doesn't like. However he admits it through ridicule.

But there is more; *"But the Floyd had done it, with the title track of that album (Saucerful of Secrets), they'd coupled this classical symphonic approach with their electronic cosmic vision. And rock and roll was the loser. There is an anonymous sterility behind the music of the bands that I've mentioned (Pink Floyd, Moody Blues, Yes) which is suffocating rock, and has almost succeeded in castrating the vehemence and aggression which marked the music of the sixties...rock needs to be as abrasive as a razor cut, not as suffocating as the volumes of messianic ramblings of the new apostles like Yes and The Moodies."*

Jones like many critics is clearly of the opinion that for rock music to be of any value it must somehow be as abrasive as a razor blade? But why? It's perhaps true that in it's infancy rock music needed to someone throw it's weight around as an adolescent. However if some of the rock genre's have "grown-up" that need no longer exists, and the music can go on to tackle other adult issues. It no longer needs to be bent solely on rebellion. There will always be the juvenile rock forms determined to do that. Furthermore if anybody is doing any suffocating of any form of music, it is closed minded critics who continue to disparage progressive rock as if they were the arbiters of what constitutes good and bad. Jones makes the observation that the music of the sixties contained vehemence and aggression. Well, if that's his musical preference, fine. But that's no reason to take out his frustration by ridiculing an entire genre of music. As a matter of fact Ian MacDonald's book **Revolution In The Head**, puts to rest any notion that The Beatles were full of vehemence and aggression. Yet The Beatles were pretty much what the sixties were all about.

Finally Jones' concludes his piece this way; *"There's an emptiness at the heart of such music because the musicians have avoided the face of reality and deadened the instincts of individuality. Suppressed our sense of the real to paraphrase, Mailer, and avoided the consequences. I'd sooner have Iggy Stooge vomit in my lap and stand on my head, than go down under the weight of Close To The Edge or To Our Children's Children Children or whatever. At least with Iggy you know what you're fighting."*

Thus he sums up his article. If in fact Jones has experienced the 'emptiness' he talks about while listening to this music, he should probably stop listening to it. But to sit and suggest that it is the music that's empty, is a judgement that many might question he's in any position to make. This is after all an observation coming from one who would sooner have Iggy vomit in his lap! While it's evident Jones can make these judgements, foisting them on others is what's in question. He certainly can and should make these judgements for his own life, but not for the listening habits of others.

After having taken so much space to express my own thoughts in response to this article, let's take a look at the comments of others who read this piece of journalism back in June of 1974 and find out what they thought:

"I don't know much about the Moodies music and/or pet philosophies, so I won't pass judgement on them, but I'd like to point out that I didn't pay 3 odd for an album like Tales From Topographic Oceans because it's so meaningful! I bought it and listen to it because I like the way it sounds. And I think this applies to most other people, too. Jones seems to imply that bands which incorporate classical influences into their music, or attempt large scale compositions are trying for some sort of cultural respectability. No way. Rightly or wrongly, the cultural establishment of this country, apart from the occasional enlightened personality like Malcolm Arnold or John Williams, still regard any kind of rock as a threat to, or a criticism of it's artistic standards....Although the concept of rock-as-art has largely been discredited thanks mainly to the Tony Palmers of this world. What's wrong with rock musicians being openly intelligent, intellectual even, about their music? Are they any less important or relevant to rock because they take care in their composition and presentation of their music, exploit the full range of instrumental sounds and textures available to them and don't bellow obscenities at the audience when they get on stage. If Iggy Pop and Syd Barrett are the only names Jones can drop to spike the guns of progressive rock, he's on to a loser right from the start. And if Iggy puking over you gets you off, well that's your thing Jonesy. Just stay downwind of me that's all....And besides, there's just no way progressive rock is sterile. Just get an earful of Yessongs, Genesis Live or the live album from Ummagumma, if you want proof. And if they don't get you off, you're probably dead, so you'd best have yourself buried before you go off."
   - Phil Harding, Manchester.

"The suggestion that bands like Yes are suffocating rock is ridiculous...They have given it the kiss of life. The significance of classical rock is that it provides a much

needed alternative to the drab repetitive music to be found in the singles charts. Bands such as Yes and Focus have broadened rock's audience, and finally dispelled the myth that rock has no serious musical value."
- Ian Leight, Stokenchurch.

"The think piece was notable for two points. It's excellent style and facile content. The basic assumption behind the grandly worded whole appears to be that rock has deviated from it's beginnings and hence lost it's virility. Rock represents an attempt by the entertainment industry to sell various fantasies to audiences of varying sophistication, aged between eleven and thirty. That is why Melody Maker can feature and promote both Gary Glitter and Led Zeppelin in one issue. No serious contradiction occurs and no one is surprised. Unlike the industry of ten years ago, no particular group or individual can dominate and influence all sectors. Creatively, rock is a many headed hydra, only the body remains similar to those previous years. The rock establishment as such, musical publications like your own, record companies, managers, even venues remain just as they were, with some exceptions.

"However technological advances and increased affluence allow the actual artists to produce a greater variety of work and have provided a public that can afford to buy it. Because this situation has arisen this does not mean that Mr. Jones can take one of those creative areas and vilify it because it deviates from the original. The very fact that Lou Reed, Iggy or any number of other individuals can be pointed out as examples of basic rock aggression, should indicate that a choice is available. If the function of the rock industry is to entertain and success is indicated by record sales, the offerings of Pink Floyd etc. are valid."
- Robert Pringle, Mitcham.

"We greeted think piece expecting a balanced argument over some important aspect of today's music. It was with some dismay that we waded through columns of practised cynicism directed at Pink Floyd, Moodies and Yes. Far from presenting any cohesive argument, Mr. Jones merely coughs out frenziedly -it ain't rock and roll- at several points in his lengthy discourse. He finishes up by saying - at least with Iggy you know what your fighting. In other words, Close To The Edge is too heavy for me, so it must be bad. It seems to us that Jones doesn't really know what Yes, their contemporaries or anyone else, except Iggy are/were up to, so how can he hope to criticise objectively and constructively? Jones' type of thinking could only result in a total uniformity of the music scene in which everyone sounds like Iggy. Sure enough, the heavy metal bands will never go away as long as Mr. Jones and his friends buy their records. But if music is to progress, to become worthy of the progressive music tag, rock and roll will have to be left behind. It could be rock and roll that they'll be playing in supermarkets in ten years time not Topographic Oceans. At least the new heroes will make their dollars with a foot in heaven and not with both feet in Iggy style decadence."
- Tom White, Holoway Little Stoke.

Jumping ahead more than a decade, let's examine more closely an article written by Alan Jones in 1983 that appeared in the **Rock Years Vol IV**. It is clear that his feelings towards the progressive rock genre had changed little over the intervening ten years

"..Everywhere there was a mood of seriousmess; rock and roll was all at once upwardly mobile, moving out of the gutters and into the suburbs relinquishing it's working class snootiness for middle class respectability....These groups were playing for what they thought were higher stakes. The comparison they were often looking for was one with classical music, and to force home the point of their aspiration, the population was made to endure their preposterous orchestral inclinations".

To touch on some of the highlights of this article by Jones, his observation of this type of music wanting to elevate itself to a higher level, may or may not be true depending on who you talk to. In some cases it tried and probably worked, in other cases not. It seems that what's important here though is that these rnusicians tried. Jones says the population was made to <u>endure</u> their preposterous orchestral inclinations. Well judging by the various Melody Maker polls that same population was very happy hearing progressive rock music and made it's opinion known for a number of years by voting many progressive rock bands like Yes and Emerson Lake & Palmer, tops in any number of categories. Clearly a good percentage of the people were not on Jones' side.

But while the general public were quite happy with the efforts of Keith Emerson, Alan Jones was less enthusiastic:

"As a member of The Nice, ELPs Keith Emerson was forever plundering the classics...Encouraged by Emerson's example— Dough Heads like Deep Purple's Jon Lord started knocking out blundering efforts like Concerto For Group And Orchestra (the latter conducted by Malcolm Arnold, who like Joseph Egar should have known considerably better than to get involved in the first place)."

As for Keith Emerson plundering the classics, it must be remembered that Mozart himself borrowed heavily from other composers, just ask Haydn. Mozart admitted his efforts didn't always tend toward originality. The point is when dealing with any form of art or entertainment the artist or perforrrer can and should feel free to build on the shoulders of what has gone before, and all through the effort, giving credit where credit is due. Jones' comment that people like Malcolm Arnold and Joseph Egar should have known better, makes it seem that they were doing something they shouldn't have done, (i.e. working with progressive rock bands). Clearly Alan Jones feels he could have suggested a better path for these gentlemen to follow. My own view is that if both these men felt they were contributing to the development of some new form of music what's wrong with that?

Having taken on the oldguard of progressive rockers. Jones then went on to tell his views on the mid-eighties revival of neo-progressive rockers, in particular Marillion.

"Marillion are most often compared to Genesis, and no little wonder their album owes virtually everything to that group, whose emphasis on a kind of symphonic terrorism and taste for straining narrative excursions they share. Marillion's music is full of grandiose suffering and glib sentimental wallowing in pain and various miseries."

In Jones' mind

"What all these groups lack however, is a Vasco da Gama to give them a sense of direction they don't have a wit themselves, of a genuine explorer, and every time they actually get somewhere they find someone else has been there before them. The territory is littered with references to their predecessors most obviously Floyd, Genesis or Yes."

Truth is this was the "line" most critics took towards the progressive rock movement. Virtually all of them felt the need to malign the genre, not so much for what it was, I feel, but for what it represented. As explained elsewhere, progressive rock was not part of the historical rebellious rock n' roll tradition And for that it was criticised.

Finally on the matter of critics, there is another aspect to "criticism" that we need to be aware of. Noted film critic Michael Medved has written about how extended exposure often warps a person's perspective. The nature of the job causes so much exposure to a product that the product become predictable. What this means is that after a while anything that is different or daring is what's required to break the tedium and generate a response. Not unlike an addict who needs more and more of a substance to get the same desired effect and unfortunately it's an almost unavoidable consequence.

Dangerous as it sounds I think the same applies to music critics. Not in everyone's case of course, but the critic has to always be on guard to be on roughly the same wavelength as their audience or they become out of touch and irrelevant. Typically we have seen this happen in the movies where audiences have by and large come to disregard what the critics say and many times, happily fill theatres attending movies the critics have trashed.

This strange phenomenon has shown itself to be evident in the music business as well. A quick scan of the critics columns in most of the music trades will show how far out the critic is in relation to the music the general consumer listens to and purchases. In closing what this means is when we read what a critic has to say it needs to be taken with a grain of salt. Keeping in mind that their level of exposure is going to be much greater than you or I experience and this is bound to have some effect. The best advice is to find a critic you can relate to and use their writings to guide you in exploring new musical releases.

Everybody Has A View

It's fair to say anything that requires effort, will have a harder time attracting a sizeable following. The masses tend to be more interested in passive, or light entertainment. So it's not unusual that progressive rock's following has been small. Part of the reason for this is also the fractionalization of the audience that began in the early seventies. Everyone has their own musical interests and in some cases they're not too open to music outside of their favourite genre. This perhaps is part of the reason progressive rock fans are always asking the question and tend to be so vocal about what is and what isn't prog.

This divergence of opinion has even been voiced by the artists involved. Take for example the idea of merging classical music with rock, Russell Unwin writing in **Melody Maker** in the seventies drew this comparison; *"Curved Air are probably the nearest pop has come yet, apart from the King Crimson experiments, to being linked with the contemporary classics. Most of their music is directly associated with the classical world through their excellent violinist Darryl Way."* Unwin goes on to add, now talking about Barclay James Harvest; *"The experiment of using group plus orchestra here is much more successful than for instance Deep Purple's attempt. The orchestral backing actually contributes to the group's sound rather than being a separation of two musical identities."*

Talking about that fusion in an interview, Tony Kaye had some thoughts of his own; *"I was totally out of that. I had no inclination to join classics with rock and roll. I didn't oppose it, but I really didn't like the idea either. I was always very much for one thing being one thing and the other thing being the other thing. I don't think jazz and classics make a good marriage together either."*

Having mentioned Curved Air initially in this matter it's fitting to get the comments of the other classical influence in that band besides Darryl Way, and that would be Francis Monkman, who spoke to **Melody Maker's** Chris Charlesworth in 1971; *"I thought the Nice were terrible. People were saying look what Emerson has done with the Karelia Suite but it wasn't much really. Emerson Lake & Palmer are a lot better. There are some very musical things on their album. Emerson still has a tendency to jump into Bach when there is no reason for it and it always spoils things. I think Deep Purple were working the wrong way with their orchestra thing. There is no point in pitting an orchestra against a group."*

The name Deep Purple, may conjure their classic **Deep Purple In Rock**, or maybe **Machine Head**, but there was a time when even Deep Purple attempted to overturn the boundaries of rock. This was done mostly through the efforts of keyboardist Jon Lord. So what are Jon's thoughts on the experimentation of yesteryear, in particular his **Gemini Suite**. Says Lord; *"Ah bless it's little heart, it's very naive. I thoroughly enjoyed doing it, and it was amazing to work with the London Symphony Orchestra. The thing that Deep Purple did before that, Concerto For Group And Orchestra was great fun, and a great event. To have been there and seen it was enjoyable, but musically it was very naive. I've come a long way since then."*

Lord was asked, if this was an attempt to fuse rock with the classics he'd have to admit that it failed because the rock and the orchestral sections generally alternated, with minimal amount of blending. Lord's reply; *"Yes exactly. That's why it was a naive attempt. I did one album in Germany in 75 which again I don't think was ever released in America called Sarabande, where I think I succeeded. I did it all in the studio, as opposed to a concert hall, so I was able to have greater control. I had the group actually playing with the orchestra a good deal. But one had to make concessions in the orchestra because of that. I do believe now that never the twain shall meet, at least not with each style having it's own terms. One or the other, the rock or the classical side would have to make concessions. In the end, I became disenchanted with the whole idea, although I had a hell of a lot of fun trying to make it work."* Whether or not efforts such as those described were successful or not is best left to the listener. But there is no denying that these efforts went a long way to shaping the sound of progressive rock.

Peter Gabriel was interviewed in **Musician** magazine in December of 1992 and asked how he looked back on his days in Genesis. Rather than dismiss the work of his early days, Gabriel took a more objective and sentimental approach. His overall feeling was both a sense of love and loathing. Some of the early Genesis material he said seemed very good, while some of it was a little embarrassing: *"The dividing line is always whether it had the right emotion. Was it done with some genuine passion, however naive it may seem, or was it just a shot at writing another song? I cringe a lot when I see some of the pictures. I don't think dressing up in flowers on-stage, painting my face and wearing masks is particularly good if you want to be taken seriously, but I think people missed the point. To me a lot of that was emotion being expressed, however simply and bizarrely it may look now."* It's easy to look back through "wizened" eyes and try to dismiss the early efforts. Every artist must surely go through the same analyses. The point that can be easily overlooked is not only how we feel about the creative effort today, but rather the effect that creative effort had on others listening to it at the time. There is no denying it provided a great deal of listening pleasure then, as well as today. For many progressive rock fans of the nineties, early Genesis is still the launching point and in some cases the yardstick other material is measured by. To say it inspired others to create music in the same vein would be an understatement. The music of early Genesis was not only the spark for other British bands, but also launched a massive progressive rock scene in Italy and greatly influenced many of the neo-progressive rock bands of the eighties and nineties around the world.

None-the-less, this divergence of opinion continues to exist today. Some within the progressive rock community feel that there is still an element of intellectual snobbery associated with the genre. Chris and Paul McMahon who were originally two thirds of Haze and metamorphosed into the almost funky World Turtle have taken this view. Interviewed in **Mojo** magazine Paul said: *"I've read some really stupid definitions. It's got to be in complex time signatures, it's got to have lots of key changes, lots of tempo changes. Arty lyrics."* Brother Chris added: *"Which is how prog started, and to be honest, that's meaningless now. The idea of bands still playing that stuff is kind of hard to call progressive."* Paul asserts: *"progressive should be an experiment, it should be about continuing to progress. What people are doing now is repeating experiments that were done 20 years ago."* Which is true if one considers the creation of progressive rock music as an experiment. By World Turtle's definition of prog no one should be creating music the same way twice. Which is quite ludicrous. I have tried to make clear progressive rock, progressive music and progress in general are entirely different concepts and the danger of confusion is great when we take to ourselves a definition we want as opposed to the reality that exists.

There are even situations where fans of progressive rock bands will attempt to distance themselves from the use of the term. In their otherwise excellent book **Genesis: A Biography**, authors Dave Bowler and Bryan Dray go to great lengths throughout the book to distance the music of Genesis from the progressive rock genre insinuating that any association would put the band in an inferior light. In their explanation of the creation of the classic twenty-three minute "Supper's Ready", a cornerstone of the progressive rock genre, they reference their own anti-prog bias by trumpeting the already stated critics response suggesting: *"It's length immediately raised the hackles of some critics — how could a song of twenty-three minutes duration be relevant to the pop kids of the day? The fact that it was so long was sufficient proof for some that Genesis were dull, pretentious prog-rockers, so why bother to listen?"* The authors then go on to explain why "Supper's Ready" was such a magnificent composition, all the while, avoiding the obvious. We've already discussed the aspects of critics or individuals not understanding what the progressive rock genre was all about, and why they were afraid to take the time to listen to it, so there is no need to do it again here in reference to Bowler and Dray. Throughout their biography on Genesis the music is referred to as soul music, and never as progressive rock. But again as referred to elsewhere, the one misunderstanding that many have regarding progressive rock was that it lacked feeling, passion and soul. In fact, because much of the lyrical content of prog dealt with deeper philosophical subject matter, the words as well as the playing tended to come from the heart and in that respect certainly had "soul". Bowler and Dray can call it what they like, but there is no denying the music of Genesis was progressive rock at it's finest. To suggest anything other than this is to ignore the fact that many Italian progressive rock bands of the seventies and virtually all of the neo-prog bands of the eighties took their cue from the musical and lyrical style of Genesis.

The music critics never seemed to "get it" when it came to progressive rock. Their feeling was anchored in the belief that rock music was born out of a rebellious spirit and needed to stay firmly planted in that attitude. Progressive rock was rarely about destructive rebellion. It did speak to changing the system but in it's own philosophical way. As I've pointed out elsewhere, if rock was the adolescent, then progressive rock was the young adult, maturing and coming to an understanding of how things work in the real world. Progressive rock still speaks to changing the system or fear of the establishment, but it's answer lies more in changing the individual, to change the system, rather than rock's naive attitude of simply tearing down the system.

For critics the idea of blending art and rock is best summed up in John Blackwell's quote at the opening of this chapter. It summons up "instinctive hostility". But one might ask, what effect did the critics have on fan appreciation of progressive rock? Katherine Charleton in **Rock Music Styles: A History** says: *"Critics of the style claimed that the melding of those two dissimilar styles was pretentious, that rock music had it's own values without holding itself up against the historical importance of classical traditions. Music listeners disagreed, however, and many forms of art rock remained popular with millions of faithful fans all over the globe for more than two decades and will probably continue to do so into the future."*

Where Is Radio In All This ?

In many respects the writings of critics like Alan Jones epitomise the type of slandering progressive rock music has withstood over the years. Music critics don't seem to recognise or understand, that there was a turning point for some, where it was no longer important for a form of music to follow the dictates of fashion or a certain lifestyle. Instead the music took on an importance all it's own.

Now print critics are not alone with this view, for the most part it was taken by all the media, many of the record companies, and by most radio stations. There were exceptions to this but generally those in the music business seemed to take exception to this "high-faluten" kind of music, and they quite simply refused to try and understand it. This has proven to be frustrating for both musician and fan alike. Take for example the fan who wrote into the April 1983 edition of **Keyboard** magazine saying;

"Why is it impossible for anyone playing or writing progressive rock to get any-

where in this country (US)? It frustrates me to see all these synthesiser groups getting record deals and national exposure when it sounds like a lot of them haven't even learned to play yet...I'm not denying anyone the right to enjoy or play new wave or anything else. I just wish that record companies would take note of the success of bands like Genesis, Asia, Pink Floyd, Alan Parsons and more recently Saga and look for similar talents closer to home...Why doesn't the industry take notice of American progressive rock musicians?"

Over the years radio has always, to some degree, exerted an influence on music. The producing technique of "fading-out" the end of the song was done specifically for radio to ensure a song was the "right" length and also to avoid the potential for "dead-air" from a song's sudden ending. Most people came to feel that all songs simply faded-out, forgetting that before radio came along songs did in fact have endings. Fading out songs in the fifties and sixties led to editing songs in the seventies when the songs started to get too long for commercial formats. We all remember the three minute truncated version of "Roundabout". Both these techniques worked against progressive rock music, which was typically longer and usually did have some form of ending. The technical side of radio that developed in the sixties was the use of limiters and compressors to ensure the sound coming out of the radio was within a certain standardised db range. Compressors and limiters were designed to ensure that a radio station couldn't accidentally turn up the volume of music or commercials so as to damage your radio speaker. These devices were eventually designed to make the station sound very up-front with a lot of presence but also very flat. The quiet parts of any song were "boosted" while the louder parts were compressed. Given the dynamic nature of progressive rock you can see how this technology totally destroys the effort placed in creating a piece of music containing both loud and soft passages. On radio it all sounds the same.

Radio in North America has had a "love-hate" relationship with progressive rock. Through the late sixties and very early seventies the place to hear new and adventurous music was on University FM stations. These student run operations were a hotbed for new music. Many a night I would fall asleep listening to the strains of King Crimson's "21st Century Schizoid Man" or Black Sabbath's title cut from their first LP. These songs along with the early Moody Blues, Pink Floyd, Frank Zappa and much of the psychedelic music coming out of San Francisco formed the core of music playlists. The very nature of the university environment is one of experimentation, and even to this day campus stations try to play material that gets little exposure elsewhere, resulting in some very unusual programs. It wasn't until the 1972 release of Yes' "Roundabout" that commercial radio picked up on progressive rock. There is a certain school of thought that during the early to mid 1970s radio played a lot of prog, but this wasn't the case. Many of the prominent bands did release singles but other than a few songs such as ELP's "Lucky Man", Yes' "Roundabout", Jethro Tull's "Teacher", or some later ones by Kansas and Styx, progressive rock has not been heard much at all on the radio. Even when it was heard it was usually in some edited form over which the artist rarely had control, which gave an untrue picture of the nature of this music. Commercial radio in many respects had to play a certain amount of progressive rock during the seventies because they saw the fan response at the concert level.

It should come as no surprise to learn that radio stations play what they THINK is popular. Radio relies on advertising. As such it has to have listeners to attract advertisers. It is a business. So naturally it feels that the only way to attract listeners is to play the hits. In all fairness this seems to work in varying degrees. But I postulate that radio plays what it <u>thinks</u> is popular. The testimony to that fact is that radio is usually the last to change formats to adapt to any new form of music. Radio inevitably plays a game of catch-up. That's because very few radio stations have the courage to play what is not yet popular. Radio just does not understand that kind of thinking. Yet history shows the radio industry does come around in the end.

Since the early 1970s radio has become extremely fragmented in an effort to win an audience. It's no longer good enough to be a Top Forty station, now you have to choose between a Hot Contemporary and a Hit Radio format, each over-compartmentalised with a very narrow play-list of artists and an even narrower list of "add-on" opportunities. Radio is first and foremost a business, and as such, does not really understand music, other than, as a tool to make money. While a few people involved at the programming level may understand music, as an industry it does not. Most music directors quite honestly wouldn't know a quarter note from a treble clef. These same individuals would insist that it does not matter, because they know a hit when they hear it. Most stations simply hire a music or program director who fulfils the role as laid out in the station's chosen format. In addition, most radio stations are programmed by what are known as "consultants". These consultants are rarely in the same town and are generally hired to make all the music decisions for the station, thereby reducing the risk of playing "un-popular" material. Certainly progressive rock comes under even greater scrutiny than other forms of music because of i'ts complexity and it's length. Commercial radio has to play commercials, so if the music isn't in neat little three minute packages, there is a problem. For most radio station progressive rock just doesn't fit.

Little of what's released actually makes it to air, so you can expect a lot of material to just end up being ignored. Typically there are well over one hundred music releases each month and yet listeners may only ever hear four or five of them that make it onto a station's playlist. The rest are left unplayed and unexposed to the listener. In 1970 for example, out of 5,685 singles, only 242 made an appearance on the Billboard Hot 100 chart. Things haven't improved. Instead of radio providing the listener with choices, the listener is constantly bombarded by a series of safe musical releases, most of which they've probably heard before. After all, it's so much safer for radio to pick and play only a couple of sure things rather than run the risk of trying something new. Because of that not only radio, but the listener suffers.

Radio attempts to reflect what's popular, and yet how does something get to be popular if people aren't allowed to hear it? The music that is played over and over again by well intentioned individuals who say, 'It's in the grooves', or 'you can tell a hit' is just so much industry ego stroking. Ultimately, we are left up to the narrow minded business men who program the airwaves.

But having said that, the record companies also share in this problem. Bands like Tamarisk, Pendragon, Twelfth Night and many of the first wave of progressive rock, really struggled to get that recording contract, the record companies ended up, then and today, releasing so much that is simply mediocre. As in most business it's not what you know, it's who you know...most of the time anyway.

The Pressure to Conform

Unlike so much of what was happening on the popular radio stations, progressive rock found it's home on University or Pirate radio stations playing to a small but select audience. While the music business took hold of the pop side of the business they were never able to come to terms with, let alone understand progressive rock music. In many respects the music business has been the 'kiss-of-death' for progressive rock.

As long as the music business and radio stations rely on hits, there will always be pressure on bands to write them. This pressure is not only felt by the new bands. Take for example Yes at the time of recording **90125**. Chris Squire interviewed in **Guitar World** magazine relates a typical story: *"Ahmet Ertegun came down to the studio and said, "We have to have a hit single this time. You have to work on it. It is your responsibility, Chris, to make sure it happens. And fortunately we did it."* When a band is signed to a major label, it's hard to say no in a situation like this. And it's this kind of pressure that can split a band apart.

Another interesting example of the pressure to conform is IQ who produced some excellent neo-progressive rock and released several independent LPs from 1983 to 1985. They were eventually picked up by Polygram and each album became more and more commercial. Was this a function of their new vocalist or pressure from the major label? Who knows, a bit of both perhaps. In fairness it should be stated, according to the band, pressure from the record company was non-existent. IQ keyboardist Martin Orford explains: *"Despite what some people might think, we have never written a commercial song because a record company told us to do. Much as I am an out-and-out prog rocker, I have my own ideas about what I think constitutes a good pop song and I will always want to write the occasional commercial song. I am quite aware that songs such as "Drive On" seem to offend the prog rock purists but I am just as proud of that song as I am of something like "It All Stops Here", "Nostalgia" or any of the other epic songs I've written or co-written. Squawk records never imposed any restrictions on our writing. What a shame that such a healthy attitude could not have been rewarded with a hit record!"* It is interesting to note that IQ would produce some of their best material with the return of Peter Nichols in 1991. Their independent release **Ever**, showed the IQ in fine form with a return to their earlier style.

Fair enough, but to drive the point home with another example, the U.S. band Echolyn had released three independent CDs in the early nineties and were generating a tremendous amount of talk in prog circles. They were signed to Epic records a division of Sony Music and released one CD, **As The World** and then for whatever reason split-up. Did the record company try to shift their musical direction? It doesn't seem so. But for whatever reasons, intentional or unintentional, coincidental or not, it's strange that just as the band is poised to make it big, they fold instead. While it's anyone's guess as to whether the band would have remained together former Echolyn keyboardist Chris Buzby explained it from his side in **Progression** magazine: *"I think we would have been better off as a band if Sony never happened. Sony was trying to be visionaries - they lit the torch and started running with it, then got scared. They suddenly realised it was going to be hard for them to break a whole new genre of music into this whole industry they helped create. But even without the Sony deal, I don't think we'd be together now. The musical differences would have happened over time. Sony dropping us after one album just accelerated it."* The story is familiar, it's not the first and probably won't be the last time it happens. Fortunately this story has a happy ending, of sorts. While Echolyn lost it's bass and keyboard players the core trio of Brett Kull, Ray Weston and Paul Ramsey would continue with the assistance of guest musicians for future releases.

It should be added that there will always be bands who decide to change their musical style on their own for a variety of valid reasons. That kind of "internal" development or maturity is to be expected. What's being discussed here however is "external" pressure applied to a band to make changes not for artistic reasons but for profitability's sake.

In the context of radio exposure, it could be argued that a band like Barclay James Harvest could never exist in the United States. Here is a band that continues basically to maintain a cult following after being in the recording business since 1969. Over 20 albums to their credit with virtually no radio exposure. If there were a band in the United States or Canada they would very likely have given up some time ago, or as in the case of so many like Styx or Starcastle, modified their sound to fit into what either the record company or the radio stations wanted, in order to get airplay. This simple example has happened so many times and more than anything explains why progressive rock has such a difficult time in America.

These are some of the elements that have hindered the growth and popularity of progressive rock. While it's true to say prog is not as accessible as most other forms of pop music and it does require a little more effort to listen to it, these have not been the factors working against it. It's more a matter of close minded critics serving their own agenda and a media that failed to understand the genre, that meant many people never had the opportunity to hear progressive rock music, and decide for themselves whether they enjoyed it or not.

FILE #4 - Progressive Rock Today

"I think overall, record companies should take more risks in order to generate more interest in music. Let's not be brainwashed by too much media and let's stop listening with our eyes. Progressive rock is like a monster waking from a long sleep, with the right support and management it could be more glorious than ever."

Rich Berends of Mastermind interviewed in **Expose'** December 1994

Not Just An English Thing

Sometimes it's easy to think of progressive rock as solely a British musical genre. Yet, as has been clearly documented here, progressive rock musicians around the world may have taken their cue from the British but the genre very quickly started taking on an International flavour. It's true that many an American band fashioned themselves after a British look in order to find a market. Take for example a band like Fireballet, posing on the back of their album jacket decked out in their medieval best. It was a blatant attempt by the band and or record company to appeal to the progressive rock buyer in America who'd only ever heard of British bands like Yes and Genesis. However, if they had dug just a little deeper into the import record bins, they would have found a whole world of progressive rock music. It turned out that many countries had been influenced by the progressive rock happening in Britain. They were able to purchase albums by all the key bands and in turn they recorded and released their own albums. These unfortunately rarely made it out of their home countries.

As a result of the European musical heritage many of the countries on the continent have provided us with a lot of fine progressive rock bands. Countries, such as Germany, Switzerland, France, Spain, Italy, Sweden and Norway. And you needn't stop there because it's spread around the world to places like Japan, and South America. An added bonus is the inclusion of instruments or musical styles that are indigenous to specific countries. From Spain come the various Flamenco progressive rock styles, and Japan gives us material with a decidedly oriental sensibility. In fact each country, whether it be Scandinavian, Oriental or American was able to infuse not only it's own musical influences but cultural ones as well.

Consider the fact that Genesis found themselves on the record charts of Italy before anywhere else. It's fascinating to look at the top five albums on the Italian charts for 1972. They include: #1 Van Der Graaf Generator's **Pawn Hearts**, #2 PFM's **Storia Di Un Minuto**, #3 ELP's **Pictures At An Exhibition**, #4 Genesis' **Nursery Cryme** and #5 King Crimson's **Islands**. Just for the record Yes' **Fragile** was #11. Why such a strong interest in progressive rock? Well, given that nearly the whole written language of classical music is Italian, they more than any were able to appreciate the depth of what progressive rock bands were attempting to create.

Italy was a hot-bed for progressive rock with more than 50 contemporary bands existing at the same time, vying for the public's attention with each having made at least one recording. It certainly wasn't all PFM and yet that was perhaps the only band to make a mass market impact in North America. A quick scan of the listing at the back of this book reveals how significant an impact Italy had, when it came to progressive rock. Unfortunately the big push came to a slow end by the middle to late seventies, a victim of the economic and political turmoil that ravaged the country in 1976. There for a while things got very tenuous. Franco Falsini of Sensations Fix emigrated to the US and recorded the band's final LP there, Le Orme went to France and others like Banco got work doing movie soundtracks. Fortunately progressive rockers are a hearty bunch and the seed survived and today Italy once again is giving us not only some great reissued material but exciting new prog rock as well in the form of bands like Deus Ex Machina, Asgard, Barrock, Eris Pluvia, Il Trono Dei Ricordi, Finisterre and a host of others.

The French progressive rock scene was very different from the Italian one. Understanding that culture and to some degree history play a large part in prog, you can understand the different influences French musicians felt. There are two aspects that distinguish French progressive rock. They are; a strong theatrical sense and in general a non-melodic vocal style. The use of vocal theatrics was initiated and made popular by Christian DeCamps of the band Ange. This theatrical style has led to some Genesis comparisons but musically these bands are quite dissimilar. Partially due to the second "generalised" aspect of non-melodic style. The uninitiated, upon first listening to bands like Ange, Alice, Atoll are struck by the fact the vocalist isn't really singing the melody, but rather speaking or many times yelling the story line. Whereas vocalists in Italy came from a stronger operatic or melodic vocal style, many French bands did not and as a result the singing style is harsher and more guttural. The French prog scene took off slightly after the Italians in about 1972, with the first wave of bands lasting until the late seventies. Unlike Italy however, France began producing a new wave of bands in the early eighties at a much quicker rate than the Italians. Today we're treated to wonderful symphonic music from Minimum Vital, Afterglow, Halloween, Eclat and others.

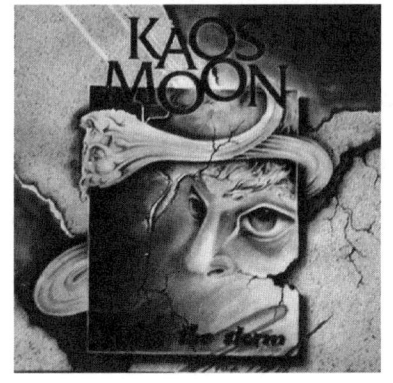

In Canada the province of Quebec proved to be quite prolific in this genre producing such notable bands as Octobre, Maneige, Morse Code, Harmonium and most recently new bands such as Visible Wind, Kaos Moon, Miriodor and a half dozen others. The Quebec cultural experience is unique in Canada. The eight million people who reside in that province are extremely supportive of home grown talent. Sadly the rest of Canada can hardly account for two or three prog bands while Quebec has almost a dozen currently making the rounds. Part of the reason is their strong reliance on ethnic/folk input in the music. This was more true of the earlier bands like Harmonium but is still a factor today. It's this diversity that allows for the creation of music other than corporate, alternative rock. English speaking Canadians today can count on Rush, Saga and FM to create their own version of progressive rock.

In Eastern Europe, behind the "Iron Curtain" (when one still existed), progressive rock was very much a part of the overall underground music scene. In Hungary bands like Omega and East, Poland's Exodus and SBB, while in Czechoslovakia there was Collegium Musicum, Modry Efekt, Synkopy, and in Russia itself bands like In Spe, Dawn Dialogue and others existed. All of these countries could boast a strong folk culture and it's not surprising that this ethnic quality would find it's way into much of this music. The classical influence came from composers such as Rimsky-Korsachov and Dvorak. Recent progressive bands from Eastern Europe have been rare. One band of note is After Crying from Hungary whose symphonic sound is influenced by ELP and King Crimson. Their CD **De Profundis** released in 1996 contained epic suites displaying a very accomplished compositional style.

In South America progressive rock has a more recent history, but what they lack in history they've made up for in volume. The progressive rock communities in places like Argentina and Brazil are second to none. At the time of this writing it was possible to listen to at least three different progressive rock radio shows each week on different radio stations in Buenos Aires city. There are record shops and labels devoted exclusively to progressive rock and there are at least three or four well produced prog magazines produced to keep the fans informed of the latest bands and tours. Older bands such as Bacamarte, Banana, Espiritu and Tellah, find their older material re-released on CD while new bands such as Apocalypse, Blezqi Zatsaz, Cinema Show and Kaizen, are finding their material snapped up not only by fans in South America but throughout the world.

The Japanese progressive rock scene had it's share of impressive bands in virtually all genres from Canterbury to RIO. Many of these band formed and became popular during the late seventies and early eighties. On the symphonic side, spurred on by influential labels such as Made In Japan and Belle Antique and publications notably Marquee Moon, bands such as Bikyoran, Kenso, Outer Limits, Mr. Sirius, Gerard and many others have and are still creating some of the finest progressive rock music available.

It's true to say that if you looked hard enough virtually every country has at least one progressive rock band whether that's Iran's Revival or Iceland's Pursaflokkurinn. It's a genre that may be small in terms of following but is truly international in scope.

The Fans Multi-Media Response

In contrast to the critics disdain, if there is one thing that typifies the fan's emotional response to progressive rock, it is the fervour with which they have worked to spread a positive word. Nowhere is this more prevalent than on the Internet in the nineties and in the production of progressive rock fanzines that began during the progressive rock revival of the early eighties. Some of these were of near magazine quality while others were little more than amateur efforts to contribute in some form of passionate response, and many of them only continued into the mid eighties.

During the height of the neo-progressive rock scene in and around London, the best fanzine going was **Afterglow** produced by Roger and Russell Morgan. It was produced with great photo reproduction and graphics and originally focused on the band Genesis. It became the voice for neo-progressive rock bands happening in England by issue #11 in 1983. The list of contributors to each issue was lengthy and as a result there was coverage of just about every aspect of the prog-rock scene. Interviews with the hottest new bands, reviews of live concerts and LP releases. It managed to survive for about 15 issues. The next batch of fanzines fall into the fan's passionate response category more than any others. Usually assembled by one individual with little if any help, but again put together and sent out to any who might listen about progressive rock from a positive light. These include Kim McClelland and Dave Hillage's **Northwest Progressive Music News**, Ronnie Larkins' **Exposure**, Jeremy Ewing's **Court Jester**, David Pickering and Andrew Wright's **Slogans**, and Keith Holden's **Revelatory**. These and many others have come and gone, along with band specific fanzines like **Relayer** (Yes), **Amazing Pudding** (Pink Floyd), **Higher And Higher** (Moody Blues). The list is long and illustrious of the individuals who made an honest and sincere effort to counteract the negative publicity coming from the rest of the print media.

Around the early eighties the Japanese publication **Marquee Moon** came into existence and continues to this day to be the slickest of all progressive rock publications. Each issue is roughly 80 pages with colour photos and all the latest news and information in the world of prog-rock. Unfortunately for prog fans by 1997 **Marquee Moon** had turned into more of an alternative/pop magazine leaving only a few pages of coverage for fans of progressive rock. A relative newcomer to the prog publishing world is Korea's **Art Rock**. Much like Marquee Moon, this is a very professionally produced publication with lots of photos and many in colour. Keep in mind both these are written in their native language. One of the other long-running prog-rock fanzines was **Eurock** published by Archie Patterson in Portland. His publication was more a catalogue of records new and old for sale, but for a while it contained descriptions of each release along with a healthy amount of commentary and interviews. It covered the whole gamut of progressive music, from electronic to avant-garde. In 1992 The **Music News Network** came on the scene published in Tampa Florida. With a by-line calling itself the International Monthly Progressive Rock Newsletter it has been the only publication to boast a regular monthly output. Each issue is approximately 10 to 14 pages packed with the latest news and information, tour dates and record releases as well as one feature interview or in depth article. **MNN** is put together by Lisa Mikita and Christine Holz and it's regular publication has proven to be a lifeline for prog fans around the world. The English language **Background Progressive Rock Magazine** is still published in Holland. They bill themselves as an international non-profit magazine reporting on known and unknown progressive rock. It's now over sixty issues and contains interviews, reviews and information on musical developments and is published six times a year. You can now find their band index on the Internet. Currently one of the best British magazines is **Audion** published in the UK. It usually runs about 40 pages per issue with articles on all facets of progressive music including many historical articles. **Audion**'s prime focus tends to be more on the prog-sub genres such as RIO, Zuehl, ambient etc.. From France come a couple of excellent publications. The English language **Acid Dragon** boasts of being the only progressive rock fanzine connected with a progressive radio program. Each 40 page digest-size issue contains three or four in-depth articles or interviews on mostly current bands and includes dozens of reviews. For the French language readers there are **Harmonie**, **Big Bang** and **Musea Magazine**. Each a quality publication in it's own right.

While there are many other publications the two most comprehensive English language magazines devoted to all aspects of progressive rock would be **Expose'** and **Progression**. Both are available by subscription for about $20 and well worth every penny.

PROGRESSION - The Journal of Progressive Music came on the scene in 1992 and since that time has built a sizeable, international subscriber base. Each issue is 80-120 pages and is published quarterly. This magazine is devoted to news, reviews, interviews and features involving progressive rock artists new and old, in the United States and overseas. They cover the so called "mainstream" progressive acts such as IQ, Yes, ELP, Jethro Tull Marillion, etc. but also include occasional features and reviews on more "fringe" prog artists such as Univers Zero and Richard Pinhas. A typical edition of the magazine includes exclusive, in-depth interviews with progressive rock artists plus dozens of concert and album reviews, tour itineraries and information on new album and video releases. Feature articles will include a biography of a particular artist or a history of progressive music in a particular country. **Progressions** strengths lie in it's magazine style and regular columnists.

Expose is also a quarterly publication roughly 80 pages in size jammed full of interviews, reviews etc. covering all aspects of the genre. **Expose** is not quite a magazine but it's much more than a newsletter. There is what's called Media Look where they spotlight the progressive releases from specific labels or record companies. You come away with a tremendous amount of information to help track down those bands you've been searching for. The other thing unique to **Expose** is their Reviewer's Roundtable, where specific releases are reviewed by more than one staffer. From this you'll glean insights missed by one but caught by another. All in all an excellent publication. **Expose**'s strengths are in the number of reviews in each issue and the Media Look section which goes a long way to bringing a person up to date on progressive rock releases.

Clearly, whatever your field of interest in the world of progressive rock, there is undoubtedly a magazine being produced to satisfy your thirst for information.

A Home On The Internet

With the advent of the Internet, progressive rock fans around the world found a whole new means of communicating that has delivered a tremendous shot of adrenaline into the whole genre. The Internet by it's ability to target a specific market has been able to reach out to a growing number of fans around the world. Now instead of isolated pockets of interest, musicians, record companies, publishers and fans are able to communicate as a group as easily as being in one community. In fact they have created a progressive rock community that is primed to propel the genre into much greater acceptance. Given that one of the primary reasons the interest in progressive rock has been small is as a result of not having access to the band's material, the Internet provides a pipeline to millions who might not otherwise ever be exposed to this music. As a result instead of interest in progressive rock declining, it's growing as more individuals come in touch with the different web sites.

Another aspect the Internet provides is access. Not only to information but to the artists. Many progressive rock artists actively participate in various newsgroup discussions or have mailing lists where fans can subscribe to receive answers to questions and the latest news on their favourite musicians.

One element of the Internet that can be very engaging at times or downright obnoxious, is the newsgroups. This aspect of the Internet is populated with many people who sometimes have nothing better to do than disseminate gossip, rumours and in some cases falsehoods. Still if you are prepared to weed through the copious entries made weekly, you can generally find some interesting threads of information. Not only do most bands have dedicated newsgroups, you'll also find two devoted to the general discussion of progressive music. They are;

alt.rock-n-roll.metal.progressive - (posts relating to harder, metal progressive)
rec.music.progressive - (posts relating to symphonic progressive rock etc.)

As you might expect there is a lot of cross-posting going on, but for fans of progressive rock, it's the last one, rec.music.progressive that seems to contain the most applicable postings. Everything from fans discussing which was the first progressive rock LP to whether the Beatles were progressive or not. As mentioned some of the discussion is quite informative, but as in any large group there will always be those obnoxious types who fail to add to the discussion but are vocal none-the-less. There are currently over 15,000 different newsgroups, and they come and go, with new groups added weekly. This can be a fine arena for discussion, debate and many times buffoonery, but when it comes to legitimate information you'll need to slide onto the Web.

Typically the Web side of the Internet provides a more authorised source for individuals to track down information on progressive rock bands, labels, publications, new releases, history and on and on. Perhaps the best place to start is with Adam Levin's The Progressive Rock Web Site. This comprehensive one-stop shopping site has everything you need to bring yourself up-to-speed. The latest releases, links to hundreds of dedicated band home pages, information on labels or vendors, and even struggling musicians.
It resides at: <URL:http://www.ari.net/prog/>

Next stop on your list might be the **Gibraltar Encyclopaedia of Progressive Rock**. This site is an exhaustive listing of bands and recordings with multiple contributors each posting their reviews of the bands and albums listed. The attempt has been to make this site as inclusive as possible, so it's natural you'll find listings for many fringe artists as well as established ones. The idea of having multiple contributors enhances the appeal of the listings. Like much of this work, the GEPR is a living and growing entity that has found it's way to one print press run. Another is in the works.
It resides at: <URL:http://www.ari.net/prog/GEPR/gepr.html>

Recently the good people at Gibraltar have taken to producing a monthly "webzine" devoted to the latest news regarding progressive rock. This impressive website is pretty much an internet prog lovers dream site with all the latest news, releases, tours, reviews, Q&As, regular columns, feature stories, label profiles, cover art profiles and even a place for fan to email their responses, requests and classified ads.
It resides at: URL: http://prog.ari.net/prog/gibraltar/gibraltar.html

Fans of progressive rock in the nineties have a much easier time keeping up with what's happening in the genre. In the seventies unless you knew someone in a band, heard a band on the radio or spent time in the import record bins you wouldn't have known that progressive rock existed around the world. Today, they say the world has become a smaller place, and that's certainly true of the progressive rock world. These days finding out what's happening on the other side of the globe is as easy as turning on the computer and downloading some audio files. Instant access to a growing world of music. While prog on the mass media, radio or TV is non-existent, it's presence on many of the alternative media sites is very high, be it in print, on CD or on the Internet.

Progressive Rock Is Here To Stay

Some have said the best years of progressive rock were the early seventies. Derek Jewell in his essay **Pomp And Circumstance**, labelled the "Golden Age" of progressive rock as 1970 to 1975. To my way of thinking this five year spread is extremely limiting when you consider that by 1969 The Moody Blues and Procol Harum were already on their fourth albums, and King Crimson had released their second, **In The Wake Of Poseidon**. As to the other end of the scale - the years 1976 through 1979 saw the release of some of the best progressive rock music by such bands as Jethro Tull, UK, Yes, Genesis etc..

Russ Summers in **Keyboard** magazine said: *"For whatever reason, progressive rock with it's grandiose symphonic sonorities, odd time signatures and overt classical references, never caught on, on this side of the Atlantic quite the same way it did in England. Only a few American bands could really claim to be musical descendants of groups like Genesis and Yes, and fewer still achieved any great popularity."*

As to why this is true, we've attempted to discuss here. Progressive rock was never heard much on radio in the United States or Canada. Only for a few short years in the early seventies when the climate was right, when FM radio was only starting to break out of it's classical shell. But it didn't take very long for FM to become the hit oriented radio we see around us today. Gone is the experimenting, now programmers concern themselves more with providing enough commercial time.

Perhaps another reason progressive rock never had much of a chance in America is the great distance involved in covering the continent. In England a band might record independently and service the record shops of most of the country from the back of their van within a week. This allows them a vast amount of exposure to millions of people. In Canada and the United States the distribution of a product is left up to the major record companies to handle as they see fit. Tours tend to be few and far between. Here, there is rarely the opportunity for a band to develop a nation-wide cult following, as happens in Britain. Here the followings tend to be very regionalized.

Fortunately for those of us who do enjoy more adventurous music, progressive rock has never died and gone away. There have been some rather bleak moments, but it has survived to this day. It lives on in bands like Glass Hammer, Deus Ex Machina, IQ and dozens of other bands in Japan, Europe and South America. **Keyboard** magazine: *"Anyone who fears for the survival of progressive rock will be reassured by the success of Saga. Though not as overtly preoccupied with classical structure as the founding* fathers of the style, this Canadian band sculpts it's music in a scale comparable to the most grandiose efforts of ELP and Yes, with synthesised shadings that can subtly colour each musical episode even while satisfying a stadium full of hard core rockers."

So while the music may sound a little different for some, and change it must, it will continue to be progressive. Jim Gilmore talked about joining Saga: *"I went down and played a lot of classical stuff that I'd written. After they took me in, it was pretty frustrating because they wouldn't let me play as fast as I wanted to. I wasn't able to do as many solos as I would have liked, so I had to learn to fall back a little from the kind of progressive rock I had been doing. Now, even though we're getting popular and we have a steady beat, I think we're maintaining a good degree of musicality, I'm happy with that."*

It is good to see there are more than the fans who feel the progressive era never died completely. **Keyboard** magazine: *"There's another way of looking at this. You could say the progressive era never really disappeared, it was just pushed to the side for a while, and here there's a certain amount of truth in this. Genesis are still enormously popular, their following almost fanatical...The faithful perceived the seismic reverberations of the new wave as a direct assault on the values they held so dear; a peculiar allegiance to a concept of musicianship that relied over heavily on notions of technical dexterity rather than taste and feel, and a fondness for styles based loosely on European classical music."*

In some ways the above statement is true, other than the slanted innuendo that somehow progressive rock does not rely on feel. When in fact musicians who have honed their craft to such a skill perhaps are able to feel their art, their music, more than those just starting out. It's strange that whenever there is an art form critics have trouble figuring out, they say it lacks feeling. The critic for some reason feels it's imperative to put the onus on the artist to relate to their audience, when perhaps looking at it more objectively, the audience or listener has a sense of responsibility to take what the performer is giving, and then decide whether they like it or not. It is very much the listener who must be responsible for making any compromise.

The artist must first and foremost be doing what pleases, or is true to his own self, or skill. The artist, musician, painter whatever, can never attempt to simply sell out to do only what pleases the audience. This is no longer art, it is simply parroting, simply bland pabulum for the masses. This is where in some respects progressive rock is very different from other forms of popular music. It relies less on mass appeal and more on musical self fulfilment. And just like the artist who gives their 100%, the listener is required to give their 100% in search of listening pleasure.

One of the bands that in some people's eyes have attempted to bridge the gap between pop or commercial music and progressive rock, is the Scottish band Simple Minds. While this is probably overstating their influence they have gone so far as to tour with Peter Gabriel, and even recorded the Gabriel song Biko on their 1989 album Street Fighting Years. Says keyboard player Michael MacNeil: *"When we toured Europe with Peter Gabriel, opening gigs to 40,000 people at a time, we were playing to a lot of early Genesis fans, probably aged in their mid-thirties. It was good, because those people are pretty sensible. It's not like they're out to see a punk group or someone like the Clash.*

They're mature adults and they take music seriously. It's not just a bit of entertainment to them. They stand there and really listen instead of jumping about and screaming. You feel like you've got their complete attention, and that you're doing something for them."

Throughout the course of this book I have tried to demonstrate that progressive rock has always been with us in some form or another. I don't believe that it's "golden years" were in the early seventies. I do believe that was the time period where it matured as a genre and came of full-age. That was the time where all of the elements crystallised into a musical form. But to suggest that it's best work existed only at that time and the rest has been downhill since, causes me to think of Mark Twain's quote; *"The rumours of my demise are greatly exaggerated."*

To suggest that Yes' **Close To The Edge** was the peak of their creativity is an unfair assessment since the band is still producing material. Their peak cannot be judged until they are no longer around. But then there are still some who feel The Beatles best work was **Rubber Soul** or **Revolver** which ignores **Sergeant Pepper**. But to suggest that even **Sergeant Pepper** was their crowning achievement ignores what a great album **Abbey Road** is. Similarly with any artists still around and producing progressive rock. As I pointed out with the critics, it's one thing to have your "favourite" recordings, it's another thing entirely to call them the "best". I choose to see creativity as a cycle or a continuum, and it's entirely possible to come around on the cycle to periods of higher creativity. History is full of individuals who waited until very late in life to accomplish their most lasting creative output. If these periods must be quantified, we can call it a high-point, but to call it a peak and imply everything else from that point on was downhill, is, in my view overstepping the bounds of proper evaluation or appreciation and simply being judgmental. Bands mature, line-up's change, new directions are charted. Genesis became more commercial after Gabriel left, but after the pop influence of Collins left, they reverted to a darker moodier sound once again. After Trevor Rabin left Yes, they reformed as one of their earlier incarnations to produce the spectacular **Keys To Ascension**, very much in their older style. Only when that creative cycle is complete can one sit back and retrospectively say: "this appears to be their best work."

I suggest the above is equally applicable to the genre of progressive rock. Until it is finished it's creative cycle (if it ever does), we can't in all fairness sit back and smugly suggest it's best days are over. Country, jazz, reggae, pop, classical, and many other musical genres have been around for many years and all have gone through less-creative patches. It's a good sign that many of the original prog supergroups like Yes, Genesis, Jethro Tull, ELP and King Crimson are still with us. Additionally from the world-wide perspective there are undoubtedly more progressive rock bands producing music than ever before. Why would we want to put such a negative limit on the genre's creative ability. As long as there are musicians who choose to go beyond the pop norm, and as long as their music gets in the hands of fans who want to listen to something more adventurous, progressive rock will be with us.

JETHRO TULL
Ring Out, Solstice Bells · March, the Mad Scientist
Christmas Song · Pan Dance
BARCLAY JAMES HARVEST
LIVE
SIRE
Bleu Disque Music (ASCAP) Time 3:25
℗ 1973 RTM
STEREO
SAA-704
MB 27190-S
Produced by Mike Vernon for RTM
HOCUS POCUS II
(Akkerman-Van Leer)
FOCUS
Cotillion
COT 44151
Arr. by Emerson, Lake & Palmer From Cotillion LP 66666
℗ 1972 Atlantic
Side 1
Instrumental
Pub., Room Seven Music (BMI) 3:43
NUTROCKER
(Kim Fowley)
EMERSON, LAKE & PALMER
Prod. by Greg Lake for E.G. Records
ATLANTIC
Topographic Music/ Warner Bros. Music Ltd.
45 RPM
SIDE 2
K 11047
K 11047 B*
(MS 1769X)
℗ © 1977
6 min 40
STEREO
AWAKEN PT. I
(Anderson/Howe)
(Edited from the Album K 50379 'Going For The One')
YES
Arranged and Produced by Yes
COLUMBIA
45 R.P.M.
DUNMO MUS., NCB
7XCA 27877
℗ 1967
DB 8156
SOLD IN U.K. SUBJECT TO RESALE PRICE CONDITIONS, SEE PRICE LISTS
ARNOLD LAYNE
(Syd Barrett)
THE PINK FLOYD
Produced by Joe Boyd for Blackhill Enterprises
MADE IN GT BRITAIN
Mooncrest
Produced by Atomic Rooster by arrangement with Geff Masters Ltd
Orchestration directed by Vincent Crane
MOON 52
MOON 52-A
℗ 1971
G.H. Music Ltd
Made in England
DEVIL'S ANSWER
(Cann)
ATOMIC ROOSTER
HONKY TONK TRAIN BLUES
KEITH EMERSON

GENESIS
THE LAMB LIES DOWN ON BROADWAY

KATE BUSH
THE KICK INSIDE

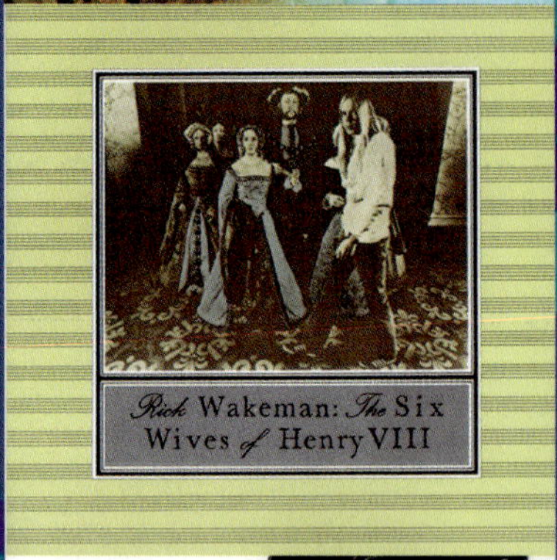
Rick Wakeman: The Six
Wives of Henry VIII

yessongs

So
Peter Gabriel

ON.... AMON DÜÜL II.... LIVE IN LONDON.... AMON D

MANFRED MANN'S
EARTH BAND
Glorified Magnified

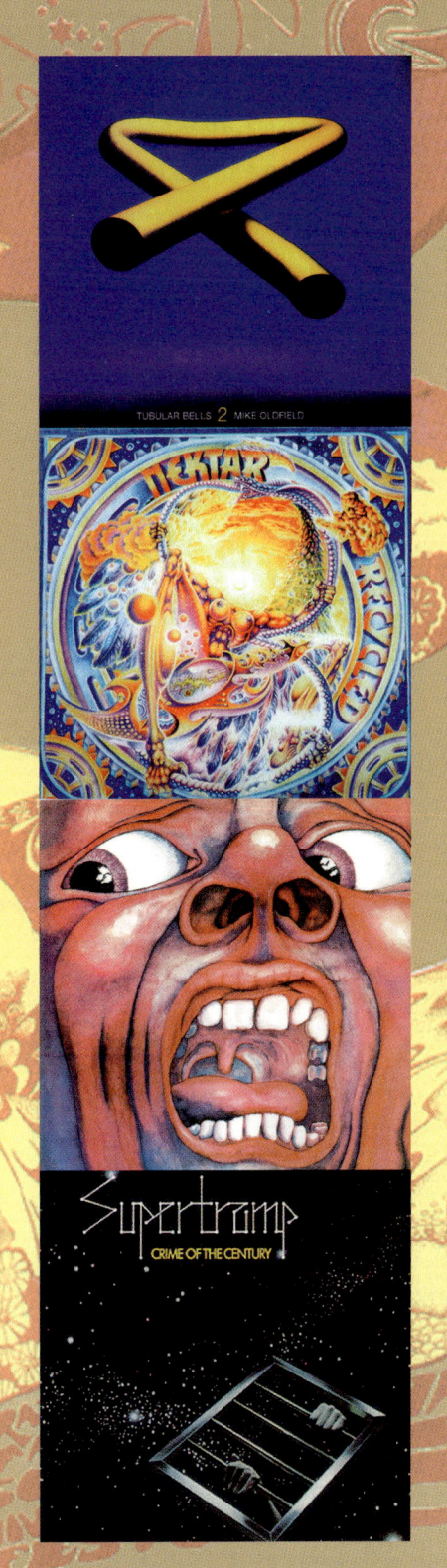

- **Grey Lady Down** — *The Crime*
- **Peter Banks**
- **Mike Oldfield** — *Tubular Bells 2*
- **Nektar** — *Recycled*
- **Focus 3**
- **King Crimson** — *In the Court of the Crimson King*
- **Primitive Instinct** — *Floating Tangibility*
- **Supertramp** — *Crime of the Century*

bande originale du film de J. LAPERROUSAZ
PHILIPS
CONTINENTAL CIRCUS
musique par GONG avec DAEVID ALLEN

SYNERGY
Electronic Realizations for Rock Orchestra

Voyage of the Acolyte
Steve Hackett

JOHN WETTON
BATTLE LINES

10 cc
SHEET MUSIC

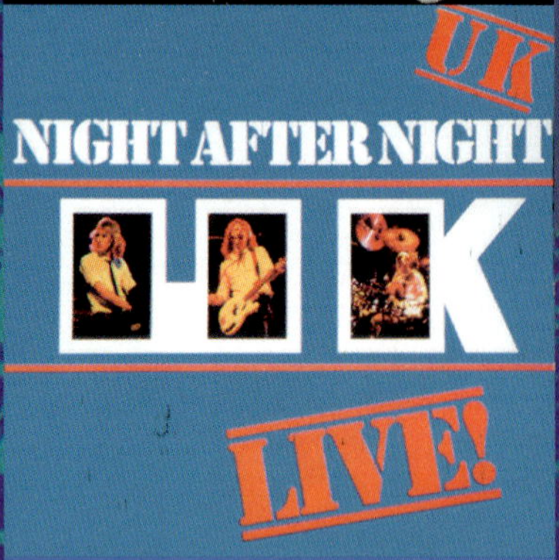
UK
NIGHT AFTER NIGHT
UK
LIVE!

instrumentals
FORCEFIELD
featuring
JAN AKKERMAN
RAY FENWICK
BERNIE MARSDEN
MARIO PARGA
DON AIREY
COZY POWELL

JUNE 1, 1974
KEVIN AYERS-JOHN CALE-ENO-NICO

TODD RUNDGREN'S
utopia

PENDRAGON
THE WORLD

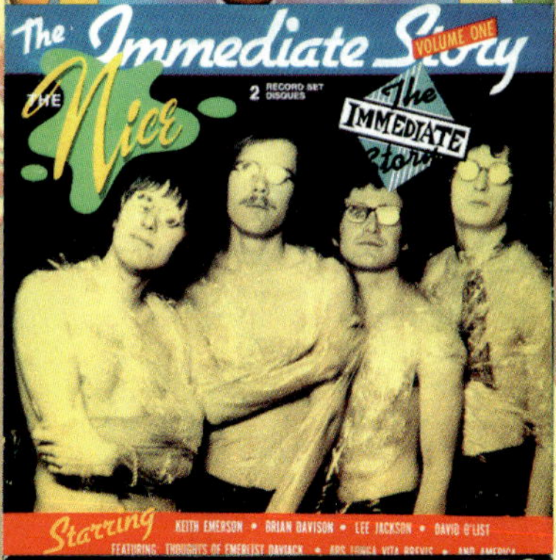
The Immediate Story
VOLUME ONE
THE Nice
2 RECORD SET DISQUES
The IMMEDIATE Story
Starring
KEITH EMERSON • BRIAN DAVISON • LEE JACKSON • DAVID O'LIST

CHRIS SQUIRE
Fish Out Of Water

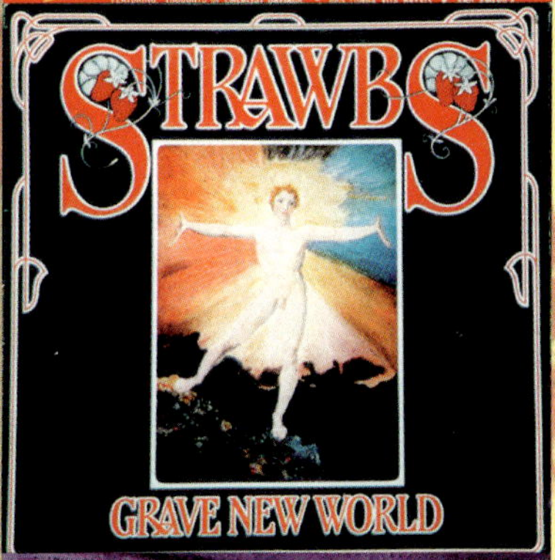
STRAWBS
GRAVE NEW WORLD

MAGICIANS HAT
BO HANSSON

TANGERINE DREAM
FORCE MAJEURE

JETHRO TULL

Hatfield and the North

VARIATIONS
ANDREW LLOYD WEBBER

Starline
BARCLAY JAMES HARVEST
EARLY MORNING ONWARDS

MARILLION
SCRIPT FOR A JESTER'S TEAR

BBC RADIO ONE LIVE
STEVE HILLAGE
LIVE IN CONCERT

Roy Harper
Lifemask

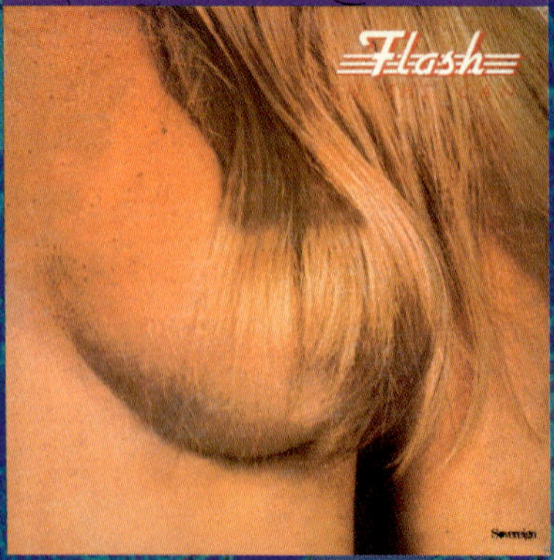
Flash

DAVID GILMOUR
ABOUT FACE

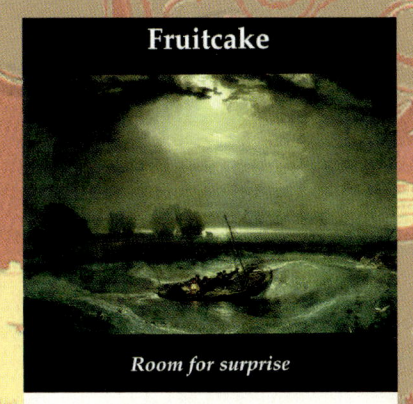

FRUITCAKE
Room for surprise

BUDGIE / SQUAWK

Queen
A Night At The Opera

RUSH
Moving Pictures

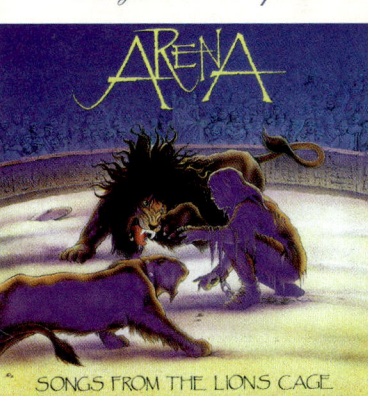

ARENA
SONGS FROM THE LION'S CAGE

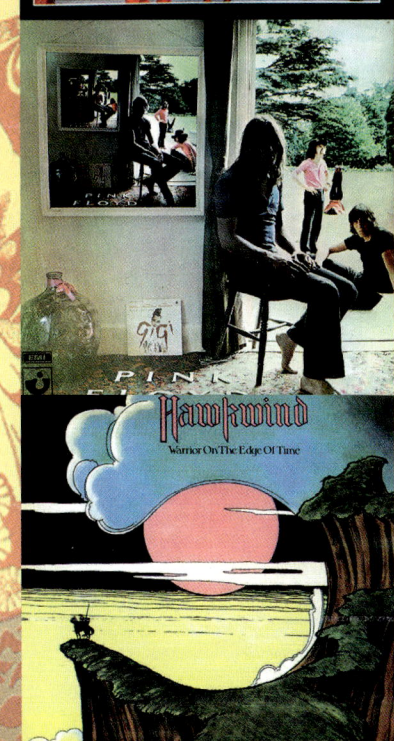

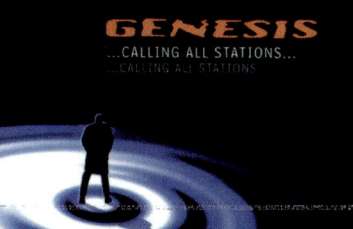

GENESIS
...Calling All Stations...

Hawkwind
Warrior On The Edge Of Time

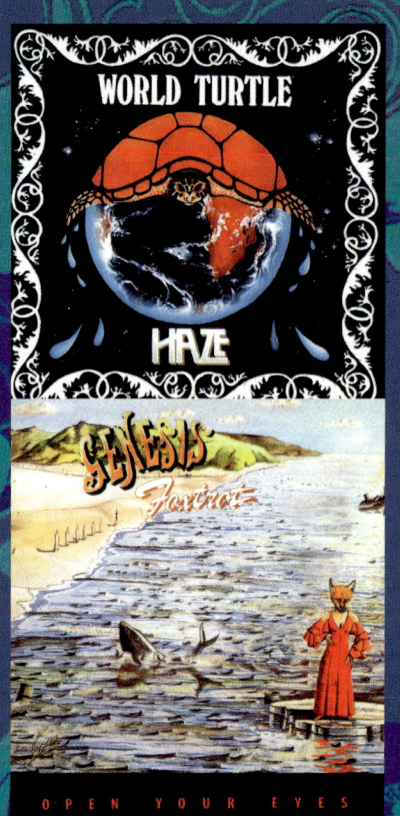

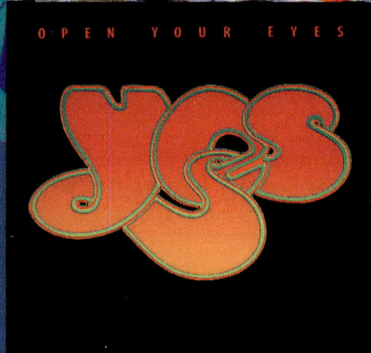

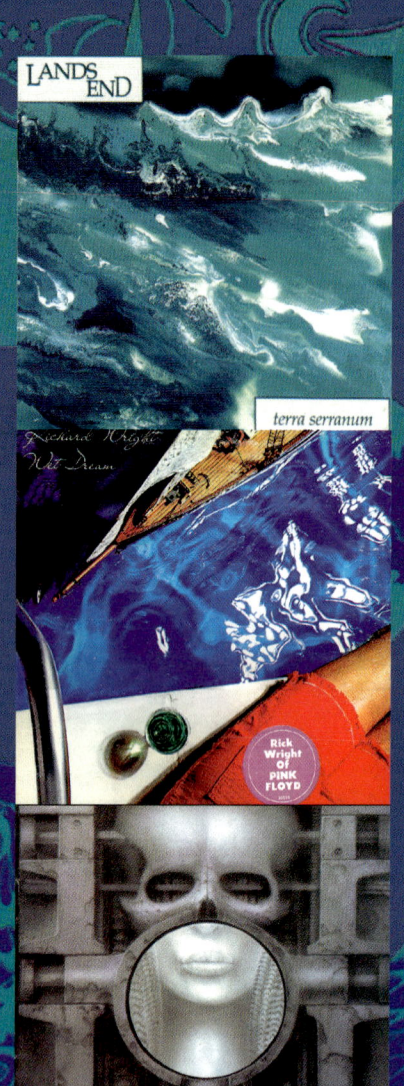

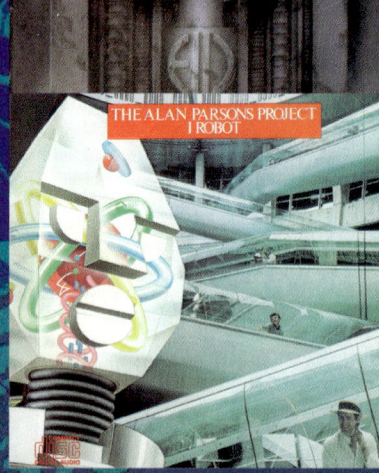

- WORLD TURTLE — HAZE
- LANDS END — terra serranum
- GENESIS — Foxtrot
- Richard Wright — Wet Dream
- YES — OPEN YOUR EYES
- Emerson, Lake & Palmer — Brain Salad Surgery
- THE SOFT MACHINE — Jet Propelled Photographs
- THE ALAN PARSONS PROJECT — I ROBOT

FILE #5 - The A - Z Listing

Introduction To The Listing

The very idea of putting together an A-Z listing of progressive rock bands is daunting enough let alone when you start getting into the qualifiers of who belongs and who doesn't. Suffice it to say this listing is not complete. It probably never will be. But it's pretty close, and I'll simply keep adding to it in future editions.

However there does need to be some clarification for bands you may think belong, but are missing. I have tried to include all bands that fall under the definitions of classical, pomp, neo-prog and symphonic (orchestrated) progressive rock. I have tried to include a good many from the Canterbury sub-genre as well. These have been the prime focus of my work over the last decade. There are bands listed from other progressive sub-genres but I have admittedly not included all. For example bands that are predominately RIO or avant-garde have been left out for the most part. Some bands that performed fusion or jazz-rock, where it had close ties to prog have been included, Brand X for example.

In other cases I have intentionally included bands that initiated certain sub-genres such as Egg, or Hatfield & The North but may not have included modern descendants. There are probably specialised books to be written about those sub-genres any how. While I may have listed some, to include them all here is beyond the scope of my endeavours.

I have attempted to locate and identify as many progressive rock bands and individuals as possible, even going so far as to include bands that may have only released a demo tape or in some cases just existed for a short time with no recorded material. Given that fact, it's very possible that a band may be listed but will have no recorded output to track down. If this is known I've tried to make mention of it. After saying this, there will still be bands or individuals I've missed, so if one of your favourites is not listed, it's nothing personal. They may show up in some future edition.

A word about the discography. The first edition of **The Progressive Rock Files** included a discography however it was dropped for the next two editions. It makes a return here at the request of many who've written wishing it was there to help in the quest of progressive rock music. While it is quite comprehensive, it is selective. As a rule I have avoided listing "Best of.." releases or compilations. In most cases release dates of the country of origin have been included although for some of the more obscure bands they're unknown. Where an album was recorded in one year and released many years later it's listed with both dates thusly (74/93).

Periodicals

Down Beat, "Bill Bruford A Drummer's Discipline". Art Lange, Charles Doherty. February 1984.
Eurock, Issues #26, 35,
Eurock Supplements, 11/88, 1/89
Expose', Issues #2, 4, 5, 6, 7, 8, 9, 10, 11, 12, 13
Gavin Report, Anderson Bruford Wakeman & Howe Review. June 9th, 1989
Guitar Player, "Asia, Side two" Steve Howe Intv. Jim Schwartz, September 1982
International Musician & Recording World, "Genesis: Under The Big Top" Ron Bienstock, Paul Galotta. February 1984
Keyboard, Article on Keith Emerson. September 1980.
_____, "The Deep Purple Legacy Lives On" Interview with Jon Lord. Bob Doerschuk. March 1983.
_____, "Around the World with Saga" Interview with Jim Gilmore. Bob Doerschuk. July 1983
_____, Article on Kit Watkins. July 1983
_____, "Michael MacNeil of Simple Minds" Bob Doerschuk. September 1983
_____, Article on Geoff Downes. Dominic Milano. November 1983
_____, Article on Tony Kaye. July 1984
_____, Article on Rick Wakeman. Bob Doerschuk. September 1989
_____, Vintage Synths: "The Mellotron: Pillar of a Musical Genre" Mark Vail. May 1991
_____, Article on Keith Emerson. June 1992
_____, "More Mellotron". September 1993
_____, "Digital Dinosaurs: Progressive Rock On The Internet" Daniel J. Barrett, June 1996
Los Angeles Times, Calendar: "Asia Says Yes To Pop Stardom" Michael Watts. Sunday December 19, 1982
Melody Maker, "Something In The Air" Monkman talks to Michael Watts. September 11th 1971
_____, "Birth Of The New Yes" Chris Welch, Mark Plummer. August 28th, 1971
_____, "State Of Rock". September 25th, 1971
_____, "Contemporary Classics-Rock & The Classics Continued" Russell Unwin. March 13th 1971
_____, "Renaissance Is Born Again". Mark Plummer, February 20th, 1971
_____, "Curved Air's Classical Keyboard Man" Chris Charlesworth, March 13th, 1971
_____, "Genesis: fun time in New York City" Chris Welch, December 23, 1972
_____, "Moodies, Floyd a Bore!" Allan Jones, June 22, 1974
_____, "Planet Marillion" Lynden Barber. April 9th 1983
Mojo, "Welcome Back My Friends, The Songs That Never End" Rob Chapman Issue #39 February 1997
_____, "Hello Atlantis" (Yes) Dave Rimmer. Issue #39 February 1997
Music Express, "The Marillion Mystery" Interview with Fish. Tarin Elbert. Issue #71 1983
Musician, Frontman Column "Peter Gabriel". December 1992
Progression: The Journal of Progressive Music, Issues #20, 21, 22, 23, 24
Record, London Calling Column, Chris Welch. April 1983
Record Collector, "Biography of IQ" Justin Beaney. February 1983
_____, "Interview with Rick Wakeman" Mark Paytress. December 1995
Record Review, "Eddie Jobson: Curved Air, Roxy Music, Zappa, UK and Jethro Tull's not so secret weapon" Jon Sutherland. December 1983
Trouser Press, "Italy: The Decline and Fall of Progressive Rock" Ted White. October 1980
_____, "The Genesis Autodiscography" Jon Young. March 1982 *Up Front*,
"The Brits Are Back" Peter Goddard
Willis Riley Reports From New York (British Paper)

So Where Does This Leave Us?

We've talked about the origins of progressive rock, what's happened to it over the years, what people have said about it. How this music more than most has been slandered by the critics and yet lives on. It beats in the hearts of fans and in the composers who continue to write and perform this non-conforming music. The desire to create progressive rock urges them to stretch their composition skills to the limit...to master their instruments, to hone their song writing or musical abilities. Thankfully some still take up the challenge. Bands may come and go but at the very least their music lives on for us today.

In the end what are we talking about? You would think by the tirade of "negative-press" progressive rock has received over the years it was something evil. But it's not. After all what's wrong with musicians taking their music seriously, what's wrong with writing long songs, what's so wrong with really playing your instruments? Regardless of what anybody says or writes, nothing really, absolutely nothing.

Many of you having read this far may already know how to acquire the LP's, cassettes or CD's recorded by the progressive rock bands listed here. But for those who don't, other than coming across some of these bands by chance at your local independent music store, be aware there are many progressive rock mail-order vendors that have sprung up over the last 10 years and for the most part all of them can be considered very reputable. Of course it's always better if you know of someone who has conducted a transaction but that's not always possible. Listed here are four sources that I am personally familiar with. They can be your starting point if you choose. They are:

EUROCK
PO Box 13718
Portland OR
97213
USA

SYN-PHONIC
PO Box 2034
La Habra CA 90631
USA

ZNR Records
PO Box 58040
Louisville KY
40268-0040
USA

Musea
68 La Tinchotte
57117 Retonfey
France

Cyclops
33A Tolworth Park Rd
Tolworth Surrey
KT6 7RL
UK 0181 339 9965

Each of these independently run operations have been in the mail order business for many years and you can be quite safe is sending your orders to them although you may want to call first to find out about availability because a lot of this material is in short supply.

The addresses for the progressive rock magazines mentioned earlier are:

EXPOSE'
6167 Jarvis Ave.
#150
Newark CA
94560
USA

Progression
PO Box 7164
Lowell, MA 01852
USA

Acid Dragon
20 rue ferrandiere
69002 Lyon
France

To help you decide what to order, I've created the rest of this book. The A-Z listing of bands is quite literally a 'work-in-progress' because it is by no means complete. It can never be, as there will always be new bands formed and old ones rediscovered. Don't be alarmed if you find 'contradictions'. Some art-rock, fusion or even space-rock bands are included where they may have had significant impact on progressive rock as a whole. I've tried to make the listings as complete as possible, providing some detail as to the nature of the band's style. This will help others who are looking for this music to better understand which bands they may want to seek out. Have fun!

Progressive Rock Files Sources:

Books
All Music Guide To Rock, edited by Michael Erlewine, Vladimir Bogdanov, Chris Ruhlman. San Francisco: Miller Freeman Books, 1995
Book Of Genesis, Hugh Fielder. London: Sidgwick and Jackson, 1984
Book of Music, The. edited by Gill Rowley. London: New Burlington Books, 1977
Future Rock, David Downing. Panther Books, 1976
Genesis: A Biography, Dave Bowler, Bryan Dray. London: Sidgwick and Jackson, 1993
Genesis: I Know What I Like, Armando Gallo. Los Angeles: DIY Books, 1980
Genesis: Peter Gabriel, Phil Collins and Beyond, Philip Kamin, Peter Goddard. Toronto: Stoddart, 1984
Genesis - Turn It On Again, Geoff Parkyn. London: Omnibus Press, 1983
Harmony Illustrated Encyclopaedia of Rock, edited by Ray Bonds. 3rd Ed. New York: Harmony Books, 1982
History of Rock, Tony Russell. 197??
History of Rock #88, "Pomp And Circumstance" Derek Jewell. London: Orbis Publishing, 1983
Intergalactic Trading Company, Catalogue, Original 3 Ring Binder ed. 1977/8
La Disgraphie du Rock Francais, Francis Grosse, Bernard Gueffier. Musea, 1984
Marillion In Words & Pictures, Carol Clerk. London: Bobcat Books, 1985
NME Book of Rock 2, edited by Nick Logan, Bob Woofindon. London: W.H. Allen & Co., 1977
Pink Floyd: A Visual Documentary by Miles, Miles. London: Omnibus Press, 1980
Pink Floyd: The Illustrated Discography, Miles. London: Omnibus Press, 1981
Revolution In The Head, Ian MacDonald. New York: Henry Holt and Company, 1994
Rick Wakeman: The Caped Crusader, Dan Wooding. London: Granada, 1979
Rock Family Trees Vol I, Pete Frame. New York: Quick Fox, 1980.
Rock Family Trees Vol II, Pete Frame. London: Omnibus Press, 1983.
Rock Music Styles: A History, Katherine Charleton. Dubuque: Wm. C. Brown Publishers, 1990
Rock Record, Terry Hounsome. 3rd Ed., New York: Facts On File, 1987
Rock Yearbook 1984. edited by All Clark. "Tales From Soporific Oceans" Alan Jones. London: St. Martin's Press, 1983
Role of Rock, Don Hibbard, Carol Kaleialoha. Englewood Cliffs: Prentice-Hall, 1983
Rocking the Classics, Edward Macan. New York: Oxford University Press, 1997.
Rolling Stone Encyclopaedia Of Rock And Roll, Perelis, Romanowski. New York: Rolling Stone Press, 1983
Rolling Stone Illustrated History of Rock & Roll, 1976
Saucerful Of Secrets: The Pink Floyd Odyssey, Nicholas Schaffner. New York: Dell Publishing, 1991
Say Yes! An Autobiography, Rick Wakeman. London: Hodder & Stoughton, 1995
Year by Year in the Rock Era, Herb Hendler. Westport: Greenwood Press, 1983
Yes: The Authorised Biography, Dan Hedges. London: Sidgwick and Jackson, 1981
Yes Stories, Tim Morse. New York: St. Martin's Press, 1996

A word of explanation is necessary regarding the idea of comparing a band's "sound" to that of another. This seems to be unique to progressive rock, where upon discovering a new band fans will quickly identify them by saying they sound like some other band. This technique has been employed throughout to help newcomers identify bands they may be most interested in listening to. However, a word of caution; by saying a band sounds like Yes or sounds like King Crimson does not *always* mean that the band sounds like them. It would be a mistake to read that they sound like some other established band and assume they're "sound-alikes" in a negative sense. It may mean that the one band produces music that is "angular" like King Crimson, or uses a Mellotron like KC. To say a band sounds like Camel may simply mean that they produce a more melodic style with long instrumental passages or to hear of a band sounding like ELP may mean they use a similar organ style and that's all. The reference is simply that, a reference point. Some bands have the knack of incorporating many diverse elements and therefore a sound-alike description is more difficult but in most cases I've tried to identify a musical style of each band listed to help in your discovery. Enjoy!

FESTIVAL MUSIC EVOLUTION 70
LE BOURGET AIRPORT   EXHIBITION PARK   PARIS

SATURDAY, MARCH 28TH

AIRFORCE
ATOMIC ROOSTER
PRETTY THINGS
WILD ANGELS

SUNDAY, MARCH 29TH

PROCUL HARUM
RENAISSANCE
TREES
COCHISE
HAWKWIND
HIGH TIDE
SKIN ALLEY

MONDAY, MARCH 30TH

AL STEWART
BRIDGET ST. JOHN
EDGAR BROUGHTON BAND
FORMERLY FAT HARRY
KEVIN AYERS
+ THE WHOLE WORLD
THIRD EAR BAND
DADDY LONGLEGS

plus SURPRISE GUESTS

ALSO INTERNATIONAL EXHIBITION OF MUSICAL INSTRUMENTS AND AMPLIFICATION
AND
POP VILLAGE ENTERTAINMENT CENTRE - BARS, SHOPS, STANDS, RESTAURANTS, FILM SHOWS
FREE COVERED CAMPING SITE, ALL FACILITIES WITH SLEEPING BAGS FOR HIRE
DETAILS ON APPLICATION
FESTIVAL AND AIR TRAVEL TICKETS £17 PER PERSON

Le Bourget Pop Festival in Paris - The surprise guests were Pink Floyd.

5uu's - United States
Inspired by the Rock In Opposition movement, 5uu's create their own brand of highly complex and challenging progressive music. Utilizing a different arrangement of instruments with each recording, their music goes from dark and industrial at times to something more akin to 20th Century classical, very angular and dissonant. If you enjoy the music of bands such as PRESENT or UNIVERS ZERO you will likely enjoy what you hear.

Bel Marduk & Tiamat (84), Elements (88), Hungers Teeth (94), Point of View (96), Crisis in Clay (97), Regarding Purgatories (00)

XII ALPHONSO - France
The brothers, Francois and Phillippe Claerhout are the masterminds behind this outfit, and they produce a dreamy Celtic symphonic prog sound. Imagine IONA meets MINIMUM VITAL, with a little MIKE OLDFIELD for good measure.

The Lost Frontier (96), Odyssees (99)

A BOLHA - Brazil
One of Brazil's first prog bands who produced a hard sounding, simply arranged prog from a four-piece line-up that included guitar organ drums and bass. They display a strong British blues influence.

Um Passo a Frente (72)

A PIEDI NUDI - Italy
An Italian five piece who've managed to assimilate the seventies Italian influences well and craft their own sound. It's reminiscent of IL BALLETTO DI BRONZO. They play well with lots of musical twists and turns, and a host of experimental and jagged time signatures.

A Piedi Nudi (93), Creazione (94), Eclissi (97)

A TRIGGERING MYTH - United States
A mix of old and contemporary prog sound, somewhat like HAPPY THE MAN or CAMEL. The two key members are primarily keyboard players who create a sound that is rhythmically very deliberate, always rolling along similar to some of the solo work of KIT WATKINS. With the '98 release Sins of Our Saviours they worked with members of Italian proggers Deus Ex Machina which gave their sound a decidedly seventies Italian prog flavour.

A Triggering Myth (90), Twice Bitten (93), Between Cages (95), The Sins of Our Saviours (98)

AARDVARK - Great Britain
Uncomplicated progressive rock with some early YES keyboard flavour. The album was produced by David Hitchcock who would later go on to work with GENESIS, CAMEL and CARAVAN. Overall not heavily prog sounding but good to capture the early seventies sound.

Aardvark (70)

ABACUS - Germany
They come from the same school of music as bands like Karthago and SCARAMOUCHE, who were basically straight ahead rock bands who managed to incorporate some progressive rock tendencies.

Abacus (71), Everything You Need (72), Just a Days Journey Away (72), Midway (73), Anyway We Can (76)

ABBFINOOSTY - Great Britain
Heavy neo-prog with influences ranging from MARILLION to PINK FLOYD to Led Zeppelin.

Future (94), The Storm (9?)

ABEDUL - Spain
One of the few Spanish progressive rock groups to feature English vocals.

ABEL GANZ - Great Britain
Neo-progressive rock band very much in

the vein of IQ & PENDRAGON. Their early GENESIS influenced material was originally available only on cassette but has since been mastered to CD. At least four discs worth of material, in the A Trick of the Tail or Wind & Wuthering vein with a slight eighties slant.

Gratuitous Flesh (84), Dangers of Strangers (85), Gullibles Travels (87), Deafening Silence ( )

ABIOGENESI - Italy
A darker, sinister style that hearkens back to an early seventies sound with great Hammond work and hints of BLACK WIDOW, PINK FLOYD and CAMEL.

Abiogenesi (95), Il Giocoscuro (96)

ABISSI INFINITE - Italy
Tunnell (71)

ABRAXAS - Poland
A sound similar to early MARILLION or mid-period GENESIS. A mixture of neo-prog, some pop and a couple of more adventurous pieces. The music is at once melodic but full of a melancholy feel, punctuated by louder dynamic accents. Throw in a little dissonance and you get the picture.

Abraxas (96), 99 (99)

ABSOLUTE ELSEWHERE - Great Britain
Their only album features Bill Bruford on percussion. Should appeal to fans of PINK FLOYD. The project was conceived by Paul Fishman who would later go on to form the dance band Reflex. He was a student of electronic music and with his father produced this album.

In Search of Ancient Gods (76)

ACADEMIA - Sweden
A style that is very reminiscent of Mike Oldfield with it's symphonic guitar and synth driven compositions. While the compositions are not overly complex they are highlighted by the vocals of Sara Lofgren. Melodic and lyrical.

The Tale of Ocean Waves (97)

ACCIDENTE - Brazil
Mainly longish instrumental material influenced by PINK FLOYD and CAMEL.

Quebre Este Disco (8?), Gloomland (8?)

ACHARD, CYRIL - France
Musically here, each composition begins in a somewhat new-agey fashion but quickly develops with drums, guitars and synths into what can best be described as a combination of symphonic prog with fusion overtones.

Confusion (97)

ACHE - Denmark
A fusion of progressive keyboards with pop songs and harmonies.

De Homine Urbano (70), Green Man (71), Pictures from Cyclus 7 (76), Bla Som Altid (77)

ACINTYA - France
Formed in Nancy, Acintya only recorded one self-produced album with a symphonic style inspired by WAPASSOU in its use of violin and keyboard. The instrumental album features some elaborate and complex themes.

La Cite des dieus Oublies (78)

ACQUA FRAGILE - Italy
Sounds like early GENESIS. Two LPs produced by PFM and it shows in their sound.

Acqua Fragile (73), Mass Media Stars (74), Live in Amelia 1975 ( )

AD INFINITUM - United States
Former CATHEDRAL keyboardist Todd

Braverman decided to put together a prog band that would play classic seventies symphonic prog with all the analog keyboard sounds. The compositions are all pretty much over ten minutes in length but the writing emphasis was always to create well crafted songs with the emphasis on melody. He succeeds and the groups two vocalists share duties at the microphones. Great playing, lots of Mellotron and still 'hummable', what more can you ask for.

Ad Infinitum (98)

ADISOS - Greece
A symphonic prog band from the eighties who managed to retain a seventies sound in their style.

Aperis Nai Alla (84)

ADVENT - United States
Their music combines many elements of seventies progressive rock including STEVE HACKETT, HAPPY THE MAN and GENTLE GIANT. They typically avoid a harder edge, choosing instead to inject a lighter more whimsical tone to their work. The CD released in 1997 was actually a cleaned up version of their tape.

Advent (93 TAPE), Advent (97)

AELIAN - Italy
From the guitar style, drums and vocal harmonies, they show a strong YES influence.

The Watcher (92), Meeting...the Watcher Live (93), A Tree Under the Colours (00)

AETHER - Brazil
This is very lush symphonic progressive rock with the emphasis split equally between keyboards and guitar. While the songs tend to hover in the 5 minute range the band manages to pack a lot of elements into such a confined space and still seem to convey an epic scale sound in their compositions.

Visions (99)

AFTER CRYING - Hungary
Long tracks with music built around cello, synth, flute, piano, percussion and full orchestra. Vocals are in Hungarian. A very smooth, soft sound reminiscent of PINK FLOYD's Atom Heart Mother. Their influences also include KING CRIMSON and ELP which lead them to create some very powerful symphonic prog.

Overground Music (90), Megalazottak es Megaszomoritottak (92), Fold Es Eg (94), De Profundis (96), Elso Evitzed (97), After Crying 6 (97), Almost Pure Instrumental (99), Struggle for Life [Live] (00)

AFTERLIFE - United States
Trio whose musical efforts are to take the early RUSH sound and take it into the new millenium. Essentially guitar, bass and drums with just enough synth work to keep things interesting.

Afterlife (98)

AFTER THE FALL - The United States
This Connecticut trio performs on keyboards, guitars and drums. Their style is fairly placed in the neo-progressive realm although they display a wide range on influences. Any accessibility is overcome by great musicianship.

In a Safe Place (97), Before (98)

AFTERGLOW - France
A band on the Musea label creating neo-prog music in the vein of GENESIS, IQ and MARILLION.

Yggdrasil (95)

AGAMEMNON - Switzerland
Symphonic flavoured progressive rock band with one recording to their credit.

Parts 1 & 2 (81)

AGENESS - Finland
Post SCARAB neo-progressive rock with symphonic touches and heavier guitar work. Their sound contains a mixture of old and new GENESIS. If you enjoy listening to SPOCK'S BEARD, MAGELLAN or DREAM THEATRE you will very likely enjoy Ageness.

Showing Places (92), Rituals (96), Imageness (98)

AGITATION FREE - Germany
Michael Hoenig was with Tangerine Dream for a while. This group features very nice spacey electronics mixed with some dynamic progressive moments. Hints of early PINK FLOYD.

Malesch (72), 2nd (73), Last (76), Fragments (95), At The Cliffs of River Rhine [Live 74] (98), The Other sides of Agitation Free [1974] (98)

AGNUS - Argentina
A mixture on Andean folklore, male and female vocalists and improvised spacey PINK FLOYD musicianship. Keyboards are used sparingly, but show up throughout along with some well placed flute.

Pinturas y Espreciones (77)

AIN SOPH - Japan
Canterbury/fusion inspired progressive rock. Primarily instrumental music that ranges from high energy BRAND X to pastoral quiet moments in the style of PINK FLOYD.

A Story of Mysterious Forest (80), Hat & Field (86), Marine Menagerie (91), Five Evolved From Nine (93)

AIRBORNE - United States
Studio musicians with a style of music that easily falls into the pomp-rock style. A bit on the heavier side, but some interesting moments.

Airborne (79), Burn in Hell (83)

AIRBORNE - Canada
Band formed on Canada's West coast with a sound that is a progressive folk blend.

Songs for a City (77)

AIRBRIDGE - Great Britain
They came together in 1980 in Norwich, originally known as No Parallax. Most of the neo-prog material on their only album was written by COUNT LORENZO BEDINI. Keyboards get a back seat in this band, but it doesn't seem to hurt because the songs are written well.

Paradise Moves (83)

AIRLORD - Australia
Early GENESIS style with well written songs and carefully thought out arrangements. Good guitar work that is reinforced by layers of symphonic keyboards.

Clockwork Revenge (77)

AJALON - United States
A neo-prog Seattle band discovered by RICK WAKEMAN with a sound that's a cross between YES and MARILLION. As a three piece their prime influence comes from bands like RUSH but they've developed more of a sound akin to ARENA.

Light at the End of the Tunnel (96)

AKASHA - Norway
Sounds like early PINK FLOYD with lots of Mellotron. With a vocalist who sounds like GREG LAKE, some solid Mini-Moog lines and a strong GENESIS influence, symphonic fans will truly enjoy this.

Akasha (77)

AKKERMAN, JAN - Holland
Outstanding guitarist from FOCUS always manages to create a unique blend of classical, jazz and progressive rock styles.

Profile (72), Guitar For Sale (73), Tabernakel

(74), Eli (77), Jan Akkerman (78), Aranjuez (78), Live (79), A Phenomenon (79), 3 (79), Transparental (80), All in the Family (81), Meditation ( ), Can't Stand Noise (83), 10,000 Clowns on a Rainy Day (98)

AKRITAS - Greece
A band influenced by ELP but also sounding a bit like GRACIOUS. Over-all style is a mixture of jazz, fusion and progressive rock.

Akritas (73)

AKTUALA - Italy
Complex progressive jazz rock with a fair bit of ethnicity thrown in to boot.

Aktuala (73), La Terra (74), Tappeto Volante (76)

ALAMBIC - France
Instrumental progressive rock with great technique incorporating elements of folk and jazz. Fans of MINIMUM VITAL or QUIDAM will enjoy this band.

Numero Deux ( )

ALAMEDA - Spain
They sound a lot like TRIANA.

Alameda (79), Misterioso Manantial (80), Dunas (8?)

ALAN PARSON'S PROJECT - Great Britain
Parsons started out at Abbey Road Studios as one of their producers and managed to work a bit on the Beatles Abbey Road album and then PINK FLOYD'S Dark Side of the Moon. This gave him the confidence to go and work on his own projects which have always been collaborative efforts with Eric Woolfson. The two of them have assembled an ever changing group of studio people and performers to perform the material created. Great playing, usually lots of orchestra and some interesting concepts.

Tales of Mystery and Imagination (76), I Robot (77), Pyramid (78), Eve (79), Turn of a Friendly Card (79), Eye in the Sky (83), Ammonia Avenue (84), Vulture Culture (84), Stereotomy (85), Gaudi (87), Tales of Mystery and Imagination Remix (88), Try Anything Once (93), On Air (96)

ALARCEN, JEAN-PIERRE - France
The former guitarist of SANDROSE has produced two solo albums on which he fails to show his incredible talent as a guitarist but builds up a music centred on creating atmosphere. Like VANGELIS this is symphonic music with superb orchestral movements and delicate lyricism.

Jean Pierre Alarcen (78), Tableau No. 1 (80), Tableau No. 2 (98)

ALAS - Argentina
Trio consisting of keyboards, drums, bass and occasional guitar. A slight jazz influence makes the sound more than just an ELP clone. If you're a fan of LE ORME, TRIUMVIRAT you should enjoy this.

Alas (76), Pinta Tu Aldea ( )

ALASKA - United States
This Pennsylvanian duo on keyboards and drums create a very dramatic, panoramic style of symphonic progressive rock. Lots of longer tracks with plenty of twists and turns and even a little guitar work here and there, but overall you don't miss it. The vocals are very JON ANDERSON like but are well done.

Alaska (98)

ALBATROSS - United States
Mid-seventies group influenced by bands such as YES, GENESIS, Albatross played the standard analog synths of the time including Mellotron, crafting longish songs in fine symphonic style. They incorporated a varied tempo and mood throughout from mellow piano to dueling guitars and keyboards.

Albatross (76)

ALBION - Poland
A symphonic style that sounds a bit like TALE CUE and MARILLION. A combination of shorter melodic songs with some longer, more adventurous epics as well.

Survival Games (94), Albion (95)

ALEMBIC VIRTUAL - Italy
Dark and sinister heavy sounding neo-progressive rock with constant rhythm changes. A metallic approach that resembles the work of ASGARD and GARDEN WALL. The keyboards are heavy on string synths which tends to balance out the aggressive side.

Musikaal (94)

ALEPH - Australia
Classically influenced, dual-keyboard symphonic masters in the same style as SEBASTIAN HARDIE or AIRLORD. Lead vocalist Joe Walmsley's high pitched tenor voice bears a striking resemblance to JON ANDERSON. Somewhat similar to Yes but with more diverse and well assimilated influences.

Surface Tension (77)

ALFY BETZ - United States
An American keyboard player whose work leans more to classical than rock. Long tracks with one being a piano concerto and the other a symphony. Only a few guitar parts, but if you like your symphonic prog in the style of The Enid, you'll like this.

Symphony in B (97)

ALGARAVIA - Brazil
Influenced by the Discipline era KING CRIMSON this band also incorporates elements of Keith Tippett and Latin touches. There is also a strong jazz element. Imagine the band KRAAN only not as spacey.

Breve e Interminavel (96)

ALGEBRA - Italy
They go so far as to record medleys of GENESIS material, so that should give you a clue.

Storia Di un Iceberg (8?)

ALIAS RUDY - France
Dynamic and well played neo-prog material in the vein of SAGA, PALLAS or PENDRAGON.

ALICE - France
They were the first supergroup from France. As such they created a very original and melodious music which was refined and spontaneous, beautiful and touching with elegant and elaborate arrangements. It was part of the progressive rock trend of the early seventies represented by groups like Traffic and JETHRO TULL, but with it's own undeniable personality. After the first two albums the group members changed from being primarily French to Italian.

Alice (70), Arretez le Monde (72), La Mia Poca Grande (75), Cosa Resta um Fiore (78), Mi Chiamo Alice (79), Caponord (80), Cosa Testra (81), Azimut (82), Falsi Alarmi (83), Gloielli Rubati (85)

ALLEN, DAEVID
An Australian who lived in England, he was a founding member of Soft Machine, before he encountered passport problems which led him to Paris where he formed Gong. He remained with Gong until the release of Gong Est Mort in 1977, before venturing off to pursue his solo efforts. He rejoined Gong in the nineties.

Magick Brother, Mystic Sister (70), Banana Moon (71), Good Morning (76), Now Is The Happiest Time (77), N'Existe Pas (79), About Time (80), Divided Alien Playbox 80 (80), Alien In New York (83), Death Of Rock and Other Entrances (84), Don't Stop (84), Trial By Headline (88), Stroking The Tail Of The Bird (89), The Australia Years (90), She/Australia Aquaria (90), Seven Drones

(91), Magenta - She Made The World (93), Twelve Selves (93), Live (Recorded 1963) (93), Who's Afraid (93), Radio Sessions (94), Dreaming A Dream (95), Hit Men (96)

ALLIANCE - United States
Instrumental fusion in the vein of EDHELS. Some of the work falls close to synth based new-age pop.

Alliance (91)

ALLUMINOGENI - Italy
Trio sounding somewhat like THE NICE or ELP or countrymen THE TRIP and LE ORME on their first releases. The more recent material has a modern neo-prog feel to it with elements of YES' Big Generator. While not experimental, they have a good sound that is easy to get into.

Scolopendra (72), Geni Mutante (93), Green Grapes (94)

ALLUSA FALLAX - Italy
Gentle and romantic progressive rock with a classical feel incorporating many old synth sounds, Hammond organ, flute as well as acoustic and electric guitar. Musically they're in the same style as CELESTE with a vocalist similar to LOCANDA DELLA FATE.

Intorno Alla Cattiva Educazione (74)

ALPHA III - Brazil
Eurock says Amir Cantusio Jr. is one of the few composers in Latin America who refuses to compromise his musical ideas. He has at least nine albums to his credit, ranging from electronic to symphonic progressive rock. Classical guitar, organ, electric piano, synthesisers, etc., combine to create a mystical and primitive sound that's musically dense and filled with deeply emotional playing.

Mar De Cristal (84), Sombras (86), Argartha (87), Ruinas Circulares (88), Temple of Delphos (88), Aleph (89), The Seven Spheres (90), Voyage to Ixtlan (92), The Edge (9?)

ALPHA CENTAURI - France
This group's symphonic style is very reminiscent of groups such as ANGE, ATOLL, MONA LISA.

Alpha Centauri (76)

ALPHA RALPHA - France
This short lived group was founded by Claude Alvarez-Pereyre of Malicorne and Michael Mareska. They recorded one album with a number of guests including members of TAI PHONG. The music follows in the same vein as TAI PHONG and MIKE OLDFIELD. Everything from symphonic prog to floating jazz rock.

Alpha Ralpha (77)

ALPHATAURUS - Italy
Classic Italian progressive rock with a heavier almost bluesy feel. Similar to IL BALLETO DI BRONZO only a bit more symphonic like BANCO or PFM.

Alphataurus (73), Dietro L'Uragano [unreleased 1973] (92)

ALQUIN - Holland
Dual keyboard progressive rock with jazz leanings. Take a little bit of FOCUS or EARTH AND FIRE and mix in just a little SOFT MACHINE.

Marks (72), The Mountain Queen (73), Nobody Can Wait Forever (74), Crash ( ), Best Kept Secret (76), On Tour (76)

ALTAIR - Spain
ELP influenced keyboard and drum duo from Spain. Thinly produced material relying on two people to fill the sound. If you like ELP, ARSNOVA or CRAFT you'll appreciate this.

Altair (90), Fantasias y Danzas (98)

ALTER ECHO - Sweden
Seventies style symphonic prog band with great multi-part harmonies. The band

existed originally in the seventies but never recorded, they reformed in the nineties to re-record much of their old material. Vague influences include YES and GENTLE GIANT but nothing specific of these bands stands out.

Alter Echo (97)

ALTURA - United States
This Charlotte, North Carolina based four-piece are clearly in the progressive metal group. Good production from Robert Berry adds a nice touch. Fans of DREAM THEATRE should like this band.

Mercy (96)

ALVARADO, CARLOS - Mexico
The keyboardist of CHAC MOOL creates an electronic soundscape of complex prog.

Archivos ( )

ALVAREZ, SERGIO - Argentina
A solo artist who creates a grand symphonic prog that is reminiscent of YES, GENESIS and TERU'S SYMPHONIA. This mostly instrumental work features some very accomplished arrangements, melody and musicianship.

Pasaje A La Revelacion (99)

ALWAYS ALMOST - United States
Former members of ECHOLYN became STILL and then changed their name to Always Almost. This version of the band went in a more straight-forward approach to their music drawing on influences such as The Beatles, Steely Dan etc. This is great sounding material that is well played and still manages to sound like Echolyn at times, but contains the least amount of progressive influence yet.

God Pounds His Nails (97)

AMANITA - Italy
They've borrowed influences from the early to mid seventies with their heavy progressive style with a distinct JETHRO TULL touch. Musically there's lots of sombre tones with some interesting guitar, flute and organ interplay.

L'Oblio (96)

AMAROK - Spain
Beautiful melodic progressive rock with female vocals. Flowing material that is somewhat low key.

Els Nostres Petits Amics (94), Canciones De Los... (9?)

AMAZING BLONDEL - Great Britain
Great medieval folk sound with acoustic guitars and flutes. Fans of GRYPHON will appreciate this style.

Amazing Blondel (70), Evensong (70), Fantasia Lindum (71), England 72 (72), Blondel (73), Mulgrave Street (74), Inspiration (75), Bad Dreams (76), Live in Tokyo (77)

AMBER ROUTE - United States
One of the USA's best know space rock ensembles. Primarily a duo of Walter Holland on guitar and synth and Richard Watson on clarinet with other people augmenting on bass, guitar and drums etc. Their sound is somewhere between PINK FLOYD and early to mid Tangerine Dream.

Snail Headed Victrolas (80), Ghost Tracks (83),

AMBROSIA - United States
Formed in 1971 and based in the Los Angeles area. Their music can best be described as pop with progressive tendencies. Some of their albums feature progressive rock material, others will be more pop oriented. Overall very well played and written material. Somewhere I've Never Traveled was produced by Alan Parsons.

Some members appear on Parsons solo efforts.

Ambrosia (75), Somewhere I've Never Traveled (76), Life Beyond L.A. (78), One Eighty (80), Rhode Island (82)

AMENOPHIS - Germany
Symphonic keyboard work with stinging guitar with some interesting male and female vocalists. Some long instrumental passages where they really stretch out, particularly on their first album. Their second release was more commercial. Same vein as IVORY, FLYTE and GENESIS.

Amenophis (83), You & I (87)

AMERICAN TEARS - United States
Their music, especially on the first two albums tended to be a bit more adventurous. The music was always of a harder edge but along the lines of old STYX. Their third LP streamlined the sound a little.

Branded Bad (74), Tear Gas (75), Powerhouse (77)

AMON DUUL II - Germany
In many ways one of the first German rock bands to make any kind of impact on the rest of Europe. Many times described as foreboding and perhaps a little bleak, they forged their own sound based on a certain amount of electronic gadgetry. Some have put them in a group with bands like Faust and Can but in many cases they are much more melodic and musical.

Phallus Dei (69), Yeti (70), Dance of the Lemmings (71), Carnival in Babylon (72), Wolf City (72), Vive La Trance (73), Live in London (74), Hijack (74), Lemmingmania (75), Made In Germany (75), Pyragony X (76), Almost Alive (78), Only Human (78), Hawk Meets Penguin (83), Meeting With Men Machines (82), Surrounded by the Bars (93), Nada Moonshine # (95), Eternal Flashback (95), Kobe [Reconstruction's] (95)

ANABIS - Germany
Eurock says the group's sound is best characterised as gothic-progressive rock. Multi-keyboards and guitars are arranged into delicate overlapping melodic themes. This isn't simply a seventies progressive rehash. Symphonic prog that sounds like: ELOY, GENESIS.

Heaven on Earth (84), Wer Will (85), Theatre (88)

ANALOGY - Switzerland
German musicians who moved to Switzerland. The music holds a lot in common with EARTH AND FIRE featuring female vocals, flute and bluesy Hammond organ, that created a dark, symphonic sound.

Analogy (72), The Suite (7?)

ANCIENT VEIL, THE - Italy
Former members of ERIS PLUVIA producing a similar style of music.

The Ancient Veil (96)

ANCIENT VISION - United States
Symphonic progressive rock influenced by JETHRO TULL, MOODY BLUES or early KING CRIMSON. Some displays of instrumental prowess, good solid songs and fine arrangements.

The Vision (91), Focus or Blinders (95), Ancient Promises (97)

ANDERSON, BRUFORD, WAKEMAN, HOWE - Great Britain
One album that sounded like the best stuff YES had created to date, though they couldn't use the name. Even comes with a Roger Dean cover. Great stuff, more like Close to the Edge than their later stuff. This eventually led to the 'union' of all former members.

Anderson Bruford Wakeman & Howe (89), An

Evening of Yes Music Plus (94)

ANDERSON, IAN - Great Britain

Out on his own, Ian breaks away from JETHRO TULL but releases a very unconvincing first solo effort. His best work is still in the band. His first solo release reflected the digital synth sounds of the early eighties a little too much for some fans. By the time of his next solo in 1996 he established a more confident and mature style which includes outstanding lush keyboard orchestrations.

Walk Into Light (83), Divinities (96), The Secret Language of Birds (00)

ANDERSON, JON - Great Britain

Lead vocalist and primary composer of so many YES classics on his own with a very personal style.

Olias of Sunhillow (76), Song of Seven (80), Animation (82), Three Ships (85), City of Angels (88), Deseo (94), Change We Must (94), Angels Embrace (95), Toltec (96)

ANEKDOTEN - Sweden

A symphonic style similar to Red era KING CRIMSON especially on their first CD. Their sound includes a cellist who doubles on Mellotron. The music is filled with intense gothic images, and a somewhat heavy, melancholy feel. Highly recommended, and well received of the latest wave of progressive rock groups.

Vemod (93), Nucleus (95), Live EP (97), Official Bootleg Live in Japan (98), From Within (99)

ANGE - France

Probably the only French band along with MAGMA to have any amount of international attention. Ange's sound is nothing like MAGMA, instead it's built around Christian Decamps' vocal and theatrical presence. Great guitar and keyboard work that epitomise the best of symphonic progressive rock. Recommended.

In Concert (71), Caricatures (72), Le Cimetiere des Arlequins (73), Au dela du Delire (74), Emile Jacotey (75), Par le fils de Mandrin (76), Tome IV (77), En Concert (78), Guet Apens (78), Vu d'un Chien (80), Moteur! (81), A Propos de (82), La Gare de Troyes (83), Fou (84),

ANGEL - United States

Only the first album had any amount of material that could be called progressive rock. They sprang from the glam-rock era and quickly changed their sound to accommodate the masses. Much of their material is pomp stadium rock, very aggressive, guitar oriented. However there are some longer pieces with well placed Mellotron where the band's more prog side comes through.

Angel (75), Helluva Band (76)

ANGLABARN - Sweden

ANGLAGARD have been compared to this early seventies band, but some might disagree. Anglabarn's sound tends to be in a somewhat folkier MOODY BLUES style.

Anglabarn (73)

ANGLAGARD - Sweden

Early KING CRIMSON meets early GENESIS with loads of flute and Mellotron. They use a traditional line-up of instruments playing traditional seventies symphonic rock but recorded with a clean modern production quality. Hailed by many as one of the best progressive rock groups of the nineties.

Hybris (92), Epilog (94), Buried Alive (96)

ANGIPATCH - France

This line up of five musicians from Lyon plays a music in the same vein as ANGE or GENESIS. It's particularly built around the singers presence and the theatrical aspect of the compositions. Because of this style of writing music and this vocal emphasis, Angipatch's music evokes ANGE but also today's music by integrating modern sounds and instrumental combinations, laying the emphasis on the keyboards and using the studio as judiciously as possible.

Vie (81), Delirium (82)

ANGRA - Brazil

More on the progressive metal side but with great symphonic style. Progression magazine says they're a cross between Queensryche and the London Philharmonic. Lush orchestrations and plenty melody and musical dynamics.

Angel's Cry ( ), Holy Land (96), Holy Live ( ), Fireworks (99)

ANIMA - Brazil

Heavy techno guitar style that sounds like TISARIS or EDHELS. Some of their material leans more to the spacey side with a strong Meddle era PINK FLOYD influence, at other times a folk influence predominates with a sound similar to the pastoral moments of YES and GENESIS. Given so many influences they've incorporated them very well to produce their own sound.

Tempus Stetisse (9?), Singularities (96)

ANIMATOR - United States

From the Chicago area, this band play music very much in the style of RUSH, IQ or PENDRAGON. Not that they sound like them, it's just that they keep their roots firmly planted in the English symphonic prog school and play their own material.

Gallery (90)

ANKH - Poland

The music here is hard-edged, aggressive, with strong psychedelic influences. The progressive elements come from the violin, numerous keyboards and long multi-part arrangements in their compositions. If you enjoy bands like ANEKDOTEN, this will be of interest to you.

Bedzie Tajemnica (97)

ANNALIST - Poland

Their sound follows in the footsteps of COLLAGE.

Memories (94), Artemis (95), Eon (97)

ANOMALY - Holland

Instrumental progressive rock with strong fusion element. The band's influences are metal, fusion and classical but the metal portion really takes a back seat. Instrumental compositions that are complex yet accessible, interesting and challenging. Great guitar and keyboard interplay.

Anomaly (00)

ANOXIE - France

A group from Perigord, formed by Pascal Lachaize (keyboards) in July 82 and in the same vein as ANGE and BARCLAY JAMES HARVEST. Many tours in the South West of France before recording their first single in 1986 and a cassette titled The Returning.

Visa for another Earth SP (86), The Returning (86 TAPE), Pastales ( )

ANTARES - Italy

A mystical floating progressive sound.

Sea of Tranquillity ( )

ANOTONIUS REX - Italy

Post JACULA haunting progressive material.

Zora (77), Ralefun (78)

ANUBIS - France

Their style is influenced by both the old French school represented by ANGE, ATOLL, MONA LISA and by a mid eighties sound. The group's style is based on carefully selected vocal harmonies, the singers high voice and the energetic straight forward themes during which the guitarist plays some very original solos.

Anubis (83)

ANYONE'S DAUGHTER - Germany

Symphonic progressive rock in the truest sense of the word. They took their name from a song on DEEP PURPLE'S-Fireball LP. First appearance was in 1974. Their albums were sung in English initially, and later in German. A lot of instrumental work, with long songs and lots of keyboard and guitar interplay.

Adonis (79), Anyone's Daughter (80), Piktors Verwandlungen (81), In Blau (82), Neue Sterne (83), Live (84), Last Tracks (86)

APHRODITE'S CHILD - Greece

A band of musicians from Greece who wound up recording in France. This was one of the first groups for, at the time unknown, keyboard player VANGELIS. The band has a strong jazz rock influence.

End of the World (69), It's Five O'clock (69), 666 (72), Aphrodite's Child (75)

APOCALYPSE - Argentina

Symphonic neo-progressive rock with longer tracks, especially on the second release. Reminiscent of MARILLION on the vocal side and PINK FLOYD on the guitar side. Outstanding musicianship accompanied by some very effective song writing. As one might expect lots of twists and turns with longer songs unfolding in a very traditional manner. Their '97 CD is a reissue of their first LP.

Apocalypse (91), Perto Do Amanhecer (95), Aurora Dos Sonhos (96), Lendas Encantadas (91/97)

APOGEE - Germany

German multi-instrumentalist Arne Schafer creates symphonic-gothic progressive rock that holds up to scrutiny quite well. The songs, all in the ten minute range are very well composed and arranged.

The Border of Awareness (95), Sisyphos (98)

APOTEOSI - Italy

Melodic symphonic progressive rock with female vocals in the style of RENAISSANCE or CAMEL.

Apoteosi (75)

APPLETWIG CUTTER - Great Britain

Short-lived outfit based in the Northeast of England who produced music with all the hallmarks of early GENESIS and hints of JETHRO TULL. Instrumentation included flute and 12 string guitar. They released a cassette in the early eighties which included a mixture of short and long tracks.

AQUARELLE - Canada

Excellent prog-fusion band from Quebec. The violin and winds are particularly effective. Think of a jazzier version of MANEIGE.

Live at Montreux (79)

AQUELARRE - Argentina

Prog rock with a strong folk influence. You'll hear bits of JETHRO TULL, LE ORME and PINK FLOYD.

Aquelarre (74), Brumas (74), Siesta (7?), Lo Mejor (7?)

APRES LA PLUIE - France

Roger Lombardot, well known for having written the lyrics of one track (Dignite) off ANGE'S first album, wrote this album's lyrics. Here he makes a comeback with a line-up from Ardeche, singing the lyrics on this album which are halfway between political songs and theatrical with texts in the same vein as ANGE or MONA LISA.

La celebre ascension abyssale de Joseph Celsius (79)

ARACHNOID - France

A group who only produced one promising progressive rock album on which the influence of symphonic groups like KING CRIMSON, GENESIS or ANGE is incorporated into their own ideas which are perfectly mastered and exploited. Their music is a bit more dark and sinister.

Arachnoid (79)

ARAGON - Australia
Australia's leading neo-progressive rock band, with at least four recordings to their credit. In the style of MARILLION, with unique vocals. Their material is dramatic and bombastic full of energy, featuring tight musicianship with lots of guitar and keyboard interplay.

Don't Bring the Rain (87), The Meeting (92), Rocking Horse (92), Mouse (95), Mr. Angel (97)

ARAUJO, MARCO ANTONIO - Brazil
As a cellist, Antonio brings a strong classical sense to his music. Great use of acoustic guitar and other string instruments. Compositions tend to be longer with flute and even some horns.

Influencias (81), Quando a Sorte te Solta um Cisne na Noite (82), Entre um Silencio e Outro (83), Lucas (84)

ARC - Great Britain
Early seventies prog with a decidedly rock edge.

At This (7?)

ARC - France
A group in the same vein as ANGE, MONA LISA or SYNOPSIS with a lots of vocals and keyboards but with a certain lack of maturity.

Maquette (80)

ARCADELT - Italy
A symphonic style reminiscent of ERIS PLUVIA.

Enjoy (96)

ARCADIUM - Great Britain
Very early sounding prog with lots of organ, longer songs with a bit of psychedelic flavour.

Breath a While (69)

ARCANE - Spain
Very promising band with a cassette-only release, Suite Dreamside Stroll. Their style is similar to fellow countrymen GALADRIEL. They have good male & female vocals (in English).

Suite Dreamside Stroll (95 TAPE)

ARCANGEL - United States
Two members of Connecticut prog legend JASPER WRATH, Jimi Christian and Jeff Cannata went on to form this band. Similar to the STYX or ANGEL school of aggressive, pomp, progressive rock. They display some prog tendencies but for the most part focused the band in the stadium rock style.

Arcangel (83)

ARCANSIEL - Italy
A four piece progressive rock band who really play up a storm. Musically it's a bit less symphonic...a bit harder more intense instrumental approach.

Four Daises (88), Still Searching (90), Normality of Perversion (94)

ARCHITECTURAL METAPHOR - United States
They create a spacey-psychedelic-prog, and have been labelled as Boston's answer to Hawkwind and PORCUPINE TREE.

Odysseum Galactis (94), Creature of the Velvet Void (97)

ARCO IRIS - Argentina
Kind of folky-ethnic progressive rock with a bit of a PINK FLOYD sound.

Sudamerica (72), Manana Campestre ( ), Agitor Lucens V (75), Arco Iris (77)

AREA - Italy

Complex progressive music with a jazz-rock feel to it from a band led by Demetrio Stratos, who died of Leukaemia in 1979. Their style was experimental and eclectic, with the most unique feature being Stratos' flamboyant vocal style.

Arbiet Macht Frei (73), Caution, Radiation Area (74), Crac (75), Are(A)zione (75), Maledetti (76), Anto/Logicamente (76), 1978 Gli Dei se ne Vanno, Gli Arrabbiati Restano (78), Event '76 (79), Tic & Tac (79), Area '70 (80), Parigi - Lisbona (96), Gioria e Rivoluzione (96)

ARENA - Great Britain

Clive Nolan (PENDRAGON), and Mick Pointer's (MARILLION) latest effort. The compositions are grand in scale with a vocalist whose singing style is very similar to Fish. A MARILLION and PALLAS styled neo-prog sound. Good Moog, Mellotron, bass, guitar and drums on some symphonic epic scale long tracks with huge introductions, many shifts in tempo and style, culminating in even larger endings.

Songs From the Lions Cage (95), Pride (96), The Cry EP (97), Welcome to the Stage (97), The Visitor (98)

ARGENT - Great Britain

Their roots go back to the Zombies, where Rod Argent and Jim Rodford thought it would be nice to put together the next phase, thus Argent came into being in 1969. They ran the whole gamut of music from harder edged rock in extended material, into more cosmic keyboard oriented pieces. All through this Argent was ever present with the keyboards.

Argent (70), Ring of Hands (71), All Together Now (72), In Deep (73), Nexus (74), Circus (75), Counterpoints (76)

ARIA PALEA - Italy

Italian styled progressive rock with haunting flute and a very theatrical feel.

Zoicekardi'a ( )

ARK - Great Britain

Best described as almost neo-progressive. Not for the adventurous listener. Their material has some good moments, but borders on the edge of prog and is pretty mainstream AOR.

Spiritual Physics (9?)

ARKUS - Holland

Mellow progressive rock a bit like CODA. Arkus create a type of thematic symphonic sound similar to CAMEL'S Snow Goose era.

1914 (81), Win or Lose ( )

ARMAGEDDON - Germany

Heavy progressive rock.

Armageddon (70)

ARMAGEDDON - Great Britain

After leaving RENAISSANCE, Keith Relf created this group and their compositional style is decidedly heavier. The songs tend to longer and bear the pre-heavy metal influences of DEEP PURPLE etal. There's a good blend of guitars and the standard keyboards of the day. Keep in mind much of this bands style came from long bouts of jamming, unlike the structure of many prog bands.

Armageddon (75)

ARPIA - Italy

This trio from Rome produces symphonic progressive rock with lots of keyboards adding texture and harmony to the dynamic vocals.

Liberazione (95)

ARRAKEEN - France
Good sounding symphonic progressive rock with a female vocalist. As such the vocalist may remind some of RENAISSANCE while the music has an underlying harder edge similar to MARILLION.

Patchwork (90), Mosaique (92)

ARS NOVA - United States
New Jersey based band who released one mini album entitled Turning The Tide, influenced by GENESIS and MARILLION. Changed their name to NEPETHE.

Turning the Tide (9?)

ARSNOVA - Japan
Dynamic three piece female instrumental symphonic progressive rock with traces of ELP and CRAFT and a hint of RIO influences. Their complex, dramatic style features many abrupt tempo changes and may also bring to mind some of the more intense moments of ANGLAGARD.

Fear & Anxiety (92), Transi (94), The Goddess of Darkness (96), Six Singular Impressions (97), The Book of the Dead (98)

ART AND ILLUSION - Italy
Four-piece who produce a melodic, theatrical progressive rock fusing traditional folk instruments with a strong pop sensibility.

Monolith (9?), Seasons (95)

ART IN AMERICA - United States
Rather interesting band made up of two brothers, Chris & Dan Flynn along with their sister, Shishonee who along with providing back-up vocals plays the string harp. A unique sound. Songs are not overly complicated but reveal a certain depth in musicianship and lyrics. Perhaps best described as melodic-art rock with classical influences. Sound a bit like YES and ELP.

Art in America (83), From the Vaults (97)

ART ZOYD - France
Initially their music had a lot in common with the kind of music created by Frank Zappa but latter went on to create their own sound as purveyors of the Rock In Opposition sub genre. Their style is a neo-gothic avant symphonic music based on a 20th century European classical influence, very intricate and powerful.

Symphonie Pour Le Jour (76), Musique Pour L'oyssee (79), Generation Sans Future (80), Phase IV (82), Espaces Inquiets (83), Le Mariage du ciel et de l'enfer (84), Faust (96) Haxan (97)

ARTCANE - France
Strongly influenced by KING CRIMSON'S Larks Tongue in Aspic with an atmosphere reminiscent of this album in the search for tension and the development of anguish. The album also includes some long passages of floating symphonic rock evocative of PULSAR.

Odyssee (77)

ARTIE MESTIERI - Italy
Jazz-rock, fusion, although on their first release Tilt, the keyboards lean to a more symphonic style.

Tilt (74), Giro di Valzer per Domani (75), Live (90)

ASFALTO - Spain
A band with seven LP's to their credit, they created a symphonic prog sound with a harder edge.

Asfalto (7?), Al Otro Lado (78), Lo Mejor De (80)

ASGAERD - Great Britain
Sounds a lot like some material from the MOODY BLUES. A six man group from the west country, signed to the Moodies' Threshold label and produced by Tony Clarke hence the similarity in sound.

In the Realm of Asgaerd (72)

ASGARD - Italy
Predominantly symphonic neo-progressive rock material. They feature a strong IQ influence and are even vaguely reminiscent of MARILLION. After four albums their sound has taken on a bit more edge.

Gotterdammerung (91), Esoteric Poem (92), Arkana (92), Imago Mundi (93)

ASIA - United States
This band was in existence before the British supergroup came along. In fact the CD booklet explains how the British ASIA in no uncertain terms forced the US band to retire. Having said that, the music here is more pomp-progressive rock like STYX or KANSAS with lots of guitar and even some Mellotron.

Asia (78), Armed to the Teeth (80)

ASIA - Great Britain
Billed as a super group because of the history of it's members. The list of previous bands is long and illustrious; YES, Roxy Music, ELP, KING CRIMSON, Family etc.. Asia played a streamlined pomp progressive rock. Short songs with very restrained musicianship. It really sounded like they were trying very hard to get hit material under the pretext of progressive rock. In many respects, disappointing. Fortunately the material they started to produce in the mid nineties started to improve.

Asia (82), Alpha (83), Astra (85), Then and Now (91), Aqua (92), Live in Moscow (92), Aria (94), Archiva Volume I (96), Archiva Volume II (96), Live In Nottingham (97)

ASIA MINOR - France
A very elaborate and original style, built on the alternately delicate and fiery chords of the guitar, on the majestic flourishes of the flute and on the clear and nostalgic singing of Setrak Bakirel. One of the best symphonic progressive rock bands of the eighties. Sound like- JETHRO TULL, early KING CRIMSON, FOCUS or perhaps JADE WARRIOR.

Crossing the Line (79), Between Flesh and Divine (81)

ASLAN - Japan
A nineties era band who call themselves direct descendants of seventies YES. A quintet featuring a female lead vocalist. Most of their material consists of copies or covers of YES material.

ASTRAL NAVIGATIONS - Great Britain
Early rudimentary styled progressive rock with simple arrangements.

Holyground (70)

ASTURCON - Spain
Their sound is very much like Celtic influenced progressive rock.

ASTURIAS - Japan
Melodic progressive rock in the style of KENSO, HAPPY THE MAN and MIKE OLDFIELD. Their material comes close to being new age at times but not offensively so.

Circle in the Forest (88), Brilliant Streams (90), Cryptogram Illusion (93)

ATARAXIA - Japan
An original neo-progressive rock sound. While influenced by bands such as GENESIS, they have carved out their own style. Twin keyboards of mostly digital synths help create a lavish symphonic sound. If you like OUTER LIMITS, you'll like Ataraxia.

Adolescence of an Ancient Warrior (86)

ATAVISM OF TWILIGHT - United States
This Southern California band created powerful symphonic progressive rock with great flute and guitar. Their music is instrumental, moody and even contains elements of jazz. On a par with other American bands such as BABYLON and EASTER ISLAND!

Atavism of Twilight (92)

ATHENA -Italy

Multi-part songs with several different parts, changing time signatures, heavy metal guitar, pounding double bass drums, super fast unison parts, saw wave keyboard solos, long instrumental breaks between vocal section culminating in abrupt endings. Harder edged prog like DREAM THEATRE.

Inside the Moon (95)

ATILA - Spain

They produced two instrumental albums, with strong classical influences. The earlier material tends to be more guitar driven.

The Beginning of the End (75), Intencion (76), Reviure (78),

ATLANTIDE - France

A band that recorded on the Crypto label sounding somewhat like YES except there doesn't appear to be a keyboardist although the lead guitarist plays some Mellotron. Speaking of the guitarist he's got STEVE HOWE'S style mastered. Lot's of Close to the Edge references.

Atlantide (76)

ATLANTIDE - Italy

Early seventies heavy styled progressive rock.

Francesco Ti Ricordi (7?)

ATLANTIS - United States

Imagine a blend of ELP and UK that really works well together and that would be Atlantis. Lots of solid musicianship with powerful and intense compositions bearing all the hallmarks of symphonic progressive rock.

Atlantis (98)

ATLANTIS PHILHARMONIC - United States

Classic early seventies progressive rock similar to ELP.

Atlantis Philharmonic (74)

ATLAS - Sweden

Dual keyboard instrumental symphonic progressive rock with Mellotron. In the same style as HAPPY THE MAN, KENSO or FINCH. Complex rhythmic structures and ever changing styles.

Bla Verdag (78)

ATMO - Italy

Relaxed melodic folk influenced progressive rock. Beautiful playing and singing from Mario Gulisano (EDITH) on guitar and vocals. He has help from Salvo Condorelli on keyboards and drum programming. Sound is similar to HARMONIUM.

Atmo (92 TAPE), The Sea and the Dark Land ( )

ATOLL - France

Atoll is another major French progressive rock band. They were first influenced by ANGE but quickly went on to create their own personal sound and a specific style. They are perfect technicians and inspired soloists. Atoll produced an intricate, vigorous, energetic and inventive music, both wonderfully arranged and played. One of the best and one of the most original symphonic prog bands.

Musiciens-Magiciens (74), L'Araignee Mal (75), Tertio (77), Rock Puzzle (80), Cosmic Trips (81), Tokyo C'est Fini ( )

ATOME - France

A symphonic prog rock group influenced by ANGE and GENESIS. Rich well constructed music.

Les Herbes Bleues Iere Partie SP (78)

ATOMIC ROOSTER - Great Britain

Formed in late 1969 by Vincent Crane and Carl Palmer, their early prog sound was dominated by Crane's crunchy organ style. The trio consisted of guitar, drums and keyboards with Crane handling all the bass chores with his foot pedals. Musically the early albums have a lot in common with bands such as THE NICE and early ELP. Many consider Death Walks Behind You their most proggy LP.

Atomic Rooster (70), Death Walks Behind You (70), In Hearing Of...(71), Made In England (72), Nice 'N Greasy (73)

ATOMO PERMANENTE - Brazil

An offshoot of the band III MILENIO, creating a very melodic, softer progressive rock.

Projecao (93)

ATON'S - Italy

Elements of melodic folk and progressive rock. Not overly complex but interesting compositional style.

Caccia Grossa ( ), H ( ), Dr. Faust ( ), Klein & Wagner (96)

ATRIA - France

Spacey symphonic progressive rock material with strong keyboard and guitars throughout. Longer tracks with a neo-prog leaning featuring soaring melodies and strong symphonic swells.

Boulevard of Broken Dreams (92), Hide (96)

ATTILA & DAVE PROJECT - United States

This trio from San Francisco produce a psychedelic music that hearkens back to early PINK FLOYD. Other influences include some early sixties folk-rock and even a bit of light jazz. Very eclectic.

Songs of Innocence and Experience (96)

AUCAN - Argentina

Melodic, progressive folk sound that comes across like an early PFM mixed with a little KING CRIMSON. Nice symphonic melodies beautifully played and some wonderful instrumental interplay.

Aucan (77), Brotes del Alba (80)

AUDIO - Italy

Symphonic progressive rock from the early eighties. Hints of YES, GENESIS and GENTLE GIANT.

Audio (8?)

AUFKLARUNG - Italy

A five piece band featuring the lead singer from ASGARD. A full symphonic sound, acoustic guitars together with fat Mellotron-ish string synths all sound a bit like RED JASPER. All together the sound reminds you of STRAWBS Bursting at the Seams or Hero and Heroine.

Aufklarung (9?), De' La Tempsta...L'Oscuro Piacere (95)

AUGUST - Japan

Melodic symphonic prog that sounds like RENAISSANCE or SOLSTICE. There is no violin but there is an element of folk in their sound, as well as a female vocalist.

August (90)

AUNT MARY - Norway

Classic early style heavy progressive rock with lots of guitars and Hammond organ.

Aunt Mary (70), Loaded (71), Janus (73), Bluesprint ( ), Live Reunion ( )

AUTUMN - Great Britain

A group consisting of at least two former ENID members namely Nick Magnus (keyboards) and Robbie Dobson (drums) with others creating some excellent instrumental symphonic progressive rock. Layers of keyboards including Mellotron and some great drumming create a very vintage sound that is still breathtaking. If you enjoy listening to bands such as THE ENID, GREENSLADE or DRUID you'll enjoy Autumn.

Oceanworld (76/99)

AVALON - Canada

Their music is similar to bands like STYX or KANSAS. Harder edged progressive rock, but with a lot of attention to detail in some interesting songs. They produced one album and then faded from the scene.

Voice of Life (77)

AVE ROCK - Argentina

They produced two albums of progressive rock in a heavier style than most of their country-mates. With a sound that is dominated by organ and guitar they play in a style similar to CRUCIS or EL RELOJ.

Ave Rock (75), Espacios (77)

AVIARY - United States

One album with some nice pop that was closer to the art rock of 10cc at times than prog. Side one shows the band being a little more adventurous, side two is basically a return to stadium rock.

Aviary (79)

AVIATOR - Great Britain

Progressive rock with fusion featuring keyboard/woodwind work from JACK LANCASTER and guitar work from former MANFRED MANN'S EARTHBAND member Mick Rogers.

Aviator (78), Turbulence (80)

AVIOLINEE UTOPIA - Italy

Yet another Italian band that manages to incorporate the feel of the seventies prog bands but does it in a very convincing and personal style. You'll hear elements of early KING CRIMSON and VAN DER GRAAF. If you like bands such as FINISTERE or APIE-DI NUDI you'll appreciate the musical accomplishments here.

Aviolinee Utopia (97)

AWAKEN - United States

Upbeat compositions that have a pop-ish edge layered with good harmony. This is balanced by the fact that four of the five members take part in the dramatic keyboard playing. A melodic neo-prog style, fans of SPOCK'S BEARD will enjoy.

Awaken EP (96 TAPE)

AXIS - Greece

A Greek group which emigrated to France and produced a progressive rock album obviously influenced by the Canterbury school on certain tracks with this saturated organ sound dear to those groups. Some beautiful themes plus this superb organ sound. The group's music subsequently gave way to more variety. Sound like - EGG or CARAVAN.

Osanna (71), Axis (73)

AZAZELLO - Russia

With influences ranging from DREAM THEATRE to Fates Warning, you might expect this to be prog metal, but instead it's much more than that. There is a lot more going on in each of these tracks that will appeal to symphonic prog fans as well. There is also a charming quirky-ness that is most engaging. Sung in Russian there is a lot to enjoy here.

Black Day (00)

AYERS, KEVIN - Great Britain

One of the premier members of the Canterbury sound that emanated from the area of England that gives it's name to the music. Ayers spent time in SOFT MACHINE before going solo with a style that focused on his over the edge writing style and very characteristic voice. Material is on the edge of progressive rock with jazz and electronic influences.

Joy of a Toy (70), Shooting at the Moon (71), Whatevershebringswesing (73), June 1, 1974 (74), Confessions of Doctor Dream (74), Sweet Deceiver (75), Yes, We Have No Mananas (76), Rainbow Takeaway (78), That's What You get Babe (80), Diamond Jack and the Queen of Pain (83), Too Old to Die Young (98)

AYREON - Holland
Multi-instrumentalist Arjen Anthony Lucassen creates panoramic symphonic concept albums with guest vocalists and musicians galore. Sort of like ALAN PARSONS on steroids. This is dramatic stuff with the guitar solidly up front supported by a wall of keyboards. Bombastic at one moment, poignant the next and it all works perfectly.

The Final Experiment (97), Into the Electric Castle - A Space Opera (98)

AZAHAR - Spain
The group was formed by two Spaniards, a Uruguayan and an Egyptian. Their first LP had no drums, but did have two keyboard players and was every bit symphonic with lots of solos and time changes. It contained some southern Spanish or Flamenco influences. Their second LP added an American drummer of Spanish ancestry.

Elixir (77), Azahar (79)

AZABACHE - Spain
This band is an offshoot of the band AZAHAR. While their first album was somewhat similar to that group their second was really not progressive at all.

AZTEC JADE - United States
Straddling the line between symphonic prog and prog metal, this group manages to create epic compositions full of sweeping, panoramic bravado. Lots of great guitar and keyboard interplay spiced with lush orchestrations.

Frame of Mind (98), Paradise Lost [Compilation] (99)

BABE RUTH - Great Britain
Formed in 1971, they played a progressive rock that leaned heavily to the jazz side of things.

First Base (72), Amar Caballero (73), Babe Ruth (75), Stealin' Home (75), Kids Stuff (76),

BABYLON - United States
A mid-seventies symphonic band that hailed from Florida. Their original studio LP was inventive and well produced. The compositions, vocals and instrumental sections will remind the listener just how much of an influence early GENESIS were. The band tended to record longish multi-part songs with tons of keyboards including Mellotron. Live recordings made of the band at the time were eventually released in 1989.

Babylon (78), Night over Never (89), Better Conditions for the Dead (89)

BACAMARTE - Brazil
Great guitar work, is the highlight of this Brazilian symphonic progressive rock group. Fans of the classic Italian symphonic sound will enjoy this. Sound like YES, PFM and RENAISSANCE.

Depois Do Fim (83)

BACHDENKEL - Great Britain
Early English heavy progressive sound, that borrows a lot from the psychedelic style of bands like quicksilver Messenger Service.

Lemmings (73), Stalingrad (78)

BACHWEIB - Japan
A quartet featuring female vocals. The band describes themselves as wrapped in a symphonic sound filled with lyricism and romanticism. A nineties band that hearkens back to seventies style GENESIS and PINK FLOYD.

BADGER - Great Britain
Tony Kaye's efforts after leaving YES.

Badger performed material in long form but took it's influence from a solid R&B background. As a result the material is not at all complex, but rather simple with lots of pseudo jamming. Nice Roger Dean cover through.

One Live Badger (73), White Lady (74)

BAG - France
Symphonic fusion with lots of jazz and World Music influences.

Soudain L'Elephant (93)

BAGSBY, DAVID - United States
Solo artists Bagsby creates a blend of symphonic prog with elements of space-iness and Zappa-esque quirkyness.

Transphoria (99)

BAHAMAS - France
The music is sometimes cool, aerial, soft with a melancholic atmosphere and along with the inflections of the singers voices evoke a little of ANTHONY PHILLIPS first albums or PINK FLOYD and even some ATOLL or CAMEL when their music turns toward more complex developments.

Le Voyageur Immobile (76)

BAIRD, KEN - Canada
Baird's compositional style is sqaurely in the symphonic progressive pop realm. The addition of female vocalist Susan Fraser adds a nice touch. If you enjoy the work of ALAN CASE or ALAN PARSONS you'll find much to like here.

Fields (98)

BAKU - Germany
A neo-progressive rock sound with basic song structure and few tempo changes. A melodic style that is similar to some of the work of NOVALIS or SCHWARZBEIT.

Sequences of My Bequest (94), Dirge on the Pyre (9?)

BAMBIBANDA E MELODIE - Italy
This is an offshoot of GARYBALDI playing some decent progressive rock.

Bambibanda E Melodie (74)

BANANA - Argentina
Progressive rock in the style of early Italian bands. Material contains long tracks sounding like a cross between YES and PFM. Melodic singing with progressive style soloing from guitars and synths.

Aun es Tiempo de Sonar (78)

BANCO DEL MUTUO SOCCORSO [BANCO] - Italy
One of the finest Italian progressive rock bands ever. They formed in Rome in 1971 through the amalgamation of two top Italian bands Fiori Di Campo and Experience. Dual keyboards and operatic vocals are the highlights. The band focuses on very classically oriented piano and keyboard solos but are able to rock out much the same way PFM might. While the recordings seemed to end in the early eighties, the band continued to exist mostly doing live gigs, which they continue doing as of this writing.

Banco Del Mutuo Soccorso (72), Darwin (73), Io Sono Nato Libero (73), Banco (75), Garofano Rosso (75), Come in un'Ultima Cena (76), Di Terra (78), Canto Di Primavera (79), Campolinea (80), Messere si Domina Valle (91), Banco Del Mutuo Soccorso - Live (93), Papagayo Club '72 (94), Nudo (97)

BANDA ELASTICA - Mexico
Progressive with a blend of fusion and RIO influences. Complex and challenging material, fans of bands like Congreso and SAMLA will enjoy.

Banda Elastica (85), II (91), Los Awakates de Nepantla (94), Maquizocoatl (96)

BANKS, PETER - Great Britain
He first came to prominence as guitarist for Yes. After he was let go, he went on to form Flash who produced three LPs. He then moved on to a solo career.

Two Sides of Peter Banks (73), Instinct (93), Self Contained (95), Reduction (98), Can I play You Something (99)

BANKS, TONY - Great Britain
Keyboardist with GENESIS, Bank's solo efforts have not been a big hit with progressive rock fans. While the playing has been good, other than his first solo effort much of the material has been based on shorter pop oriented songs. see: GENESIS.

A Curious Feeling (79), The Fugitive (83), The Wicked lady (83), Soundtracks (86), Bankstatement (89), Still (91), Strictly Inc. (96)

BANZAI - Belgium
The band is led by the organ playing of Peter Torfs and features high-pitched tenor vocal harmonies. One known LP of pop influenced symphonic prog which features long instrumental passages accompanied by tight musicianship. Overall impression is something like YES' Time and a Word, only more complex with stronger keyboard parts.

Hora Nata (74)

BARCLAY JAMES HARVEST - Great Britain
Over the years they've tried all styles but mostly progressive rock, especially their early material. BJH sprang from the merger of two semi-pro bands in the Manchester area in the mid sixties. They feature a unique blend of Beatles harmonies with great guitar, keyboards and interesting lyrics. Many have simply labelled them a poor man's MOODY BLUES which is a great injustice. The band had some fun with that by writing a song using that as the title.

Barclay James Harvest (70), Once Again (71), Other Short Stories (71), Baby James Harvest (73), Everyone is Everybody Else (74), Live (74), Time Honoured Ghosts (75), The Best of... (75), Octoberon (76), Gone to Earth (77), Live Tapes (78), XII (78), Eyes of the Universe (79), The Best of...Vol. II (79), Turn of the Tide (81, Berlin Live (82), Ring of Changes (83), Victims of Circumstance (84), Face To Face (87), Welcome to the Show (90),

BARDENS, PETER - Great Britain
Former CAMEL keyboardist, however his solo career bears little resemblance to his work with them. His early material tended to focus on shorter blues tinged songs while his work in the eighties tended to be more spacey and almost new age keyboard oriented work.

The Answer (70), Peter Bardens (71), Write my Name in the Dust (71), Heart to Heart (79), Seen One Earth (87), Speed of Light (88), Watercolours (91)

BARRIO, JUAN DEL - Argentina
Classical based symphonic music.

El Alma De Las Cosas ( )

BARROCK - Italy
Symphonic progressive rock with two female lead singers. At times sounding very much like THE ENID, although not as intense.

L'Alchimista (90), Oxian (94)

BASS, COLIN - Great Britain
CAMEL's bassist goes solo and with help from Andy Latimer it's a treat. Much of the material here has all the hallmarks of CAMEL to some degree. Fans will certainly appreciate it.

As Far As I Can See [EP] (99), An Outcast of the Islands (99)

BASSO, LUCIANO - Italy
Symphonic keyboard work and composi-

tional style that may remind you of bands such as LE ORME, THE NICE. There are some nice violin and cello segments that hint of WAPASSOU. Fans of Italian prog, and others will enjoy his work.

Voci (76)

BATT, MIKE - Great Britain

Self trained keyboardist who spent time in the kids band The Wombles before going out on his own producing adventurous symphonic concept albums. Most of his work has him conducting, arranging and using full orchestras to augment more traditional rock instruments. The material tends to be somewhat jaunty and stop and go, but comprises some very strong, melodic themes and complex arrangements.

Schizophonia (77),Tarot Suite (79),Waves (80),Six Days in Berlin (81),Zero Zero (82)

BATTIATO, FRANCO - Italy

He made a string of experimental albums through the seventies. Started out as pretty straight forward pop, but by the release of Pollution he moved into the realm of SENSATIONS FIX and LE ORME only a little spacier. The next release was similar but with a more electronic flavour and even more so on his release Clic.

Fetus (72),Pollution (72),Sulle Corde Di Aries (73),Clic (74),L'Egitto Prima delle Sabbie (7?),M.lle Le Gladiator (75),L'era Del Cinghiale Bianco (79),Patriots ( ),La Voce Del Padrone (81),L'arca di Noe (82),Orizzonti Perduti (83),Mondi Lontanissimi (85),Fisiognomica (88),Giubbe (89),Caffe' de la Paix ( )

BAUMAN, PETER - Germany

Ex of Tangerine Dream, Bauman went on to produce a mixture of work that was either quite electronic or included symphony orchestra. Most recently he has formed a record label that produces new age music and other slightly progressive rock material.

Romance 76 (76),Trans Harmonic Nights (79),Repeat Repeat (81)

BEAUGARDE - Belgium

Rather simple arrangements of something like SUPERTRAMP sounding like ELO.

Solo Mortale (79)

BEDFORD, DAVID - Great Britain

He worked with KEVIN AYERS as arranger before joining his group on keyboards for a couple of albums. Went on to produce a number of solo efforts and work with other prominent people in the progressive rock world. Bedford's work tends to concentrate on full orchestras playing material bordering on progressive and the orchestrated avant-garde.

Stars End (74),Tubular Bells (75),The Rhyme of the Ancient Mariner (75),The Odyssey (76),Instructions For Angels (77), Great Equatorial (95)

BE-BOP DELUXE - England

Band leader Bill Nelson came out of a folk background to create a rather interesting art-rock group based around his unique pop song writing sensibilities and guitar playing.

Axe Victim (74),Futurama (75),Sunburst Finish (76),Modern Music (77),Drastic Plastic (77),Live in the Air Age (77)

BEGGAR'S OPERA - England

Hailing from Scotland their early material was very classically oriented. Their later material, where they started becoming more proficient at writing, began taking on more of a unique sound. Big users of the Mellotron, which showed up nicely on their third album.

Act One (70),Pathfinder (72),Waters of Change (71),Get Your Dog Off Me (73),Sagitary (76),Beggars Can't Be Choosers (79),Lifeline ( )

BEGGAR'S FARM - Italy
A nineties band who recorded on the harder edged Black Widow label with a seventies sound.

Beneath the Moon of Ilsacon (9?)

BELAIR - Germany
A wall of keyboard sound with dual guitars and flute. Some longish tracks where the instrumental virtuosity shines. A dreamy symphonic progressive rock.

Welcome Home (86), A Golden Dream (8?), The Sleeping Beauty (87)

BELLAPHON - Japan
Instrumental symphonic progressive rock reminiscent of FINCH or the Moonmadness period CAMEL. A strong emphasis on melodic content and heavy interplay between guitars and keyboards.

Firefly (78), Delphi ( )

BEN - Great Britain
Early seventies band whose style is in the progressive fusion end of things.

Ben (71)

BERKERS, JERRY - Germany
Solo work featuring most of the musicians from WALLENSTEIN.

Unterwegs ( )

BERRY, ROBERT - United States
Most remembered for his stint in 3 with KEITH EMERSON and Carl Palmer. His work since then may be of interest to fans because of his associations. Fans of GTR and 3 will like his work.

Pilgrimage to a Point (93)

BHATIA, AMIN - Canada
Solo keyboard artist who produced a very dramatic, symphonic album called The Interstellar Suite. The LP is a virtual soundtrack for an imaginary movie. Tons of keyboards and sampled sounds.

The Interstellar Suite (87)

BIBBO, PIERPAOLO - Italy
Good sounding material featuring organ, violin and flute.

Diapson (8?)

BIDDULPH, RICK - Great Britain
Former roadie for several Canterbury bands strikes out on his own multi-instrumentalist project. The material on his first solo outing, Second Nature is more relaxed sounding a bit like PETER BARDENS mid-eighties work. Several tunes have a dark and mysterious feel while others have the traditional Canterburian jazz feel.

Second Nature (94)

BIG BIG TRAIN - Great Britain
Melodic progressive rock. Nice marriage of pop and progressive styles in the vein the later IQ and PENDRAGON.

From The River To The Sea (91 TAPE), Goodbye to the Age of Steam (94), English Boy Wonders (98)

BIG ELF - United States
Crunchy organ, and long songs that hearken back to the early days of prog and bands like DEEP PURPLE.

Closer to Doom (97)

BIG PICTURE - United States
Neo-progressive rock sound, that is firmly planted with an eighties YES influence. Medium length songs with abbreviated solo sections with an emphasis on melodic hooks.

Big Picture (93)

BIGLIETTO PER L'INFERNO - Italy

Classic Italian symphonic progressive rock. Their first album was a little on the heavier side, while the second has more emphasis on the organ and generally a more progressive feel. In the style of PFM. The second LP was recorded in 1974 but not released until 1991.

Biglietto Per L'Inferno (74), IL Tempo Della Semina (74/91)

BIKINI - Hungary

They sound similar to OMEGA.

Bikini (86)

BI KYO RAN - Japan

Virtually unknown in the USA, they fully deserve the title the Japanese KING CRIMSON circa the Red era. Fabulous Fripp-style guitar work, excellent drumming and incredible arrangements make their records worthwhile. Their later work started to display more of a Zeuhl influence.

Bi Kyo Ran (82), Parallax (83), Who-Ma (88), Fairy Tale-Early Live Vol. 1 (87), Wo Ma-Live Vol. 2 ( ), Ran - Live Vol. 3 ( ), Madoromi - Live Vol. 4 ( ), Go-Un (95), Deep Live (96), A Violent Music (98)

BIRDSONGS OF THE MESOZOIC - United States

Multiple keyboards and saxes, along with guitar drive the sound here. The band combines elements of classical, progressive, avant-garde and hints of industrial to create a unique urgent sound. A bizarre and unusual sense of composition.

Magnetic Flip (84), The Beat of the Mesozoic EP (86), Sonic Geology (88), Faultline (89), Pyroclastics (92), The Fossil Record (93), Dancing on A'A (95)

BIRTH CONTROL - Germany

Along with AMON DUUL II, these guys are perhaps the most prolific German progressive rock band with seventeen releases to their credit. Their style centres aroundswirling organ and strong vocals. As you might imagine an earlier, simpler progressive rock sound.

Birth Control (69), Operation (71), Hoodoo Man (72), Rebirth (74), Live (74), Plastic People (75), Backdoor Possibilities (76), Increase (77), Titanic (78), Live 79 (79), Deal Done at Night (80)

BIXO DA SEDA - Brazil

Alternates between straight ahead rock and prog. A bit inconsistent, but the good cuts are quite good.

Bixo Da Seda (76)

BLACK JESTER - Italy

Nineties band who create a heavy neo-progressive rock that borders on progressive metal.

Diary of a Blind Angel (92), Welcome to the Moonlight (94), The Divine Comedy (97)

BLACK SEPTEMBER - United States

Keyboard oriented progressive rock in the ELP direction featuring MICHAEL WEST. No guitars, rather it's keyboards, violin, sax and drums all the way, produced by MASTERMIND'S Bill Berends.

Black September (94)

BLACK SPIRIT - Italy

A seventies era band who create heavy sounding progressive rock.

Black Spirit (7?)

BLACKWATER PARK - Germany

Organ driven heavy prog from the early seventies.

Dirt Box (71)

BLACK WIDOW - Great Britain
Heavy sounding early seventies prog band with long songs, simple arrangements and flute work similar to JETHRO TULL.

Sacrifice (70), Black Widow (70), Three (71)

BLACKFOOT SUE - Great Britain
Early progressive rock sound with predominant rock overtones, particularly their on their second LP.

Nothing to Hide (73), Strangers (74), Gun Running (75)

BLAKULLA - Sweden
The sound here is a symphonic prog blend of YES and KAIPA. Imagine the high tenor in the vocals ala JON ANDERSON and the guitar work of ROINE STOLT mixed with some keyboard work from a heavy organ, blend together with some folk and classical influences and you'll know what to expect here. The CD reissue of the 1975 LP contains some unreleased material.

Blakulla (75/97)

BLEZQI ZATSAZ - Brazil
A four-piece symphonic progressive rock group with the emphasis on keyboards. The keyboardist is FABIO RIBEIRO and he plays a mountain of keyboards in a style heavily influenced by RICK WAKEMAN. The music is all instrumental, massive and bombastic and at times remind you of UK or ARSNOVA and at other times dreamy like VANGELIS.

Rise and Fall of Passionate Sanity (92)

BLIND OWL - United States
One of the first neo-progressive rock releases in America. It has little in common with the British neo-prog sound. Full of swirling keyboards with hints of STARCASTLE, ASIA and even some of the more prominent Italian bands of the seventies like BANCO and RDM.

Debut at Dusk (87)

BLOCCO MENTALE - Italy
A textured melodic progressive rock, in a symphonic style similar to CELESTE.

IIOA (73)

BLODWYN PIG - Great Britain
Formed by original JETHRO TULL guitarist and produced a mixture of blues with hints of early progressive rock with some jazz flavour thrown in by JACK LANCASTER.

Ahead Rings Out (69), Getting to This (70), The Modern Alchemist [Live] (97)

BLONDE ON BLONDE - Great Britain
An unusual band with an even more unusual blend of mostly rock with some classical influences. A fine example of early English style progressive rock.

Contrasts (69), Rebirth (70), Reflections on a Life (71), Blonde on Blonde (72)

BLOQUE - Spain
The band released four LP's, with their third one El Hijo Del Alba being the most progressive. They tended to jump from straight forward symphonic progressive to hard rock. Like GRANADA or IBIO.

Bloque (78), Hombre, Tierra Y Alma (79), El Hijo Del Alba (80), Musica para La Libertad (81)

BLUE MOTION - Switzerland
Post CIRCUS dual keyboard progressive rock.

Blue Motion (80)

BLUE ROSE - France
Essentially a three piece under the guidance of violinist and vocalist David Rose, they come from the CAFE JACQUES school of art rock, pop with prog undertones. Not overly adventurous.

Blue Rose (83)

BLUE SHIFT - United States
They create a musical symphonic prog style similar to YES circa 90125 or Big Generator, including a vocalist with the same tenor tone. Their material is modern, well played and benefits from superior arrangements. Their advertising claims they record in the tradition of the masters of progressive rock.

Not the Future I Ordered (98)

BLYNDSIDE - Great Britain
Nineties neo-progressive rock of a heavy nature. Influences include RUSH and YES circa Big Generator.

Where Extremes Meet (91 TAPE), Into the Storm of the Eye (9?)

BODIN, TOMAS - Sweden
Keyboardist for THE FLOWER KINGS, whose solo material could easily be labelled a Flower Kings instrumental effort, only some what more eclectic. Epic material played in grand style.

An Ordinary Night in My Ordinary Life (96)

BODKIN - Great Britain
Early seventies progressive rock band whose sound is dominated by heavy organ work.

Bodkin (72)

BODY - Great Britain
Spacey progressive rock.

The Body Album (81)

BOFFO, JEAN PASCAL - France
Rich synthetic textures with the extensive use of wind and string instruments. Lush and orchestral material that retains enough of an edge. His early material is in the same category as STEVE HACKETT and ANTHONY PHILLIPS. The later material contains much stronger elements of Zeuhl.

Jeux de Nains (86), Carillons (87), Rituel (88), Nomades (94), Offrande (95), Vu Du Ciel (98)

BONDAGE FRUIT - Japan
A cross between HAPPY FAMILY and KENSO. No keyboards, but the inclusion of eclectic instrumentation reinforces the Canterbury-ish nature of their material. A strong ethnic, jazz and Zeuhl influence is also present in their music.

Bondage Fruit (95), Bondage Fruit II (96), Recit (97), IV (99)

BONFIRE - Holland
Crazy progressive rock like SUPERSISTER. Instrumental material in the GENTLE GIANT vein with hints of FINCH and FOCUS.

Bonfire (74), Bonfire Goes Bananas (75)

BOOK OF HOURS - Sweden
They create a musical style that is similar to bands like ANEKDOTEN that have been influenced Red era KING CRIMSON. They feature two guitars, but still have plenty of room for organ and Mellotron.

Art to the Blind (99)

BOOKER, ANDREW - United States
Solo multi-instrumentalist Booker produces a well crafted sound of mostly instrumental prog.

Ahead (96)

BOOZ, EMMANUEL - France
The title of one of his songs, La Symphonie Catastrophique is fairly descriptive of his style. KING CRIMSON meets Zappa meets UNIVERS ZERO with highly emotional French vocals a la ANGE. Not as inaccessible as you may think. Powerful and

certainly interesting music.

Le Restaurant d'Alice (70), Le Jour ou les Vaches (74), Clochard (76), Dans Quel etat j'erre (79),

BORAG THUNG - Great Britain
A band with superior musicianship, who released a ten track cassette and a live tape in the mid eighties. Their sound is very GENESIS influenced, especially in the keyboard department. A good quality production with long instrumental sections and lyrics of a more Christian nature.

BORNE - Spain
An instrumental fusion group with southern Spanish influences. Some jazz, but otherwise some very progressive moments.

Exprime la Naranja (79)

BORT, EDUARDO - Spain
Progressive rock classic with lots of Mellotron featured.

Eduardo Bort (74)

BOTTEGA DELL'ARTE - Italy
Soft melodic symphonic progressive rock.

Bottega Dell'Arte ( )

BOUD DEUN - United States
Virginia based band creating a guitar, bass, drums and violin instrumental progressive sound in the DIXIE DREGS and KING CRIMSON vein with a strong Mahavishnu Orchestra influence, melding together in a jazz-rock style.

Fiction and Several Days (95), Astronomy Made Easy (97), The Stolen Bicycle (98), A General Observation [Live] (98)

BRAINDANCE - United States
What started out as a one-off studio project turned into a band that fuses the technical bombast and complexity of progressive metal, the delicacy and intricacy of atmospheric new age ambience and the breath-taking cerebral spectre of gothic mayhem and madness. That's what their web-page says. Their music has elements of PETER GABRIEL, YES and others to form an original sound still their own.

Shadows (94 TAPE), Fear Itself (95)

BRAINFOREST - United States
Nineties band who create a classic seventies progressive rock sound with Mellotron intertwined with guitar, bass, drums and organ.

Brainforest (95)

BRAINSTORM - Germany
Complex progressive rock incorporating elements of SOFT MACHINE and CARAVAN.

Smile a While (72), Second Smile (74)

BRAND X - Great Britain
A seemingly never ending revolving door of musicians that included Phil Collins, Peter Robinson, Percy Jones and others playing a mixture of a little progressive rock with a healthy dose of fusion jazz. Some great musicianship and interesting songs.

Unorthodox Behavior (76), Moroccan Roll (77), Livestock (77), Masques (78), Product (79), Do They Hurt (80), Is There Anything About (82), X-Communication (92), Manifest Destiny (97), Missing Period (98)

BRASSE - Holland
Nineties band led by Marc Brasse's keyboard style, whose work is reminiscent of ALAN PARSONS or PINK FLOYD. Noted for strong melodies and complicated arrangements.

Pawn (93), Sand, Water and Heroes (9?)

BREAKWIND - Japan
Nineties band with members coming from other hard prog bands Seilane and

Lavender so the musicianship is top-notch. The material tends to be more upbeat featuring some great Hammond and Moog playing.

BREATH OF GOD - United States

The newspaper called them a mixture of '70s progressive rock and Jesus Christ Superstar which just about paints the picture. The inclusion of a hot violinist gives some of their material a KANSAS feel. Many of their compositions feature some intricate keyboard work mixed with some fiery guitar work...one minute they rock and the next they breathe.

Breath of God (99)

BRETT, PAUL[SAGE] - Great Britain

Guitarist who started out on the folk side of things, formed a band that started producing more rock oriented pieces. Then after Sage disbanded Brett carried on working on some major progressive rock concept LP's. In fact some might say his later material is the best yet.

Paul Brett Sage (70),Jubilation Foundry (71),Schizophrenia (72),Paul Brett (73),Clocks (74),Phoenix Future (75),Earthbirth (77),Interlife (78),Eclipse (79)

BRICE, COLIE - United States

Multi-instrumentalist Brice creates grand, panoramic symphonic prog that is mixed a liberal dose of psychedelic influences and it's very impressive. Lots of orchestral dynamics, a mix of soft and aggressive, electric and acoustic it's all here to enjoy.

Chameleon (99)

BROGUIERE, PATRICK - France

Solo artist performing everything from keyboards to drum programming. His first recorded work was loosely based on King Arthur and sounded like some of MIKE OLDFIELD'S early work. The music is wrapped in the uniquely romantic French symphonic perspective.

Broceliande (94), Icones (96), Mt. Saint Michel (98)

BROSELMACHINE - Germany

Early seventies progressive folk sound.

Broselmachine (71)

BROWN, ARTHUR - Great Britain

A product of England's psychedelic summer of 1967. His most progressive material came when he formed KINGDOM COME in the early seventies. Lots of Mellotron and early synthesiser in epic songs during this phase courtesy of keyboard virtuoso Vincent Crane who went on to found ATOMIC ROOSTER.

Crazy World of Arthur Brown (68),Galactic Zoo Dossier (72),Journey (72),Kingdom Come (73),Dance (75),Lost Ears (76),Chisholm in My Bosom (77),Faster than the Speed of Sound (80),Requiem (82)

BRUFORD - Great Britain

Drummer extrordinaire Bill Bruford, played with GENESIS, YES, KING CRIMSON, UK, need we say more. On his solo work, there is a decided edge of fusion blended with progressive rock. Never boring. Much of Bruford's later solo work took on much more of a distinct jazz flavour and is omitted here.

Feels Good to Me (77), One of a Kind (79), The Bruford Tapes (79), Gradually Going Tornado (80)

BUBU - Argentina

A more complex progressive style with strong classical influences that'll put you in the mind of MAGMA or KING CRIMSON.

Anabelas (78)

BUCCHERI, FRANCESCO - Italy
Electronic progressive rock with lots of Mellotron. In the Klaus Schulze/Tangerine Dream/VANGELIS style.

Journey (79), Second Journey [Unreleased 83] (9?)

BUDGIE - Great Britain
A hard rock band who produced a couple of albums of hard-edged early sounding progressive rock.

Squawk (72), Never Turn Your Back (73)

BUDKA SUFLERE - Poland
Polish progressive rockers who start out real strong. First couple albums are real good.

Cien Wielkiej Gory ( ), Przechodniem Bylem Miedzy Wami ( ), Na Brzegu Swiatla ( )

BULLFROG - Germany
They produced a harder prog sound that is sometimes compared to JANE.

Bullfrong (76), High In Spirits (77)

BUON VECCHIO CHARLIE - Italy
Progressive rock sound similar to OSANNA.

Melos (71/90)

BURANT, ALAN - Canada
This is well executed symphonic neo-progressive rock with some prog-metal elements thrown into the mix, particularly in the vocal department. If you enjoy listening to the more streamlined musical compositions of bands like SAGA you'll appreciate what's going on here.

Occam's Razor (99)

BURNESSENCE - Great Britain
Formed in the mid eightiesto promote a solo album by Tim Burness. A second group effort followed. Influences include GENESIS, FLOYD, STEVE HILLAGE and STEVE HACKETT.

BURNING RED IVANHOE - Denmark
Late sixties and early seventies jazz-rock spotlighting more of a psychedelic style with just a few early progressive influences.

M144 (69), Burnin' Red Ivanhoe (70), 6 Elefantskovcikadeviser (71), WWW (71), Miley Smile (72), Right On (74), Burnin' Live 1970/72 (74)

BUSH, KATE - Great Britain
First discovered by DAVE GILMOUR in 1975. Bush's work is as adventurous as much of the material coming from PETER GABRIEL, to whom she's sometimes compared with. Thinking music, for the thinking person, lyrically and musically. Bush is a consummate performer/artist.

The Kick Inside (78), Lionheart (78), The Live EP (79), Never For Ever (80), The Dreaming (82), The Hounds of Love (85), The Whole Story (86), The Sensual World (89), The Red Shoes (93)

BYZANTIUM - Great Britain
Early YES sound with a hint of country influence.

Byzantium (72), Seasons Changing (72)

CAFEINE - France
Highlights of this band include some good musicianship and better than average compositional skills. Promising symphonic progressive rock band rooted in the style of ANGE or ATOLL but with a nineties flair.

La Citadelle (94)

CAFE JACQUES - Great Britain
A unique pop and art rock band with progish undertones. With the assistance of Phil Collins they produced two LPs with a sim-

ple BRAND X style and a vocalist who resembles KEVIN AYERS. The music is interesting although not overly adventurous.

Round the Back (77), Cafe Jaques International (78)

CAFEWIEN - Italy
Four piece consisting of guitar, bass, drums and keyboards with guest sax work who create a jazz-rock fusion inspired progressive rock, sounding like BRAND X or mid period KENSO.

Terrae Motus (94)

CAI - Spain
A group from Southern Spain who released three LP's. The first two were classic symphonic Spanish prog while the third wound up sounding very commercial. These guys have been described as a jazzier TRIANA. You'll hear lots of keyboards with plenty of folk influences.

Noche Abierta (80), Cancion De La Primavera (82)

CAIRO - United States
Dramatic and epic scale melodic compositions with plenty of longInstrumental selections from a band influenced by YES, ELP, SPOCK'S BEARD and PENDRAGON. A very satisfying, modern bombastic prog sound over all.

Cairo (94), Conflict and Dreams (98)

CALIFE, I - Italy
Complex progressive rock and usually, highly recommended.

Fiore di Mentallo (73)

CALLIOPE - Italy
Symphonic progressive rock with lots of Mellotron. Like PFM but more intense. The first two albums are in a similar style of GARDEN WALL and EZRA WINSTON. Their third release added a female vocalist along the lines of a timid ANNIE HASLAM. Their music is now in the realm of ERIS PLUVIA or KERRS PINK.

La Terra Dei Grandi Occhi (92), Citta di Frontiera (93), La Madrigale Del Vento (95)

CAMEL - Great Britain
They came together in the early seventies and their first break was to be included on the charity benefit album GREASY TRUCKERS 2 which featured an entire side of live CAMEL, but they really hit the big time with the release of The Snow Goose. Their music is instrumentally based, with vocals used sparingly. This is certainly true of their early releases. Their material focuses on their talents as instrumentalists in the development of melodic passages and extends the members to their limits in the more free, almost improvised sections.

Camel (73), Mirage (74), The Snow Goose (75), Moonmadness (76), Rain Dances (77), A Live Record (78), Breathless (78), I Can See Your House From Here (79), Nude (81), The Single factor (82), Stationary Traveller (84), Pressure Points Live (84), Echoes (91), Dust and Dreams (92), On the Road 1972 (93), On the Road 1982 (94), Never let go [Live] (94), Harbour of Tears (96), Coming of Age (98), Rajaz (99)

CAMPO DI MARTE - Italy
Searing flutes and fuzz guitar dominate but the material still holds a rich romantic feel in the style of early seventies Italian progressive rock.

Camp Di Marte (73)

CANARIOS - Spain
They performed a classical electronic style of fusion. Some have said they were the most advanced fusion of rock and classics for the time. They take up where RDM left off with Contamination.

Ciclos (74)

CAN - Germany
Leading edge, avant-garde group from Germany who set the tone for a host of bands that would follow in the musical genre that's become known as Kraut Rock. Their music has less in common with rock than it does with 20th century classical composition. Instead of recording short concise pop songs, Can experimented with electronic music, non-traditional music, noise and everything else they could cram into the studio. They created an aggressive, challenging and experimental music with a sparse style, repetitive rhythms and simple harmonies. Never achieving more than cult status with a group of loyal fans, the band split in 1978.

Monster Movie (69), Deep End (70), Tago Mago (71), Ege Bamyasi (72), Future Days (73), Soon Over Babaluma (74), Landed (75), Opener (76), Flow Motion (76), Saw Delight (77), Out Of Reach (78), Can (79)

CANO - Canada
Melodic ethnic influenced folk music with hints of progressive rock. Their early material contains a bit of Mellotron.

Tous Dans L'meme Bateau (76), Au Nord De Notre Vie (77), Eclipse (78), Rendezvous (79), Spirit of the North (80), Visible (85)

CAPITOLO 6 - Italy
Early progressive rock material inspired by JETHRO TULL.

Frutti Per Kagua (72)

CAPSICUM RED - Italy
Classical progressive similar to TRIADE and LE ORME.

Appunti per Unidea Fissa (72)

CAPUANO, ENZO - Italy
Unusual symphonic progressive rock that resembles a movie soundtrack. While the vocals are rather formulaic in the pop style, the instrumentals are more in the classic Italian prog style with dramatic key changes and rich analog synth sounds.

Storia Mai Scritta (75)

CARAVAN - Great Britain
In the late sixties THE WILDE FLOWERS split in two spawning CARAVAN and SOFT MACHINE. CARAVAN helped create a musical style that has become known as the Canterbury sound, a name that has stuck to this sub-genre ever since. Surrealist lyrics, humour, and a progressive style that incorporated elements of PROCOL HARUM and SOFT MACHINE, Canterbury was a jazzy-classical-folk-ish sound that was unique. Definitely one of the founding progressive rock bands.

Caravan (68), If I could Do it Again (70), In the Land of Grey and Pink (71), Waterloo Lily (72), For Girls Who Grow Plump in The Night (73), Caravan and The New Symphonia (74), Cunning Stunts (75), Blind Dog at St. Dustans (76), Better By Far (77), The Album (80), Back to Front (82), The Battle of Hastings (95), All Over You (96), Songs for Oblivion Fishermen (98), Etherway (98)

CARAVAN OF DREAMS - Great Britain
Richard Sinclair's version of his former band.

Richard Sinclair's Caravan of Dreams (92)

CARDEILHAC - Switzerland
An early, heavier progressive rock sound similar to GAA or KAPPUTER HAMSTER.

Cardeilhac (71)

CARGO - Holland
Heavy sounding progressive rock with some long winded psychedelic guitar passages. Perhaps a little more like Golden Earring.

Cargo (72)

CARMEN - Spain
Imagine a bit of JETHRO TULL, CURVED AIR, and a lot of Flamenco styled music all mixed together.

Fandangos In Space (73), Dancing on a Cold Wind (74), The Gypsies (76)

CARNEVALE, TONY - Italy
Classical rock with members from BANCO.

La Vita Che Grida ( )

CARPE DIEM - France
Part of ANGE'S generation but differs by the importance the group gives to the search for melodies and by the beauty of the music to the detriment of the words. Their mainly instrumental albums show their strengths as arrangers, composers and orchestrators and are masterpieces of finesse, invention and spontaneity evoking CAMEL'S The Snow Goose or that sophisticated English school which plays a light and subtle chamber rock (CARAVAN, FRUUPP).

En Regarant Passer Le Temps (75), Cueille Le Jour (77)

CARRE BLANC - France
A nineties group consisting of former members of TERPANDRE. Sound like a cross between ANGE and the familiar English progressive rock feel. Energetic, well orchestrated and arranged material.

CARRION, ALFREDO - Spain
Classical symphonic material

Andares Del Alquimista (76)

CARTOONE - United States
An American band that borrows heavily from the Frank Zappa school of avant-garde music. Most of their falls into the jazzy-fusion field. A mixture of short and long compositions with many unexpected musical twists and turns.

Cartoone (81), Music From Left Field (83)

CASA DAS MAQUINAS - Brazil
Their one recording has been called one of the best Brazilian releases of great progressive rock.

Lar de Maravilhas (75)

CASE, ALAN - Holland
Symphonic prog material that is a compositional blend of ALAN PARSONS and TONY BANKS. Very upbeat and almost pop oriented in a good way. Even the shorter songs contain interesting moments. Easy to listen to with lots of keyboard textures and interesting arrangements.

Wide Awake (97), Dark Matter (00)

CASINO - Great Britain
Geoff Mann and CLIVE NOLAN formerly members of TWELFTH NIGHT and PENDRAGON respectively, created this band. If you're a fan of Nolan's The Key and Twelfth Night's Fact and Fiction you'll have a good idea of what to expect here. Sort of a cross between PINK FLOYD mixed with GENESIS and a hint of MARILLION.

Casino (92)

CAST - Mexico
This band has been writing and performing since 1978 with music influenced by the sound of Wind & Wuthering GENESIS and a vocalist that sounds like Peter Nichols of IQ, Cast feature a melodic and flowing style, in a keyboard dominated setting. Highly recommended to fans of British neo-prog.

Landing In a Serious Mind (94), Sounds of Imagination (85/94), Third Call (89/94), Four Aces (95), Endless Signs (95), Beyond Reality (96), A View of Cast [Live] (96), Angels and Demons (97), Imaginary Window (98), A Live Experience (99), Legacy (99), Laguna De Volcanes [Spanish] (99)

CASTANARC - Great Britain
Neo-progressive rock band from the mid eighties. Swirling, multi-layered keyboards and melodic guitar support vocalist Mark Holiday. More melodic than many of the bands of the era. Heavily influenced by YES' quieter side and GENESIS' Wind & Wuthering period.

Journey to the East (84)

CASTELLANO, TONY - United States
The music here is best described as melodic prog with a strong pop influence similar to some of TODD RUNDGREN's early work. The overall feel reminds one of a STEVE HACKETT style.

Fun Size (97)

CASTELLO DI ATLANTE - Italy
Symphonic prog in the vein of BANCO, PFM, LOCANDADELLE FATE.

Sono Io il Signore (92), Passo Dopo Passo [Live] ( ), L'Ippogrifo (95)

CATAPILLA - Great Britain
Complex jazz influenced progressive rock in the vein of GENTLE GIANT and GNIDROLOG.

Catapilla (71), Changes (72)

CATHARSIS - France
A French version of PINK FLOYD. Their style is one that incorporates long dreamy, ethereal passages.

Masq (71), Les Chevrons (72), Rimbaud C'est Toi (72), Pop Poems (73), 32 Mars (75), Le Bolero Du Veau Des Dames (75), Et S'aimer et Mourir (76),

CATHEDRAL [1] - United States
Legendary Mellotron based progressive rock band with brilliant guitar. One of the best! The guitar work is a pastiche of HOWE, HACKETT and Fripp. Sounds a bit like YES, KING CRIMSON.

Stained Glass Stories (78)

CATHEDRAL [2] - United States
A newer band with a much harder edged, more neo-progressive rock sound. This group shows a strong influence from MARILLION and DREAM THEATRE. Their material is longish tracks, mini-epics with extended instrumental sections. They eventually broke up and keyboardist Todd Braverman went on to form AD INFINITUM. No relation to CATHEDRAL [1].

Kingdom of Ends (92), There in the Shadows (93)

CATWEAZLE - Sweden
Symphonic sound with organ, Mellotron and bass pedals. Their style is from the neo-prog side and they've injected a lot of originality to keep it fresh. Their approach is based around early IQ and MARILLION with a strong early GENESIS influence.

Ars Moriendi (96)

CELESTE - Italy
They were influenced by early KING CRIMSON, but their sound is very original. You'll hear elements of GENESIS circa Trespass and even bits of PFM'S Per Un Amico. A very beautiful, symphonic pastoral result. Lots of Mellotron. One of the genre's highly rated bands.

I Suoni in Una Sfera (74), Celeste [Principe Di Un Giorno] (76), Second Plus ( )

CELI, FABIO E GLI INERMIERI - Italy
Early seventies Italian progressive material with dual keyboards and lots of Hammond organ.

Follia ( )

CELLULOID - United States
Famous for their use of Mellotrons.

Mercury ( ), Neptune ( ), Jupiter ( )

CERAFIM - Canada
Progressive pop with a sound influenced by bands such as SAGA.

Sides of a Different Kind (95)

CERVELLO - Italy
Italian group consisting of former members of OSANNA, who made one LP with a heavy symphonic progressive sound. Features Corrado Rustici of NOVA on guitar and produced by OSANNA.

Melos (73)

CHAC MOOL - Mexico
Jorge Reyes' eighties group, their music is inspired by the likes of PINK FLOYD.

Nadie En Especiale (8?), Suenas De Matal (8?)

CHAKRA - United States
Symphonic prog band from California that will appeal to fans of bands like LIFT or PENTWATER.

Chakra (79)

CHANCE - France
Melodic instrumental neo-progressive rock with Vincent Fis from NOW. The sound is reminiscent of eighties style neo-prog bands and even brings to mind fellow countrymen MINIMUM VITAL.

Dunes (9?), Escape to Horizon (00)

CHANDELIER - Germany
One of Europes most accomplished neo-progressive rock bands with a sound that is similar to ARAGON or MARILLION. They perform mostly mid-tempo songs with long instrumental introductions.

Fragments (88 TAPE), Pure (90), Facing Gravity (92), Time Code (97)

CHANGES - Italy
Heavy progressive rock.

The Growing Number ( )

CHANGING IMAGES - Germany
Electronic influenced symphonic progressive rock in the SFF vein.

The Castle (91), Virtuality (93)

CHAOS CODE - United States
They create a mostly instrumental music that resembles the style popularized by Scandanavian bands such as ANEKDOTEN or FRUITCAKE. There are many long brooding or melancholy passages that turn into lush symphonic panoramas. Many angular crashing guitar chords that make way for a soft and gentle flute. If you enjoy the Scandanavian prog style you'll enjoy Chaos Code.

A Tapestry of Afterthoughts (99)

CHAR-EL - United States
One of a growing number of solo synthesists emerging on the music scene. However Char-El is included here because of the solid symphonic progressive rock foundation on which he constructs his music. Much like SYNERGY these soundscapes are fully realized compositions with all the dynamics and twists and turns you would expect from any prog band. As a bonus many of the tracks feature the Mellotron.

Worlds Without End (97), Heaven and Earth (00)

CHARACTER - United States
Nineties band with a heavy neo-progressive rock sound.

Demon Child (9?)

CHEMICAL ALICE - Great Britain
One of the first of the neo-progressive rock bands formed in the early eighties. Essex-based and most influenced by PINK FLOYD, Frank Zappa and YES. Keyboardist

Mark Kelly would later join MARILLION. Only one debut EP on their own label.

CHEOPS - Great Britain
A strange mixture of psychedelic and progressive rock incorporating tablas, sitars and bazouki.

A Most Peculiar Pancake ( )

CHERRY FIVE - Italy
One album that is a keyboard lovers delight. This band was the fore-runner to Goblin so there is a lot of Hammond, Mellotron, Grand Piano etc. The sound is similar to very early YES or BANZAI, in fact Expose' says ...imagine RICK WAKEMAN playing on The Yes Album...

Cherry Five (75)

CHOTEM, Neil - Canada
Chotem was a member of the final incarnation of HARMONIUM and a member of the FIORI-SEGUIN project, and as you might expect his music is very similar to both those bands. One album to his credit released in the late seventies, that utilises members from previous projects including Marie-Clare Seguin on vocals.

CHRISTMAS - Canada
Pre-SPIRIT OF CHRISTMAS group playing a more folk oriented, psychedelic progressive rock.

Christmas (70), Heritage (71)

CHRONICLE - Japan
The band came together in a garage in California, headed by two members formerly with the FAR EAST FAMILY BAND. It seams all members had fled Japan because of 'artistic frustration'. Their music contains all the hints of being oriental, atmospheric and passionate.

Live at the Whisky A Go Go (75), Ima Wa Toki No Subete (75), Like a Message From the Stars (77)

CICO - Italy
Mid seventies outfit featuring ex-FORMULA 3 drummer Tony Cicco. Progressive with a pop edge.

Notte (74)

CID, JOSE - Portugal
Concept material with lots of Mellotron from an artist who's released many pop albums but only one progressive one. From the early PINK FLOYD, PULSAR school.

10,000 Anos Despois (78)

CINDERELLA SEARCH - Japan
Melodic progressive rock

Cinderella Search ( )

CINEMA - Japan
Former members of FROMAGE along with two keyboardists, and an operatic female vocalist. They have opted for a more simple approach with material full of gothic ambience, together with some Mediterranean flourishes. Like some of RENAISSANCE'S ballads, they opted for a simple, classical-based sound rich in orchestral colours, but serve mainly to support the voice.

The Seven Stories (9?)

CINEMA SHOW - Brazil
Symphonic, neo-progressive rock sound, but still incorporating prominent acoustic guitar and flute. As you might expect by the name a strong early GENESIS influence.

Danca Dos Ventos (95)

CIRCLE OF FAIRIES - Italy
Symphonic material a la FANCYFLUID with long tracks. Lots of analog synths and Mellotron that bring German band's IVORY, NOVALIS and GROBSCHNITT to mind.

As the Years go by (95)

CIRCUS - Switzerland
Complex progressive rock, with excellent musicianship. Sounds a bit like CAMEL meets JETHRO TULL with a touch of jazz. Great flute and sax work, fine acoustic guitar and inventive drumming.

Circus (76), Movin-on (77), Fearless, Tearless and Even less ( )

CIRKEL - Holland
Dutch progressive rock band specialising in elaborate keyboard and guitar arrangements. Eurock says The spirit of early GENESIS refused to go away as a whole new generation of eighties bands continued to pay homage to that group's sound.

The First Goodbye (83)

CIRKUS - Great Britain
Legendary early seventies band who musical style included tons of organ and Mellotron. The material is in the style of MOODY BLUES and CRESSIDA.

One Plus (71/98), 2 ( ), 3 ( )

CITADEL - United States
A group who produced a concept album with a sound similar to RUSH, or KANSAS.

The Citadel of Cynosure (90)

CITIZEN CAIN - Great Britain
Neo-progressive rock in the style of IQ, MARILLION & GENESIS. This is keyboard dominated, somewhat complex symphonic prog that is quite engaging. Like most neo-prog bands the group places more of an emphasis on songs and as such there are lots of vocals. If you enjoy modern prog you'll enjoy the intricate nature of Citizen Cain.

Citizen Cain (91 TAPE), Serpents in Camoflage (92), Somewhere But Yesterday (94), Ghost Dance ( ), Raising the Stones (98)

CITTA FRONTALE - Italy
Complex progressive rock that sounds a bit like GENTLE GIANT.

El Tor (75)

CITY BOY - Great Britain
Art rock band with symphonic prog elements. They started out with a bit more of an acoustic sound but became more guitar oriented with each album. Solid guitar and keyboard layering with lots of interesting multi-part harmonies set in multi-movement pieces that rock. Fans of SPLIT ENZ and 10cc will certainly enjoy what's going on here.

City Boy (76), Dinner at the Ritz (76), Young Men Gone West (77), Book Early (78), The Day the Earth Caught Fire (79), Heads are Rolling (80)

CLARION - Italy
Melodic progressive keyboard and flute duo sounding a bit like CAMEL but incorporating a host of influences from progressive rock bands of the seventies.

Clarion ( ), Bourree (97)

CLEAR BLUE SKY - Great Britain
Early blues based three piece. Long songs but simply arranged. More notable for being one of the first Roger Dean album covers.

Clear Blue Sky (71)

CLEARLIGHT SYMPHONY - France
Cyrille Verdeaux's group began by following in the footsteps of MIKE OLDFIELD but managed not to lose its own personality. The group produced mainly instrumental music which was both beautiful and dreamlike, alternating soothing and serene atmospheres with more violent, more tormented passages sometimes drifting towards a delicate cosmic floating rock. Albums featured many guest musicians

including STEVE HILLAGE and others.

Clearlight Symphony (75), Forever Blowing Bubbles (76), Les Contes du Singe Fou (77), Visions (78), Offrandes (80), Nocturne Digitales (80), Prophecy (82), Moebius (82), Shambala (82), Heart Visions (83), Remembrance (83), Kundalini Opera (84), Messenger of the Son (85), Rhapsody for the Blue Planet (90), Clearlight Symphony II (90)

CLEPSYDRA - Switzerland

One of the many MARILLION influenced neo-prog bands displaying superb musicianship. Strong guitar solos and nice keyboard work in longer songs showing a lot of musical diversity and dynamics.

Hologram (91), More Grains of Sand (94), Fears (97)

CLIFFHANGER - Holland

Dutch four piece group who create a dynamic and moderately complex progressive rock in the CAST or GENESIS vein. Their use of analog synths, bass pedals and the like give them a strong seventies flavour. One of the more accomplished symphonic prog bands.

Cold Steel (95), Not To Be or Not To Be (97), Mirror Site (98)

CLOUD NINE - United States

Nineties band who create a blend of heavy fusion ala Mahavishnu Orchestra and the dark, complex moods of KING CRIMSON.

COBWEB STRANGE - United States

A combination of poetic lyrics, instrumental dexterity in a progressive rock musical style with hints of jazz. Influences include the likes of KING CRIMSON, GENTLE GIANT, RUSH and YES.

The Temptation of Successive Hours (96), Sounds From the Gathering (99)

COCHRANE, STEVE - United States

As a solo artist his compositions fall squarely in the symphonic progressive rock side of things with influences ranging from THE MOODY BLUES, GENESIS and RENAISSANCE. Epic songs with lots of drama and plenty dynamics to keep things interesting.

The Purest of Designs (98)

CODA - Holland

A melodic symphonic progressive rock sound. The album Sounds of Passion is considered a Dutch classic. The music features an emphasis on lush keyboards mixed with a CAMEL-ish guitar sound.

Sounds of Passion (86), What a Symphony()

CODICE - Mexico

Well crafted symphonic progressive rock influenced by YES, GENESIS and ELP.

Alba Y Ocaso (99)

COENBITE - Great Britain

My Habit ( ), Castles in the Air ( )

COLLAGE - Poland

MARILLION style progressive rock with a great symphonic, wall-of-keyboard sound, and English vocals. The music is keyboard and drum heavy but incorporates many acoustic guitar and piano segments, with just enough tempo shifts to keep it interesting.

Basnie (89), Nine Songs of John Lennon (92), Moonshine (94), Zmiany [Changes] (93), Safe (96)

COLLEGIUM MUSICUM - Czechoslovakia

One of the first classical-rock bands in Eastern Europe. Headed by keyboardist Marian Varga, they have a sound that can be described as a bohemian version of THE NICE.

Collegium Musicum (7?),Konvergencie (71),Na Druhom Programe Sna ( ),Zelena Posta ( )

COLOSSEUM -Great Britain

A band born out of the British blues era, who then got into the jazz-fusion scene with a vengeance. Trendsetting in their style of composition. The band was Jon Hiseman's vehicle for musical expression.

For Those About to Die We Salute You (69),Valentyne Suite (69),Daughter of Time (70), Live (71)

COLOSSEUM II - Great Britain

By 1975 Hiseman was the only one left interested in carrying on so he formed II. They produced some excellent material in the fusion-progressive rock sense.

Strange New Flesh (76),Wardance (77),Electric Savage (77)

COLTSFOOT - Great Britain

They formed in 1983 as a four piece outfit. Originally their music was based around the early seventies hippy style. Although they didn't mind the 'hippy' tag, none of the members looked the part. Their newer material tends to be softer and keyboard oriented, almost in the New Age vein but still manages to contain some edge. They list their influences as GENESIS, TULL, KING CRIMSON and BJH.

2 cut EP (85),From Within Stone Circles (85 Tape),A Winter Harvest (96)

COMEDY OF ERRORS - Great Britain

Neo-progressive rock similar to IQ and PENDRAGON.

Comedy of Errors ( )

COMPAGNIA DIGITALE, LA - Italy

Late seventies band who created music in the style of OZRIC TENTACLES. Features the keyboardist from CELESTE.

La Compagnia Digitale (7?)

COMPANYA ELECTRICA DHARMA - Spain

This is mainly folk-prog, with the emphasis on folk (Catalonian folk, not Flamenco).

Ordinaries Adventures (79),20 Anys 74 (93)

COMUS - Great Britain

On the Dawn label, Syn-Phonic calls this a classic of gothic progressive rock.

First Utterance (71),To Keep From Crying (74)

CONSCIENCE - Canada

Featuring a female vocalist this group reminds some of the Polish group QUIDAM.

Sortilege ( )

CONSORZIO ACQUA POTABILE - Italy

The band was around during the seventies but has only in the nineties released an album. As such it is a melodic romantic BANCO influenced symphonic neo-progressive rock sound. They reformed in the early nineties and the material they've produced has been top-notch. Their use of dual keyboards in epic compositions will win over any lover of the classic Italian prog style.

Salsa Borsa '77 (78), Nei Gorghi Del Pempo (93), Robin delle Stelle (98)

CONTRAPPUNTO - Italy

This is five member group with a dedicated female vocalist creating music that is largely neo-progressive rock with pop overtones. Nothing overly adventurous, but some of the songs have interesting arrangements packed with some solid musicianship.

Subsidea (98)

CONTREVENT - Canada
Classically influenced progressive rock-fusion with violin and vibraphone. Elements of MANEIGE and Dixie Dregs may be heard.

Jeu De Paume (86), Youkali (89), Terre De Feu (93)

CONVENTUM - Canada
Classically influenced mixture of folk-fusion. Similar to Malicorne in that they use primarily acoustic instruments, and a lot of them. The compositions are quite complex and might be described as progressive chamber folk.

A L'affut d'un Complot (77), Le Bureau Central des Utopies (79)

COOPERATIVA DEL LATTE - Italy
Their style is one of prominent organ weaving in-and-out of complicated arrangments with the bass, guitar and drums. There are few vocals to interupt the musical flow which is break-neck at times only to evaporate in places making room for some softer piano work. The music is high on melody and the musicianship is top-notch.

Il Risveglio (98)

CORTE DEI MIRACOLI - Italy
Dual keyboard symphonic progressive rock wonder work similar in many ways to the work of BANCO. They had only one studio release, but some archive material has come out in the nineties.

Corte Dei Miracoli (76), Dimensione Onirica [73-74] (92), Live at Lux 1974 (9?)

COS - Belgium
The Belgian answer to the band ZAO. In the style of Canterbury/jazz/progressive rock, ala CARAVAN.

Postaeolian Train Robbery (75), Viva Bomma (78), Babel (79), Passions (83), Hotel Atlantic (84)

COTO-EN-PEL - Spain
A progressive band from Eastern Spain. They fuse that sound with elements of Spanish folk melodies using lots of Mellotron, organ and guitar work. Sort of a cross between PINK FLOYD and KING CRIMSON

Holocaust (78)

COUNT LORENZO BEDINI - Great Britain
Former guitarist with the band AIR-BRIDGE. Wound up releasing a couple of singles in the mid eighties which were more in the shorter song pop category.

COUNTRY LANE - Switzerland
Substratum (73)

COURT - Italy
Neo-progressive rock incorporating an oboe. The almost medieval material goes from acoustic pieces with flute and oboe to more heavy passages with screaming guitar. However the many acoustic instruments tends to bring out a folk-ish feeling. Imagine a cross between Queensryche and GRYPHON.

Court (96), Distances (97)

COVENANT - United States
Intense keyboard driven sound created by Dave Gryder. There are elements of metal in the drumming and the keyboards present a dark gothic feel. Gryder has used Mellotron, church organ and some great musicianship to produce some very listenable progressive rock.

Natures Devine Reflection (93)

COZMIC CORRIDORS - Germany
Spacey progressive rock with lots of organ.

Cozmic Corridors (72)

CRACK - Spain
No real Spanish influences here in this band even though they come from Southern Spain. What you will find some of Spain's finest examples of majestic and powerful symphonic progressive rock. Crack was a very Anglo styled band, with flute, keyboards and female vocals.

Si Todo Hiciera Crack (79)

CRACK THE SKY - United States
Creative and underrated American progressive rock band. Quirky, jazzy, with great guitar and keyboard interplay all describe the different sides of the band. The band's core member John Palumbo, heavily influenced by the Beatles often shares their love of strong melodies and perverse lyrics, wrapped up in jaunty little musical packages with a fair share of tempo and style changes. Everything from atmosphericaly soothing to orchestrally bombastic.

Crack The Sky (75), Animal Notes (76), Safety In Numbers (78), Live Sky (78), White Music (80), Photoflamingo (81), World in Motion (83), Raw (86), In The Greenhouse (89), Dog City (90)

CRAFT - Great Britain
Band features former members of THE ENID with lots of classical training. Their playing abilities shine through the music. Sound like a more aggressive version of THE ENID, with not so many soft and subtle parts. Perhaps a little more ELP thrown in. The band formed in 1983 and created only the one LP.

Craft (84)

CREDO - Great Britain
They were formed out of the ashes of Casual Affair and Armageddon in London. Similar to early TWELFTH NIGHT.

Field of Vision (94)

CRESSIDA - Great Britain
One of progressive rock's pioneer bands featuring an organ/Mellotron based sound much like their contemporaries BEGGAR'S OPERA, FANTASY and SPRING. Symphonic material featuring long songs with lots of flute and minor chords particularly on their second release.

Cressida (70), Asylum (71)

CROMWELL - Germany
Solid, well played neo-progressive material featuring female vocalist Anke Taeffner and a keyboardist who excels at creating epic scale panoramic atmospheres. A combination of ballads, mid-tempo songs and a few instrumentals.

Burning Banners (97)

CROSS - Sweden
A five piece, featuring two drummers heavily influenced by KING CRIMSON, with hints of YES and GENTLE GIANT in spots. Lots of minor chords and angular guitar, but overall a less complicated style making for a bit of sameness throughout.

Paradox (88), Second Movement ( ), Changing Poison Into Medicine (93), Gaze (96), Dream Reality (97), Visionary Fools (99)

CRUCIBLE - United States
From the state of Connecticut, this is a nineties group whose sound is heavily influenced by early GENESIS although their vocalist brings his own unique sound and style to the compositions. Their compositions also hold elements of early KANSAS and STYX without getting into the arena rock stuff. Great musicianship on both short and epic length tracks.

Tall Tales (97)

CRUCIS - Argentina
South American band in the same symphonic vein as FINCH, FOCUS or YES. One of Argentina's best.

Crucis (75), Los Delerios Del Mariscal (76)

CRYSTAL HAZE - United States
Obscure symphonic progressive rock band.

Crystal Haze (77)

CRYSTAL MAZE - Germany
Symphonic progressive rock showing influences from MARILLION and ELOY on their first LP. They released a second LP seven years later that was more of a pop direction.

Waiting in the Spider's Web (86), Forever (94)

CRYSTAL PHOENIX - Italy
The material here comes in two forms, heavy at times with lots of metalloid guitar and at other times melodic, acoustic guitars with lots of keyboards.

Crystal Phoenix (93)

CULPEPPER - Denmark
Progressive material featuring an eclectic mix of styles and instruments. Highly rated and highly innovative at what they did...incorporating everything from DEEP PURPLE to PROCOL HARUM.

Culpeper's Orchard (71), All Dressed Up & Nowhere to Go (77)

CURIOUS DREAM - Great Britain
Early eighties, fourpiece band with only a couple of known demo cassette recordings. The music is reminiscent of A Trick of the Tail GENESIS with hints of YES and SKY.

CURIOUS WORKS - United States
New Jersey based outfit featuring a powerful female vocalist with a melodic music influenced by YES' guitar and bass sound. Fans of RUSH and RITUAL will enjoy.

Where Fables Die (94)

CURVED AIR - Great Britain
Formed the winter of 1970 spotlighting the alto voice of Sonja Kristina and musicians DARRYL WAY on violin, and FRANCIS MONKMAN on keyboards, and eventually in it's final formation included Stewart Copeland on drums and EDDIE JOBSON on violin and keyboards. The classical training shone brightly in this band as they reworked many of the classics and created some of their own.

Airconditioning (70), Second Album (71), Phantasmagoria (72), Air Cut (73), Live (75), Midnight Wire (75), Airborne (76), Love Child (90), Live at the BBC (95), Alive 1990 (98)

CYAN - Great Britain
English symphonic neo-progressive rock duo with material very reminiscent of PENDRAGON, JADIS, CAMEL. There are lots of time and tempo changes, many musical textures, in songs that feature solid musicianship.

For King and Country (93), Pictures From the Other Side (94), The Creeping Vine (99)

CYE - Switzerland
Neo-progressive rock in a style similar to MARILLION, but with a strong CAMEL circa Dust and Dreams influence, particularly in the melancholy vocals and plaintive guitar style.

The Final Touch (92 EP), Tales (94)

D.C.P. - Germany
Eighties era neo-progressive rock group with lots of keyboards. A bit on the heavy side.

DFA - Italy
Their musical style is classic Italian symphonic progressive rock, with all the hallmarks. The music is long and involved with many textures and moods. They create music that is a cross between KENSO and DEUS EX MACHINA. Lots of Mellotron, Hammond organ, synths, guitar and few vocals.

Lavori In Corso (96), Duty Free Area (99)

D.I.M. [Diabolos In Musika] - Norway

This group creates prog metal that is firmly in the progressive rock mould. While the music tends to proceed at the usual breakneck pace, there are moments or interludes where the keyboard work calms the mood. A note of caution regarding the lyrical content, it is sexually very explicit and violent and so you may want to give it a miss.

Natural Needs (95)

DAGA BAND - Great Britain

Originally formed in 1975 and stayed together until about 1978. Reformed in 1980 with a sound like ELP meets The Who. They recorded only a couple of EPs.

Second Time Around EP (82)

DAKOTA - United States

They sound very STYX like, perhaps with a bit more melody. Went on to make a second album that was more hard melodic rock.

Dakota (80), Runaway (83)

DALI'S DILEMA - United States

This is progressive metal in the DREAM THEATRE vein. Lots of guitar pyrotechnics interspersed with a fair amount of keyboards. The compositions are complex with plenty of twists and turns.

Manifesto For Futurism (99)

DALL'AGLIO, GIANNI - Italy

Early seventies solo artist who played with IL VOLO, crafts soft melodic songs with lots of Mellotron.

Sera, Mattina (72)

DALTON - Italy

Early JETHRO TULL like sound. Very much in the style of METAMORFOSI.

Riflessioni: Idea D'Infinito (72)

DAMMICCO, CIRO - Italy

Early seventies solo symphonic material.

Mittente (72)

DARIUS - Holland

Symphonic neo-progressive rock that seems to put all the elements in the right place. Lots of vocals go into the concept nature of the album but they don't detract from the musicianship. The music contains the epic scope and interesting arrangments to propell the compositions through a number of interesting twists and turns. if you enjoy bands such as IQ, ARENA and PENDRAGON you'll like this.

Voices from the Crowd (98)

DARLING - United States

A mixture of RIO, symphonic, neo-prog, Canterbury and a little KING CRIMSON for good measure.

Darling (96)

DARK AETHER PROJECT - United States

Adventurous material incorporating drums, guitar and Stick to create a complex musical tapestry of loops and sounds that may remind the listener of KING CRIMSON during the eighties. They fall into the same school as DJAM KARET.

The Dark Aether Project (98), Feed the Silence (99)

DARK SUN - Finland

A mixture of psychedelic and progressive with material that is heavily influenced by PINK FLOYD and Hawkwind.

Dark Sun EP (96)

DATURA - France

A group influenced by the English progressive rock school and a certain trend in French rock. They offer an excellent progressive rock with a symphonic tendency, that emphasises a musical sophistication and complete mastery of the musical instruments. Sound like - GENESIS, YES, ELP.

Mr. Untel (82)

DAWN - Germany
MARILLION influenced neo-progressive rock.

Night Tales EP (89)

DAWN DIALOGUE - Russia
Wall of keyboards and fiery guitar. YES influenced in the WAKEMAN-esque keyboard work and overall sound but there are elements of GENESIS too. Vocals are in Russian. Started out in the early eighties and in the nineties they became known simply as Dialog.

I Put the Spell on the Fire (87), Cry of the Hawk (93)

DAY OF PHOENIX - Denmark
One of the earliest forms of progressive rock, with jazz overtones to come out of Denmark.

Wide Open N-Way (70), Neighbours Son (72)

DEADWOOD FOREST - United States
Symphonic progressive rock and like fellow Texas progsters HAND this features elements of YES, GRYPHON and GENTLE GIANT. Lots of great arrangements with solid musicianship in music that is busy one moment and pastoral the next. Plenty of keyboards including Hammond and Mellotron.

Deadwood Forest (99)

DEAMBRA - United States
Very accessible symphonic progressive rock with nice vocal harmony. California based band formed by guitarist Alex Diambrini influenced by YES, GENESIS and MARILLION but creating music in a nineties vein.

Deambra (96)

DEATH & TAXES - United States
This California trio create a unique blend of progressive rock mixed with hardcore thrash and even some speed metal. The prog influence is certainly there, but be prepared for an aural onslaught.

Paradigms for a New Century (96)

DECAMERON - Great Britain
Folk with a hint of progressive rock. Only a few albums would be of interest to symphonic fans.

Decameron (73), Mammoth Special (74), Third Light (75), Beyond the Light (75), Tomorrow's Pantomime (76)

DECAMPS, CHRISTIAN - France
Founding member and main writer of the band ANGE.

Le Mal d'Adam (79), V'soul Vesoul V'soul ( ), Merlin & Les Dragons ( ), Nu ( )

DECAMPS, FRANCIS - France
Brother and co-founding member of the band ANGE.

Histoire de Fou (79), Vie En Positif (90), Epicier Marchand d'Rock (93)

DECENNIUM - Holland
Song of the Sad Times (74)

DECIBEL - Mexico
Eighties era group who create complex progressive music influenced by HENRY COW.

El Poeta Del Ruido (80), Contranatura (8?)

DECKO - France
This keyboardist creates a music unlike the floating spacey style and instead goes for an original, varied inventive electronic sound which mixes and blends the grand organs, flute like sounds etc. Sounds like VANGELIS.

Mythe Xero (82)

DE DE LIND - Italy
Overall a heavy guitar oriented style, with flute bringing to mind hints of JETHRO TULL.

Io Non So Da Dove Vengo (73)

DEEP PURPLE - Great Britain
Started out more of a hard rock band but quickly fell in line with the experimentation of the times. They were one of the first bands to play with orchestra. Only some of their earlier material qualifies as progressive rock, the rest tended to be pretty much interesting hard rock. Some great guitar playing interlaced with some great organ from JON LORD. Although Lord always seemed to take a back seat in the band.

Book of Taliesyn (69), Deep Purple (69), Deep Purple with the Royal Philharmonic (70), In Rock (70), Fireball (71), Machine Head (72), Who Do We Think We Are (73), Deep Purple in concert with The London Symphony Orchestra (00)

DEJA VU - Japan
ELP influenced symphonic progressive rock with MOTOI SAKURABA on keyboards.

Baroque in the Future (88)

DELIRIUM - Italy
Progressive rock in the flavour of the seventies Italian bands. Similar to FORMULA 3.

Dolce Acqua (71), Lo Scemo E Il Villaggio (72) ,III: Viaggio Degli Arcipelaghi Del Tempo (74)

DELIRIUM - Mexico
Symphonic progressive rock reminiscent of ICONOCLASTA along with hints of other European bands such as FINCH or even SHYLOCK. Complex prog with solid musicianship and composition. Their second release actually pre-dates the first.

Delirium (85), El Teatro Del Delirio (84/96)

DELTA CYPHEI PROJECT - Germany
A very eclectic sound ranging from Pat Metheny to Jeff Beck in the guitar department and Iggy Pop to JON ANDERSON in the vocals and some WAKEMAN-esque style keyboard work. A majestic neo-prog style, with a dose of jazz and electronics.

Virtual World (93), Supernova (94)

DEMBY, CONSTANCE - United States
She has released two albums the first being firmly in the new age category, while the second is a sixty minute concept work that will delight fans of symphonic keyboard work.

Set Free ( ), Novus Magnificat - Through the Stargate (86)

DEMON THOR - Germany
Symphonic progressive rock band with some mainstream tendencies who produced a couple of albums, one being a concept work featuring lots of Mellotron.

Anno 1972 (74), Written in the Sky (74)

DEN FULE - Sweden
Progressive folk rock.

Skalv ( ), Lugumleik ( )

DESEQUILIBRIOS - Brazil
Symphonic progressive rock with FABIO RIBEIRO on keyboards. A combination of a vocalist who sounds like ANGE, solid neo-progressive instrumentation and a GEN-

TLE GIANT like compositional style.

Desequilibrios (92)

DEUS EX MACHINA - Italy
A group with roots in the older Italian sound. Heavy keyboard and guitar arrangements spiced with violin form their foundation. This is full fledged progressive rock with lots of odd time changes, great arrangements and great playing on long tracks. The vocals and some of the musicianship have been compared to AREA, however with their '98 release they moved away from symphonic prog and ventured more into the realm of avant-garde prog.

Gladium Caeli (90), Deus Ex Machina (93), De Republica (94), Diacronie Metronomiche (96), Non Est Ars Quae Ad Effectum Casus Venit (97), Equilibrismo Da Insofferenza (98)

DEVIL DOLL - Italy
More on the symphonic side making use of violin and accordion at times to create a dark and sinister style of music. Like a soundtrack to a scary movie, there's tons of minor chords and lots of songs about death, grimness and evil. Not for everyone.

The Girl Who Was Death (88), Eliogabolus (90), Sacrilegium (92), Sacrilege of Fatal Arms [remake of Sacrilegium] (92), Dies Irae (96)

DEYSS - Switzerland
From the art work to the music, very inspired by MARILLION. Their first album At King was quite derivative of the neo-progressive style, but their second release a few years later Vision in the Dark showed a much more polished band in terms of writing, singing and musicianship.

At King (85), Vision in the Dark (87), For Your Eyes Only ( )

DICE - Sweden
Classical symphonic progressive rock. Imagine the best instrumental parts of YES, throw in a little ELP organ work and then mix in elements of FOCUS and GENTLE GIANT and you might have a feel for the sound of this band.

The Four Riders of the Apocalypse (77), Dice (78), Live Dice (93)

DIFFERENCES - Holland
Nice sounding early eighties neo-progressive sound. Very much in the GENESIS vein circa And then there were Three or in some parts of Wind & Wuthering. Great symphonic keyboard arrangements and guitar parts. A good mixture of short and long songs.

The Voyage (82), A World of Difference (92)

DIFFERENT TRAINS - Great Britain
Damon Shulman, son of Philip Shulman and nephew of Derek Shulman of GENTLE GIANT, gets a go at his own group. At times a grunge band there are nevertheless those moments in each song where they betray their musical heritage. It might be the use of glockenspiel, violins, trumpets etc. or the inclusion of Baroque musical breaks.

On the Right Track (96)

DILEMMA - Holland
Diverse neo-prog material along the lines of IT BITES or TWELFTH NIGHT or to put it another way a more progressive sounding Simple Minds meets MARILLION.

Imbroccata (95)

DILLINGER - Canada
Hints of early ELP and TRIUMVIRAT, even a little JETHRO TULL flute and blues feel to some of the songs. One known LP featuring longish songs (7-8 minutes), with a bit of Mellotron in parts.

Don't Lie to the Band (76)

DISCIPLINE - United States
From Detroit, they are a symphonic, progressive rock band that has managed to capture the brooding style of Peter Hammil's VAN DER GRAAF GENERATOR and blend it with the bright and harmonic style of YES. Their sound is also influenced by KING CRIMSON, Zappa, and GENTLE GIANT. In fact a listen to their material and you may be struck by the fact that each song is very different from the other.

Push & Profit (93), Unfolded Like Staircase (97), Discipline Live...Into the Dream (99)

DISCUS - Indonesia
Symphonic progressive rock with Indonesian ethnic influences. This eight piece group features two keyboadists along a variety of reed and string instruments. The music showcases a variety of motifs such as jazz, folk pop. You'll hear elements of HAPPY THE MAN and MINIMUM VITAL

1st (99)

DIVAE - Italy
Their sound incorporates the best of the seventies Italian symphonic prog groups with a distinct British rock style. They feature twin keyboard players who make use of the best vintage gear including Hammond and Mellotron. Mostly instrumental, their music is full of compositional tempo twists and turns.

Determinazione (95)

DIVINE REGALE - United States
A New Hampshire based six-piece who create a heavier progressive rock with lots of atmosphere and solid musicianship. The compositions feature plenty of time and tempo changes with lots of good guitar work and layers of keyboards along the same lines as DREAM THEATRE. the songs tend to be on the shorter side with the longest clocking in at just over eight minutes.

Ocean Mind (97)

DIXIE DREGS - United States
One of the classic Ameri-prog bands from the seventies, whose members have gone to be so influential in any number of other modern prog outfits. Their compositional style came more strictly from a jazz-rock fusion school which allowed for tremendous musicianship to shine.

The Great Spectacular (75), Free Fall (77), What If (78), Night of the Living Dregs (79), Dregs of the Earth (80), Unsung Heroes (81), Industry Standard (82), Bring'em Back Alive (92), Full Circle (94), King Biscuit Flower Hour (97), California Screamin' (00)

DJAM KARET - United States
They've been known to produce two forms of music, one, a moody electronic style and the other a jagged edged progressive rock. Excellent guitar based instrumental material, with superb keyboards including Hammond and Mellotron. Highly recommended to fans of PINK FLOYD and KING CRIMSON.

McMusic For the Masses (82), No Commercial Potential (85), The Ritual Continues (87), Reflections From the Firepool (89), Burning the Hard City (91), Suspension & Displacement (91), Collaborator (94), The Devouring (97), Still No Commercial Potential (98), Live At Orion (99)

DR. FOLAMOUR - France
Guitar driven progressive rock with a World Music influence in style and instrumentation. The use of flutes, violin and native chants provide an exotic element to the music.

Dr. Folamour (96)

DOCTORS OF MADNESS - Great Britain
A strange progressive rock, that's a cross between Roxy Music/Eno and The Velvet Underground.

Late Nite Movies (76), Figments of Emancipation (76), Sons of Survival (78), Doctors of Madness (78), Revisionism (81)

DOGMA - Brazil
Instrumental symphonic progressive rock with MARCUS VIANA guesting on violin. Sounds like CAMEL or EDHELS. Their strong neo-progressive sound puts them on a par with MARILLION and IQ.

Album (92), Twin Surprise (95)

DOG SOLDIER - United States
Semi-progressive style sounding a bit like the simpler KANSAS material.

Dog Soldier (75)

DOLPHIN - Great Britain
Symphonic progressive rock style.

Molecules (80)

DOM - Germany
Early seventies group who created a dreamy, drifting, spacey progressive rock sound.

Edge of Time (72)

DONSI, MIKE - United States
A solid mix of many symphonic progressive rock ideas and motifs go to make up this music. Donsi handles most of the instruments but gets primary assistance on from others on guitar. You'll hear elements of spacey-ness as well.

Parallel Skies (99)

DORACOR - Italy
Solo artist Corrado Sardella handles all the musical chores to create a symphonic neo-progressive rock effort. No vocals, but plenty of great playing using both analog and digital keyboards. He includes a 'thanks' to bands like IQ, ARENA, LE ORME and THE FLOWER KINGS, which indicates generally the type of compositions you'll find here.

The Long Pathway (97), Segni Premonitori (98), Antiche Impressioni (99)

DORIAN GREY - Germany
They produced an underground style of progressive rock.

Idaho Transfer (76)

DOWNES, GEOFFREY - United States
Former keyboardist of the Buggles, YES and ASIA goes solo and comes up with a quasi new age progressive rock album that manages to avoid being just another boring keyboard album.

The Light program (86), Vox Humana (94), Evolution (96)

DRACMA - Spain
Epic symphonic material, strong on melody and elaborate arrangements. Fans of MARILLION and IQ will enjoy this band. Musically their material contains lots of alternating loud and soft parts, fast and slow sections, and interplay between electric and acoustic instruments.

Limits (94), A Fine Stormy Weather (96)

DRAFT & BILL - Italy
Early eighties style GENESIS sound with shorter more streamlined songs. More pop than prog.

Reported Missing (92)

DRAGON - Belgium
Similar to the early British bands like CRESSIDA. Elements of symphonic prog mixed with a little hard-rock and psychadelics underscored with some hard-edged guitar.

Dragon (76), Kalahen (77/86)

DRAGON - New Zealand
They have a very seventies British feel. Symphonic progressive rock of very good standards. Not unlike their countrymen RAGNAROK.

Scented Gardens For the Blind (74),Dragon (74),Running Free (77),Gragon (77),O Zambesi (78),Powerplay (78),Body & The Beat (84),Rain (84)

DRAGONFLY - Switzerland

Symphonic flavoured prog rock. Lots of guitar and keyboard interplay, with beautiful piano and synth work. Hints of TULL, YES and PFM.

Dragonfly (81)

DRAMA - United States

Instrumental symphonic progressive rock and some fusion. A little Like KENSO. Two members would later form LEGER DE MAIN.

Strange Expression (93 TAPE),Drama (93)

DRAMA - France

The good people at Musea have discovered a group that incorporates mid-period CAMEL, STEVE HACKETT, and ROUSSEAU styles creating a melodic progressive rock. The compositions are complex and challenging yet accessible.

Drama (96), Flying Over the 21st Century (98)

DRAPER, ALAN - Great Britain

Keyboardist and composer Draper creates a pleasant and uplifting form of symphonic progressive rock. He's assisted on the CD with guest playing guitar, flute and additional keyboards. The material contains lots of tonal variety with medieval motifs, marching sequences and more dramatic elements. If you enjoy GLASS HAMMER, THE ENID or JEREMY you'll enjoy the material here. The CD is actually his first, but is a compilation of material recorded privately over the past 15 years.

Ascention Day (99)

DREAM THEATER - United States

Changing styles from each album, but predominantly harder edge. Metal meets progressive rock. Imagine a blend of RUSH and KANSAS with Queensryche and Fates Warning.

When Dream and Day Unite (87),Images and Words (92),Awake (94),A Change of Seasons (95) Falling Into Infinity (97)

DREAMWORLD - Germany

Post -YATHA SIDRA symphonic new age sound.

On Flight to the Moon (80)

DRIFTING SUN - Great Britain

Four piece that started out with only a subtle prog influence and with their second release matured into neo-progressive outfit with emphasis on the keyboards. All in all a nice progression.

Drifting Sun (96), On the Rebound (99)

DRUGI NACIN - Yugoslavia

Melodic progressive rock with lots of guitar flute and organ.

Drugi Nacin ( )

DRUID - Great Britain

The band won the 1974 Melody Maker Rock/Folk Contest. They are from Berkhamstead, and got a lot of support from the press. They released two albums of some very fine material. They sound a lot like YES, but their song writing differs enough to create their own mark. Their drummer went on to play with Gary Numan and Dramatis.

Toward the Sun (75),Fluid Druid (76)

DUELLO MADRE - Italy

Energetic and complex progressive rock with constant guitar and sax duels.

Duello Madre ( )

DUN - France
They feature a refined superbly arranged French style chamber rock perhaps better recognized as the Zeuhl sub-genre. Beautiful and complex music with a hint of fusion, dominated by Pascal Van-Denbulke's flute work. Sound like-MANEIGE, SUPERSISTER.

Eros (81)

E.A.S. - United States
Trio of guitar, bass and drums that have incorporated many RUSH elements, although the synth work here tends to get more time. Lots of unusual time signatures and interesting guitar work dominate.

Absolute Presence (96)

E-MOTIVE - United States
Originally known as Love and Death, this nineties era New Jersey based band produces symphonic progressive rock with a strong EMERSON style keyboard flair. Their style of progressive rock shows influences from such bands as STYX and KANSAS and others from the mid seventies. Lots of guitar interlaced with Hammond in a solid neo-progressive sound.

E-Motive (99)

EARDANCE - United States
The band comes from the Chicago area. Besides the Robert Fripp influenced guitar, they also use the 'stick' like later KING CRIMSON.

Eardance (82)

EARTH AND FIRE - Holland
Formed originally in 1968. It wasn't until their seventies releases that they hit their progressive rock stride. Female vocalist Jenny Kaagman helped establish their unique sound. The band has often just been seen as pop band, but most of their material has complete sides devoted to concept pieces, with liberal amounts of Mellotron, multiple tempos and sonic dynamics thrown in.

Earth and Fire (69), Song of the Marching Children (71), Atlantis (73), To the World of a Future (75) Gate to Infinity (77), Reality Fills Fantasy (79), Andromeda Girl (81), In a State of Flux (82), Phoenix (83)

EARTH AND FIRE ORCHESTRA - Holland
Two original members of EARTH AND FIRE reformed in the nineties to revive some of the magic with more up-to-date production values. This is virtually all instrumental and more electronic that their earlier material, but still with some symphonic flourishes.

Frames (88)

EARTHSTAR - Germany
Space-rock music, with only some slight symphonics, some of it produced by Klaus Schultz.

Salterbarty Tales (78), French Skyline (79), Atomkraft? Nein Danke! (81), Humans Only (82)

EARTHSTONE - Great Britain
Formed from the remnants of two bands, Silas and Ranata Spirit both of whom had released cassettes. Generally keyboard based with some good guitar solos, straddling the line between CAMEL and RUSH.

Seed (94)

EAST - Hungary
Melodic progressive band that leans toward the symphonic realm. Great arrangements, and keyboard work similar to SOLARIS.

Jatekok (81), Huseg [Faith] (82), Resk A Falon (83), Az Alldozat [The Victim] (84), 1986 (86), Ket Arc [Live] ( ), A Szerelem Sivataga (88), Radio Babel ( ), Taking the Wheel ( )

EASTER ISLAND - United States
The band was from Kentucky. Their first LP released in 1979 featured lush symphonic textures that start with a wall-of-keyboard sound and build from there. Vocalist Rick Bartlett has great range and control. Sounds like CAMEL and GENESIS with lots of Mellotron. One of the best US bands, in the same league as BABYLON. Original guitarist Mark Miceli reformed the band in the late nineties and released a CD in 1999 featuring a more modern sound with just a few nods to YES in the vocal department.

Easter Island [Now and Then] (79), Mother Sun (99)

EAST OF EDEN - Great Britain
One of the pioneering progressive bands incorporating electric violin and dual saxes contributing to the creation of that early Anglo sound in a style similar to GRYPHON or RARE BIRD. Melodic, organ and guitar dominated music.

Mercantor Projected (69), Snafu (70), East of Eden (71), New Leaf (71),

ECHOLYN - United States
Pennsylvania based group with a varied sound. Sort of a cross between YES and GENTLE GIANT. Their trade mark sound was the use of complicated three part harmonies. They gave new hope to the future of progressive rock without falling into the mainstreaming tendencies of some neo-prog bands. Shortly after signing a deal with Epic Records they released As the World, then went into hiatus while members went on to form STILL and FINNEAUS GUAGE. Late in 1999 they came back together to create their first studio album in four years. The new material shows the influences of the intervening years solo efforts, and yet still features all the trademark Echolyn sounds.

Echolyn (91), Suffocating the Bloom (92), ...and Every Blossom (93), As the World (95), When the Sweet Turns Sour (96), Cowboy Poems Free (00)

ECLAT DE VERS - France
Progressive rock five-piece with beautiful guitar work. Sound like ANGE, SYNOPSIS, combined with the modern folk style incorporated by MINIMUM VITAL. Their early work featured more vocals while their later work tends to be more jazz-rock-fusion instrumentally based. They shortened their name to simply ECLAT

Eclat De Vers (92), Eclat II (94), Volume 3 (97), En Concert (99)

ECLECTIC MINDS - Canada
Nineties era neo-progressive band from Montreal with influences ranging from SAGA, MARILLION, IQ and even a bit of GENTLE GIANT.

EDEN - France
Keyboard and drum duo similar to BO HANNSSON or SFF.

Aura (79)

EDEN - Germany
RENAISSANCE inspired prog style.

Perelandra ( ), Erwartung ( ), Heimkehr ( )

EDGAR ALLEN POE - Italy
Early seventies melodic romantic prog sound in the classic Italian style.

Generazioni [Storia Di Sempre] (73)

EDGE, THE - Great Britain
Talented group sounding similar to RENAISSANCE with beautiful female vocals and seamless classical style arrangements. There is also a hint of CAMEL. Melodic and quite unique.

Suction 8 (86), Sarcastic Fringeheads (90)

EDGE OF WATER - Italy
U2 inspired with more progressive leanings.

EDHELS - France

Very melodious and memorable symphonic instrumental compositions, brilliantly performed, constructed and arranged and punctuated by splendid guitar parts. Sound like - KING CRIMSON, QUIET SUN, MANZANERA.

Oriental Christmas [LP](86), Still Dream [LP](88), Still Dream (88), Oriental Christmas (89), Astro-Logical (91), Marc Ceccotti - M.A.S.C. (93), Angel's Promise (97), Universal (99)

EDITH - Italy

Neo-progressive rock in the MARILLION vain. Nice guitar parts and good keyboards but best of all is their vocalist Mario Guilisano. His voice has the quality that many Italian singers of late try to suppress, a light, warm quality as in early PFM. Laid back melodic progressive rock.

A Space Between Ever and Never (89), Ice (91), Dreams (9?), Livetime (9?), Blue (9?)

EELA CRAIG - Austria

Successful Austrian band, highly interesting with much keyboard work and classical influences.

Eela Craig (71), One Nighter (76), Hats of Glass (77), Missa Universalis (78), Virgin Oiland (80)

EGAWA, TOSHIO - Japan

see GERARD

EGDON HEATH - Holland

Late eighties Dutch symphonic progressive rock band with lush keyboard work. They sported two keyboard players as well as the normal bass, guitar and drums. Influenced by later day GENESIS.

In the City (87), The Killing Silence (91), Him, The Snake and I (93), Nebula (9?)

EGG - Great Britain

Formed in late 1969, they established quite a reputation for themselves by bringing together jazz and that infamous Canterbury sound. Dave Stewart, later of HATFIELD AND THE NORTH started here. The public support was very short lived and they split in 72. Some serious instrumental music here, that takes a little listening to, but in the end worth it.

Egg (69), The Polite Force (70), Civil Surface (74)

EGO BAND - Italy

Symphonic progressive rock with big lush keyboard and harder edged sound. Their music contains elements of early PINK FLOYD, ELOY and AMON DUUL II with long repetitive instrumental passages and pastoral acoustic elements.

Trip in the Light of the World (91), Fingerprint (93), We Are... (96), Earth (99)

EIK, ALF EMIL - Iceland

Hrislan og Straumurinn ( ), Joys and Breath of Eternity (79)

EILIFF - Switzerland

A German-sounding progressive rock style, incorporating some left over psychedelic and jazz rock influences. Fans of bands like SATIN WHALE, EAST OF EDEN and GNIDROLOG will enjoy this.

Eiliff (71), Girlrls (72), Close Encounters with their Third One [live] (72/99)

EINSTEIN - Germany

A band that managed to incorporate the elements of SAGA, ELP and even KANSAS into their own style and managed to keep a sound that was their own. A mixture of all the above.

First Principles (79)

EINSTEIN - United States

Headed up by drummer Jonathan Mover, this three piece create a heavy and melodic style of what they call aggressive progressive rock. Influences include Led

Zeppelin, DREAM THEATRE and PINK FLOYD.

Einstein (97)

EKSEPTION - Holland

In some people's eyes this band was simply the jumping off point for Rick van der Linden to go and form TRACE. This band spent much of their time reworking or incorporating the classics into more of a rock format. Some wonderful experiments here, although they did prove to be a little hot and cold.

Ekseption (69), Beggar Julias Time Trip (69), 00.04 (71), Ekseption 5 (72), Trinity (73), Bingo (74), Mindmirror (75), Ekseptional ()

EKUS - Argentina 1990s

EL PUENTE DE ALVARADO - Mexico

Two former members of ICONOCLASTA and CHAC MOOL keyboardist join up for their unique blend of shorter instrumental progressive rock with a slight fusion influence.

Conquista Y Destruccion (96)

EL RELOJ - Argentina

While their later work is more in the heavy metal vein, progressive fans should look to their second album released in the seventies for one of the genre's finest recordings. Complex guitar oriented in the vein of CRUCIS.

El Reloj (75), II (76), Santos Y Verdugos (94), Hombre De Hoy (99)

ELECTRA - East Germany

Classical tinged progressive rock influenced by JETHRO TULL. Their LP Die Sixinische Madona is their most symphonic.

Electra Combo (74), Adaptionen (74), 3 (79),
Die Sixinische Madona (80), Ein Tag Wie Eine Brucke (81), Augen in Der Sehnsucht (85), Tausend und Ein Gefuhl (87)

ELECTRIC FRANKENSTEIN - Italy

Complex progressive rock.

Electric Frankenstein (75), What Me Worry? (76)

ELECTRIC LIGHT ORCHESTRA - Great Britain

Developed out of The Move, to incorporate all the best of the experimental mood of the times and a strong heritage left by the Beatles sound and came up with something virtually every critic felt was different. Over the years they carved out their own sound incorporating the ever present sawing cello and violin. Sadly even these left as Jeff Lynne became more and more obsessed with writing the next pop hit. At the end very little progressive rock remained.

Electric Light Orchestra (72), ELO 2 (73), On the Third Day (73), Eldorado (74), Face the Music (75), A New World Record (76), Out of the Blue (77), Discovery (79), Time (81), Secret Messages (83), Balance of Power (86)

ELECTRIC SANDWICH - Germany

Early sound produced by Conny Plank featuring lots of Mellotron. A little more on the rock side.

Electric Sandwich (73)

ELEGANT SIMPLICITY - Great Britain

Melodic symphonic prog with an up-front keyboard sound but the guitar is nevery very far away. Many long compositions full of melody and swelling orchestrations. If you enjoy CAMEL, BARCLAY JAMES HARVEST and PENDRAGON you'll enjoy what you hear here.

Improper Advances (92), Nocturnal Implications (93), Blinded by Time (93), Inside the Hurting (94), Crying to the Future (94), Endless Longing (94), Natural Instinct (95), The Nature of Change (96), Reversal of Time (97), Purity and Despair (98), Moments of Clarity (99), The Story of Our Lives (00)

ELEPHANT AND CASTLE - Great Britain

Late eighties band with a musical style like later material from IQ in that it fuses neo-progressive and modern pop into a different genre. Nice full arrangements of melodic progressive rock.

The Green One ( )

ELIXIR - France

Formed in the late eighties they created a dramatic progressive rock similar to ANGE or ATOLL with hints of IQ and STEVE HACKETT. Nice melodies based on energetic rhythms, with good interplay between the keyboards, guitars and vocals.

Sabbat (87), Indifference (90)

ELOHIM - France

The second band to hold this name and follow in the tradition of the French progressive rock scene. Sound like - ANGE, ATOLL.

Le Mana Perdu (83)

ELOY - Germany

At various points in their career they paid homage to PINK FLOYD in sound, but quickly went on to carve out their own type of symphonic-progressive rock. The albums tended to be rather big screen concept works. Eloy create mood through not only the keyboard work but through their lyrics and story telling.

Eloy (71), Inside (73), Floating (74), Power and the Passion (75), Dawn (76), Ocean (77), Live (78), Silent Cries and Mighty Echoes (79), Colours (80), Planets (81), Time and Turn (82), Performance (83), Metromania (84), Ra (88), Rarities (91), Destination (92), The Tides Return Forever (94), Ocean 2 (98)

EMERALD WEB - United States

A duo consisting of Bob Stohl and Kat Epple who combine electronics and acoustics to superb effect. Music is on the exotic side. Ethereal, yet progressive, delicate yet dynamic, old and new, their music is a balance of many elements. A bit new-agey but not annoyingly so.

Dragons Wings and Wizard Tales ( ), Lights of the Ivory Plains (84), Whispered Visions ( ), Sound Trek ( ), Aqua Regia ( ), Valley of the Birds ( ), Nocturn ( )

EMERAUDE - France

Melodic and symphonic, folk oriented progressive rock.

Geoffrey ( )

EMERGENCY - Germany

A mixture of jazz, rock, and a bit of prog. The band featured the saxophone prominently with organ and keyboards behind.

Emergency (71), Entrance (72), Get to the Country (73), Hideaway (73), Gold Rock (74), No Compromise (74)

EMERSON, KEITH - Great Britain

Emerson, along with Wakeman have been singled out as creating the keyboard ethic for progressive rock music. They have influenced more keyboard players than all the others combined. From his groundbreaking work in THE NICE incorporating the classics to his keyboard and orchestra experimentation's in ELP, Emerson has created a legacy of music that will continue to inspire future keyboard players.

Inferno (80), Night Hawks (81), Murderock ( ), Changing States (96), The Christmas Album (99)

EMERSON, LAKE & PALMER - Great Britain

One of the first supergroups, this trio evolved from THE NICE, ATOMIC ROOSTER and KING CRIMSON. They went on to become a standard of measurement for other progressive rock bands. Their style of incorporating classics into a new format set the benchmark for others.

Emerson Lake & Palmer (70), Tarkus (71), Pictures at an Exhibition (71), Trilogy (72), Brain Salad Surgery (73), Welcome Back My Friends (74), Works (77), Works Vol. 2 (77), Love Beach (78), In Concert (79), Emerson Lake & Powell (86), Black Moon (92), Live at the Royal Albert Hall (93), Return of the Manitcore [Box Set] (93), In the Hot Seat (94), Live at the Isle of Wight Festival (97), King Biscuit Flower Hour Presents (97), Then & Now (98)

EMOND, REDJY - Canada

This keyboard player from Quebec brings his classical skills to bear in compositions that will appeal to fans of ELP and ARSNOVA. The interesting orchestrations feature strong melodies, interesting tempo shifts and rich synth colours.

Spheres (96)

EMPEROR - United States

One of the few bands to incorporate the pomp style with such grace. Their material includes a mini-epic that should satisfy many progressive rock fans. Sound a little like a softenedup STYX or ANGEL.

Emporer (77)

EMPIRE - Italy

A trio featuring a female singer with a sound that borrows from UK and ELP. Musically they have a modern symphonic neo-prog sound that should go over well with fans.

Back to Knowledge (94)

EMTIDI - Germany

Floating psychedelic progressive rock sound with beautiful female vocals.

Emtidi (72), Saat (72)

ENBOR - Spain

Perhaps the least folk inspired of the Spanish progressive rock groups, they're more a rock group with some Anglo-progressive rock tendencies.

Enbor (79), Katebegiak (80)

ENCHANT - United States

Their first CD was produced by MARILLION guitarist Steve Rothery, they create a solid, guitar heavy, neo-prog sound based on the Duke period GENESIS. With Wounded the band began to explore more mellow moments to provide a heightened contrast to their music. Also sounds like JADIS, IQ.

Enchant (91), A Blueprint of the World (93), Wounded (97), Time Lost (97), Break (99)

ENEIDE - Italy

Early seventies sounding band.

Eneide (72), Uomini Umili Popoli Liberi [recorded 1972] (91)

ENGEL DER VERNICHTUNG - Italy

Traditional classical progressive rock sound.

ENGLAND - Great Britain

Robert Webb formed this band in 1976 and on their first album they created some very fine symphonic progressive rock. Webb's fascination with the Mellotron used throughout the LP helps create a sound for them a bit like YES and a bit like GENESIS during the Wind & Wuthering period. A plus for a band that manages to compose and record all that is great about symphonic prog. A second LP was finally released in 1995 after being held in storage since 1979.

Garden Shed (77), Last of the Jubilees (79/95)

ENGRENAGE - Canada
Instrumental space-rock from this nineties Quebec band, in the same vein as OZRIC TENTACLES, HAWKWIND, PORCUPINE TREE and early PINK FLOYD. Most songs are in the four - six minute range.

ENID, THE - Great Britain
One of the most unique bands ever. Using all the latest instruments they create a sound so symphonic it'll fool you into thinking it's a full orchestra. Their music is mostly instrumental with a very classical sense of arrangement and structure. They create such a sense of power one moment and yet can be so pastoral the next. A must for all collections.

In the Region of Summer Stars (76), Aerie Faerie Nonsense (77), Touch Me (79), Six Pieces (79), Live at the Hammersmith 1 (83), Live at the Hammersmith 2 (83), Something Wicked This Way Comes (83), The Stand (84), The Spell (84), Fand (85), Lovers and Fools (86), Salome (86), The Seed and the Sower (88), The Final Noise (88), Tripping the Light Fantastic (94), Sundailer (95), White Goddess (98)

EPICA - Italy
Five piece from the Venice area producing progressive metal in the style of DREAM THEATRe. Nice song structure but the keyboards do take a back-seat.

Confini (95)

EPIDAURUS - Germany
Dual Mellotron/keyboard symphonic progressive rock. Beautiful CAMEL-RENAISSANCE inspired music with lots of keyboards, great guitar playing and superb female vocals. They reformed in 1994 to record their second album, which shows a similar although more commercial style.

Earthly Paradise (77), Endangered (94)

EPIDERMIS - Germany
Masterful GENTLE GIANT flavoured sound. They compose a combination of longer progressive tracks with shorter hard edged material. But the mixture of oboe in a digital environment really works.

Genius of the Original Force (77), Feel Me (90)

EPILOGUE - Great Britain
Material is pretty poppy for the most part. They combine the more accessible elements of neo-prog and the style of a lot of mid eighties synth rock bands. The lead singer sounds similar to Steve Hogarth of MARILLION. Similar to GRACE, PENDRAGON or IQ.

Hide (94)

EPISODE - United States
Melodic symphonic material from San Francisco similar to RENAISSANCE. Other influences include YES and PINK FLOYD but in some cases the material is more simply arranged.

Fortunes (85 TAPE), Into the Epicentre (89), Edge of the Sky (91 TAPE), Starlight Tales (93)

EPITAPH - Germany
Started out as a hard rock band and later turned into blues and heavy metal. Their first recording had a bit of Mellotron and incorporated some hints of prog.

Epitaph (71), Outside the Law (74), Stop, Look and Listen (75), Return to Reality (78), See You in Alaska (80), Live (81), Danger Man (82)

EPOS - Russia
Symphonic prog with some ethnic musical elements.

Ilya ( )

EQUINOX - Panama
A five piece Panamanian band with a very professional symphonic prog style. Featuring a traditional instrument line-up their sound hearkens back to all that was great about seventies prog, but updates it nicely, all the while injecting an enjoyable ethnic feel. Their second CD took a slightly more agressive and darker tone and introduced female vocalist Dalys Toruno. There's lots to like about this band.

Equinox (98), Spirits of Freedom (00)

ERA DI ACQUARIO - Italy
Melodic progressive rock with nice acoustic guitar and flute interplay.

Antologia (73)

ERGO SUM - France
Early seventies French progressive rock of the Zeuhl variety with sinister vocals.

Mexico (72)

ERIS PLUVIA - Italy
Highly rated symphonic progressive rock. Their music is based around acoustic guitars, keyboards, flutes and most notably a recorder to evoke a very period sound to the music. This gives their music a very light texture that is very appealing. They became THE ANCIENT VEIL.

Rings of Earthly Light (85), Ancient Veil ( )

EROC - Germany
Main member of the band GROBSCHNITT goes off on his own to create a couple of rather unusual LPs. Lots of sound effects both natural and electronic, and are very percussive in spots.

Eroc (75), Zwei (77), 3 (79), 4 (82), Wolkenreise ( ), Changing Skies ( )

ERRATA CORRIGE - Italy
A seventies band that reformed for the nineties. Symphonic progressive rock in the ELP or GENESIS vein.

Mappomondo (75), Siegfried, Il Drago E Altre Storia (76),

ERROBI - Spain
One of several bands from the Basque region of Spain that mix folk with prog. Excellent flute and acoustic guitar work. If you like the other Basque groups (ITOIZ, LISKER, SAKRE, etc.) then you should enjoy this.

Errobi (78), Gure Lekukotasuna (78), Ametsaren Bidea (79), Bizi Bizian (82)

ERTLIF - Switzerland

Ertlif (7?)

ESPERONTO ROCK ORCHESTRA - Great Britain
They performed a complex style of prog rock with many time and tempo changes.

Esperonto Rock Orchestra (73), Danse Macabre (74), Last Tango (75)

ESPIRITU - Argentina
Mid period YES-GENESIS like symphonic progressive rock. Their best known work is Crisalida which features a complex guitar and synthesiser sound that is reminiscent of SEMIRAMIS. Their later work moved to a less complicated style more resembling PABLO EL ENTERRADOR.

Crisalida (73), Libre Y Natural (76), Live En Obras (82)

ESQUIRE - Great Britain
Band fronted by Chris Squire's wife, along with two other members. Sounds like a cross between RENAISSANCE (vocals) and YES (Bass). Shorter songs but still interesting.

Esquire (87), Coming Home (96)

ESTRUCTURA - Venezuela
A symphonic progressive rock style.
Mas Alla de tu Mente (78)

ET CETERA - Canada
One of the prime Quebecois bands that released one self-titled album featuring an intricate jazz-fusion style. They were heavily influenced by GENTLE GIANT and many of the seventies Italian progressive bands such as BANCO or PFM, and it shows in their male and female vocals and compositional style.

Et Cetera (76)

ETCETERA - Denmark
A mixture of many influences. You might hear early MOODY BLUES, a bit of TONY BANKS or KEITH EMERSON, a small sampling of GENTLE GIANT and even some NATIONAL HEALTH. Lots of variety, great production with plenty to listen to.

Fin De Siecle (99)

ETERNIDAD - Argentina
This is a folk influenced symphonic prog with a slight YES influence. You'll hear lots of pleasant harmonies with swelling keyboards in some well arranged compositions.

Apertura (77)

ETHOS - United States
American symphonic progressive rock that is influenced heavily by early KING CRIMSON. Some say their second album is a little more accessible. They also manage to blend a bit of STYX and YES into their sound. An American classic with dual keyboards. The Relics release features some unreleased material along with alternate versions of existing material.

Ardour (76), Open Up (77), Relics (99)

EURHYBIA - France
Nineties era neo-progressive rock band with hints of MARILLION or IQ.

Eurhybia (96)

EVENT - United States
If you like your prog with a heavy slant, Event will be just for you. Taking a page out of DREAM THEATRE's progressive side these compositions betray enough prog flouishes to keep things interesting.

Electric Skies (99)

EVEREST - Canada
Interesting band that tried to fill the gap between SAGA and MARILLION. Attempted to use all the progressive rock elements in a way that was not as obvious to the average ear. The band truly felt people liked the old style progressive rock even if they were not prepared to admit it.

Everest (84)

EVERON - Germany
Hard hitting symphonic progressive rock in the style of RUSH, SAGA or PALLAS. Very dynamic songs all around six minutes in length with some much longer. Great melodies and themes. The vocalist sounds like GREG LAKE at times. Their style emphasises a wall of keyboards and lots of good guitar work.

Paradoxes (93), Flood (95), Venus (97), Fantasma (00)

EVIDENCE - France
Similar to VDGG and PETER HAMMILL.

Heart's Grave (96)

EVOLUTION - Great Britain
See: SENIOR, KEN

EXAMPLE OF LIFE - Japan
A nineties trio who's sound hearkens back to KING CRIMSON'S Larks... and Red period. Instrumental compositions performed in a more aggressive style.

EXISTENCE - Canada
English singing band from Quebec who createa neo-progressive rock. Their influ-

ences range from KANSAS to SUPERTRAMP. A combination of long and short songs with good musicianship. Their first release suffers from poor production.

EXIT - Switzerland
A mid seventies band that produced an organ dominated progressive rock sound.

Exit (75)

EXODUS - Poland
Poland's best known classical-progressive rock band, with some distinct YES influences including a high tenor lead vocalist. The second album is not as strong musically as the first.

The Most Beautiful Day (79), Supernova (81)

EXPERIENCE - France
Early seventies styled progressive rock with an organ dominated sound.

Experience (70)

EXPLOIT - Italy
Nice melodic progressive rock. Their album Crisis contains a 20 minute suite.

Crisis (72)

EXPLORERS CLUB - United States
This studio project was masterminded by Trent Gardner of MAGELLAN. He composed the material and then enlisted the help of a whos-who of prog and prog metal to bring it to fruition. It features members of DREAM THEATRE and many others even including STEVE HOWE. The material is heavily guitar oriented and bombastic. If you're a fan of the bands mentioned and prog metal in general this will be right up your alley.

Age of Impact (98)

EXVITAE - France
A cross between jazz-rock and progressive rock with original and attractive themes on which inspired instrumentalists express themselves. A lot of ideas and a great variety of instruments including sax, violin, keyboards, percussions, flute and guitar.

Mandarine (79)

EZRA - Great Britain
Up-tempo three piece, progressive rock in the style of IT BITES and SAGA. The style is very close to pop but contains enough prog flourishes and musicianship to bring it all together.

Shapes (94), Big Smiley Sun (98)

EZRA WINSTON - Italy
Hailed by many as Italy's best symphonic progressive rock group of the eighties and nineties. Their style incorporates soft and subtle, intricate guitar and flute work, which builds to more fanfare-ish themes.

Myth of the Chrysavides (90), Ancient Afternoon (90)

FAITHFUL BREATH - Germany
Symphonic music with hints of PINK FLOYD and ELOY in long song arrangements. This is an early German progressive Mellotron masterwork. NOTE: they turned into a heavy metal band later.

Fading Beauty (73), Back On My Hill (80), Rock Lions (81)

FAIRY - Japan
Symphonic progressive rock.

Hesperia ( )

FALLEN FOE - Germany
A solid neo-progressive rock style.

Fallen Foe (9? TAPE), Separating Air and Fire (9?)

FAMILY - Great Britain
One of the early British bands that helped

shape progressive rock, Family's compositions are not overly complex but they did their fare share of musical experimentation for the times. While their list of records is long it's really only their first two recordings that will interest prog fans.

In a Dolls House (68), Family Entertainment (69)

FANCYFLUID - Italy
Symphonic neo-progressive rock that sounds a bit like CAMEL or IQ at times. Their early material shows a strong Marillion influence. They matured into one of the more respected groups on the revitalised Italian prog scene.

FancyFluid (89 TAPE), Weak Waving (91), King's Journey (92), The Sheltering Sea (95)

FANTASIA - Finland
Independently released symphonic prog material.

Fantasia (75)

FANTASY - Great Britain
A fine example of the early British progressive rock sound ala THE MOODY BLUES. They released a now, legendary melodic album, Paint a Picture with plenty of Mellotron.

Paint a Picture (73), Beyond the Beyond (74), Viviratium (76)

FAR EAST FAMILY BAND - Japan
Keyboardist KITARO'S first band of note. They created a New Age sound even then with this album produced by Klaus Shultz. Japanese legends! Sounds like some of the best PINK FLOYD.

Nepporjin (75), The Cave Down to Earth (75), Parallel World (76), Tenkeyin (77)

FAST, LARRY - Great Britain
Keyboardist virtuoso Fast made a reputation in the studio and went on to join Peter Gabriel's band. Often found in the company of Robert Fripp and others of the old British prog school, Fast released his first solo album until the title SYNERGY. The album was the electronic equivalent of Tubular Bells with all instruments played by Fast but entirely synthesised. Programming for the album was done by Rick Wakeman. Synergy became a moderate success on both sides of the Atlantic.

Electronic Realisations for Rock Orchestra (75), Sequencer (76), Cords (78), Games (79), Computer Experiments Vol. 1 (81), Audion (81), The Jupiter Menace (82), Metropolitan Suite (87)

FELLOWSHIP - Italy
Progressive folk material in the Malicorne vein.

La Sorciere et Le Villageois ( )

FESTA MOBILE - Italy
Progressive rock in the classic Italian style.

Diario di Viaggio (73)

FIELDS - Great Britain
Graham Field, following the split of RARE BIRD, formed this band creating a mixture of 'good songs' and neo classical rock. A short-lived band with an ELP-ish classical flavour and even a bit of Mellotron.

Fields (71)

FIG LEAF - Norway
Sometimes grouped with prog-metal bands, Fig Leaf's musical palet is a little more broad than that. While the over all sound certainly has its heavy moments they're more along the lines of DEEP PURPLE. Add to this the inclusion of instruments such as flute and saxaphone and you get the impression there is a little more going on here.

Fearless (99)

FINAL CONFLICT - Great Britain

Nineties era neo-progressive rock group similar to GALAHAD or IQ. Thier material is generally in the six to eight minute range with a few shorter instrumentals.

Redress the Balance (91), Quest (92), Stand Up (97)

FINCH - Holland

Long instrumental sections spotlighted with some sharp guitar and keyboard work throughout. Their second release features a guitar style very similar to STEVE HOWE. Known for their tight playing, complex composition and splendid musicianship.

Glory of the Inner Force (75), Beyond Expression (76), Galleons of Passion (77), The Making of Galleons of Passion/Stage '76 (99)

FINISTERRE - Italy

Symphonic progressive rock with long tracks containing restrained hints of bands like CELESTE or BANCO. They've chosen to create a moody and atmospheric sound that relies more on the classical style than neo-prog alone. Long passages of dissonant harmonies and jazzy chord voicings.

Finisterre (95), In Limine (96), Al Margini Della Terra Fertile [Live] (98), In Ogni Luogo (99)

FINNEGANS WAKE - Belgium

Classically influenced symphonic prog with a violin style similar in sound to ENGLAND and CRESSIDA.

Yellow (94), Green (96)

FINNEUS GAUGE - United States

The nineties offshoot project headed by former ECHOLYN keyboardist/songwriter Chris Buzby. Their material incorporates elements of jazz, Canterbury fusion and soaring multi-part vocal harmonies reminiscent of Chris' writing with ECHOLYN. If you are a fan of GENTLE GIANT and the previously mentioned ECHOLYN, you'll enjoy this.

More Once More (97), One Inch of the Fall (99)

FINNFOREST - Finland

More of a fusion band than anything, should appeal to fans of that style. A reference point might be PEKKA POHJOLA'S B The Magpie and FINCH's Beyond Expression. Fans of NATIONAL HEALTH and KENSO will enjoy this.

Finnforest (75), Lahto Matkalle (76), Demon Nights (79)

FIORI SEGUIN - Canada

A musical effort from Serge Fiori and Richard Seguin. Folk and rock styles combine to make a distinctive French-Canadian progressive rock which contains musical elements of MANEIGE and HARMONIUM.

Deux Cents Nuits a l'heure (78)

FIRE - Great Britain

A band who produced a wonderful progressive rock concept piece.

Magic Shoemaker (70)

FIRE MERCHANTS - Great Britain

FIREBALLET - United States

The band did their part to further the cause of American progressive rock by producing their own versions of some of the classics. The use of good solid guitar and Mellotron along with complicated arrangements and vocal counterpoint make their two efforts very enjoyable. Sound borrows from the early KANSAS school of music.

Night on Bald Mountain (75), Two, Too (76)

FIRST AID - Great Britain
Fusion music.

Stumbling Boldly Forward ( ), Nostradamus (77)

FIRST MYSTERIOUS APPEARANCE - Holland
Softer progressive rock in the vein of later CAMEL.

FISH - Great Britain
Former lead vocalist with Marillion, he left to pursue a solo career, most of which picks up where he left off with the band although perhaps not as musically adventurous. While some of his solo material has tended to be somewhat more pop oriented, Sunsets on Empire showed a slight return to his prog roots. Thought provoking lyrics about the state of the world written from his own unique perspective.

Vigil in a Wilderness of Mirrors (90), Internal Exile (91), Song From The Mirror (93), Suits (94), The Acoustic Session (94), Yin (95), Yang (95), Krakow [Live] (96), Sunsets on Empire (97), Raingods With Zippos (99)

FITZPATRICK, GREGORY ALAN - Sweden
From the band SAMLA.

FIVE FIFTEEN - Finland
They create a style that incorporates psychadelic, hard rock and a very keyboard driven progressive rock.

Six Dimensions of the Electric Camembert (98)

FLAMBOROUGH HEAD - Holland
Formed in 1995, this group features twin keyboard players which provide more than just a wall of keyboards. There are many textures at work in their material and while it has moments where its lound and bombastic there are just as many subtle elements at work. Their material is strong on melody and includes 3 instrumentals so if you enjoy IQ, PENDRAGON or JADIS you'll enjoy Flamborough Head.

Unspoken Whisper (98)

FLAME DREAM - Switzerland
A quartet that came on the scene during the late seventies and produced a symphonic prog with elements of early GENESIS, YES and GENTLE GIANT. The music is relatively complex for the time and while there are many long instrumental passages they are never annoying. While not every album features a guitar they do incorporate Mellotrons, flutes and even a sax.

Gaatea ( ), Elements (79), Out of the Dark (80), Supervision (82), Travaganza (82), 8 On 6 (86)

FLAMEN DIALIS - France
A mixture of MIKE OLDFIELD, some electronic and progressive rock with a bit of Celtic music. Musea calls it totally original.

FLAMING BESS - Germany
Symphonic progressive rock in a style similar to CAMEL or EPIDAURUS.

Tanz der Gotter (79)

FLAMING YOUTH - Great Britain
The band that Phil Collins was in before joining GENESIS. Longish but simply arranged material.

Ark 2 (69)

FLASH - Great Britain
A band that was the result of two former YES members putting their heads together. The three albums they produced sounded very much like early YES, with different songs. Good to have in the collection.

Flash (72), In the Can (72), Out of Our Hands (73)

FLASHMAN - Great Britain
One album art-rock-ish sounding like a cross with ALAN PARSONS and glam rock. Long concept work.

Flashman (79)

FLEA - Italy
Seventies era guitar oriented progressive rock group with hints of JETHRO TULL.

Top O Uomini (72)

FLEA ON THE HONEY - Italy
Early seventies group featuring a mix between pop and progressive with nice melodies.

Flea on the Honey (71)

FLOWER KINGS, THE - Sweden
Symphonic prog band created by ROINE STOLT, former guitarist with KAIPA. Their sound is influenced by YES, ELP and CAMEL, with lots of nice long instrumental sections featuring some HACKETT style guitar and tons of Hammond organ and Mellotron. Long tracks with a very dynamic and dramatic style. see: ROINE STOLT

Back in the World of Adventure (95), Retropolis (96), Stardust We Are (97), Scanning the Greenhouse [Compilation] (98), Flower Power (99), Alive on Planet Earth (00), Space Revolver (00)

FLUX
Solo artist Jim Lotkin masters all sorts of instruments and comes up with a sound that is both ambient, spacey and industrial with hints of eighties KING CRIMSON. Lots of dynamics, twists and turns, changing tempos all with a somewhat dark almost gothic feel. Processed vocals are suppled by Ruth Collins.

Protoplasmic (97)

FLYING CIRCUS - Germany
This seven member German outfit takes the heavier path which incorporates keyboards but the main emphasis is guitar. The vocalist is rather high-pitched, sort of resembling David Surkamp of PAVLOV'S DOG.

Seasons (98)

FLYNN, ANTHONY - United States
Progressive rock mixed with acoustic guitar instrumentals and a tinge of jazz fusion. Like ANTHONY PHILLIPS hits Pat Metheney.

Angel's Breath (90)

FLYTE - Holland
A six piece outfit who created a symphonic progressive rock sound rich in melodies, driven by guitar, two sets of keyboards, bass and drums. Sounds similar to MACHIAVEL and CASTANARC.

Dawn Dancer (79)

FM - Canada
A trio whose music has become more pop over the years. Their early albums were great progressive rock, with unusual instruments like violin or mandolin used instead of guitar. Lots of long instrumental passages with great solos. Their LP City of Fear was produced by Larry Fast.

Headroom (77), Black Noise (78), Surveillance (79), City of Fear (80), Contest (86) Retroactive: FM Archives Volume 1 (95)

FOCUS - Holland
Formed in Amsterdam in 1969, they became a major concert attraction in Europe playing extended songs with lots of classical bits thrown in. Over the years their music matured and some say peaked with the LP-Hamburger Concerto. Some great guitar, keyboard and flute work.

In and Out of Focus (71),Moving Waves (71),Focus III (72),At The Rainbow (73),Hamburger Concerto (74),Mother Focus (75),Ship of Memories (76),Focus Con Proby (78),Akkerman & Leer (85)

FOGLIE DI VETRO - Italy

Another of the new Italian bands that hearken back to the classic seventies sound. Their material is original with hints of PFM and A PIEDI NUDI.

Foglie Di Vetro (96)

FONYA - United States

This is essentially a one-man show, a product of Chris Fournier. A flowing symphonic sound that is a merger of CRAFT, ELOY and OZRIC TENTACLES. A sometimes spacey progressive rock with well developed, highly structured compositions. An unabashed fan of bands such as GENESIS and YES he has included covers of tunes from them on his solo releases.

Wanderers of the Neverending Night (92), Soul Travels (93), In Flux (95), Earth Shaper (96), Perfect Cosmological Principle (97), Upper Level Open Space (98)

FOOL'S GARDEN - Germany

Perhaps better labelled as closer to prog-pop. Nicely crafted songs with a strong Beatles influence. Good melodies and harmonies. Progressive fans will however appreciate the use of Mellotron, good guitar solos and some interesting effects.

Dish of the Day (9?)

FOR ABSENT FRIENDS - Holland

A very melodic neo-progressive band whose sound is similar to mid-late period IQ.

86/88 (88),Live (89),Nerd Illusion (90),Illusions (90),Both Worlds (91),Running In Circles (94),Faf out of Hal (95),Tintinabulation (96)

FOR YOUR PLEASURE -

Sounds similar to GENESIS of the nineties.

Scattered Pages (93)

FORCEFIELD - Great Britain

Formed in the late 1980's by Ray Fenwick, Cozy Powell and Pete Prescott. Forcefield featured a rotating line-up of musicians from Focus, Colosseum, Rainbow and the Spencer Davis Group amongst others. The band's instrumental album is the most progressive with outstanding contributions by Focus' Jan Akkerman and legendary keyboard player Don Airey. Imagine Focus meets Deep Purple.

Forcefield (87), Instrumentals (88), Forcefield III (89), Forcefield IV (90)

FOREVER EINSTEIN - United States

Very distinctive sound from this trio playing bass, drums, and amplified acoustic guitar. Musically they inhabit territory pioneered by the mid seventies KING CRIMSON of Larks Tongue in Aspic. Lots of musical twists and turns with many unexpected pleasures. A combination of both short and long instrumental works that are quirky and catchy.

Artificial Horizon (90), Opportunity Crosses the Bridge (92), One Thing After Another (98), Down With Gravity (00)

FORMULA - Germany

A six piece group who show a MARILLION influence. Lots of good guitar-keyboard-flute interplay

Signals (90),Blue (92)

FORMULA 3 - Italy

Progressive trio in the same vein as ALUMMONGENI or TRIADE. Their first two albums showed them moving slowly away from a psychedelic sound to a more progressive rock style.

Dies Irae (70), Formula 3 (71),Sognando E Risognando (72),La Grand Casa (73)

FOUNDATION - Sweden

This mid eighties band's instrumentation included the Chapman stick and some cello, which set it apart then and still makes for some interesting listening today. The compositions stick pretty close to the GENESIS style, but there's also some interesting VANGELIS like keyboards happening. Their solo release was re-issued in 1999 with some bonus tracks including a 16 minute epic composition.

Departure (85/99)

FOUNTAIN OF TEARS - United States

This is a five piece band featuring a female vocalist. Their musical style is clearly symphonic progressive rock. Along with the lush keyboard work comes intense, driving orchestrations with loads of drama.

Fountain of Tears (99)

FOURTH ESTATE - United States

A power guitar trio from Colorado from the same school as the STEVE MORSE BAND. The material is distinctly melody driven, not overly complicated, sometimes more rock than prog, but never dull.

Finesse and Fury (92),See What I See (95),War of the Worlds (98)

FOXTROT - Norway

Featuring ex-members of KERRS PINK and as you can imagine this has a GENESIS feel to it.

A Shadow of the Past (84)

FRAGIL - Peru

This late seventies band's goal was to recreate the sound of early YES and GENESIS and to varying degrees they succeeded on their sole release.

Avenida Larco (81/99)

FRAGILE GLASS - United States

A California group who create music in the vein of PENDRAGON or MARILLION. Good song writing and impeccable playing highlight this slightly commercial sounding band.

Farewell Father Analogue (89)

FRAME - Germany

Early Bellaphon label progressive band with good organ and Mellotron sound. Hints of DEEP PURPLE.

Frame of Mind (72)

FRANCO MARIA GIANNINI - Italy

Early folk-ish progressive rock with Mellotron and flute accents.

Affresco ( )

FREDERA - Brazil

CAMEL influenced progressive rock.

FREEHAND - United States

Tight musicianship is the key to this band of multi-instrumentalists. Progressive rock with a bit of fusion. A mixture of KING CRIMSON, GENTLE GIANT and Allan Holdsworth. They changed their name to Smokin Granny.

Thinking Out Loud (88)

FRENCH, SALLY - Great Britain

Fans of female vocalists will like what they hear with Sally French. While the music is primarily in the folk-pop realm, the arrangements are heavy in the symphonic keyboard department including Mellotron.

The Other Side (94)

FRENCH TV - United States

A band formed in Kentucky. Real solid instrumental progressive rock with plenty of symphonic moments. This fusion, Canterbury influenced group is more in the prog-rock vein while still retaining their spirit of fun and musical adventure.

French TV (83), After a Lengthy Silence (87), Virtue in Futility (94), Intestinal Fortitude (95), After a Lengthy Silence (96), Live: Yoo-Hoo (97), The Violence of Amateurs (99)

FRITSCH, ELOY - Brazil

Keyboardist with the band APOCALYPSE, his symphonic solo material is equally as good. Eurock says:...some of the most dynamic electronic music I've heard. The rhythms are high powered and energetic, and the melody arrangements are crisp and full of bright synthetic tone colours.

Dreams (95), Space Music (98), Behind the Walls of Imagination (99)

FROMAGE - Japan

Symphonic progressive rock is the style of TAI PHONG. Great emotional style.

Ondine (84), Tsukini-Hoeru (85), Ophelia (88),

FRUITCAKE - Norway

The band features male and female vocalists, two keyboardists and two guitarists. They concentrate on the melodic elements of a song with minimal lyrics. Like many Scandanavian groups there is a certain melancholy to their style with many memorable musical motifs. A cross between PENDRAGON and ANGLAGARD.

How to Make it (94), Room For Surprise (96), One More Slice (97), Power Structure (98)

FRUUPP - Great Britain

Formed in Belfast in the early seventies. Hints of YES and GENESIS but for the most part the band developed their own delicate sound with flowing melodies punctuated by folk-ish instrumental sections. Longish songs with nice keyboard work.

Future Legends (73), Prince of Heavens Eyes (74), Seven Secrets (74), Modern Masquerades (75)

FSB - Bulgaria

Dual keyboard band featuring loads of synthesisers whose influences include jazz, rock and classical elements. They create a symphonic music in a style similar to OMEGA. Their first album features a classical violinist.

Non Stop (77), 2 (78), Kula (80), 8 Obratow (81), Po Dziesiecu (83), Vi (8?), In Concert (8?)

FUHRS AND FROHLING - Germany

Two-thirds of SFF. Real good instrumental dreamy progressive rock feel.

Ammerland (78), Strings (79), Diary (81)

FUSION ORCHESTRA - Great Britain

They created a very dynamic, jazz-influenced hard rock with lots of instrumental prowess. The group featured a female vocalist and might be best compared to BABE RUTH.

A Skeleton In Armour (73)

FUSIOON - Spain

A fusion of progressive rock with classical music and folk. They are from the Balearic Islands in the Mediterranean. They have three very rare albums all since re-released on CD. The first LP shows the band just finding their footing, while the second shows them stretching our with more involved compositions and then the third firmly establishing them as one of the premier Spanish symphonic prog bands.

Fusioon (72), Fusioon II (74), Minorisa (75)

FYREWORKS, THE - Great Britain

Unknown prog artist of the seventies Danny Chang unites with Robert Reed of

CYAN in the nineties to produce some classic progressive rock in the best British tradition. Their style borrows from the mid-period GENESIS sound, in particular you'll hear STEVE HACKETT and ANTHONY PHILLIPS influences.

The Fyreworks (97)

GAA - Germany
Progressive rock with some space-rock elements incorporating a heavy organ sound. In the style of KAPUTTER HAMSTER or SUBJECT ESQ.

Auf Der Bahn Uranus (74), Alraunes Apltraum [Compilation] (98)

GABRIEL, PETER - Great Britain
Gabriel was the lead vocalist with GENESIS, and in 1975 left to pursue a solo career. The music he creates today is full of ethnic rhythm sections that provoke exotic flights of fantasy. Highly percussive and full of sampled sounds Gabriel remains at the forefront of progressive rock in attitude if not completely in musical style.

Peter Gabriel I (77), Peter Gabriel II (78), Peter Gabriel III (80), Peter Gabriel IV (82), Plays Live (83), So (86), US (92)

GALAAD - Switzerland
A sound featuring long tracks in the seven, nine and eleven minute range. Their vocalist has the same kind of expressive and passionate delivery of ANGE while the musicianship shows a MARILLION or neo-prog influence.

Premier Fevrier (92), Debout...Le Coeur Ouvert (95), Vae Victis (96)

GALADRIEL - Spain
Eurock says they carry on the seventies tradition of GENESIS. Lush keyboard orchestrations and ornate guitar lines provide the thematic structure and a tight rhythm section take the arrangements through a complex series of changes. Echoes of Selling England by the Pound resonate throughout.

Muttered Promises From an Ageless Pond (88), Chasing the Dragonfly (92), Mindscapers (97)

GALAHAD - Great Britain
Five piece band in the same vein as IQ and COLLAGE. Lots of atmosphere and great musicianship. Their material features many instrumental interludes featuring solid keyboard work and biting guitar.

A Moment of Madness (89), Nothing is Written (91), Other Crimes and Misdemeanours (92), In a Moment of Complete Madness (93), Sleepers (95), Classic Rock Live (96), Following Ghosts (98), de-constructing ghosts (99)

GALAXY - Switzerland
Symphonic arrangements with super guitar and keyboard work. Overall influences of YES and GENESIS.

Natures Clear Well (78)

GALERE - France
Early eighties group featuring superb female vocals surrounded by fiery guitar performances. Sounds like ATOLL or MONA LISA.

Epilogue (8?)

GALIE - Mexico
Keyboard based progressive rock from the late eighties that bears some resemblance to UK with its light symphonic arrangements. English vocals, even though the titles are in Spanish.

Galie (85), 1986 (86)

GALIJA - Yugoslavia
Karavan (7?)

GALLANT FARM - Italy
Nineties symphonic neo-progressive rock group with EZRA WINSTON connections. Style is similar to PALLAS or PENDRAGON.

Leverage (9?)

GALLEON - Sweden

Acid Dragon magazine says, a superb blend of PALLAS-style prog, that is energetic and bombastic music with symphonic crescendos. Imagine RUSH with a Mellotron.

Lynx (92), Heritage and Visions (94), King of Aragon (95), At This Moment in Time EP (95), The All European Hero (96), Mind Over Matter (98)

GANDALF - Austria

This multi-instrumentalist creates epic concepts in both music and story. A unique sound that hearkens back to MIKE OLDFIELD with a bit of Kitaro. A nice blend of natural acoustic sounds with synthesisers.

Journey to an Imaginary Land (81), To Another Horizon (83), Tales from a Long Forgotten Kingdom (84), Fantasia (87), The Universal Play (87), More than just a Seagull (88), From Source to Sea (88), Invisible Play (89), Symphonic Soundscapes (90), Reflection (91), Gallery of Dreams [with Steve Hackett] (92), Colours of the Earth (94), To Our Children's Children (94)

GARDEN WALL - Italy

One of the best neo-progressive rock Italian bands showing a GENESIS influence that has been well assimilated into their own sound which at times borders on prog-metal. Their vocalist borrows a lot from PETER HAMMILL'S throaty style. A powerful style with elements of DREAM THEATRE, KING CRIMSON and a little HAPPY FAMILY.

Principum (93), Path of Dreams (94), The Seduction of Madness (95), Chimica (97)

GARYBALDI - Italy

Creative prog rock for the early seventies. Very inventive guitar work from P.N. Fassato along with some powerful Mellotron.

Astrolabia (73), Nuda (72), Bambi Comes Alive ( )

GATHERING, THE - Holland

Prog metal band with a subtle symphonic touch. The second album features a female vocalist and is somewhat of an improvement over the first.

Always (92), Mandylion (94), Nightime Birds (97)

GEE, PETER - Great Britain

PENDRAGON'S bassist began releasing solo work. The first of which was very melodic and not as progressive sounding as his work with PENDRAGON. The solo work also takes on more of a spiritual tone lyrically.

Heart of David (94), Visions of Angels (97)

GENESIS - Great Britain

Without a doubt one of the founders of the progressive rock genre. They carved out a sound that stands as a bench mark to this day. Genesis pioneered progressive rock at a time when the instruments themselves were going through development from simple synthesisers to Mellotrons to samplers...The music was always textured and exquisitely crafted. Always a good place to start. Their work following Abacab became more pop oriented.

From Genesis to Revelation (69), Trespass (70), Nursery Cryme (71), Foxtrot (72), Selling England by the Pound (73), Genesis Live (73), The Lamb Lies Down on Broadway (74), Trick of the Tail (76), Wind & Wuthering (77), Spot the Pigeon EP (77), Seconds Out (77), And then there were Three (78), Duke (80), Abacab (81), Three Sides Live (82), Genesis (83), Invisible Touch (86), We Can't Dance (91), The Way We Walk: The Shorts (92), The Way We Walk: The Longs (93), Calling All Stations (97), Archive 1967-75 (98)

GENESIS BY THE LONDON SYMPHONY - Great Britain

Part of a series of albums produced by David Palmer. It lovingly recreates the power and strength of GENESIS' material. Orchestrated versions of some of the classic material featuring guest appearances by some band members. See also his work with JETHRO TULL, PINK FLOYD and YES.

We Know What We Like - The Music of Genesis (87)

GENFUOCO - Italy

Progressive rock in a similar fashion to PFM or BANCO.

Dentro L'Invisible (79)

GENTLE GIANT - Great Britain

One of the first bands to manage to successfully merge medieval madrigals with snippets of classics into some of the most unique sounding progressive rock. They created a style of almost traditional sounding early English music that seemed to hop around from verse to chorus. Giant have been labelled one of the most complex groups of any age.

Gentle Giant (70), Acquiring the Taste (71), Three Friends (72), In a Glass House (73), Octopus (73), The Power and the Glory (74), Free Hand (75), Interview (76), Playing the Fool (77), The Missing Piece (77), Giant For a Day (78), Civilian (80), Out of the Woods (95), Under Construction (97), King Biscuit Flower Hour Presents (98), Out of the Fire (98)

GERARD - Japan

Dynamic and dramatic keyboard oriented symphonic progressive rock with lots of soaring guitars. They create music that is at one moment majestic solo piano and the next a large grandness with multiple keyboards and guitar interplay. Imagine the best parts of EMERSON and WAKEMAN.

Gerard (84), Empty Lie, Empty Dream (8?), Irony of Fate (90), Save Knight by the Night (94), The Pendulum (96), Pandora's Box (97), Evidence of True Love [EP] (98), Meridian (98), Live in Marseilles-Battle Triangle (99)

GERMINALE - Italy

Seventies style Italian progressive rock. Five piece line-up that nicely mixes up an older sound with a nineties instrumentation. Flute and Hammond play a big part in the overall sound which is a mixture of elements of VAN DER GRAAF and KING CRIMSON in terms of style.

Germinale (94), E Il Suo Respiro Ancora Agila Le Onde (96)

GIALMA 3 - Italy

Very original sounding progressive rock sound with beautiful guitar.

L'Isola Del Tonal ( ), Rain's Dream (99)

GIGI PASCAL - Italy

Early sounding progressive rock.

Debut (7?)

GILA - Germany

Early seventies group who crafted long tracks with strong keyboards and guitars. Includes members who have played in both POPOL VUH and AMON DUUL II.

Free Electric Sound (71), Bury My Heart at Wounded Knee (73), Night Works (72/99)

GILGAMESH - Great Britain

Smooth, multi-textured jazz rock produced by Dave Stewart. Fans of EGG and NATIONAL HEALTH will enjoy this.

Gilgamesh (75), Another Fine Tune You've Got Me Into (78)

GILMOUR, DAVE - Great Britain

Guitarist with PINK FLOYD goes out on his own for a couple of solos. The first was a bit more pedestrian, while the second seemed to be more reminiscent of Floyd's style.

Dave Gilmour (78), About Face (84)

GILTRAP, GORDON - Great Britain

Giltrap started out as a rather traditional folk guitarist working the small clubs in Great Britain. It wasn't until Visionary that he seemed to discover the full orchestra along with electric guitar and realise what he could do with them. The music he went on to create was an amazing blend of folk, classical and rock Instrumental music around. Full panoramic symphonic prog soundscapes that paint pictures in your mind.

Testament of Time (71), Giltrap (73), Visionary (76), Perilous Journey (77), Fear of the Dark (78), Peacock Party (79), Live (81), Airwaves (82)

GIRAFFE - United States

San Francisco band featuring Kevin Gilbert, that injected a bit of fusion as well as pop in their progressive rock style.

The View From Here (89), The Power of Suggestion (94)

GIUFFRIA - United States

Keyboard player and founding member of the band ANGEL, Giuffria wanted to bring a band together that would write and perform the best of what ANGEL did. Unfortunately the material sounded like so many other hard rock bands.

Giuffria (84), Silk and Steel (86)

GIZMO - Great Britain

Nineties era neo-progressive rock group but with some ELP influences as well. In the mould of MARILLION and IQ.

GLACIER - Great Britain

A five piece band from the North of England who originally formed in 1979 but split up in 1982, only to reform in 1984. They were known to have released at least one cassette. Their sound is a cross between ELP, UK and Cream.

GLASS HAMMER - United States

Their style of symphonic prog incorporates elements of YES, ELP, CAMEL or MIKE OLDFIELD influences. They are a duo based in Tennessee producing progressive rock in the best tradition of RICK WAKEMAN and KEITH EMERSON. Their first release Journey to the Dunadan is a musical interpretation of a Tolkien book and contains a wide spectrum of musical styles, sound effects and narration. Yet another did the same treatment to material from C.S. Lewis. If you're a fan of Moogs, Hammonds and Mellotrons look no further!

Journey to the Dunadan (94), Perelandra (96), Live and Revived (97), On to Evermore (97), Chronometree (00)

GLEEMEN - Italy

Early seventies, pre-GARYBALDI group and very similar in style.

Gleemen (70)

GLOVER, ROGER - Great Britain

Roger played bass with DEEP PURPLE for a few years and went on to play a lot of sessions and produce albums. On the LP Elements he took up keyboards with a vengeance along with bass guitar. The album is epic in proportion, utilising a full orchestra for effect.

Butterfly Ball (74), Elements (78), Mask (84)

GNIDROLOG - Great Britain

Blues-rock early style of progressive rock in the same vein as early JETHRO TULL. Longish songs with plenty of starts-and-stops featuring flute and organ predominate. A very intense vocalist also has some comparisons to VDGG. Members of the original group got back together again in the late nineties with the goal of recording more progressive rock..

In Spite of Harry's Toenail (71), Lady Lake (72), Live 1972 (72/00), Gnosis (00)

GOBLIN - Italy
Described by many as a blend of symphonic prog and horror movie soundtrack music. Lots of eerie keyboard work with various sound effects blended in.

Profondo Rosso [Soundtrack] (75), Roller (76), Suspiria [Soundtrack] (77), Il Fantastico Viaggio Del Bagarozzo Mark (78), Zombi [Soundtrack] (78), Amo Non Amo (79), Patrick [Soundtrack] (79), Squadra Antigangstern [Soundtrack] (80), Contamination (82), Volo (82), Tenebre (82), Phenomena (87)

GODFREY, ROBERT JOHN - Great Britain
Godfrey was responsible for the orchestral arrangements in early BJH recordings and did this solo album before forming THE ENID. It was clearly a sign of things to come. Like THE ENID'S material it may require a bit of effort to sit through because of the musical complexity.

Fall of the Hyperion (74)

GODLEY & CREME - Great Britain
The other side of 10cc. It was the artistic side of these two blending with the pop side of Stewart and Gouldman that worked so well. Here the material is hit and miss. When they're good, they're really good.

Consequences (77), I (78), Freeze Frame (79), IsmIsm (81), Birds of Prey (83), History Mix Vol I (85), Goodbye Blue Sky (88)

GOLGOTHA - Great Britain
They've released a coupleof albums of concept work that favours a heavy side of progressive rock. Another view is keyboard driven symphonic progressive-metal complete with ARTHUR BROWN style vocal. Their second album Symphony in Extremis is a little more symphonic in nature. Imagine THE ENID meets RUSH.

Unmaker of Worlds (90), Symphony in Extremis (93)

GOMA - Spain
A five piece mixing hard rock and folk elements to create a typically Spanish flavoured complex prog-rock sound. They incorporate sax and guitar trade-offs giving them a distinct style. If you like TRIANA and BLOQUE, you'll enjoy this.

14 Abril (75)

GOMORRAHA - Germany
Early seventies styled progressive rock.

Gomorrha (70), Trauma (72), I Turned to See Who's Voice it Was (72)

GONG - France
Pioneering progressive band working in the jazz-rock, space-fusion, percussive side of things. Excellent musicians playing in an adventurous format. Critically acclaimed and highly popular, especially in Europe. They went through many different group formations, the discography is based on releases for both Gong and Pierre Moerlen's Gong.

Magick Brother (70), Camembert Electrique (71), Continental Circus (71), The Flying Teapot (72), Angels Egg (73), You (74), Shamal (75), Gazeuze [Expresso] (76), Live Etc. (77), Gong est Mort (77), Floating Anarchy (77), Expresso 2 (78), Downwind (79), Time is the Key (79), P. Moelen's Gong Live (79), Leave it Open (80), Radio Gong Pt. I (84), Radio Gong Pt. 2 (84), The Owl and the Tree (86), Breakthrough (86), Second Wind (88), The History & Mystery of Planet Gong (90), Gong Live on TV (90), Live at Bataclan 73 (90), Live at Sheffield 1974 (90), Je N'Fume pas de Bananes (92), Shapeshifter (92), Camembert Eclectique (95), The Birthday Party: Oct. 8th, 9th 1994 (95), The Peel Sessions 1971-1974 (96), Pre-Modernist Wireless [early BBC sessions] (96), Family Jewels (99)

GORDI - Yugoslavia
Heavy rock with a bit of prog influence.

Pakleni Trio ( )

GORDIAN KNOT - United States
Progressive metal music that is complex and listenable. Lots of musicianship packaged with some great ideas. It's all instrumental so there is plenty of room for the players to display their abilities.

Gordian Knot (98)

GOTHIC LUNCH - Italy
Material sounding similar to eighties PINK FLOYD, ASIA, and ALAN PARSONS.

Gothic Lunch (92)

GOTHIQUE - Great Britain
Originally an instrumental group, that quickly changed their name and began performing non-stop supporting such bands Hawkwind, THE ENID and even BUDGIE. Their music has hints of a medieval nature to it. They released a few self-produced cassettes before calling it a day.

Kristina (84 TAPE), 3 Cuts Live (85 TAPE), Face of Ages (85 TAPE)

GOTIC - Spain
Their only release was an instrumental LP with flute and keyboards producing a CAMEL inspired symphonic prog rock.

Escenes (77)

GRACE - Great Britain
A band from Stoke that created music that was a cross between MAGNUM on the hard side and GENESIS on the progressive side. Well crafted songs with a hint of Celtic influence.

Grace (81), Live (81), The Poet, The Piper, and the Fool (91), Pulling Strings and Shiny Things (94), Poppy (96), Gathering In The Wheat [Live] (98)

GRACIOUS - Great Britain
Lots of Mellotron here, that might take you back to some early style KING CRIMSON. The second album flows a lot better musically, but is a little more blues based. A third album released in 1996 features the original rhythm section along with a new guitarist/keyboardist. The music is strikingly similar to the material from the seventies. As good or better than before.

Gracious (70), This is...Gracious (72), Echo (96)

GRANADA - Spain
Three LPs of Spanish rooted progressive rock. The first two had southern influences, the third had north-western Spanish influences. They featured bagpipes.

Espana, Ano 75 (75), Hablo de Una Tierra (75), Valle Del Pas (76)

GRANDBELL - Brazil
A sound that is based around mostly a twelve string acoustic guitar and flute and a vocalist with a strong JON ANDERSON influence. Keyboards and electric guitar are used but subtlety. The material is not overly complex but is strong on melody. If you like the softer elements of YES, you'll like this.

The Sun and the Embyro (96)

GRANDSTAND - Sweden
They credit GENESIS and THE FLOWER KINGS as inspiration and consequently their compositions bear those same hallmarks right down to the use of Mellotron. Not overly adventurous but certainly pleasant to listen to.

In the Middle, On the Edge (98)

GRAVE - Germany
Early heavy progressive rock which may appeal to fans of bands such as DEEP PURPLE and GROBSCHNITT..

Grave I (75)

GRAVY TRAIN - Great Britain
Progressive rock with flute and so there are the obvious comparisons to early JETHRO TULL.

Gravy Train (70), Ballad of a Peaceful Man (71), Second Birth (73), Staircase to the Day (74)

GREATEST SHOW ON EARTH - Great Britain
Early seventies styled progressive style with a strong heavy psychedelic influence.

Horizons (70), The Going's Easy (70), The Greatest Show on Earth [Compilation] (75)

GREEN SPACE - France
A more pop oriented neo-progressive band. Some would say a little too commercial.

Behind (90)

GREENSLADE - Great Britain
Dave Greenslade and Tony Reeves were both in COLISEUM. Coming out of London's R&B scene, The music of Greenslade was complex in its arrangements and like most progressive rock bands incorporated a number of musical styles. Wonderfully creative songs and top notch musicianship featuring bass, drums and two keyboard players.

Greenslade (73), Bedside Manners are Extra (73), Spyglass Guest (74), Time and Tide (75), Live 73-75 (99)

GREENSLADE, DAVE - Great Britain
After the demise of the band GREENSLADE, Dave continued to create some marvellous music. The first album Cactus Choir was very much a continuation of the Greenslade style, while the second was a double record set with book. It not only featured Greenslade on keyboards but Phil Collins on some vocals and drums.

Cactus Choir (76), Pentateuch of the Cosmogony (79), From the Discworld (94)

GREENWALL - Italy
Italian style prog featuring long compositions. The arrangements tend to simple based around upbeat and mid tempo themes.

Il Petalo Dei Fiore E Altre Storie (99)

GRENDEL - France
Nineties era, MARILLION influenced neo-progressive rock.

Au Dela du Reve...La Solitude (9?)

GREY LADY DOWN - Great Britain
Neo-progressive rock sound, like MARILLION. They strive for a more direct, aggressive and some would say accessible sound than some of their contemporaries. Lots of keyboards in a musical structure that contains many instrumental passages. If you enjoy bands such as GENESIS, IQ, JADIS or PENDRAGON you'll enjoy this.

The Crime (94), Forces (95), Fear (97), Live-Official Bootleg (98), The Time Of Our Lives [Live] (98)

GRIMALKIN - Italy
Fluid symphonic progressive rock melodies with a slight neo-prog feel. They create a primarily instrumental sound, with some English vocals. Their music is characterised by a combination of soft and delicate parts punctuated with slowly building crescendos. At times you'll hear a hint of THE ENID style.

The Drifting Sailor (96)

GRIME - France
Music based on the lead singers vocal presence and theatrical elements as well as melodies built around the chords of the organ, saxophone or flute in a musical style very close to ANGE or ATOLL.

Grime (79)

GRITS - United States
Complex progressive rock with elements of CARAVAN or even Zappa. A unique blend of jazzy-fusion and symphonic prog with a liberal dose of energetic jamming.

As the World Grits (93), Rare Birds (76/97)

GROBSCHNITT - Germany
Long running German band with a traditional line-up. Music of top quality symphonic progressive rock style. Lots of keyboard and guitar interplay. Their later LPs tended to be more mainstream.

Grobschnitt (72), Ballermann (74), Jumbo (75), Rockpommel's Land (77), Solar Music Live (78), Merry Go Round (79), Volle Molle (80), Illegal (81), Razzia (82), Die Grobschnitt Story (94)

GROON - Great Britain
Fusion material for fans of XAAL or BRAND X.

Refusal to Comply (95)

GROUP, THE - Finland
Scandinavian jazz-rock that leaned a little towards progressive rock.

The Group (78)

GROWING DREAM - Canada
From the Province of Quebec this is a group with influences from GENESIS and RENAISSANCE. They create a folk tinged prog with male and female vocals.

Seeds (9?)

GRUPO SINTESIS - Cuba
A nine member group consisting in part of three guitarists and two keyboard players who create a mellow symphonic style. Influences include bands such as PFM, PINK FLOYD and YES. While the music has definite Anglo prog overtones there is no mistaking a romantic Latin feel.

En Busca de Una Nueva Flor (78), El Hombre Extrano ( )

GRUPPO 2001 - Italy
L'alba di Domani (72)

GRYPHON - Great Britain
A mix of traditional early English instruments and musical style with a more contemporary style. The sound of the bassoon and krumhorn stand out a mile. They formed in 1972 with this distinctive musical style however over the years changed into something a little more mainstream as far as progressive rock is concerned. Their later material consisted of longer multi tempo, multi-theme pieces.

Gryphon (73), Midnight Mushrumps (74), Red Queen to Gryphon Three (74), Raindance (75), Treason (77)

GTR - Great Britain
One assumes it stands for guitar because the band was formed by STEVE HOWE and STEVE HACKETT. The music seemed a little restrained for two such accomplished guitarists. It ended up sounding only slightly more adventurous than ASIA.

GTR (86), King Biscuit Flower Hour - GTR Live (96)

GUALBERTO - Spain
Spanish guitarist plays everything from folk to Flamenco to progressive rock. His second album, Verecuetos comes highly recommended. Great sounds from violin, sitar and string-synth and no vocals. Five long tracks with many mood changes, some complex rhythms and great musicianship.

A La Vida - Al Dolor (75), Verecuetos (75), Otros Dias (79)

GUIZER JARL - Great Britain
A short-lived band influenced by the YES-GENESIS school who released a cassette of very Tolkien sounding neo-prog in the early eighties. Good keyboard work, lots of powerful chords interlaced with a STEVE HACKETT style guitar sound.

GULISANO & DI LORENZO - Italy
Some connections with the band EDITH and sound a bit similar.

Somewhere In Between ( )

GUNN - Great Britain
Hard rock trio that played more a hard rock blues type of music than progressive rock. They went on to play with MOODY BLUES drummer Graeme Edge on his solo LPs. One of the first Roger Dean covers.

Gunn (68), Gunnsight (69)

GUNN, RONNIE & DAVID THOMAS - Great Britain
See: THOMAS, DAVID

GURNEMANZ - Germany
Progressive folk music with mostly acoustic instruments

No Rays of Noise (77)

GWENDAL - France
Predominantly Celtic folk mixed with some jazz and progressive rock. Sounds like GENTLE GIANT or MANEIGE, but in a folk rock style.

Gwendal (74), Gwendal 2 (75), A Vos Desirs (77), Gwendal 4 (79), En Concert (81), Locomo (83), Danse La Musique (85), Glen River (90)

H2O - Italy
Italian symphonic progressive rock of the highest kind. A fine blend of Wind and Wuthering era GENESIS with modern bands such as IQ. They create long and involved compositions containing many moods and styles. Many rich acoustic portions sandwiched between large dramatic panoramas in songs sung in Italian. A wonderful blend of old and new symphonics.

Unopuntosei (97)

HACKETT, STEVE - Great Britain
Former guitarist with GENESIS. Some excellent material here with lot's of Mellotron on the earlier LPs. Everything from rock to romance to quirky to jazzy. Good guitar and keyboard work in both short and long song formats.

Voyage of the Acolyte (75), Please Don't Touch (78), Spectral Mornings (79), Defectors (80), Cured (81), Highly Strung (82), Bay of Kings (83), Till We have faces (84), Momentum (88), Time Lapse Live (92), Guitar Noir (93), Blues With a Feeling (94), Many Sides to the Night (95), Genesis Revisited (96), The Tokyo Tapes (97), Darktown (99)

HADES - Norway
Early seventies JETHRO TULL like sound.

Hades (7?)

HAIRY CHAPTER - Germany
Heavy progressive sound similar in style to BLACK WIDOW or DEEP PURPLE.

Eyes (70), Can't Get Through (71)

HAIZEA - Spain
Folky-progressive rock not unlike the second release by ITOIZ. Sort of a psychedelic electric folk.

Hontz Gaua (79)

HALEY, DENNIS -
Interesting space-rock which will appeal to fans of TANGERINE DREAM and NEURONIUM.

Seven Seconds After (99)

HALLOWEEN - France
Originally a trio whose sound combined drums, keyboards and violin/guitars into a neo-CRIMSON-ATOLL style that's complex and intense. The instrumental work is technically as well as emotionally adventurous. They have expanded to a five piece and continue to produce excellent sym-

phonic progressive rock. Their Merlin CD featured a small string and horn section as not only accompaniment but incorporated to create a very period sounding work.

Part One (88), Laz (90), Merlin (94), Silence...Au Dernier Rang! [Live] (98)

HAMMER, JAN - United States

Keyboardist with Weather Report, Hammer came to national prominence by creating the synth soundscapes for the hit TV series Miami Vice. Some of his solo work is quite interesting although not all of it would qualify as progressive rock.

The First Seven Days (75)

HAMMILL, PETER - Great Britain

Founding member of VAN DER GRAAF GENERATOR had a very uneven solo career. Some people love'em, some hate'm but say what you will Peter took chances. His solo work never really equalled his work with the band in terms of progressive rock style.

Fools Mate (72),Chameleon in the Shadow (73),The Silent Corner (74),In Camera (74),Nadirs Last Chance (75),Over (77),Future Now (78),PH7 (79),Black Box (80),Sitting Targets (81),Enter K (82),Patience (83),The Love Songs (84),The Margin (85),Skin (85),Close As I Am (86),Organum (86),Let it Play (87),Spur of the Moment (88),In a Foreign Town (88),Out of the Water (90),Room Temperature Live (90),Fall of the House of Usher (91),Fireships (91),The Noise (93),Roaring Forties (94),X My Heart (96), Everyone You Hold (97), This (98), Typical (99)

HAMONET, JEAN-LUC - France

At first he sounds like a bit of CAMEL, then FOCUS, then perhaps ROUSSEAU and even some hints of JETHRO TULL. A fine mixture of classical, Celtic-folk, and even a little jazz. Came on the scene in the mid eighties with a very melodious music with subtle arrangements with a great variety of instrumentation.

HANDS - United States

This is a late seventies band from Texas who create prog in a style that is a blend of GENTLE GIANT and early KANSAS. A good number of instrumentals and interesting use of instruments. Some times they rock with great guitar and violin interplay and other times they create a very medieval sound. The material on the CD is mostly from 1977-78. They used to go by the name PRISM before changing their name to Hands and their archive release is listed here.

Hands (96), Prism-Live 75-77 (97), Palm Mystery (99)

HANGER 18 - United States

Their guitarist calls them a refreshing alternative to the grunge and punk stuff heard on radio. The band boasts of great musicianship, vocals with multi-part harmonies and thought provoking lyrics. Influences listed include MARILLION, RUSH, YES, and ASIA.

Need to Know (96)

HANSSON, BO - Sweden

Legendary symphonic keyboardist.

Lord of the Rings (72),Magician's Hat (73),Attic Thoughts (75),Watership Down (75),

HAPPENSTANCE - United States

Melodic vocal oriented pop-rock with neo-progressive tendencies and symphonic flourishes. Not overly challenging, but well played.

Happenstance EP (96)

HAPPY FAMILY - Japan

Progressive with a strong avant-garde feel. First time listeners will immediately pick up on the MAGMA and UNIVERS ZERO influences. Happy Family rank right up there with IL BERLIONE and TIPOGRAPHICA.

Happy Family (95),Toscco (97)

HAPPY THE MAN - United States

Another one of the few American progressive rock bands, this time from Virginia who forge their own sound. Not as rocky as CRACK THE SKY, not as Top 40 as STYX turned out to be, and not quite as unusual as Zappa. Add it all up throw in a liberal dose of jazz-rock and you wind up with Happy the Man. The most accomplished American seventies prog band.

Happy The Man (77), Crafty Hands (78), Better Late... (83), Beginnings (92), Live (97), Death's Crown (99)

HARLEQUIN MASS - United States

Symphonic progressive rock with influences from RENAISSANCE and GENESIS. They also feature some fine flute and oboe parts lending to a slight Canterbury element.

Harlequin Mass (78)

HARLIS - Germany

Former members of Scorpions & JANE come up with a good hard rock style incorporating some progressive rock elements.

Harlis (75), Night Meets the Day (76)

HARMONIUM - Canada

One of the first French Canadian symphonic bands to become popular with a unique mix of folk and rock with a dash of ethnic flavour. Some say a bit like GENTLE GIANT. They used the Mellotron to good effect.

Harmonium (74), Les Cinq Saisons (75), L'heptadeD' Harmonium (76), En Touree (80)

HARNAKIS - Spain

A symphonic group whose sound is more Italian or English than Spanish. Heavily influenced by MARILLION.

Numb Eyes: The Soul Revelation (91)

HARPER, ROY - Great Britain

Folkie turned rocker then mellowed out again. His distinctive voice got him a song on Led Zeppelin III as well as a guest spot on PINK FLOYD'S - Wish You Were Here LP. Roy is a real 'folk' hero in some parts. The material that falls into the progressive rock area was very interesting, particularly the releases listed below. Lyrically he always had something important to say and was able to tell some great tales. Musically he went from using full orchestras to solo guitar.

HQ (75), Bullinamingvase (77), The Unknown Soldier (80), A Work of Heart (82), Whatever Happened To Jugula (85)

HASLAM, ANNIE - Great Britain

Various artists come to the assistance of Haslam on a variety of solo releases. Her solo work since she left RENAISSANCE has been rather spotty. Unfortunately she has tended to link up with people who try to bring out more of a pop influence than the type of material she's best remembered for.

Annie in Wonderland (78), Lily's in the Field [with Steve Howe] (96), Blessing in Disguise (96)

HATFIELD AND THE NORTH - Great Britain

Formed in 1972 as part of the Canterbury sound. Although this band was far more jazz inclined. Each of the members was an accomplished musician. The band featured Dave Stewart, Dave Sinclair, Pip Pyle and Phil Miller.

Hatfield and the North (73), The Rotters Club (75), Afters (79)

HAWKWIND - Great Britain

Surpassing GONG and SOFT MACHINE for personnel changes with ex-members of AMON DUUL, GONG and the Pink Fairies passing through the ranks. Hawkwind's first album was produced by the Pretty Thing's Dick Taylor and was compared immediately to Pink Floyd. Hawkwind helped define the term space-rock, with their long spacey, improvisational musical jams and science-fictiony lyrics. While the keyboards are ever present the Hawkwind sound was based on helmsman Dave Brock's searing guitar work.

Hawkwind (70),In Search of Space (71),Doremi Fasol Latido (72),Space Ritual (73),Hall of the Mountain Grill (74),Warrior on the Edge of Time (75),Road Hawks (76),Masters of the Universe (77),Quark Strangeness and Charm (77), PXR5 (78), Live 79 (79), Levitation (80), Sonic Attack (81), Choose Your Masques (82), Friends & Relations (82), Friends & Relations II (83), Zones (83), Stonehenge (This Is Hawkwind Do Not Panic) (84), Chronicle Of The Black Sword (85), Friends & Relations III (85), Live Chronicles (86),Angels Of Death (86), Out & Intake (87),The Xenon Codex (88), Space Bandits (90), Palace Springs (91), Electric Tepee (92), California Brainstorm (92), It is the Business of the Future to be Dangerous (94), Psychedelic Warriors The White Zone (95), Alien 4 (95), Love In Space (96), Future Constructions (96), Live In Chicago 1974 (97), Distant Horizons (97) The Elf and The Hawk (98) In Your Area (98),Thrilling Hawkwind Adventures (00)

HAZARD - France
Sounds like ANGE, ATOLL or MONA LISA. Progressive rock in the classic French mould.

Le Chemin de L'oubli SP (74)

HAZE - Great Britain
They were formed in 1978 and built a large local following in the Sheffield area. Their material as one might expect incorporates changing rhythms, tempos and styles. Short and longish songs with a heavier guitar edge. They changed their musical style and their name to World Turtle in the early nineties.

The Cellar Tapes (83 TAPE), C'est la Vie (84), The Cellar Replay (85 TAPE),The Ember (85 EP), Stoat and Bottle (87), In the End 1978 - 88 (92),World Turtle (94), 20th Anniversary Show (98)

HAZE - Germany
Early seventies styled heavy progressive rock

Hazecolor Dia (71)

HEAD POP UP - Japan 1990's
A trio consisting of drummer and two keyboardists creating a jazz influenced sound similar in many respects to HAPPY THE MAN. Complicated rhythms and arrangements.

HEADS IN THE SKY - Canada
First self produced album was a cross between some PINK FLOYD and some ALAN PARSONS, very good. The second was an EP and turned out to be far to pop oriented, not very good at all.

Heads In the Sky (82),Poetry and Science (83)

HECENIA - France
Symphonic progressive rock. Powerful GENESIS influence from the Wind & Wuthering era especially on their first release. A very keyboard dominated sound, with lots of breathing room. A second album was a little more like ARSNOVA and early ENID.

Legendes (89),Le Couleur Du Feu (94)

HELDON - France
More on the electronic side of things here. The first album was full of heavy guitar textures and dense aggressive electronics. Each album that followed showcased very different sound styles but all of them featured leader Richard Pinhas' Fripp influenced guitar sound. The addition of Mellotron on some albums should appeal to fans.

Electronic Gorilla (74),Allez Teia (75), Its

Always Rock and Roll (75), Agneta Nilsson (76), Un Reve Sans Consequence Speciale (76), Interface (76), A Dream Without (78), Heldon IV (79), Stand By (79)

HELMERSSON, ANDERS -
Finland

Early eighties symphonic progressive keyboardist influenced by YES, ELP and KING CRIMSON. One album full of rich analog synth sounds as well as input from many guest session players contributing guitars, bass, drums and violin work.

End of Ilussion (82)

HENRY COW - Great Britain

In their day they were one of the more popular progressive bands in Great Britain although only achieving cult status in America. Highly politicised lyrics in a nearly improvisational musical format. Their drummer, Chris Cutler came up with the musical sub-genre RIO standing for Rock-In-Opposition. An uncompromising and technically complex musical style.

Legend (73), Unrest (74), Desperate Straights (75), In Praise of Learning (75), Concerts (76), Western Culture (78)

HERBS - Great Britain

They patterned themselves after the hippy bands of the seventies. Strange psychedelic mixture of sound effects and music.

3 Cut EP (84 TAPE)

HERE AND NOW -
Great Britain

Similar in nature to the type of psychedelic music produced by GONG.

What You See is What You Get (78), Give and Take (78), A Dog in Hell (78), All Over the Show (79), Fantasy Shift ( ), Theatre ( )

HERETIC - Japan

Solo artist Hiro Kawahara's synthesiser-guitar work featuring a wide assortment of instruments with influences from VANGELIS, HELDON and KING CRIMSON.

Interface (85), Escape Sequence (88), Past in Future (96), Drugging For M (97)

HERNANDEZ, FRANCISCO -
Mexico

Guitarist from CAST with a solo effort that carry's with it the same symphonic prog feel. Mostly longer compositions with lots of excellent guitar work. If you enjoy CAST you'll certainly like this.

Whispers From the Wind (98)

HIAKARA - Finland

Early seventies progressive rock style.

Hiakara (7?), Gearfar (7?)

HIGH FIDELITY ORCHESTRA -
Mexico

Complex and jazzy progressive rock with a KING CRIMSON and HENRY COW influence. Fans of RIO will enjoy.

High Fidelity Orchestra (82)

HIGH WHEEL - Germany

A couple of releases of solid neo-progressive rock material with elements of MARILLION, PENDRAGON and CAMEL. Their third release There is a more adventurous concept with a strong PINK FLOYD influence.

1910 (93), Remember the Colours (94), There (9?)

HILLAGE, STEVE - Great Britain

A product of the Canterbury school of progressive rock. Spent time playing guitar with SOFT MACHINE, and KEVIN AYERS but gained notoriety when he joined forces with Daevid Allen's GONG with whom he recorded several successful albums for Virgin. Music holds over bits from the seventies hippy era combined with the early jazz of the progressive rock era.

Fish Rising (75),L (76), Motivation Radio (77),Green (78),Live Herald (78),Open (79),Rainbow Dome Musick (79),Aura (80),For to Next (83), BBC Live In Concert (92)

HILLMAN, STEVE - Great Britain
Known for more electronic, TANGERINE DREAM style compositions, Hillman branches out with a more traditional progressive rock opus with Convergence. The material here is more structured featuring flute, keyboards, drums and of course Hillman's biting guitar work.

Convergence (98)

HINN ISLENSKI PURSAFLOKKUR - Iceland
Imagine a Scandinavian GRYPHON mixed with elements of GENTLE GIANT. Odd meters, constant time changes, lots of dynamics, quirky rhythmic and melodic motifs are all elements of their material.

Hinn Islenski Pursaflokkur ( ),Pursabit (79),A Hljomleikum ( ),Gaeti Eins Verid ( )

HIRAYAMA, TERUTSUGU - Japan
An early solo effort from the leader and guitarist of TERU'S SYMPHONIA, that is very much in the same rich symphonic style.

Castle of Noi (88)

HITCHINGS, TRACY - Great Britain
Female prog vocalist who has worked with QUASAR, CLIVE NOLAN and others. Her solo work is very reminiscent of her work of STRANGERS ON A TRAIN.

From Ecstacy to Fantasy (91)

HODGSON, ROGER - Great Britain
Former key member of SUPERTRAMP, Hodgson took a real chance with his first solo outing. On it are some progressive pieces much in the same vein as a SUPERTRAMP of old.

In the Eye of the Storm (84), Hai Hai (86), Rites of Passage (97)

HOELDERLIN - Germany
One of the great traditional sounding German prog rock bands. A lot of instrumental passages with some very pastoral images. Great keyboard work. Songs of changing tempo and themes.

Hoelderlin's Traum (72), Hoelderlin (75), Clown and Clouds (76), Rare Birds (77), Traumstadt Live (78), New Faces (79), Fata Morgana (81)

HOLE IN THE WALL - Norway
An early seventies progressive band with a distinct West Coast influence.

Hole In the Wall (7?)

HOLDING PATTERN - United States
Early eighties band whose material is very reminiscent of early GENESIS and YES with a bit of HAPPY THE MAN thrown in. The first release was an EP while the second is a compilation and remix of lost tracks. The mostly instrumental and very melodic material features a prominent guitar and rich analog synths and Mellotron playing in symphonic style with hints of fusion.

Holding Pattern EP (81), Majestic (90)

HOLY LAMB - Latvia
Their musical style is symphonic progressive rock with influences such as YES and CAMEL.

Holy Lamb (00)

HOME - Great Britain
Mixture of hard and soft progressive rock. Lots of good guitar work here. The keyboards showed up on their third release, a concept album called, The Alchemist.

Pause For a Fresh Horse (71), Home (72), The Alchemist (73)

HOPO - Italy
Symphonic progressive rock material.

Senti ( ), Dietro La Finestra (91)

HORIZONTE - Argentina
Classic seventies style progressive rock in the same style as CRUCIS and EL RELOJ incorporating a strong ethnic element. Here the compositions tend to be a little shorter and little rockier but there is no denying the influence of bands such as YES and JETHRO TULL.

Horizonte (77), Senales Sin Edad (79)

HORUS - Italy
Sounds like LE ORME or PROCESSION.

Horus ( )

HOSEMOBILE - United States
According to the press release, this material is mostly instrumental band of dual guitars (one doubling on Fender Rhodes piano), bass and drums...A stunning mix of 90's post-rock with a progressive/experimental edge. The end result is a fusion of fiery aggression with complex structures and intense layering of musical ideas.

Six Foot Hater ( ), What Can and Can't Go On (99)

HOST - Norway
Heavy progressive rock.

Pa Sterke Vinger (74), Hardt Mot Hardt (76), Live and Unreleased ( )

HOSTSONATEN - Italy
The bassist from FINISTERRE creates a symphonic prog that is very much along the lines of early GENESIS and PFM. Overall there is a very plaintive quality to the compositions with lots of recurring musical motifs, lush Mellotron and simple progressions. If you're a fan of bands like those mentioned or even ERIS PLUVIA you'll enjoy this.

Mirrorgames (98)

HOUSE OF USHER - United States
Melodic progressive rock with a host of influences from old and new prog bands. These influences mostly on the symphonic side of things have been incorporated quite well and what stands out is House of Usher's own unique brand of prog. Not overly complicated but everything meshes well.

Body of Mind (98)

HOWE, STEVE - Great Britain
Guitarist of YES. Each album showcases Howe in all his guitar playing glory. Some great material.

Beginnings (75), The Steve Howe Album (79), Turbulence (91), The Grand Scheme of Things (93), Not Necessarily Acoustic (94), Mothballs (95), Homebrew (96), Quantum Guitar (98), Portraits of Bob Dylan (99)

HOWEVER - United States
The band is from Virginia featuring a sound that's a mix of jazzy Canterburian, HAPPY THE MAN and GENTLE GIANT styles.

Sudden Dusk (81), Calling (85)

HOYRY-KONE - Finland
ANEKDOTEN fans will like this band. Heavy progressive with cellos and violins incorporating a fair amount of dissonance and unusual scales creating a music that is more challenging to listen to. The strongest early influence would have to be a seventies KING CRIMSON along with a slight hint of France's MAGMA.

Hyontesia Voi Rakastaa (95), Huono Parturi (97)

HUDSON FORD - Great Britain
Two key members who split from the STRAWBS created four pop oriented albums. The first two albums contain a couple of longish songs with progressive rock overtones in a style similar to STRAWBS.

Nickelodeon (73), Free Spirit (74), Worlds Colide (75), Daylight (77)

HUMAN EXPRESSION - Italy
Formed in 1982 their material features a serious swirling organ/keyboard sound. Very Italian prog sound with rich harmonies. Long passages of solo keyboard work bridge the musical transitions and song segments. Their sound tends to be on the mellower, melodic side.

Being in the Beginning (85)

HURDY GURDY - Denmark
Early heavy sounding progressive rock.

Hurdy Gurdy (71)

HUSH - United States
Mostly a pop-rock band from San Francisco. They released one album with a couple of longer progressive rock type tracks.

Hush (78)

HYBRID - Great Britain
A combination of old and new symphonic progressive rock with a slightly heavier touch. While the guitar takes a prominent place the choir and strings are not far behind. If you're a fan of IQ, YES and RUSH you'll enjoy Hyrbid.

Chasing the Dream (99)

HYDRAVION - France
A floating electronic style of music in the manner of Jean Michele Jarre. Not just keyboards however.

Hydravion (77), Stratos Airlines (79)

I COCAI - Italy
Pleasant melodic progressive rock that sounds a bit like PFM at times.

Piccolo Grande Vecchio Fiume (77)

I GIGANTI - Italy
Strong vocals and keyboards highlight an album that's an early concept piece. They started out as a psychedelic beat group trying to break new barriers though not always very successfully. Fans of LE ORME, PFM or CELESTE may appreciate the mellower aspects.

Terra In Bocca (71)

I NOMADI - Italy
Legendary seventies band who recorded many albums incorporating elements of folk and classical into an early progressive rock sound.

Per Quando Noi Non Saremo ( ), Gordon (75), Naracauli E Altre ( ), Canzoni D'Oltremanica e D'olreoceano ( ), Mille E Una Sera ( )

I NUMI - Italy
A band that created mostly psychedelic shorter songs heavily influenced by The Beatles.

Alpha Ralpha Boulevard (71), Stroia Di Zero ( )

I POOH - Italy
Sound like an Italian Bee Gees at times, but on other occasions they create music of great beauty and majesty. They make good use of the Mellotron on many of their albums.

Alessandra (72), Parsifal (73), Rotolando Respirando (77), Viva (79), Buona Fortuna (81)

I TEOREMI - Italy
Early heavy progressive sound, with relatively complicated arrangements for the

time. Similar to early DEEP PURPLE, URIAH HEEP or CLEAR BLUE SKY.

I Teoremi (72)

IL BALLETTO DI BRONZO - Italy

Some say their album Ys is the greatest progressive rock album ever. In the tradition of mid seventies classic Italian style. Some nice Mellotron mixed in amongst the jamming and dissonance. They reformed in the late nineties as a power trio with a sound that was like a harder edged ELP. The music has remained somewhat dark and foreboding but full of symphonic flourishes.

Ys (72), Sirio 2,222 ( ), Ys [English demo 71] (96), Trys (99)

IL BARICENTRO - Italy

Progressive-fusion, with an amazing display of musicianship.

Sconcerto (76), Trusciant (7?)

IL BERLIONE - Japan

KENSO influenced but with a more complex approach. Their first release managed to avoid the exesses of RIO (noise), or jazz-fusion (soloing) but still managed to create music that was sensitive to the elements of progressive rock and melodic structures. Their second release fell more in the avant-garde fusion area.

Il Berlione (92), In 453 minutes Infernal Cooking (95)

IL CASTELLO DI ATLANTE - Italy

Symphonic progressive rock that sounds like PFM with flowing violin set in long, sometimes melancholic music. The band has been together in some form or another since the seventies.

Sono Il Signore Delle Torre a Nord (93), Passo Dopo Passo (94), L'ippogrifo (95)

IL GIARDINO DEI SEMPLICI - Italy

Soft progressive rock sound.

Il Giardino Dei Semplici ( )

IL GIRO STRANO - Italy

Italian progressive rock with long songs, great Hammond organ and sax and flute work. Ambitious compositions with a strong classical influence as well as a bit of folk and jazz.

La Divina Commedia [72-73] (9?)

IL PAESE DEI BALOCCHI - Italy

Progressive rock with a symphony orchestra. Not cliché, not overly romantic, this group has incorporated the orchestra into their sound very well. The haunting pipe organ ending side two is positively awe-inspiring.

Il Paese Dei Balocchi (72)

IL RISVEGLIO - Italy

Classic Italian symphonic progressive rock with all the seventies influences turned around and produced with a very modern sound. There are plenty of hints of early GENESIS, but the band keeps it all under their own style. Lots of drama, passion and musicianship providing plenty of prog moments.

Cooperative Del latte (99)

IL ROVESCIO DELLA MEDAGLIA [SEE RDM] - Italy

Enrico Bacalov, who produced side two of Concerto Grosso 2 by NEW TROLLS and all of Milano Calibro 9 by OSANNA has reached beyond these earlier efforts and transformed RDM into the gods of Italian progressive rock.

La Bibbia (71), Io Como Io (72)

IL SISTEMA - Italy

Early style progressive rock from yet-to-be

members of CELESTE and MUSEO ROSENBACH. Very much in the classical rock vein with fiery playing on flutes, sax, Hammond organ, bass guitars and drums. Ranges from heavy classical rock to a more blues based acid style.

Il Viaggio Senza Andata [69-71] (9?)

IL TRONO DEI RICORDI - Italy

Heavy symphonic progressive rock similar to MUSEO ROSENBACH or RDM. Great keyboard and guitar interplay in the fine tradition of Italian prog. Keyboards include Hammond organ and Mellotron.

Il Trono Dei Ricordi (94)

IL VOLO - Italy

Ex-FORMULA 3 people who released a couple of LPs before breaking up never to reform again. This is classic symphonic progressive rock with a hint of fusion.

Il Volo (75), Essere o Non Esserre (75)

IBIO - Spain

They fused the Northern Spanish mountain music with progressive rock. Loads of synths, Mellotron and weaving guitars.

Ibio ( ), Cuevas de Altamira (78)

IBIS - Italy

This band consisted of former members of the NEW TROLLS when they split in half in the early seventies. Long songs more on the heavy side, but the music is full of the lots of the warm synthesisers and dynamics Italian prog is known for. Listen and you may hear hints of YES and Led Zeppelin.

Ibis (75), Sun Supreme (74)

ICARE - France

A group of five musicians including three guitarists. Calm and ethereal compositions, serene and flowing music. Sound like - CAMEL, BARCLAY JAMES HARVEST.

Aquarelle (80)

ICE - Germany

Very heavy, at times quirky sounding progressive rock trio. Fans of bands such as HOELDERLIN, or NOVALIS will find this enjoyable to some degree.

Opus I (80)

ICE - Great Britain

More of a flowing progressive rock sound with hints of two-guitar psych-prog. The titles with fuller arrangements tend to be the stand-out tracks on their LP Saga of the Ice King.

Ice (74), Import/Export (75), Saga of the Ice King (79)

ICE AGE - United States

Formed in 1991, they were originally known as Monolith, they create a heavier prog that is from the same school as DREAM THEATRE and LEGER DE MAIN. You can expect heavy guitar riffs one minute and soft piano the next. Their melodic and well constructed compositions are a rollercoaster of prog influences including RUSH, YES and KANSAS.

Join (97), The Great Divide (99)

ICONOCLASTA - Mexico

Mexico's top symphonic, fusion, progressive rock band, full of dense keyboard/guitar work. Their guitar style is heavily influenced by STEVE HACKETT and over all their sound hints at the less jarring moments of KING CRIMSON.

Iconoclasta (85), Reminiscencias (85), Soliloquio (87), Suite Mexicana EP (87), Siete Anos (88), Adoliscencia Cronica (89), En Busco De Sentido (90), En Concierto (91), La Reincarnation Del Maquievalo (92), De Todos Uno (94)

ICU - Germany

A nineties neo-progressive rock group.

Moonlight Flit (9?), Now and Here (9?)

IE RAI SHAN - Japan
Symphonic progressive rock music that sounds a bit like OUTER LIMITS, PROVIDENCE or MR. SIRIUS. Take a big lush, symphonic sound, mix in some harder rock elements and blend it with some unique Japanese cultural elements.

Ie Rai Shan (94)

IGRA STAKLENIH PERLI - Yugoslavia
Psychedelic flavoured progressive rock with hints of Hawkwind and Meddle era PINK FLOYD.

Igra Staklenih Perli (79), Vrt Svetlosti (80), Inner Flow [recorded 75] (9?), Drives [recorded 78] (9?), Soft Explosion Live [recorded 78] (9?)

IHRE KINDER - Germany
Heavy progressive rock.

Ihre Kinder (69), Leere Hande (70), 2375004 (70), Werdohl (71), Anfang Ohne Ende (72)

IKAREPONCHITCHIES - Japan
Strong melodies and complicated rhythm patterns dominate their sound. A nineties era band that labels themselves as hard prog Anima (tion) Rock.

IKARUS - Germany
Early seventies prog sound with dominant organ flavour. Their music is reminiscent of other bands from this period who also used the organ quite heavily, namely YES and PINK FLOYD. Typical of the times there is also a distinct jazz current running through some of the compositions.

Ikarus (71)

ILK - Great Britain
This is primarily the solo effort of Richard Youngs and while it falls into the symphonic prog category, the performance and musicianship is a little rough. The influences that surface are YES with a hint of medieval or Celtic like HORSLIPS.

Zenith (99)

ILLUSION - Great Britain
Made their debut in 1969, comprising most of the original line-up of RENAISSANCE initially, but all that changed through a major line-up shuffle. They featured Jane Relf on vocals with a sound similar to RENAISSANCE but with more of an edge.

Out of the Mist (77), Illusion (78), Enchanted Caress (79/92)

ILUVATAR - United States
If you like the Wind & Wuthering era GENESIS or MARILLION or PENDRAGON you'll like these guys. This Baltimore, MD quintet creates symphonic neo-progressive rock that should please fans to no end. Lots of keyboards, great vocals and soaring string synths. Each song features long instrumental excursions. Their material features a host of great melodies created with some fine musicianship.

Iluvatar (93), Children (95), Sideshow (97), A Story Two Days Wide (99)

IMAGES - France
This music is halfway between a certain tradition of French songs, where the text is important and a polished progressive rock which sometimes evokes folk music emphasis is laid mainly on the lyrics, with, however some beautiful musical passages which are dominated by the guitarist and flutist.

Images (77)

IMAGIN'ARIA - Italy
On the surface their sound has all the hallmarks of a heavier symphonic prog-metal Italian sound. On closer inspection however it's clear they have not forgotten about their own rich progressive heritage and they've managed to incorporate many of the classic Italian touches to their heavy style. Those heavier moments are balanced

with many delicate elements including strings and acoustic guitar.

In Um Altro Quando (96)

IMAN CALIFATO INDEPENDIENTE - Spain

Instrumental band from Southern Spain. Primarily Flamenco with Arab influences. They create a dreamy floating style of progressive rock. Their first album was more folk influenced while on their second the influence was a little more jazz.

Iman Califato Independiente (78), Camino Del Aguila (80),

IN SPE - Estonia

Longish tracks featuring dynamic and powerful symphonic progressive rock. The music influences from classical and jazz, some gripping guitar solos and even a hint of Zappa. Fans of early GENESIS and CAMEL will enjoy the symphonic style here.

In Spe (85), Concerto for Typewriter Concerto In D Minor (85)

IN THE LABYRINTH - Sweden

They create an atmospheric, almost soundtrack like music. Shorter tracks, each evoking a certain mood with hints of early GENESIS. This is mostly instrumental incorporating everything from Mellotron to Indian flutes. The second release took their sound even further creating a kind of symphonic-world music style.

The Garden of Mysteries (96), Walking on Clouds (99)

INDEED - United States

Multi-instrumentalist Brian Hirsch creates music that falls neatly into the symphonic neo-progressive style.

Inter-dimensional Space Commander (96)

INDEX - Brazil

The music here is pure seventies style symphonic progressive rock with lots of warm, rich analog keyboards sounds. Guitarist Jones Junior was formerly with QUATERNA REQUIEM and he continues their style here. If you're a fan of CAMEL and ROUSSEAU you'll find this enjoyable.

Index (99)

INDEXI - Yugoslavia

Similar to early MOODY BLUES featuring acoustic guitar, analog synths and even some narration.

Indexi (74), Indexi (77), Modra Rijeka (78), Sve Ove Godine ( )

INDISCIPLINE - Canada

From Quebec, this nineties group produce material in the same vein as KING CRIMSON and VDGG with a vocalist whose style matches PETER HAMMILL.

A Non-obvious Ride (97)

INDIGO - Austria

Late eighties, post KYRIE ELEISON group who produced a melodic progressive rock. A combination of melodic pop oriented material along with long structured prog compositions.

Herbstwind (81), Indigo (84), Short Stories (91), A Collection of Tales...From Past to Present (92), Silent Memories (8?)

INES - Germany

Melodic progressive rock fronted by a great female keyboardist. The musicianship straddles the line between old style and neo-progressive rock, with elaborate harmonies and sometimes highly complicated arrangements. The influences here include WAKEMAN, Orford and BANKS.

Hunting the Fox (94), Eastern Dawning (97)

INFINITY - United States
Mostly song-oriented material here with a strong late seventies feel in the production and arrangements. Influences in the material include YES, GENTLE GIANT and early STYX. Their one known self-titled release ends with a classic 13 minute epic.

Infinity (96)

INFRA - Sweden
Material in the KING CRIMSON vein.

Infrangible Time EP (9?)

INNER FLAME - Brazil
Formerly known as HIHIL, this new incarnation creates a prog-metal style that is full of moody, doomy, minor-key music. The keyboards are sparse and underplayed, but if you enjoy an almost goth approach you'll find it here.

Inner Flame (99)

INNER RESONANCE - United States
A prog-metal band with a wall-of-keyboards backdrop.

Solar Voices (99)

INTRA - United States
Vintage Ameri-prog featuring a blend of YES and HAPPY THE MAN. Lots of interesting playing with plenty of twists and turns to keep you on your toes.

Intra (76/98)

INTENCE - Switzerland
Out of Blue Fashion (83)

INTERGALACTIC TOURING BAND - Great Britain
Concept album featuring the talents of Larry Fast, Rod Argent, DAVID BEDFORD, ARTHUR BROWN, David Cousins, ANNIE HASLAM, Percy Jones, ANTHONY PHILLIPS and many, many others. Not the greatest work but interesting to have in the collection.

Intergalactic Touring band (77)

INVISIBLE - Argentina
They took their cue from YES but then incorporated many different styles. An emotional melodic prog style.

Invisible ( ), Duranzo Sangrando ( ), El Jardin ( )

IONA - Ireland
Celtic flavoured, Christian band with long melodic symphonic progressive songs. Robert Fripp guested on one album. Sounds like a more adventurous and progressive Clannad.

Iona (90), The Book of Kells (92), Beyond These Shores (94), Journey Into the Morn (95), Heaven's Bright Sun (97), Woven Cord (00)

IO UOMO - Italy
Heavy organ based progressive rock.

IQ - Great Britain
They were part of the resurgence of progressive rock in the early eighties. And like the first wave, IQ learned their chops on the road, performing constantly. Their music leaned at times to a certain jazzy feel ala BRAND X but certainly in their early period their music contained a hint of early GENESIS as well. By the Nomzamo release they had lost Peter Nichols on lead vocals. Fortunately after two so-so albums Nichols returned for EVER an album that found IQ back in their old style, sounding perhaps better than ever.

Seven Stories Into Eight (82 TAPE), Tales From the Lush Attic (83), The Wake (85), Nine In a Pound is Here (85), Living Proof (86), Nomzamo (87), Are You Sitting Comfortably (89), J'ai Pollette D'arnu (91), Ever (94), Forever Live (96), Subterranea

IRIS - France

This group, from ANGE'S same generation, was part of the trend in a certain French progressive rock but it's delicate and refined music also belonged to a British musical tradition. Iris played the same sensitive, sophisticated compositions built around the exquisite chords and classical reminiscence of the organ and on the polished and high vocal harmonies. Sound like - ALICE, GRACIOUS.

Litanies (72)

IRIS - France

No relation to the band from the seventies, this incarnation features the guitarist from ARRAKEEN, Sylvain Gouvernair doing double duty on guitars and keyboards to great effect. He's assisted by Ian Mosley and Peter Trewavas both formerly of MARILLION. They've created a purely instrumental album, that Acid Dragon magazine called one of the best of 1996.

Crossing the Desert (96)

IRRGARTEN - Canada

This band from Quebec City appeared on both the GENESIS and VDGG tributes CDs. It should not be a surprise that their sound is reminiscent of both those bands. If you listen carefully you'll hear some influence from mid-period ELOY. Songs are all on the longish side.

Home and Sanctuary (96)

IRRWICH - Switzerland

They appeared just before the neo-progressive rock revival, however their sound is firmly in the eighties style of the genre. A distinct classical European feeling to some of the material. Imagine a mix of GENESIS circa Abacab and TRIUMVIRAT circa Old Loves Die Hard.

Living in a Fool's Paradise (82)

ISHIZAWA, HIROYUKI - Japan

A very lush, melodic, symphonic progressive rock along the same lines as VERMILLION SANDS with a strong RENAISSANCE influence. The female vocalist will remind you of KATE BUSH or ANNIE HASLAM.

ISHTAR – Spain 1990's

Progressive rock with great guitar and keyboards.

ISILDURS BANE - Sweden

Classical symphonic progressive rock, with Swedish folk roots giving their music something special. A vague reference point might be CAMEL or GENESIS, and then a fusion with the band BRUFORD. The band has been around since the late seventies. Their earlier material tends to be more symphonic.

Sagan Om Den Irlandska Algen (83), Sea Reflections (85), Eight Moments of Eternity (87), Sagan Om Ringen (88), Cheval (89), The Voyage: A Trip to Elsewhere (92), Lost Eggs (94), Mind Volume 1 (97)

ISIS - Japan

They've incorporated elements of both versions of RENAISSANCE to arrive at a very symphonic progressive rock. The prominent piano blends well with the Anglo folk influence.

Isis (91), Image (91)

ISLAND - Switzerland

Symphonic classical influences featuring the intensity of VAN DER GRAAF GENERATOR and the complexity of GENTLE GIANT. Long tracks featuring jazz influenced saxophone and clarinet work.

Pictures (77)

ISKANDER - Germany

One of Germany's best progressive rock bands. Lush symphonic keyboard melodies, soaring guitar, overflowing with exotic instrumental coloration's and polyrhythms. Like early CAMEL or GENESIS.

Overture (84), Boheme 2000 (86), Mental Touch (88), Another Life (90),

ISOPODA - Belgium
Mid-GENESIS symphonic progressive rock sounding band, highly melodic with lots of good ideas. Vocals are in English.

Acrostichon (78), Taking Root (81)

IT - United States
Great instrumental abilities and complex melodies. Much of their music is of a spacier style, but there's also some solo acoustic work and anthemic prog songs. A style similar to Todd Rundgren's UTOPIA.

Order Through Chaos (94)

IT BITES - Great Britain
You might mistake them for just another pop band, but listen closely and you'll hear some interesting progressive rock music in a shorter format. Great stuff in particular their second release which creates a very unique sound.

The Big Lad in the Windmill (86), Once Around the World (88), Eat Me in St. Louis (89), Thank You and Goodnight (91)

ITOIZ - Spain
From the Basque country this highly recommended band shows a strong folk influenced progressive sound. Later releases began showing jazz influences as well. Similar to GOTIC, IBIO or COTO-EN-PEL.

Itoiz (78), Ezekiel (80), Alkorea (82)

IVANHOE - Germany
Neo-progressive rock with a hard edge. Imagine DREAM THEATRE and Queensryche with JADIS.

Visions and Reality (94), Symbols of Time (96), Polarized (97)

IVORY - Germany
Masterful flowing symphonic progressive rock. Sounds like AMENOPHIS, FLYTE or GENESIS circa Trick of the Tail.

Sad Cypress (79), Keen City (96)

IVORY TOWER - Germany
Power progressive metal.

Ivory Tower (98), Beyond the Stars (00)

IXT ADUX - United States
From Los Angeles, this group is most notable in that they have no keyboard player. You'll hear hints of KING CRIMSON in their guitar driven sound.

Brainstorm (82)

IZZ - United States
Hailed by some as the most exciting new U.S. prog band since SPOCK'S BEARD, Izz create classic symphonic progressive rock with a blend of melody and dissonance. There is the shimmering Mellotron and the angular guitar work backed by clever harmonies and marvelous arrangements. Mixed in are some shorter more pop oriented Beatle-ish tunes where the hum-along factor is very high. A nice blend.

Sliver of a Sun (98)

J.E.T. - Italy
Heavier English sound ala URIAH HEEP, but still with the early Italian prog flavour in the melodies.

Fede Speranza Carita (72)

JACKAL - Canada
They create a heavy psychedelic progressive rock similar to DEEP PURPLE only more complex. A mix of prog and psychedelic incorporating good guitar and organ interplay.

Awake (73)

JADE WARRIOR - Great Britain
Their first three albums were more guitar oriented with a JETHRO TULL influence, before taking on a very oriental motif that lasted four albums. Some have heard influences from KING CRIMSON and the light jazz rock world. Mostly subdued mellow instrumentals.

Jade Warrior (70), Released (71), Last Autumn's Dream (72), Floating World (74), Waves (75), Kites (76), Way of the Sun (78), Horizon (84), Breathing the Storm (91), Distant Echoes (93), Eclipse (98), Fifth Element (98)

JADIS - Great Britain
They sound strikingly similar to IQ, partially because they were founded by IQ'S keyboardist Martin Orford and he has done keyboard duty with both. The band has since gone through numerous personnel changes but still manages to produce neo-progressive rock of the highest calibre.

Jadis (90), More than Meets the Eye (92), Across the Water (94), Once or Twice EP (96), Sommersault (97), As Daylight Fades (98), Understand (00)

JANE - Germany
One of the most musically varied bands in Europe. They were formed out of what was left of HARLIS. Some of their material is great, some so-so, but if you're in an experimental mood for jazz-rock, hard rock, or space rock try them out.

Together (72), Here We Go (73), Three (73), Lady Jane (75), Fire, Water, Earth & Air (75), Live (76), Between Heaven and Hell (77), Age of Madness (78), Sign No. 9 (79), No. 10 (80), Jane (81), Germania (83), Beautiful Lady (86), Live 89 (89)

JANISON EDGE - Great Britain
This five piece symphonic progressive rock outfit is fronted by keyboardist Mike Varty and vocalist Sue Element and is fleshed out by members from SHADOWLAND, QUASAR, and LANDMARQ. Their compositional style is true blue prog with the right blend of dynamics. Lots of opportunities for the musicianship to shine through in a collection of shorter tunes and epics. If you enjoy any of the bands mentioned you should make room for Janison Edge.

The Services of Mary Goode (99)

JANYSIUM - Great Britain
They were a London based band that released a couple of cassettes in the early eighties before splitting. Some members went on to form MACH ONE.

JASPER WRATH - United States
Musically they're very much in the tradition of THE MOODY BLUES, JETHRO TULL, YES and PINK FLOYD. Their material features the mainstays of Mellotron, flute, Arp 2600 along with many other analog synths. A sound very much rooted in the early seventies, they incorporated the obligatory elements of physchadelia and jazz. Two members, Jimi Christian and Jeff Cannata went on to form ARCANGEL.

Jasper Wrath [Anthology 1969 - 1976] (97)

JEREMY - United States
Uplifting instrumental symphonic keyboard oriented progressive rock. A mixture of long and short pieces incorporating vintage synths. Sort of the American answer to ANTHONY PHILLIPS, STEVE HACKETT, MIKE OLDFIELD or GORDON GILTRAP.

Pilgrim's Journey (95), Celestial City (97), Salt the Planet (99)

JERICHO - Great Britain
Early styled progressive rock.

Jericho (72)

JESTER'S CROWN - United States
A four piece whose music is a bit on the progressive pop side with some interesting

musicianship. Occasional hints of RUSH and PENDRAGON in some of their songs. Their second release made major progressive strides.

Above the Storm (95), aWay (98)

JESTER'S JOKE - Italy
Neo-progressive rock sound similar to IQ and MARILLION.

Just a Reason to be Out There (91)

JETHRO TULL - Great Britain
Some of the best blending of blues, jazz, a bit of R & B and progressive rock elements. Oh and throw in a dash of medieval folk as well. They go back a long way but continue to produce music that is as interesting and entertaining as ever to this very day.

This was...Jethro Tull (68), Stand Up (69), Benefit (70), Aqualung (71), Thick As a Brick (72), Living in the Past (72), Passion Play (73), War Child (74), Minstrel In the Gallery (75), Too Old to Rock and Roll (76), Songs From the Wood (77), Heavy Horses (78), Bursting Out Live (78), Stormwatch (78), A (80), Broadsword and the Beast (82), Underwraps (84), Crest of a Knave (87), Rock Island (89), Catfish Rising (91), A Little Light Music (92), Roots to Branches (95), J-Tull Dot Com (99)

JETHRO TULL BY THE LONDON SYMPHONY - Great Britain
Part of a series created by David Palmer. He chose Tull because of his long association with the band. Orchestrated versions of some of their classic tracks featuring guest appearances by some band members. This is a fine record for the collection.

A Classic Case - The Music of Jethro Tull (85)

JOBSON, EDDIE - Great Britain
Violin and keyboard player who has worked with a very distinguished list of bands, namely FRANK ZAPPA, ROXY MUSIC, CURVED AIR, JETHRO TULL and UK. He then struck out on his own giving us an album that contains a little jazz, a little rock, and a whole bunch of progressive rock.

The Green Album (83)

JOHANSEN, SVERRE KNUT - Norway
Multi-instrumentalist Johansen creates lush symphonic soundscapes, well developed and fully arranged. Themes are constantly being developed so nothing repeats much. There are no jagged edges here, everything flows together smoothly.

Distant Shore (94)

JOHANSSON, BJORN - Sweden
This Swedish multi-instrumentalist creates a symphonic prog with lots of classical motifs. His material is embellished with many acoustic intruments such as flutes and mandolins providing a light and airy feel. The long compositions are suitably spiced up with electric guitar from time to time. He's assisted by Par Lindh on keyboards.

Discus Ursi (99)

JOHN CARSON'S HYPERMANIA - Great Britain
Carson, the former lead vocalist with ARENA creates a simple progressive pop style which has much in common with STYX's latter style. Not complicated but certainly melodic 'arena' rock with pomp-prog arrangements.

Down to Birth (99)

JON & VANGELIS - Great Britain
Some might have thought it an unlikely pairing, but in fact Vangelis was approached at one time to join YES so in that sense it's not too strange. The music is very elec-

tronic in nature although Jon's voice lends a very human feel to the material.

Short Stories (79), Friends of Mr. Cairo (81), Private Collection (83), Pages of Life (91)

JONESY - Great Britain
Formed in January 1972 by John Jones, lead guitarist with the group. They borrow heavily from the KING CRIMSON school of progressive rock, but forged their own style incorporating lots of Mellotron.

No Alternative (72), Keeping Up (73), Growing (73)

JOURNEY - United States
The Journey of today bears little resemblance to their founding member's efforts. This first LP has someprogressive rock moments. Too bad their later efforts didn't.

Journey (75), Look Into The Future (76)

JUMBO - Italy
They started out as a basic bluesy rock group. After 1971 they started to inject some other influences such as classical into their work. Heavy sounding.

Jumbo (70), DNA (71), Vietato Ai Minori Di 18 Anni (72), Jumbo 1983: Violini D'Autunno [83] (9?), Jumbo Live [90] (90)

JUMP - Great Britain
Neo-progressive rock featuring twin guitars and plenty of keyboards sandwiched in-between. More on the hard rock at times, if you enjoy FISH or Hogarth era MARILLION, you'll like what you hear.

The Myth of Independence (9?), Living In A Promised Land (98), The Freedom Train [Live](99), Matthew (99)

JUST, TED - United States
Multi instrumentalist whose main influence is RICK WAKEMAN. Just's style is very melodic while incorporating elements of classical, baroque and rock.

Baroquen Dreams (97)

KACZYNSKI, CHARLES - Canada
Quebecois prog with a modern approach.

Lumiere de la Nuit (80)

KADWALADYR - France
Fusion band along the lines of BAG or GWENDAL. Complex themes and melodies.

The Last Hero (94)

KAIPA - Sweden
One of Sweden's best seventies bands. Very much like GENESIS with a Scandinavian flavour thrown in. There's also hints of CAMEL and early FLOYD in some of the tunes dreamy symphonic atmosphere.

Kaipa (75), Inget Nytt Under Solen (78), Solo (78)

KAIZEN - Brazil
Ex-members of QUATERNA. A blend of superb violin playing and powerful, emotional symphonic prog rock.

Gargula (94)

KALABAN - United States
From California, they play a blend of music based on the British groups GENESIS, YES and CAMEL. Nice keyboard and guitar interplay and a fiery rhythm section.

Don't Panic (90), Resistance is Useless (93)

KAMAKI, SHIGEKAZU - Japan
The former guitarist with MR. SIRIUS creates a guitar based prog rock with elements of jazz-rock and fusion. All the prog moments are here, but there's also a lot of other musical styles blended in.

Magatama (97)

KAMELOT -
Progressive metal with early English-folk embellishments providing an almost medieval sound.

Siege Perilous (98)

KAMPAI - Germany
Neo-progressive rock sound.

Land of the Free (9?)

KANSAS - United States
The American counterpart to bands like YES or GENESIS, Kansas crafted their style of progressive rock through their many albums to great effect. They even came up with a couple of pop hits along the way. Their early material featured loads of keyboards and the violin up front while their later material has become more guitar oriented. Kansas creates some of the best musical epics heard on vinyl, check them out. They re-incorporated the violin with David Ragsdale during the mid to late nineties, before reforming with the original line-up including Livgren for the year 2000 release.

Kansas (74), Masque (75), Song For America (75), Leftoverture (75), Point of Know Return (78), Monolith (79), Audio Visions (80), Vinyl Confessions (82), Drastic Measures (83), Power (86), In the Spirit of Things (88), Live at the Whisky ( ), Freaks of Nature (95), Always Never The Same (98), Somewhere to Elsewhere (00)

KANZEON - Japan
A symphonic, instrumental prog in a similar style to OUTER LIMITS or KENSO.

Kanzeon (80)

KAOS MOON - Canada
A sound in the same vein as VISIBLE WIND, with hints of PINK FLOYD and KING CRIMSON.

After the Storm (94)

KAPUTTER HAMSTER - Germany
Progressive rock with the raw underground feel.

Kaputter Hamster (7?)

KARAT - Germany
Originally from East Germany, Karat produced a symphonic prog sound similar in style to NOVALIS or GROBSCHNITT. Their albums in the eighties were a little more streamlined, with fewer epics but good prog none the less.

Karat (77), Uber Sieben Bruecken [Der Albatros] (79), Schwanenkonig (80), Der Blaue Planet [Modra Planeta] (82), Die Sieben Wunder Der Welt (83), Live (84), Funfte Jahreszeit (8?), Karat (91), Die Geschenkte Stunde (95)

KARMA - Great Britain
Formed by guitarist Steve Wilson who released some unusual cassettes of psychedelic-progressive rock. Steve would later go on to form PORCUPINE TREE in the nineties. These cassettes contain early versions of the TREE's Small Fish and Nine Cats.

The Jokes on You (83 TAPE), The Last Man to Laugh (84 TAPE)

KAYAK - Holland
Band from Holland formed by TON SCHERPENZEEL. Their material went from Euro-pop to really great progressive rock. Ton later went on to play keyboards in CAMEL. Melodic with CAMEL influences.

See See the Sun (73), Kayak (74), Royal Bed Bouncer (75), The Last Encore (76), Starlight Dance US version (77), Phantom of the Night (78), Periscope Life (80), Merlin (81), Eyewitness (82)

KEATS - Great Britain
A project by members of the ALAN PARSONS crew when they're not working on the latest Parsons concept. Ad Colin Blunstone and PETER BARDENS who used to be in CAMEL and on the surface you'd think it a pretty heady band. Unfortunately what might have been a pop-progressive rock masterpiece comes out sounding pretty homogenised and very mainstream.

Keats (84)

KEBNEKAISE - Sweden
They create a heavily folk based progressive music that is very melodic and enjoyable.

Resa Mot Okant Mal (71), Kebnekajse II (73), III (75), Ljus Fran Afrika (76), Elefanten (77), Vi Drar Vidare (78), Electric Mountain ( )

KEN'S NOVEL - Belgium
Symphonic prog with traditional influences such as YES and GENESIS, and their arrangments are first class. Everything a prog comosition is supposed to be, dynamic, loud and soft, electric and acoustic, tempo changes it's all here and sound great. This four piece really knows their stuff.

The Guide (99)

KENSO - Japan
Progressive rock with elements of fusion. Nimble guitar lines race in and out of the keyboard arrangements. Some material is more on the jazz side of things but still very listenable. Expose' says they are the Japanese equivalent to HAPPY THE MAN.

Kenso (81), Kenso II (83), Kenso (85), Music From Five Unknown Musicians (86), Self Portrait (87), Sparta (89), Yume No Oka (91), Live 92 (93), Sora Ni Hikaru Early Live Volume 1 (94), Inei No Fue Live Volume 2 (94), Zaiya Live (96), In the West (99), Esoptron (99)

KERBEROS - Sweden
A young progressive metal band with some interesting material with hints of DREAM THEATRE.

Barbeque at Alderaan (96)

KERRS PINK - Norway
Their sound is characterised by laser like lead guitar and ornate keyboard melodies. A mixture of short and longer songs in the six minute range. They go from well crafted pop songs to more adventurous compositions. At times they sound like later day CAMEL and PINK FLOYD.

Kerrs Pink (81), Mellom Oss (81), A Journey on the Inside (93), Art of Complex Simplicity (97)

KICK - United States
Uptempo neo-prog with a strong GENESIS influence circa Duke or Abacab.

The Power and the Glory (90)

KIN PING MEH - Germany
Heavy progressive rock, with a hint of early YES and DEEP PURPLE.

Kin Ping Meh (71), Kin Ping Meh 2 (72), Kin Ping Meh 3 (73), Virtues & Sins (74)

KING CRIMSON - Great Britain
One of progressive rock's founding bands, KC pioneered the use of extended song format and Mellotron along with bands like THE MOODY BLUES. Where King Crimson picked it up was on their experimental side. KC said it was all right to create music that didn't have an instantly hummable melody. This made them sometimes difficult to listen to, but the wait for melody was worth it. For the record King Crimson's music can be divided into roughly three eras: 1 The early years devoted to symphonic prog, 2 The eighties where the sound became more streamlined no longer symphonic and 3 The nineties where they began to experiment more with sound. During the late nineties, Robert Fripp began releasing live recordings of each version of King Crimson. During this time he also seemed to disavow any connection to progressive rock!

In the Court of the Crimson King (69), In the Wake of Poseidon (70), Lizards (70), Islands (71), Earthbound (72), Lark's Tongues in Aspic (73), Starless and Bible Black (74), Red (74), USA (75), Discipline (81), Beat (82), 3 of a Perfect Pair (84), Vroom (94), Thrak (95),

B'Boom - Live in Argentina (96), Thrakattak (96), The Projekct Box (99)

KINGSTON WALL - Finland
Spacey psychedelic rock in the OZRIC TENTACLES vein.

Kingston Wall (92), II (93), III Tri-logy (94)

KITARO - Japan
From Japan comes the dramatic but predominantly new age sound of Kitaro. He has a tendency to be somewhat more melodic than VANGELIS and injects a fair bit of emotion into his music as opposed to just sounds.

Oasis (79), Silk Road (80), Silk Road II (80), Ki (82), Silver Cloud (83), Live In Asia (84), Towards the West (86),

KITE - United States
Hailing out of Idaho in the U.S. North West, Kite produce what might be termed as modern-prog with songs structured as rock compositions but then embellished with lots of prog elements. There are hints of PINK FLOYD, RUSH and even a bit of ECHOLYN.

Gravity (97), Lost All Age (00)

KLAATU - Canada
It's doubtful anyone really thought they were the Beatles. But in any case their first two albums contain progressive rock of the finest variety. Quirky, explosive, catchy, orchestral, humorous and even poignant describe their early efforts. It's too bad they started to lean more to the pop side with later albums.

Klaatu 3:47 EST (76), Hope (77), Sir Army Suit (78), Endangered Species (80), Magentalane (81)

KOPECKY - United States
Fascinating material from three brothers whose musical foundation is centred on Indian traditional influences. Add to this a host of other muscal germs such as DJAM KARET and MAXIMUM INDIFFERENCE and you get a set of music that while not too complicated, contains some nice arrangements and textures.

Kopecky (99)

KORNELYANS - Yugoslavia
Sound like the early Italian progressive rock bands. A prominent organ sound recalls DEEP PURPLE.

Not An Ordinary Life (74)

KOZMIC MUFFIN - Spain
A dual guitar and organ progressive sound.

Nautilus (96)

KRAKEN IN THE MAELSTROM - Italy
Prog rock band similar to KING CRIMSON or VAN DER GRAAF GENERATOR.

Embyogenesis (9?)

KRAAN - Germany
A combination jazz-rock-spacey band, with good strong sax, guitar and keyboards on later albums.

Winthrup (72), Kraan (73), Andy nogger (75), Kraan Live (75), Let It Out (75), Wiederhoren (77), Flyday (78), Tournee (80), Schallplatten (83)

KRAFTWERK - Germany
Often described as cold, clinical, hypnotic, repetitious and mechanical, Kraftwerk's synthesiser laden compositions are a mixture of electronic, industrial and ultimately dance music. Their immensely successful single Autobahn received lots of airplay although the single was actually edited down from the songs original 22 minute length. Much as Tangerine Dream influenced so many electronic rock bands, Kraftwerk influenced a whole genre of

electronic dance musicians.

Kraftwerk 1 (71), Kraftwerk 2 (72), Ralph & Florian (73), Autobahn (74), Radioactivity (75), Exceller 8 (75), Trans Europe Express (77), Man Machine (78), Computer World (80), Electrokinetik (81), Techno Pop (83), Electric Cafe (86), Robotronik (91), Robots (92)

KRAUTZEN, HENRY - Belgium
Solo work by the leader of FINNEGANS WAKE, in a similar style with Canterbury influences.

Iceland ( )

KULTIVATOR - Sweden
Progressive with a folk influence. They come from the Canterbury school of music with a bit of RIO and Zeuhl, so expect a little jazzier flavour to the music. Unusual harmonies and keyboard work will remind you of bands such as SOFT MACHINE, Eskaton, or MAGMA

Barndomens Stigar (81)

KYRIE ELEISON - Austria
Progressive rock similar to early GENESIS with a heavy emphasis on keyboards such as Hammond organ. The overall sound of the material is firmly in the Foxtrot era. They went on to become INDIGO.

The Fountain Beyond the Sunrise (76), Blind Window's Suite (74/94)

LA BIBLIA - Argentina
Concept album based on the Bible that includes a who's who of Argentinean prog. Very well done. The style is similar to the symphonic Italian bands.

La Biblia (7?)

LA FAMIGLIA DEGLI ORTEGA - Italy
Early Italian symphonic progressive rock style that is similar to the more pastoral moments of PFM or LE ORME.

La Familia Degli Ortega (73)

LA HOST - Great Britain
They were formed by two ex-members of AIRBRIDGE. Early eighties neo-progressive rock sound.

4 Cut EP (84 TAPE), LaHost (85 TAPE), Erotic Antiques ( )

LA MAQUINA DE HACER PAJAROS - Argentina
Folk influenced progressive rock.

La Maquina de Hancer Pajaros ( ), Peliculas ( )

LA PENTOLA DI PAPIN - Italy
In the same musical style as I FLASHMAN, I GIGANTI etc. Sort of beat-classical rock, with some spacey PULSAR like fuzz guitar.

Zero-7 (77)

LA ROSSA - France
A band much like the Swiss group CIRCUS. They perform complicated, perfectly constructed and developed compositions with an emphasis on the sophistication of the arrangements. Sound like VDGG, YES, GENTLE GIANT.

A Fury of Glass (83)

LA SECONDA GENESI - Italy
Very inventive music featuring great guitar and flute.

Tutto Deve Finire ( )

LABANDA - Spain
Instrumental Celtic Rock with some nice progressive moments featuring a French violinist.
Labanda (80), Fiestre Campestre (81), Rural Tour (92), No Todo es Seda ( ), Danza De Entrenzado ( ),

LADY LAKE - Holland

Straight ahead symphonic prog that is reminiscent of early CAMEL and GENESIS. Lots of long instrumental sections interspersed with only a few vocals. The original LP was released in 1977 so the CD released in 1997 contains a number of bonus tracks.

No Pictures (77/97)

LAKE GREG - Great Britain

Guitarist and vocalist first with KING CRIMSON, then later with EMERSON LAKE & PALMER. Lake was usually the one to inject the more song oriented elements, so it's quite natural that his solo efforts do not reflect the grand scope of the bands he has worked in. Some nice songs though. He also spent a brief time replacing John Wetton in ASIA.

Greg Lake (81), Manoeuvres (83)

LANCASTER, JACK - Great Britain

Original member of BLODWYN PIG who in later years went in a strong jazz rock vein to create some wonderful progressive rock at times. Released an LP called Marscape with all the members who would later go on to form BRAND X.

Marscape (76), Wild Connections (79), Skinnigrove Bay (87)

LANDBERK - Sweden

Dreamy, atmospheric progressive rock. Influenced by early bands like KING CRIMSON and PINK FLOYD with intelligent use of floating Mellotron and the moody melancholy sound associated with those groups.

Lonely Land (92), One Man Tell's Another (94), Unaffected (95), Dream Dance EP (95), Indian Summer (96)

LANDMARQ - Great Britain

Landmarq create a wonderful and moderatly complex symphonic progressive rock. Wall of keyboard and thick guitar sounds dominate. Produced by Clive Nolan of PENDRAGON. Sound very similar to IQ and JADIS. For their release Science of Coincidence they were joined by new vocalist Tracy Hitchings.

Solitary Witness (92), Infinity Paradise (93), The Vision Pit (96), Science of Coincidence (98)

LANDS END - United States

Symphonic progressive rock band from California with lush keyboards. Colourful and intense melodies from the EDHELS school with even some FLOYD influence on the longer tracks.

Pacific Coast Highway (93), Terra Serranum (95), An Older Land (96), Natural Selection (97), Drainage [Live] (98)

LARK ECHO - Finland

Their sound is in the early PINK FLOYD or KING CRIMSON vein.

Lark Echo ( )

LASER - Italy

A band led by organ playing influenced by QUATERMASS or THE NICE.

Vita Sul Pianeta (73)

LAST TURION - Germany

Neo-progressive rock with only hints of heavy metal. Instead they focus their efforts towards stronger melodies and heavy symphonic arrangements. Some similarity to MARILLION or CHANDELIER.

Circle Logic (92), Seduction Overdrive (96)

LATTE E MIELE - Italy

Symphonic progressive rock which, musically speaking is close to RDM. You'll hear hints of ELP or PFM.

Passio Secundum Mattheum (72), Papillon (73), Aquile E Scoiattoli (76), Vampyrs (77), Papillon [English demo 73] (9?), Live 1973 (9?), Vampyrs [demos 79] (9?)

LAURA - France
Symphonic progressive rock created in the early eighties that bears the influence of bands such as STYX and ATOLL.

Laura (80), Colis Postal (81)

LEBLANC, GUY - Canada
LeBlanc is keyboardist and founding member of NATHAN MAHL. Here his solo work incoporates much of the same traditional prog elements but also showcases a slightly more jazz influenced guitar style compliments of Scott McGill formerly of Finneus Guage. All compositions feature solid instrumental interplay with plenty of dynamics to keep the interest level high.

Subversia (99)

LEES, JOHN - Great Britain
Guitarist and main writer for BJH goes out on his own and produces material of a shorter more mainstream nature. Still good.

A Major Fancy (77)

LEGEND - Great Britain
Five piece pagan symphonic progressive rock group whose early acoustic folk style has evolved into a more electric guitar approach. They have been described in the press as being similar to early YES, RENAISSANCE and Steeleye Span.

Light in Extension (91), Second Light (93), Triple Aspect (96)

LEGENDE - France
A musical style that is similar to the classic French prog style developed by bands such as Ange. The music contains a strong acoustic, folk quality but the emphasis is on keyboards through out. They used to go by the name NORTHERN CROSS.

Departs (89), Tempus Fugit (93)

LEGER DE MAIN - United States
Ohio based trio producing material featuring long tracks. Expose' says if RUSH were really a progressive rock band, this is the type of music they'd produce. Masters of arrangement and studio technique with a dense wall of keyboards and buzzing guitars with compositions that allow plenty of room for softer acoustic elements to stand out.

The Concept of Our Reality (95), Second First Impression (97)

LEGGAT - Canada
The Leggat brothers used to be in a pop band called A Foot In Cold Water, that played some longer simple material. After that band, Leggat was formed playing a very guitar oriented hard edge progressive rock.

Illuminations (82)

LEHMEJUM - Brazil
Purely instrumental keyboard progressive rock with the spotlight on piano and organ. Their style is sometimes symphonic and sometimes more fusion based with a hint of Latin rhythms.

Lehmejum (93)

LEMUR VOICE - Holland
They come from the heavier side, influenced by DREAM THEATRE and RUSH although their style is closer to progressive rock than metal. They originally went by the name Aura. The band lists their influences as Queensryche and OZRIC TENTACLES.

Insights (96)

L'ENGOULEVENT - Canada
Folky Quebecois prog that is similar to CONVENTUM.

L'ile ou Vivent (7?)

LENS - United States
Here are three of the founding members of San Francisco's EPISODE performing flowing instrumental progressive rock material with a strong jazz-rock influence. Much of their material in this incarnation emphasizes the guitar rather than keyboard.

Sketches (97), Weaving a Tangled Web (99)

LEONARD, KEVIN - United States
The former NORTH STAR keyboardist strikes out on his own in a different vein. Unlike the neo-prog material he's best known for, the material here is more jazz influenced with an eye to 20th century classical compositional style. Solid musicianship highlight this instrumental fare.

Auto Matrix (95)

LE ORME - Italy
One of the finest symphonic progressive rock bands from Italy. Formed in the late sixties they matured musically during the early seventies settling on the musical triad of keyboards, bass/guitar and drums. Their music contains elements of classical, jazz, folk and rock creating their own brand of progressive rock which at times has hints of ELP or Traffic.

Collage (71), Uomo di Pezza (72), Felona & Serona (73), In Concerto (74), Contrapunti (74), Beyond Leng (75), Smogmagica (75), Verita Nascoste (76), Storia O Leggenda (77), Piccalo Rapsodia dell'Ape (80), Venerdi (81), Il Fiume (96)

LETHE - Italy
Material that bears a striking resemblance to JETHRO TULL or ELP, featuring longish tracks.

Nymphae (9?)

LEVIATHAN - Italy
Neo-progressive rock in the vein of MAR- ILLION and SAGA. Many of the songs don't depart too far from the 4/4 beat but there are plenty of prog embellishments to make it interesting

Heartquake (88), Bee Yourself (90), Volume (97)

LEYENDA - Mexico
Interesting band mixing pre-Colombian folk and prog. Similar to LOS JAIVAS from Chile.

Ozzo Alexion ( )

LIAISON - Great Britain
They were out of North West London in '79 underwent changes till they finally settled on a line-up in about '81. They've been called inventive and original. For a prog band their lack of keyboards is unique.

4 Cut EP (82 TAPE), Only Heaven Knows EP (83 TAPE)

LIEVAUX-TRANSFO - France
This group whose leader is the singer/composer Jean-Yves Lievaux offers a music halfway between French and English progressive rock. Sound like- ATOLL, YES, KING CRIMSON.

Public Passage (80), Porte 50 (81)

LIFT - United States
Long tracks and material that sounds like ELP with some great Mellotron. Guitar and keyboard driven symphonic material in the best tradition of YES and GENESIS. Vocals are a high tenor in the style of Jon Anderson.

Caverns of Your Brain (77)

LIGHT - Holland
They create a more guitar oriented progressive rock sound of the nineties without sacrificing any of the creative aesthetics. The guitar is backed up by solid keyboard work. Great arrangements and a unique style. Fans of PENDRAGON will

appreciate this band.

Light (95)

LIGHT, THE - United States
A nice fat progressive rock sound from a California band whose sound is firmly rooted in the late seventies. Dense keyboards in songs with big intros and extros. If you like your prog in the style of SAGA, STYX or KANSAS you'll like this band.

On a New Horizon (95)

LIGHTSHINE - Germany
Progressive sound with great fuzz guitar, dreamy atmosphere, and a slight symphonic element punctuated with pleasant flute and synth work. Fans of GROBSCHNITT will enjoy the style here.

Feeling (76)

LIGHTSPEED - Canada
A nineties band from Hamilton, Ontario whose style lies more in the pomp-rock vein.

So, Exactly Where Are We? ( ), On Second Thought ( )

LIKE WENDY - Holland
This is lush, superbly arranged symphonic progressive rock circa GENESIS Wind and Wuthering or Trick of the Tail. Lots of melody weaving in and out of solid musicianship with the usual mood changes.

The Storm Inside (98), Rainchild (99)

LIMELIGHT - Great Britain
Power trio in the same vein as RUSH, but with the added element of Mellotron.

Limelight (80)

LINDH, PAR [PROJECT] - Sweden
Classical rock featuring members of ANGLAGARD. Dramatic, keyboard heavy music that is reminiscent of some of WAKEMAN'S and EMERSON'S finest work. Loads of Mellotron and Hammond B3 are featured along with pipe organ. The music is not overly complex but very well arranged to provide plenty of depth.

Gothic Impressions (94), Rondo EP (96), Bilbo (96), Mundus Incompertus (98), Live In America (99)

LIQUID SKY - United States
A group who take their influences from both prog and non-prog sources to create a style that is a blend all their own. Their compositions are not overly complicated but layered with textures and arranged with hints of rockier bands like Led Zeppelin all the while incorporating prog elements from KING CRIMSON or YES.

Doldrums of Ecstasy (98)

LIQUID TENSION EXPERIMENT - United States
This side-line project features DREAM THEATRE guitarist John Petrucci, drummer Mike Portnoy and keyboardist Jordon Rudess along with bassist Tony Levin. Great musicianship with compositions ranging from all out jamming to more jazz or fusion inflected pieces. Not complex, and perhaps not even really prog in the strictest sense but a great display of musical prowess.

Liquid Tension Experiment (98), 2 (99)

LISKER - Spain
Twin guitar and flute fronted progressive rock sound. While no keyboards are present the dominant flute makes up for their absence. The strong guitar interplay combines elements of folk and rock with hints of JETHRO TULL.

Lisker (79)

LISTEN - United States
With songs entitled Lifecycles-Symphony #1 and running for over 20 minutes you'd

be correct in thinking this is a symphonic progressive rock band. But know there is a strong prog-metal flavour running through this material that carries a vintage old style heavy prog attitude.

Close Your Eyes and Your There (99)

LIVES AND TIMES - Great Britain
Their music has hints of early CURVED AIR and even some ENID-esque epics. The vocals will appeal to fans of KATE BUSH.

A New Idea of Heaven (90), A Pull of the Tide (93), Waiting for the Parade (94), The Great Sad Happy Ending (94), There and Back Again Lane (9?)

LIVGREN, KERRY - United States
Solo efforts from former KANSAS member that sound quite a bit like the best of what KANSAS created.

Seeds of Change (80), Time Line (83), Kerry Livgren AD (84), Art of the State ( ), Prime Mover ( ), Reconstruction's ( ), When Things Get Electric (96)

LIVING LIFE - Italy
A progressive group similar to early eighties GENESIS. Not in the classic Italian style but more a blend of space, jazz and folk influences.

Mysterious Dream (81), Let: From Experience to Experience (78)

LIVIT - Germany
A hard edged neo-progressive rock band described in Acid Dragon magazine as: A masterpiece of progressive metal music with PINK FLOYD features (the sound effects), fluid guitars in the PENDRAGON vein, heavy inventivity in the Queensryche tradition. Fans of SHADOW GALLERY should love this.

Just in Time (9?), Unspoken (96)

LIZARD - Poland
As the name might imply, influenced by KING CRIMSON, but whose sound is more in the modern neo-prog mould with hints of IQ and COLLAGE. The music also shows a strong East European prog influence that creates a style that is not only challenging but is also enjoyable.

Lizard (96), W Galerii Czasu (97)

LOAD, THE - United States
A trio from Ohio. They recorded three LPs worth of material between 1973 - 1977 but it was never released. This is keyboard driven progressive rock with influences from ELP and THE NICE.

Praise the Load (76), Load Have Mercy (95)

LOCANDA DELLE FATE - Italy
Italian symphonic masterpiece featuring dual keyboards incorporating elements of PFM, PINK FLOYD and YES. Very melodic, with many memorable musical themes. The original trio reformed in 1998 and recorded some new material that turned out to be smooth polished and even symphonic but not quite as adventurous as their material from the seventies. A tough act to follow.

Forse Le Lucciole Non So Amano Pui (77), Live (93), Homo Homini Lupus (99)

LOCH NESS - Mexico
Heavy sounding power trio playing progressive rock with influences ranging from PINK FLOYD to RUSH. The sound of the guitar may have you thinking psychadelic, but the over all structure and arrangement of the material is much closer to prog.

Ox (88), Prologue (88), Drunmadrochit (94/99)

LODGE, JOHN & JUSTIN HAYWARD - Great Britain
This release along with their individual solo efforts constitute perhaps the most effective pop song writing side of THE MOODY BLUES. As always it was the pop influence that was wrapped into the total

construction of music that made their material so recognisable and desired by fans.

Bluejays ( )

LONGSHOT -
Symphonic neo-prog influenced by mid-period GENESIS. If bands like IQ, PENDRAGON and LANDMARQ are your cup-of-tea you will enjoy Longshot

The Cosmic Bacteria's Experience (97)

LOOK - United States
Look create a pleasant pop oriented progressive rock with just enough symphonic elements to hold your attention. The music is bright and up-beat a blend of YES and some PINK FLOYD all arranged in melodic compositions you'll be humming for days.

Waiting Skies (99)

LOOKING GLASS - United States
Based in the Seattle area, Looking Glass were four individuals who came together in the nineties with a fair amount of musical background. Their style was accessible, yet intricate and layered. Influences included YES, RUSH and GENESIS. No known recorded material.

LORD, JON - Great Britain
While in DEEP PURPLE, Lord was the prime instigator for musical experimentation. Witness the band's early efforts with classical musicians. His solo work was an extension of what he felt unable to do within the band context. His work with orchestra and rock created some very enjoyable prog rock.

Gemini Suite (71), Windows (74), Sarabande (76), Before I Forget (82)

LORIEN - Great Britain
Progressive rock in a style similar to MARILLION and YES.

Children's Games (96)

LOS JAIVAS - Chile
Most well known Chilean progressive rock band. A strong cultural and ethic influence brings to mind bands such as JADE WARRIOR.

Cancion Del Sur (77), Los Javas (79), Todo Juntos ( ), Aconcagua (81), Altur As De Machu (84), Trilgia El Rencuentro (97)

LOST TALES - Italy
The music hear takes you back to the classic Italian era of the seventies and updates it nicely. The influences range from early KING CRIMSON to PINK FLOYD. Lots of acoustic guitars mixed with digital syths. A pleasant blend of symphonics with a bit of spacey-ness at times too.

A Volo Radente (99)

LOTHLORIEN - Italy
Their compositional style pays homage to the classic Italian prog of the seventies all the while maintaining a very modern sound. If you are a fan of CALLIOPE or MALIBRAN you will like what you hear.

Il Sale Sulla Coda (98)

LOWBLOW - Japan
With a line-up which includes members of TIPOGRAPHICA, you would expect this to be more of the avant-gard prog style and you would be right. Lots of dense harmonies with a free-form jazz influence. Not to be missed is the humorous approach to the song titles, just to demonstrate they don't take themselves too seriously. But keep in mind this is challenging music to listen to, and not everyones cup-of-tea.

Mister Café (97)

LUNA INCOSTANTE - Italy
Combination of guitars, reeds, bass, drums and keyboards. Their musical style displays hints of early KING CRIMSON, with lots of minor chords but not in the symphonic sense.

Senzasanti (8?), Luna Incostante (97)

LUNAR CHATEAU - United States
Progressive rock trio with solid, catchy pop elements. Melodic rock with definite prog elements and great keyboard work with hints of ELP and RENAISSANCE.

Lunar Chateau (94)

L'UOVO DI COLOMBO - Italy
Classic material from 1973, keyboard driven progressive rock.

L'uovo Di Colombo (73)

LYNNE, BJORN - Great Britain
This Norwegian musician lives in England and creates music in a style similar to MIKE OLDFIELD and GANDALF. His early material was a blend of many genres including prog and space-rock. His later releases tended to be more symphonic epic concept recordings.

Witchwood (96), The Void (97), Wizard of the Winds/When The Gods Slept (98), Wolves of the Gods (99), Revive (00)

MACH ONE - Great Britain
A band with two guitarists formed sometime in early 1981 playing mostly charity gigs in London and Birmingham. Eventually wrote enough material for a cassette release and after much struggling put together the funds to release their first album.

Lost For Words (84)

MACHINA COELI - Italy
Symphonic progressive rock with great depth and lots of emotion. The material is very adventurous and epic in scale.

Finitor Visus Nostri [EP] (99)

MACHIAVEL - Belgium
Belgium's most famous symphonic band born out of the seventies prog-rock era sounding a bit like YES. They utilise a very traditional instrument line-up including loads of Mellotron. Their early lyrics were quite cosmic, but in their later years they became more heavy metal oriented.

Machiavel (76), Jester (77), Mechanical Moonbeams (78), Urban Games (79), New Lines (80), Valentine's Day (81), Break Out (81)

MACHINES HAVE LANDED - Canada
Machines Have Landed Part 1 (81)

MACKAY, DUNCAN - Great Britain
Started out as keyboard player for Steve Harley's Cockney Rebels. Mackay spent the bulk of his time as a session player at Abbey Road where he sat in for the ALAN PARSONS PROJECT and KATE BUSH amongst others. He also played a brief time with 10CC. His first solo outing contains material far more in the progressive field than the second.

Score (77), Visa (80)

MAD CRAYON - Italy
A band with among other things, Canterbury influences. They create a lush symphonic sound and lyrically sound a bit like GENESIS. Musically they have more in common with LE ORME and LOCANDA DELLE FATE.

Ultimo Miraggio (94), Diamanti (99)

MAD PUPPET - Germany
Material geared to prog fans who like more of a moody or folk influence to their

progressive rock. A good balance of guitars and keyboards with a bit of flute. Some very good moments on their first release but then they became less adventurous with later material.
Masque (82), Not only Mad (91), King Laurin and His Rosegarden (94)

MADRAGORE - France
Instrumental music with well constructed themes. Very melodic with a definite GENESIS influence.

A Revivre Le Future (9?)

MADRIGAL - France
Symphonic-progressive rock. A neat, carefully worked out sound with elaborate arrangements, well placed harmonies and beautiful melodies. Sound like - TAI PHONG, MOODY BLUES or 10cc.

School of Time (78)

MADRIGAL - United States
Based in Spokane Washington their musical style picks up where ECHOLYN left off. Great keyboard playing with lots of interesting vocal work enhanced by flute and saxophone. Will appeal to fans of ECHOLYN and GENTLE GIANT.

Waiting (88), On My Hands (96)

MADDER LAKE - Australia
Progressive rock with a harder edge. Their music contained long instrumental passages with above average playing ability.

Butterfly Farm (73)

MAELSTROM - United States
Maelstrom was influenced by the popular prog bands of the day including GENTLE GIANT, VDGG, YES and others of that era. Their symphonic prog sound incorporates the key instruments of Hammond organ, Mellotron, flute and sax.

Maelstrom (73)

MAESTRACCI, JACKY - France
Multi-instrumentalist who crafts well thought out symphonic pieces.

Symphonia ( )

MAGDALENA - Japan
This was actually vocalist Megumi Tokuhisa's band prior to joining TERU'S SYMPHONIA. The music here is a mixture of heavy symphonic prog, pop, bombastic anthems and classical elements.

Magdalena (86), Reconstruction (91)

MAGDEBURG - Germany
A melodic, symphonic progressive rock sound.

Magdeburg [Verkehrte Welt] (80), Grande Hand (82)

MAGDALENA - Japan
Symphonic progressive rock.

Magdalena (86), Magdalena (86), Reconstruction (91)

MAGELLAN - United States
A sound that shows some RUSH influence. Strong, dramatic symphonic music that's a mixture of YES, PENDRAGON and KANSAS. Compositionally their music is very dramatic with lots of stops and starts and more than the usual amount dynamics.

Hour of Restoration (91), Impending Ascension (94), Test of Wills (97)

MAGMA - Argentina
NOT to be confused with the French band of the same name, this Magma was a symphonic progressive rock band that came from the same roots as fellow countrymen MIA. They recorded three albums mixing a symphonic sound with Andean folklore and a hint of jazz.

Canto para una Consagracion (82), La transformacion (85)

MAGMA - France
One of France's premier underground groups, Magma, guided by group founder Christian Vander produced an adventurous, complex music incorporating everything from dissonance to blues shouting to free jazz to 20th Century classical composition. Their sound gave birth to the Zeuhl sub genre.

Magma (70), 1001 Centigrade (71), Mekanik Kommandoh (73), Mekanik Destruktiw Kommandoh (73), Kohntarkosz (74), Live (75), Udu Wudu (76), Inedits (77), Attahk (78), Concert Bobino 1981 (81), Merci (84), Mythes et Legendes Vol. I (85), Theatre Du Taur Concert 1975 (94), Mekanik Zeuhl Wortz (94), Concert 1971 Bruxelles - Theatre I 40 (96), Kompila (97), London BBC Concert 1974 (99)

MAGNA CARTA - Great Britain
Progressive folk from the early seventies. Perhaps more folk than most would like.

Lord of the Ages (73)

MAGNESIS - France
Comparable to MARILLION in many ways, but they manage to retain hints of the French symphonic style made famous by bands such as MONA LISA. An interesting blend of early GENESIS, French folk and symphonic styles.

Le Miroir Aux Defauts (9?), Absintheisme (95)

MAGNUM - Great Britain
Formed in Birmingham, they play a brand of pomp-progressive rock in a style similar to STYX or ANGEL. Tony Clarken is the guitarist and songwriter and maintains a very poetic-epic style in his lyrical and musical composition.

Kingdom of Madness (78), Magnum II (79), Marauder (80), Chase the Dragon (82), The Eleventh Hour (83), On a Story Tellers Night (85)

MAGUS - United States
Vermont based Magus was essentially the brainchild of Andrew Robinson. Following a number of release that wewre pretty much solo efforts and band has been put together to carry the name into the new millenium. The music is a very full sound with lots of slow dreamy guitar parts and keyboard washes sounding like a mix of ELOY and early seventies PINK FLOYD. There are times where, while using soundclips and voice-bits the material is every bit the same as the best of ROGER WATERS.

Magus (96), Traveller (97), Highway 375 [EP] (98), Echos From the Edge of the Millenium 1987-1999 [Compilation] (99)

MAHOUJIN - Japan
Symphonic prog material from the seventies heavily influenced by the style and sound of ELP.

Babylonia Suite (77)

MAINFRAME - Great Britain
Guitar and keyboard duo consisting of Murray Munro and John Molloy who created a concept album entitled Tenants of the Lattice Work. The music was one long continuous piece with elements of STEVE HACKETT, YES and PINK FLOYD with a bit of Thomas Dolby thrown in.

Tenants of the Lattice Work (83)

MAINHORSE - Great Britain
Early progressive rock style featuring a young PATRICK MORAZ on keyboards.

Mainhorse (71)

MALIBRAN - Italy
Another Italian band who feature the classic seventies, GENESIS influenced symphonic progressive rock style. If you like JETHRO TULL, you'll like this band because of some great flute playing. Sound wise they also have something in common with CALLIOPE.

The Wood of Tales (90), La Porte Del Silenzio (93), La Citta sul Lago (98)

MALLEUS - Italy
Floating symphonic orchestrated opera material.

Opera Totale ( )

MALOMBRA - Italy
Neo-prog band featuring a combination of early GENESIS, hint's of Hawkwind's spaciness with a slight influence from OZRIC. This ultimately results in a unique blend of synthetics and symphonic rock. There is a combination of male and female vocals which provides an interesting counterpoint and produces a striking contrast between the delicate musical passages and the more powerfully arranged bits.

Malombra (93), Our Lady of the Bones (96)

MANDALABAND - Great Britain
Musician/Writer/Producer Davy Rohl created two concept albums of progressive rock. Both used many talented musicians like all of 10cc, members of BJH and plenty more. Fully orchestrated these albums truly stand out. Their style is more on the romantic and lyrical with plenty of melody.

Mandalaband (75), The Eye of Wendor (78)

MANDRAGORA - Argentina
Argentina's neo-prog answer to MARILLION, although you will hear elements of many of the older mainstream prog groups.

Pecado Tras Pecado (93)

MANDRAGORE - Canada
Nineties band creating neo-progressive rock mixed with a medieval flavour sets this bands music apart. The songs tend to be about Arthurian legends so it fits. Unfortunately the material was edited to ensure each song was under five minutes in length to try and get on radio. This hurt the arrangements and probably won't win them many prog fans or get them on the air.

MANEIGE - Canada
Complex mostly instrumental progressive rock in a GENTLE GIANT vein, with ethnic folk influences. The early work up to 1978 tends to be more symphonic while the work after 1979 tends to have a more jazz influence. They toured with such greats as KING CRIMSON, GENTLE GIANT and SOFT MACHINE.

Maneige (75), Les Porches De Notre-Dame (75), Ni vent...Ni Nouvelle (77), Libre Service (78), Composite (80), Montreal, 6 A.M. (81), Images (84)

MANFRED MANN'S EARTH BAND - Great Britain
Manfred Mann, with a background in pop and then jazz, formed the Earth Band in the early seventies. You can rely on always hearing something great on each release. Their style has lots of room for musical virtuosity through instrumentals as well as a hint of jazz on songs that build on grand musical themes. Great keyboard and guitar work.

Manfred Mann's Earth Band (72), Glorified Magnified (72), Messin (73), Solar Fire (73), The Good Earth (74), Nightingales and Bombers (75), The Roaring Silence (76), Watch (78), Angel Station (79), Chance (80), Somewhere In Afrika (82), Budapest Live (83), Criminal Tango (86), Masque (87), Soft Vengeance (97)

MANILLA ROAD - USA
They came together in Kansas playing progressive rock music in a style similar to STYX or KANSAS. Their later albums took on more of a hard rock approach.

Invasion (79), Metal (82), Metal Logic (83), Open The Gates (85), The Deluge (86)

MANNHEIM STEAMROLLER - United States

Sort of an American ENID. They started out writing jingles and ended up working with the London Symphony. Their hallmark sound is the harpsichord. The band has over the years found a solid following not only in the progressive rock side of music but now more than ever new age music.

Fresh Aire I ( ),Fresh Aire II (77),Fresh Aire III (79),Fresh Aire IV (81),Interludes (81),

MANNING, GUY - Great Britain

Manning is a part-time member of PARALLEL OR 90 DEGREES. Here his work is similar but also contains many elements of ROGER WATERS, PINK FLOYD and even ROY HARPER. Longer material crafted around modern socail concepts.

Tall Stores for Small Children (98)

MANSET, GERARD - France

Solo artist in the same vein as PETER GABRIEL although stylistically very different. Manset's work involves full orchestra, narration's and almost a sound-track-ish approach to his science fiction epic La Mort d'Orion.

La Mort d'Orion ( )

MANTICORE - Sweden

Swedish symphonic outfit with a distinct GENESIS feel to the material. Their long melodic tracks emphasise EMERSON style keyboards, HOWE-like guitar, and SQUIRE'S bass. Plenty of Mellotron and Hammond to keep up with the guitar playing.

Time to Fly (93)

MANZANERA, PHIL - Great Britain

Guitarist with Roxy Music started out on a solo career reasonably early with his own set of guests. Music is a mixture of easy jazz with a bit of avant-garde thrown in á la SOFT MACHINE. Good guitar playing throughout with lots of instrumentals.

Diamond Head (75),801 Live (76),Listen Now (77),K-Scope (78)

MAQUINA - Spain

One of the better psych-prog bands from Spain. Lots of great fuzz guitar

Why? (71)

MARATHON - Germany

Neo-progressive material.

Impossible is Possible (9?)

MARATHON - Holland

A neo-progressive style that is similar to MARILLION or IQ, but also has a strong element of SAGA circa Worlds Apart.

The First Run (93)

MARATHON - Italy

Musically they're somewhere between JADIS and DREAM THEATRE but not as heavy as IVANHOE.

Sublime Dreams (96)

MARCO - Mexico

Symphonic soloist Marco Gomez. A great mixture of styles and playing technique encompassing new age, classical, traditional Spanish and heavy metal. ICONOCLASTA fans will certainly enjoy this.

Marconceptos (94)

MARCO, ANTONIO ARAVJO - Brazil

Strong classical influences.

MARGE LITCH - Japan

Perhaps one of the best symphonic progressive rock bands in Japan. Featuring a powerful female vocalist, backed by a four piece on drums, bass, keyboards and guitar.

Rainbow Knight (86), Star Light (87), The Force of Trinity (88), Marge Litch (89), Prologue (89), Fantasien (91), The Ring of Truth (92), Crystal Heart in the Fountain (95), Fantargen 2 (97), Fantasien 1998 (98)

MARIA - Japan
Mid seventies symphonic prog band, with good guitar and keyboard interplay and Japanese vocals.

Maria (76)

MARILLION - Great Britain
The premier neo progressive rock band of the eighties. Honing a style from the school of early GENESIS and PETER GABRIEL, Marillion quickly became the spokes-band for the movement and proved if you worked hard and perfected your writing skills a progressive rock band could make it in the eighties. The material is very introspective lyrically with all the right instruments well played. Fish left in 1989 to pursue a solo career. The band continued creating great material like the 1994 album Brave. After Brave, they began focusing on more 'mainstream' material and were even quoted in one publication as saying We're more than just a prog band! Conflict continues as fans from the early days continue holding out hope that Marillion may at some point return to writing prog classics for the new millenium.

Script For A Jesters Tear (83), Fugazi (84), Real To Reel (84), Misplaced Childhood (85), Garden Party Live EP (86), Clutching at Straws (87), The Thieving Magpie [Live] (88), Seasons End (89), Holidays in Eden (91), Brave (94), Afraid of Sunlight (95), Made Again (96), This Strange Engine (97), Radiation (98), Marillion.com (99)

MARSH, HUGH - Canada
More from the school of jazz and fusion, the release Shaking the Pumpkin has some moments that might fall into a progressive rock category somewhere. Fans of Jean Luc Ponty may enjoy.

Shaking the Pumpkin (87)

MARSUPILAMI - Great Britain
Canterbury-style band.

Marsupilami (70), Arena (71)

MARTHA'S WAKE - United States
An intriguing blend of symphonic progressive rock and a heavy, folkish grunge sound. The unique vocal style of Leah Carson combined with flute, guitars, keyboards and trumpet make for an unusual style.

Colouring China (96)

MARTZ, JASUN - United States
Mellotron soaked material featuring dark classical guitar. Overall sinister sound. Martz toured with Zappa and his release The Pillory features a number of Zappa alumni contributing to the sound.

The Pillory (78)

MARY NEWSLETTER - Italy
Another of the nineties bands that has captured the true seventies feel of Italian progressive rock. This five man band with the traditional lineup of guitars, drums, bass and keyboards also incorporates just a little flute and violin to add to the symphonic prog retro sound. But don't missunderstand, these guys are pure nineties prog.

Nouve Lettere (97), Distratto dal Sole (98)

MARYSON - Holland
Dutch keyboardist W.J. Maryson has created a mythic 'sword-and-sorcery' tale with a soundtrack to match. The music is pure symphonic neo-progressive rock.

On Goes the Quest (97)

MASCARADA - Spain
This is symphonic progressive rock that is strongly reminiscent of GENESIS' Nursery

Cryme. Long compositions rich with melodic acoustic passages strengthened by lush Mellotron orchestration. The material is epic in scope with lots of musical detail.

Urban Names (99)

MASON, NICK - Great Britain
PINK FLOYD drummer goes solo. On the first album he has a lot of help from jazz friends and comes up with material that's really out in left field. On the second release he settles back into a mainstream slant with some great guitar work from Rick Fenn of 10CC fame and a guest vocal from DAVE GILMOUR.

Fictitious Sports (81), Profiles (85)

MASQUE - Sweden
Lush keyboard symphonic sound. In the same sound as MARILLION or CAMEL. Their second LP Ten Ways took a more mainstream approach and may not appeal to everyone.

Flesh the Understands (91), Ten Ways (94)

MASTER KEY - France
Featuring a strong classical influence and nice harmonies. Sound like - MOODY BLUES, ALEPHI.

Tears of Love SP (71)

MASTERMIND - United States
A trio from New Jersey which sounds very much like ELP, except they have no keyboard player. All the keyboard sounds are triggered by guitarist Bill Berends guitar while brother Rich handles the drums. The emphasis in their material is on aggressive compositions and long arrangements. Dramatic symphonic music like a harder edged ELP, or KING CRIMSON.

Volume I (86), Volume II - Brainstorm (91), Volume III - Tragic Symphony (94), IV - Until Eternity (96), Mastermind Live in Tokyo (97), Excelsior! (98), Angels of The Apocalypse (00)

MASTRO, LOUIE - United States
Multi-instrumentalist Mastro used to be in the band Lunar Sea. His solo progressive work incorporates everything from Moogs to Mellotrons. As is often the case with solo artists the material can sound a bit samey, but after repeated listening the musicianship and compositional skills here shines through. A touch new agey perhaps but still dynamic.

Mermaid in the Mist (96)

MATCHING MOLE - Great Britain
This band was spear-headed by Robert Wyatt who came out of the Canterbury school of progressive rock. It was the SOFT MACHINE that Wyatt stayed with for four albums. Naturally his work with his follow-up band Matching Mole is more jazz-avant-garde oriented.

Matching Mole (71), Little Red Record (72)

MATERIA GRIS - Argentina
This early seventies band created an very rudimentary style progressive rock which incorporated many of the psychedelic musical motifs of the sixties.

Oh Pierra Vida De Beto (72)

MATHEMATICIANS - United States
Indianapolis based band with a practised fusion sound. The incorporation of the Chapman Stick, flute and percussion brings an eighties KING CRIMSON sound to their instrumental brand of progressive rock.

Irrational Numbers (94), Factor of Four (96)

MAXIMUM INDIFFERENCE - United States
Instrumental progressive rock with a slight jazz influence. Lots of solid musicanship that still manages to find a solid groove.

Maximum Indifference (96)

MAXOPHONE - Italy
Symphonic progressive rock in the traditional Italian style which sounds a bit like PFM.

Maxophone (76)

MAYBE - Norway
Folky progressive rock.

Envelope of Time ( )

MCCHURCH SOUNDROOM - Germany
Early seventies sounding prog material.

Delusion (71), McChurch Soundroom (72)

MCOIL - Germany
Heavy rock with symphonic progressive touches.

All Our Hopes (79)

MEDICINE MAN - Great Britain
Neo-progressive rock with IQ and PENDRAGON connections.

The Journey (9?)

MEDINA AZAHARA - Spain
One of the longest living Spanish symphonic progressive rock bands with very strong flamenco and folk influences. A little like TRIANA and MEZQUITA.

Medina Azahara [Paseando Por La Mezquita] (79), La Esquina Del Viento (80), Andalucia (82), En Al-Hakim (89), Caravana Espanola (91)

MEDITERRANEAN - Italy
Progressive rock with a twist, this three piece features keyboards and some great mandolin playing.

Ecce Rock ( )

MELLONTA TAUTA - Italy
A GENESIS influenced band who even have some GENESIS medleys in their material.

Mellonta Tauta ( )

MELLOW CANDLE - Great Britain
Progressive folk material with beautiful dual female vocals. Early sound, sort of a cross between CURVED AIR and RENAISSANCE.

Swaddling Songs (72), The Virgin Prophet [demos 69-70] (95)

MELODY - France
Symphonic melodic-progressive rock. Their music is centred on the voices of Diana Chase (Sally Oldfield) and Patrick Frehner (PFM). Melody offers magnificent, beautiful and elegant compositions, immediately attractive and ethereal melodies during which the voices of the two vocalists sing out in turn. Sound like - RENAISSANCE, PFM, GENESIS.

Come Fly With Me (76), Yesterlife (77)

MEMORIANCE - France
This band creates polished, elegant compositions with complicated instrumental developments and percussive, energetic progressions. Their music is based on delicate, attractive melodies which include refined arrangements with superb guitar parts. Sound like - ATOLL, KING CRIMSON, CAMEL.

Et Apres (76), L'Ecume des Jours (79)

MEN OF LAKE - Italy
A newer Italian group with a very retro sound. Nice material with great organ and other traditional instruments. Somewhat reminiscent of PROCOL HARUM, GRACIOUS or CRESSIDA. Fans of early Hammond organ or early seventies Italian progressive rock will enjoy this band.

Men of Lake (91), Out of the Water (93), Music from the Land of Mountains, Lake and Wine (98)

MENTAL PICTURE - United States

Two man progressive rock unit from Milwaukee. Spacey and melodic with some uncomplicated work on electronics, electric guitar and drums. Musically the material borders on a new age sound with many long passages of arpegiated guitar or keyboard shifting key and then returning.

Mental Picture (84 TAPE)

MENTAUR - Great Britain

Heavier neo-prog with longer songs of epic proportions. Should appeal to fans of SHADOW GALLERY and MAGELLAN.

Try Your Brakes (90), Verdict (91), Darkness Before Dawn (96)

MERCURY RISING - United States

Intelligent progressive metal that rarely lets up. Lot's of shifts in tempo and tight arrangements compensate for the minimal keyboard work.

Upon Deaf Ears (96), Building Rome (98)

MERCY TRAIN - Great Britain

Melodic progressive material.

Presence ( )

MERLIN - Germany

Neo-progressive material featuring both male and female vocalists creating a RENAISSANCE influenced sound. Some nice guitar and flute interplay.

Vanish to the Moon (89)

MERRYWEATHER, NEIL - United States

Strange album with some progressive rock moments and lots of Mellotron. The material comes from the Mott the Hoople/CITY BOY school of art rock. They do a couple of interesting covers and some rather quirky tunes but they know how to rock out as well.

Space Rangers (74), Kryptonite (75)

MESSAGE - Germany

Only their early material would be considered progressive rock. They had the help of Taf Freeman from NEKTAR on their first album playing some beautiful Mellotron. Later material got to be pretty ordinary sounding heavy rock.

The Dawn Anew Is Comin' (72), From Books and Dreams (73), Message (75), Synapse (76), Using the Head (77), Astral Journeys (78), Miles of Smiles (80)

METABOLISME - France

A band that borrows from both the French progressive rock style as well as the British. They offer a delicate and sophisticated sound based on carefully worked out, ethereal vocal harmonies, elegant chords on the keyboards and good solos on the guitar or flutes. Sound like - MONA LISA, FRUUPP.

Tempus Fugit (77)

METAMORFOSI - Italy

Their second album Inferno is a good place to start with these guys. Long concept pieces with some very inventive synth playing for the time. Classic, dynamic Italian symphonic progressive rock, full of experimental time signatures, rich atmosphere and textures.

...E Fu Il Sesto Giorno (72), Inferno (73)

METAMORFOSIS - Spain

A mixture of progressive, jazz-rock and the kitchen sink. Exotic and ethereal.

Metamorfosis ( )

METAPHOR - United States

This San Francisco band spent a number of years as a classic era Genesis tribute band and the time on the road shows in the top-notch musicianship. The music is first class symphonic progressive rock with as you might expect a strong GENESIS flavour. Longer songs with lots of twists and turns and strong on melody. Loads of thematic build-up, changing time signatures produces a very satisfying sound

Starfooted (00)

METROPOLIS - United States
Progressive rock in the style of KANSAS or DREAM THEATRE only not quite as developed.

Unsure Destination (9?)

MEZQUITA - Spain
A band with strong Flamenco influences. Like many of their contemporaries there is a strong KING CRIMSON influence. Spanish symphonic progressive rock doesn't get much better than this.

Recuedos De Mi Tierra (79)

MIA - Argentina
One of the most established Argentinean seventies prog groups similar to the Italian gems. Their style spanned everything from folk to jazz to intense symphonic progressive rock. Their third album Cornostipicum is considered their symphonic masterpiece.

Transparencias (76), Magicos Juegos Del Tiempo (77), Cornonstipicum (78)

MIDAS - Japan
Similar to OUTER LIMITS or MUGEN. Fine arrangements with nice violin. Richly symphonic with a definite GENESIS edge - the keyboard patterns are solidly within the BANKS, Orford, Kelly style yet occasionally breaking into WAKEMAN or WATKINS like soloing.

Beyond the Clean Air (88), Midas II (96)

MIDIAN - Italy
Prog metal in the same style as DREAM THEATRE, only with some added violin.

Soul Inside (94)

MIKLAGAARD - Sweden
Progressive rock from Sweden with a keyboard sound in the same vein as ELP and SUPERSISTER.

Miklagaard (79)

MILKWEED - Canada
Very obscure band with long tracks.

Milkweed (78)

MILLPLAT - Japan
Featuring members from NOVELLA and After Dinner, they create a melodic prog that is reminiscent of GALLEON.

Millplat (94)

MINAS TIRITH - Great Britain
One of the original of the second wave of progressive rock bands to come out of Great Britain. Based in Derby they play a heavier style and released a few independent cassettes in 1983.

MIND GALLERY - Canada
Instrumental symphonic-fusion material with accomplished arrangements and strong melodies. Their compositions generally range 5 to 8 minutes in length and showcase some brilliant guitar and keyboard interplay. Their music is in a similar style to EDHELS or later period MANEIGE, but with a slight psychedelic feel. Other recognizable influences include elements of YES and GENESIS.

The Lemmings Were Pushed (92), Guilty Until Proven Rich (95), Three Meals from Revolution (99)

MINDS EYE - Sweden
One of the new progressive metal bands that follow the DREAM THEATRE school, although the compositional chops are not

quite at that level yet. There is lots of guitar, double-bass-drum and intense vocals. Prog metal fans will enjoy this.

Into the Unknown (98), Waiting for the Tide (00)

MINDFLOWER - Italy
A melodic symphonic sound.

Purelake (9?)

MINI - Hungary
Good sounding material with flute up front in their sound.

Vissza A Varbosba (7?), 25 Ev Rock (7?)

MINIMUM VITAL - France
Quite a mixture of influences here everything from CARAVAN to PFM and maybe even CAMEL, but firmly rooted in the Canterbury school of music. Mostly instrumental, and like MAGMA they create their own language for the few songs requiring lyrics. Eurock says the music is full of flowing keyboards that combine beautifully with acoustic/electric guitars and a tight rhythm section.

Envol Triangles (85), Les Saisons Marines (88), Sarabandes (90), La Source (93), Esprit D'Amor (97), Au Cercle De Pierre [Live] (98)

MINISTRY OF LOVE - United States
Based in the Seattle area, they're a five piece with such diverse influences as The Cure, MARILLION, ELP, CAMEL, GENTLE GIANT and George Winston. They recorded a couple of cassettes in the nineties featuring material with lots of emotion and dynamics.

MINK, BEN - Canada
Ben's background is with primarily the band FM. His solo outing includes a lot of guests including FM. The music is a mixture progressive rock with liberal amounts of pop and some jazz thrown in.

Foreign Exchange (80)

MINOTAURUS - Germany
Symphonic material incorporating both organ and Mellotron.

Rain Over Thessalia (70), Fly Away (71)

MIRAGE - Italy
Progressive rock with members of BANCO appearing as guests on the album Frammenti.

Frammenti ( )

MIRROR - Holland
A style that contains elements of early YES and PINK FLOYD. They go from long spacey guitar solos to slightly more symphonic arrangements with interesting use of woodwinds and oboe.

Daybreak (78)

MIRIODOR - Canada
A sound not unlike GENTLE GIANT or UNIVERS ZERO at times. Complex jazz flavoured, instrumental material incorporating sax, keyboards and drums but sounding much fuller. A mixture of long and short songs with a quirky sense of melody. Their first release was more symphonic in arrangement.

Rencontres (86), Tot Ou Tard (88 TAPE), Miriodor (88), Third Warning (91), Jongleries Elastiques (96)

MITHRANDIR - United States
Highly recommended material which features strong influences from GENESIS and GENTLE GIANT. They built their sound on multi-track keyboards, flutes and guitars. Gorgeous flute passages and walls of keyboards exist side by side with grand guitar solos and well thought out melodies.

For You the Old Woman (75)

MR. GIL - Poland
Best described as grand thematic symphonic prog. The music is very dynamic with lots of starts-and-stops. Melody is mixed with dissonance to create a dark atmosphere at times.

Alone (99)

MR. SIRIUS - Japan
Symphonic material from this multi-instrumentalist. Flute, guitar, keyboards, bass and female vocals create a cross between RENAISSANCE and SLAP HAPPY. At times the sound is like an intense jazz oriented big band and at other times similar the pastoral orchestrated passages from THE ENID.

Barren Dream (87), Dirge (90), Incredible Tour ( )

MR. SO & SO - Great Britain
GENESIS influenced symphonic neo-progressive rock. A five-piece who place importance on vocal harmonies, melodies and solid guitar work. The songs are not overly complicated but move effortlessly from idea to idea with more than few musical twists and turns. Similar musical style as IT BITES with longer tracks.

Paraphenalia (92), Compendium (94), The Overlap (97)

MK II - Great Britain
Formerly The Geoff Mann Band these guys have a wide range of musical input from CAMEL'S Moonmadness to TWELFTH NIGHT'S Live at the Target. Instrumental material influenced by ALAN PARSONS early work and MIKE OLDFIELD.

Burning Daylight (94)

MO. DO. - Italy
Hints of CAMEL and GENTLE GIANT.

La Scimmia Sulla Schiena Del Re (8?)

MODRY EFEKT [M. EFEKT] - Czechoslovakia
One of the longest lived Czech bands. Leader Radim Hladik is probably one of the finest guitarists in the country. Their history can be summed up in 3 periods; the first three LPs tend to be more jazz rock, the next two are large orchestral works and the next three from 1977 on, are symphonic progressive rock of the highest order.

Kingdom of Life (69), Coniuncto ( ), Benefit of Radim Hladik ( ), Nova Synteza 1 (71), Nova Synteza 2 (74), Svitanie (77), Svet Hledacu (79), 33 (81)

MONA LISA - France
Mona Lisa offers a very elaborate and elegant progressive rock constructed on the singers vocal assurance, power and grandiloquence, on percussive, refined and finely arranged compositions, and on an instrumental and melodic finesse. A major French rock group. In 1998, the band's original vocalist got together with modern proggers VERSAILLES to re-create all that was great about Mona Lisa. Their 1998 release proved to be a milestone of French symphonic prog. Sound like - ANGE, GENESIS.

L'Escapade (74), Grimances (75), Le Petit Violon de Mr. Gregoire (77), Avant Qu'il ne Soit Trop Tard (78), Vers Demain (79), De L'Ombre a La Lumiere (98)

MONGOL - Japan
Technical symphonic progressive rock with a fusion edge.

Doppler ( )

MONKMAN, FRANCIS - Great Britain
One of the most accomplished keyboard players in Great Britain, although he's kept a very low profile. Classically trained, he came to fame in CURVED AIR in the early seventies. He later went on to do a lot of

session work with people like ALAN PARSONS and John Williams. Eventually he wound up a member of SKY, then left to go solo again. Music is decidedly progressive rock because of the classical background, more on the romantic, lush, orchestral side of things.

Energism (80), Dweller on the Threshold (81)

MONOLITH - United States

A blend of seventies KANSAS and nineties DREAM THEATRE. Progressive rock with a heavier sound featuring plenty ELP-ish fanfares and music that gallops along and start-and-stops before going in another direction all together. Lots of great melodies wrapped in a nice blend of guitars and keyboards.

Monolith (98)

MONOPODE - Canada

Symphonic progressive rock with French vocals.

La Legende (97)

MONTEFELTRO - Italy

Dynamic duo with extended material that falls into the more melodic realm of symphonic progressive rock. Similar to their contemporaries ERIS PLUVIA, EZRA WINSTON or MALIBRAN.

Il Tiempo De La Far Di Fantasia (93)

MONTESANO, GUSTAVO - Argentina

Former CRUCIS bass player/vocalist with most of his buddies from CRUCIS recorded Homenaje shortly after CRUCIS' second (and last) album. The style is fairly similar, but with more emphasis on keyboards. The CD re-issue contains 2 previously unreleased CRUCIS bonus tracks.

Homenaje (77)

MOODY BLUES - Great Britain

Originally out of Birmingham, they were one of the most influential bands to shape progressive rock music. Famous for their lush romantic style incorporating two Mellotrons to achieve the big orchestra sound. The band that virtually created the concept of concept albums now have streamlined their sound and lean more to the pop side of things daring not to venture to far astray. Gone are the days of experimentation.

The Magnificent Moodies (65), Days of Future Past (67), In Search of the Lost Chord (68), On the Threshold of a Dream (69), To Our Children's Children's Children (69), A Question of Balance (70), Every Good Boy Deserves Favour (71), Seventh Sojourn (72), Caught Live Plus Five (77), Octave (78), Long Distance Voyager (81), The Present (83), Voices in the Sky (84), The Other Side of Life (86), Sur La Mer (88), Keys to the Kingdom (91), The Moody Blues: A Night at Red Rocks (93)

MOOM - Great Britain

According to Expose' - they combine strong elements of Canterbury with the laid-back spirit of the Grateful Dead. Similar in some ways to CARAVAN'S Land of the Grey and Pink.

Toot (95)

MOON - Great Britain

This neo-progressive concept features a host of guest artists from Al Stewart to Martin Orford and sounds like a more progressive ALAN PARSONS PROJECT. Lots of heavy duty keyboard work in long compositions

The Greatest Show on Earth (98)

MOONGARDEN - Italy

Symphonic band that uses ever changing complex song structures to good effect. Sounds a lot like CAMEL and early GENESIS.

Moonsadness (9?),Brainstorm of Emptiness (96)

MOOR, THE - Sweden
Songs are suspenseful, dark, and moody with lots of Mellotron. Most of the arrangements are sparse and spacey and the style is frequently in the OZRIC TENTACLES or Hawkwind mode.

Every Pixie Sells a Story (93),Flux (96)

MORAZ, PATRICK - Great Britain
A keyboard player who's been around. First with MAINHORSE, then replacing KEITH EMERSON in REFUGEE, then replacing RICK WAKEMAN in YES and finally replacing Mike Pinder in THE MOODY BLUES. He can play a lot of styles. His solo outing started out with the fantastic first album and then drifted a bit to simpler things. In amongst all the releases is some great progressive rock keyboard work.

I (76),Out In the Sun (77),Patrick Moraz (78),Future Memories (79),CoExistence (80),Timecode (84),Future Memories II (85),Human Interface (87),Windows of Time (94),

MORENO, EDUARD - Spain
A symphonic keyboard sound with hints of YES and VANGELIS. His material features rich textures and delicate keyboard arrangements. The release El Ultimo Hombre adds a touch of rock to the mix making it a great neo-prog album.

Cine Imaginario (9?),El Ultimo Hombre (9?)

MORGAN - Great Britain
Originally in a band called Love Affair, Morgan Fisher formed this band in the early seventies creating music with lots of dynamic contrast. Some of it was influenced by modern classical composers like Stravinsky and Bartok. Fisher spent time playing keyboards for Mott the Hoople for a while. One album called Nova Solis, recorded in Italy so it featured an influence from their style of classical rock. I.T.C claims their album to be a classic of the space rock genre.

Nova Solis (75),Brown Out (76),The Sleeper Wakes (79),

MORIA FALLS - Great Britain
Neo-progressive rock in the mould of IQ and SHADOWLAND. Lots of prog-rock clichés here but still some good material. Martin Orford makes an appearance on one track.

The Long Goodbye (96)

MORRIGAN - Great Britain
Progressive folk music featuring Cathy Alexander on lead vocals as well as recorders and keyboards. Similar in style to Mellow Candle.

The Spirit of the Soup ( )

MORNINGSTAR - United States
A band from the STYX, ANGEL and STARCASTLE with a bit more rock thrown in.

Morning Star (78),Venus (79)

MORSE CODE - Canada
One of the finest progressive rock bands to come out of Canada. Very much in the YES, GENESIS fold with a hint of GENTLE GIANT. All vocals in French. Great music, featuring lots of Mellotron on the early albums, powerful, dynamic and very satisfying.

Morse Code Transmission (71), La March Des Hommes (75), Procreation (76), Je Suis Le Temps (77), Les Grands Succes (78), Code Breaker (83), D'un Autre Monde (95)

MORSE, NEAL - United States
SPOCK'S BEARD main man with a solo outing that proves he can write some great mainstream material as well. Most everything on the recording is handled by Morse. Compositions are all in the 3 - 4

minute range and deal with more personal situations. There is one longer twenty minute piece at the end that will appeal to the prog fans in the crowd.

Neal Morse (99)

MOSAIC - Italy
Former keyboardist with ARTI E MESTIERI, Crovella has created a series of shorter symphonic tracks blended together showcasing a myriad of styles. GENTLE GIANT sounding material.

Miniatures (95)

MOSTLY AUTUMN - Great Britain
An unusual mixture of mid-period PINK FLOYD and a strong Celtic style of composition and instrumentation. Their material tends to be longish with lots of atmosphere, jamming, melodies and musicianship.

For All We Shared... (98), The Spirit of Autumn Past (99)

MOURNBLADE - Great Britain
Formed in 1982 with a strong space rock influence ala Hawkwind.

Times Running Out (85)

MOVING GELATINE PLATES - France
French underground band who created a powerful jazz rock, fusion sound. Along the same lines as SOFT MACHINE and Zappa.

Moving Gelatine Plates (71), The World of Genius Hans (72)

MUFFINS - United States
A critically acclaimed band that hailed out of the Washington DC area. Overlooked by the public they created their own brand of instrumental material featuring a mix of Canterbury progressive music with elements of fusion and improvisation.

Secret Signals (75), Chronometers (75), Manna/Mirage (78), 185 (80), Air Fiction (79), Open City (86)

MUGEN - Japan
A symphonic sound, like OUTER LIMITS that is based around keyboards and violin. Mugen sound more classical than the former. Their full keyboard sound is highlighted by Mellotron.

Symphonia Della Luna (84), The Princess of Kingdom Gone (88), Leda et La Cygne (89),

MULTI STORY - Great Britain
A mixture of progressive rock with hard rock thrown in for good measure. Nice Mellotron with great melodies. Some material reaches epic, bombastic proportions. Should definitely appeal to fans of YES' Going For the One or Tormato era.

Chimes (84), East West (85), Through Your Eyes (87)

MURPLE - Italy
Early sound with menacing vocals. Overall style is typical for the era with songs arranged in the suite format in the vein of LE ORME or LATTE E MIELE.

Io Sono Murple (74)

MUSEO ROSENBACH - Italy
They produced only one studio album, Zarathustra but it's one of the best examples of symphonic progressive rock featuring dual keyboards and STEVE HACKETT influenced guitar. Some later live material was released but the focus has always been on their one studio release.

Zarathustra (73), Museo Rosenbach - Live 72 (92), Rare & Unreleased (92)

MUSHROOM - Ireland
A blend of folk and symphonic progressive rock.

Early One Morning (73)

MUSICA RESERVATA - Japan
Solo artist Masao Inoue creates a Japanese flavoured symphonic prog with female vocals. If you enjoy bands such as TERU'S SYMPHONIA or PAGEANT you enjoy this.

Paranoiac Ocean (96)

MUSICALIA - Italy
Symphonic progressive rock with a strong classical influence.

Magicoro ( )

MUTANTES - Brazil
While their earlier LP's will appeal more to fans of psychedelic music, by the time of A Divina Comedia they were becoming more progressive. Their prog work will appeal to fans of YES and PFM. Nice arrangements, harmonies, with Hammond and Mellotron.

Os Mutantes (68), Mutantes (68), A Divina Comedia ou Ando Meio Desliggado (69), Eletrico (71), Mutantes e Seus Cometas no Pais do Bauretz (72), Tudo Foi Feito Pelo Sol (74), Mutantes Ao Vivo (76),

MYERS, MIKE - United States
A multi-instrumentalist whose work incorporates a blending of jazz-rock, progressive, pop and avant-garde elements. Influences include Zappa, TODD RUNDGREN and OZRIC TENTACLES.

Myriad (96)

MYRIAD - United States
Their advertising proclaims - if you're a fan of KING CRIMSON, RUSH and ELP you need this debut CD by Myriad. This new band create music that is mid-tempo and contain some fine prog arrangements.

Myriad (99)

MYSIA - Italy
Melodic keyboard oriented soft progressive material.

Land Ho! (91)

MYSTERY - Canada
A French-Canadian band singing in English and creating a musical style closer to STYX or ASIA. Good melodies, flute and great arrangements but other than a couple of strong cuts, not overly complicated. Their second release took on more of a guitar edge ala SAGA displaying more mature material and sound.

Theatre of the Mind (95), Destiny? (98)

MYTHIC SKY - United States
Hailing out of the Pacific Northwest, this four piece group fuses electronics with rock in the grandest of fashions. Their album contains the thirty minute suite entitled Seeds of Hope which according to Eurock: A more dynamic hybrid of electronics and rock you'll not hear anywhere as the music evolves magically from intricate themes filled with instrumental interplay elaborately arranged passages of keyboards, strings, guitar and percussion. Superb!

Seeds of Hope (9?)

MYTHOS - Germany
Progressive rock with more than a hint of space-rock and a psychedelic sound.

Mythos (72), Dreamlab (75), Stange Guys (78), Concrete City (79), Quasar (80), Grand Prix (81)

9:30 FLY - Great Britain
Progressive folk with spooky female vocals, fuzz guitar and catchy tunes.

9:30 Fly (72)

NAKAJIMA, YUHKI - Japan
Progressive with classical overtones.

The Prophecies ( )

NAOS - France
A group which is inspired by the old school. They create a direct, solid, accessible music based on carefully executed vocals, an effective instrumentation and immediate and pleasant melodies. Sound like - ANGE, ATOLL.

L'Indien SP (84), Roc et Legendes ( )

NASO FREDDO - Italy
A spacey soundtrack album produced by Franco Falsini of SENSATIONS FIX in the mid seventies. To be honest this sounds like one of their LPs.

NATHAN MAHL - Canada
Until recently the Canadian four-piece Nathan Mahl were one of those wonderful undiscovered prog bands. Their style incorporates everything you love about symphonic prog rolled into one! Long mostly instrumental compositions featuring tremendous keyboard and guitar interplay. Lots of tempo shifts, complex arrangements, great use of both acoustic and electric instruments. A strong GENTLE GIANT, KING CRIMSON, YES influence.

Parallel Eccentricities (83/97), The Clever Use of Shadows (98), Heretik [Vol. 1] (00)

NATIONAL HEALTH - Great Britain
They have become a major cult band in certain circles playing a progressive rock laced with predominantly a jazz feel and some great musicianship. Multiple time changes and superbly layered harmonies and the interplay between the two were the bands signature.

National Health (78), Of Queues and Cures (78), D.S. al Coda (82), Missing Pieces (94)

NAUTILUS - Switzerland
Eurock says they are a Swiss discovery that's sure to astound fans of more cosmic oriented rock (early ELOY, NOVALIS etc.). Their music is awash with powerfully arranged waves of keyboard sound, searing guitars and an overdose of melodrama.

20,000 Miles Under the Sea (78), Space Storm (80)

NAVE - Brazil
Symphonic progressive rock with a strong YES influence, including a lead vocalist whose style is very reminiscent of JON ANDERSON. Great compositions and arrangements along with some well chosen ethic musical elements.

Nave (96)

NAZCA - Mexico
Progressive music in a style similar to UNIVERS ZERO.

Estacion de Sombre (86)

NEBELNEST - France
These accomplished musicians create a music that shows influences raging from KING CRIMSON, PULSAR and ANGE. Featuring the classic lineup of guitar, keyboard, bass and drums, each gets a chance in the spotlight with compositions that are complicated but superbly arranged with just right balance of melody and dissonance. The bonus is lots of Mellotron.

NeBeLNeST (99)

NEGASPHERE - Japan
Considered one of Japan's best progressive rock bands. Musically like early GENESIS, with elaborate keyboard arrangements and great guitar. Lots of room in their material to stretch out musically.

Live (81), Castle In the Air (84), Disadvantage (85), Negasphere 1985-1986 (91)

NEKTAR - Germany
Formed in Hamburg in 1968 by Britons who found themselves in Germany looking for a gig. Their first albums are long concept pieces with selections running whole sides in length. Their material contained

the dynamics and feel of Hawkwind/CAMEL with a bit more of an edge. On the LP Recycled they enlisted the help of Larry Fast on keyboards. Their latter albums while still showing hints of progressive rock became much more streamlined and hard rock oriented.

Journey to the Centre of the Eye (71), A Tab in the Ocean (72), Remember the Future (73), Sounds Like This (73), Live at the Roundhouse (74), Down to Earth (75), Recycled (76), Magic is the Child (77), Live in New York (77), Thru the Ears (78), Man in the Moon (80), The Dream Nebula-The Best of 1971-1975 (98)

NEO - France
A group whose solely instrumental music was evocative of that played by CARPE DIEM with the same creative research concerning the melodies and instruments, the same care given to the elaboration and construction of the themes. Sound like - BO HANSSON, CAMEL.

Neo (80)

NEON ROSE - Sweden
Heavy prog rockers. At times more rock than prog, but all well done.

Dream of Glory and Pride (73), 2 (74), Reload (75)

NEOPHYT - France
Mid eighties melodic material ala ICARE or SYNOPSIS. A little more straight forward rock though.

NEPENTHE - United States
They used to go by the name ARS NOVA, but have changed the name and added a new vocalist. Their music is strong on melody and introspective lyrics. Musically they're a mix of MARILLION, GENESIS and COLLAGE.

Everything was Beautiful and Nothing Hurt (96)

NERO, LEO - Italy
Keyboardist from IL BALLETTO DI BRONZO with a solo album which sounds very similar to that band.

Vero ( )

NESSIE - Belgium
Symphonic progressive rock.

The Tree (78), Head in the Sand (79)

NETHERWORLD - United States
This band is from the Los Angeles area and produced some legendary symphonic progressive rock.

In the Following Half Light (81)

NEURONIUM - Spain
Mainly electronic although albums prior to Heritage are somewhat more progressive.

Heritage (84)

NEUSCHWANSTEIN - Germany
They feature a vocalist who sounds similar to PETER GABRIEL, lots of Mellotron, flute, acoustic/electric guitar interplay and compositions like the best of GENESIS' Wind & Wuthering period. Highly recommended symphonic material that also has hints of IVORY and AMENOPHIS.

Battlement (78)

NEUTRONS - Great Britain
Formed in South Wales, they play material that sounds a bit like AMON DUUL II or Hawkwind, a bit spacey with a psychedelic influence.

Black Hole Stars (74), Tales From the Blue Cocoons (75)

NEW CROSS - United States
An American band with strong KING CRIMSON influences. A musical style that incorporates strong syncopation and airy melodies.

New Cross (86 EP)

NEW GROVE PROJECT - Sweden

This special project involved some of Sweden's top progressive rock artists namely, Roine Stolt (FLOWER KINGS) and Par Lindh along with Englishman Jode Leigh (ENGLAND). The eventual concept album is classic Swedish symphonic prog that will appeal to fans of any of the bands mentioned.

The Demos (96), Fool's Journey (97)

NEW SUN - United States

Music from the RUSH school of guitar, bass and drums. Lots of interesting this happening with songs ranging from short to epic length.

Fractured (95), Affects (98)

NEW TROLLS - Italy

One of the first wave of progressive rock bands from Italy. They have worked with full orchestras on two concept albums and created some strikingly 20th century classically oriented progressive rock on other LPs. Their early albums are sometimes very challenging to listen to but well worth the investment in time.

New Trolls (70), Concerto Grosso 1 (71), Ut (72), Searching For a New Land (72), UT (72), Atomic System (73), Night on Bare Mountain ( ), Tempi Dispari (74), Concerto Grosso 2 (76), Aldebaran (78), New Trolls (79), F.S. (81), America O.K. (83), Tour (85), Amici (88),

NEXT - Italy

Progressive material with YES Big Generator and PETER GABRIEL So leanings.

The Virtual Cage (94)

NEXUS - Argentina

This five piece create a grand symphonic progressive rock with sweeping keyboards. Their compositions are dramatic and melodic hearkening back to many of the classic prog sounds of the seventies

Detras del Umbral (99)

NEXUS - Great Britain

Short-lived mid eighties band known to have released a couple of cassettes of music bearing a resemblance to STEVE HILLAGE and PENDRAGON.

NHU - Spain

NHU (78)

NIADEM'S GHOST - Great Britain

This was Peter Nicholl's band after he left as vocalist for IQ. It was more pop oriented than progressive.

In Sheltered Winds (86)

NICE - Great Britain

One of the premier pioneering progressive rock bands and one of the first to so heavily use the classics. The prime instigator for this was KEITH EMERSON whose keyboard extravaganzas were already getting mammoth headlines well before the birth of ELP.

The Thoughts of Emerlist Davjack (67), Ars Longa Vita Brevis (68), The Nice (69), Five Bridges Suite (70), Elegy (71)

NICO, GIANNI, FRANK, MAURIZIO - Italy

These guys are an offshoot of NEW TROLLS and sound just as good.

Nico, Gianni. Frank, Maurizio ( )

NIGHT WATCH - Italy

Classic neo-progressive rock from Italy. Excellent musicianship propels their intricate music through its many phases. Lots of drama and dynamics makes this truly enjoyable. Fans of MARILLION, IQ and PENDRAGON will certainly enjoy this, but it should also appeal to those looking for something more adventurous. Following a change of personel, the band changed their name to THE WATCH.

Twilight (97)

NIGHTALES - United States
Symphonic sound with the occasional Mellotron. Their style is mellow, melodic and slightly fusiony. They used to be known as PARAGONE. If you enjoy CAMEL'S Moonmadness or PINK FLOYD'S Dark Side of the Moon, you should enjoy this.

The Voyage (96)

NIGHTRIDER - France
Hard edged progressive rock, that should appeal to fans of SAGA or RUSH. The material still manages to maintain a certain flavour of the seventies.

Nightrider (79)

NIGHTWINDS - Canada
Symphonic progressive rock with Mellotron, sound a bit like GENESIS. From Toronto, the singers voice is very similar to FISH, but the material was actually recorded before MARILLION came on the scene. If you enjoy golden age GENESIS (1971-1977) you'll like this band. The album was produced by Dee Long and Terry Draper of the band KLAATU.

Nightwinds (79)

NIGHTWING - Great Britain
On the more aggressive side but with infectious melodies, Nightwing burst on the scene in 1980. Somewhat pompous at times, bombastic at others they create their own brand of progressive rock. In their later releases they worked with STEVE HACKETT on guest guitar and production.

Something in the Air (80), Black Summer (82), Stand Up and Be Counted (83), A Night of Mystery Alive (85), My Kingdom Come (84)

NIHIL - Brazil
Early GENESIS styled progressive rock. They changed their name to INNER FLAME.

Nihil (97)

NIMRODEL - Japan 1990's
Taking their name from CAMEL'S Mirage, much of their material includes CAMEL cover tunes. Their own original material bears all the hallmarks of CAMEL'S elaborate compositional style.

NIRGAL VALLIS - Mexico
Symphonic prog-rock that will appeal to fans of YES, GENESIS and JON ANDERSON'S solo work.

I Murio La Tarde (85)

NOETRA - France
Complex fusion material with a vague similarity to CARPE DIEM. Intricate arrangements that sometimes border on jazz or classical music.

Neuf Songes (81)

NOLAN, CLIVE - England
The keyboardist with PENDRAGON, he's involved with many studio projects and bands including ARENA PENDRAGON, and STRANGERS ON A TRAIN. In 1999 he worked with Oliver Wakeman, Rick's son and created the concept CD Jabberwocky

Jabberwocky (99)

NO MAN IS AN ISLAND - Great Britain
A mixture of modern rock and neo-prog. If you like Tears For Fears you might like this.

No Man is an Island (85), A Girl From Missouri (85)

NO NAME - Belgium

Their sound is firmly planted in the neo-progressive rock category. Nice symphonic arrangements with lots or chordal variety, good cross-rhythms and some nice SAGA-like guitar work. Not overly complex and easy to get into.

The Secret Garden (95), The Other Side (99)

NORLANDER, ERIK - United States

Norlander is the keyboardist for THE ROCKET SCIENTISTS, and some have pegged him to take over where KEITH EMERSON and RICK WAKEMAN supposedly left off. His all instrumental material features aggressive and symphonic compositions all centring around a science fiction theme. He uses vintage instruments such as Mellotron and Hammond to great effect. If you like either of the aforementioned keyboardists, you'll enjoy this.

Threshold (97)

NORTH STAR - United States

They formed during 1976 as a high school project. A three song EP was released in 1982 and finally the '84 cassette release. In 1992 they released a CD entitled Power. Their music is very mature and keyboard dominated with hints of MARILLION and And then there were Three GENESIS era.

Triskelion (84 TAPE), Feel the Cold (85 TAPE), Power (92)

NORTHERN CROSS - France

A compositional style that hearkens back to the classic French prog band's like ANGE. The changed their name to LEGENDE.

Same Stories Never Told (86)

NORTHWINDS - France

Doom-laden prog metal with influences ranging from Black Sabbath, JETHRO TULL and HORSLIPS.

Great God Pan (98)

NOSFERATU - Germany

Early seventies sound.

Nosferatu (70)

NOSTALGIA - Italy

Melodic progressive rock influenced by CAMEL & GENESIS.

Never Too Late (9?)

NOTRE DAME - Italy

Progressive rock that sounds like a blending of ANGLAGARD, ANEKDOTEN and ECHOLYN.

Notre Dame (96)

NOTTURNO CONCERTANTE - Italy

Melodic symphonic neo-progressive rock in the CAMEL, IQ vein.

The Hiding Place (90), Erewhon (9?), News From Nowhere (9?), The Glass Tear (9?)

NOVA - Finland

One album of some fine progressive rock featuring longish songs. Lyrics are all in Finish.

Atlantis (76)

NOVA - Italy

Featuring ex-members of the band OSANNA playing a cross of jazz and progressive rock.

Blink (75), Vimana (76), Wings of Love (77), Sun City (78)

NOVALIS - Germany

Founded in Germany in 1971 they created 'romantic rock' as they called it and committed themselves to our endangered environment in their material. Their music is based on long concepts performed in a grand style for the most part. It's all in

German. One of the most interesting and musically accomplished bands in the world of progressive rock.

Banished Bridge (73),Novalis (75),Sommerabend (76),Konzerte (77),Brandung (77),Vielleicht Bin Ich Ein Clown (78),Flossenenger (79),Visionen (80),Neumond (82),Sterntaucher (83),Blumerang (84),Nact Uns Die Flut (85)

NOVA MALA STRANA - Italy

Symphonic progressive rock with female vocals. If you like bands such as MARGE LITCH and GERARD you'll enjoy this.

Nova Mala Strana (97)

NOVELLA - Japan

Progressive rock group featuring a female vocalist, two guitarists and somewhere around fifteen keyboards. Thought of as the best parts of GENESIS (circa Wind & Wuthering), RENAISSANCE and CAMEL all with a touch of oriental melody.

In the Night (8?),Ao No Shozo EP (8?),Paradise Lost (8?),Sanctuary (8?),Secret Love EP (8?), Temple of Noi (8?),From the Mystic World Vol. 1 ( ),From the Mystic World Vol. 2 ( )

NOVEMBER - Holland

A modern PETER GABRIEL meets mid period GENESIS. Recommended for fans of JADIS, PALLAS, etc..

First of November (94)

NOW - Belgium

Post PRELUDE neo-prog sound. The material is in the vein of YES' 90215 period only with a little more complicated song structures and arrangements. Fine guitar solos and big sounding keyboards are the focal points.

Now ( ),Complaint of the Wind (87),Spheres (91),Deep (92),

NOW - United States

A California based band. Music is in the vein of KING CRIMSON and GENESIS with some uniquely American twists. Great dual guitar harmonic sound with nice melodies.

Reactions/Heaven on Earth (85),Everything is Different (86),Now What? (90),kNOW Reason (92)

NU - Spain

Started as a fairly symphonic group with guitar/Mellotron and vocals/flute much like JETHRO TULL. Their later LPs tended to sound more like hard rock. If you like BLOQUE or MEZQUITA you'll very likely enjoy Nu.

Cuentos de Ayer y de Hoy (78),A Golpe De Latigo (79),Fuego ( ),El Mensajero Del Mago (87),Dos Anos de Destierro (90),Imperio de Paletos [Live] (92),La Danza de las Mil Tierras (94),

NUANCE - France

Formed in the area of Toulouse. Nuance offers a very elaborate carefully constructed music with long, complex, polished instrumental developments with refined and original arrangements. Sound like - CAMEL, CARAVAN, FRUUPP.

Il est une L'egende (82),Ami (86 TAPE),Territories (89),Reflets (96)

NUBERU - Spain

Folk band turned somewhat progressive.

NUMEN - Spain

Symphonic neo-progressive band with primary emphasis on keyboards. Their material is not overly complex but retains a naive melodic quality.

Samsara (98)

NUMERO UENO - Japan 1990s

NUOVA ERA - Italy
One of the new group of Italian prog bands performing music in the seventies style of dramatic, romantic, symphonic rock. Featuring Hammond organ and Mellotron their material would fit in the prog releases of 1976. All their material is highly recommended.

L'Ultimo Viaggio (88), Dopo L'Infinito (89), Io e il Tempo (92), Il Passo Del Soldato (95), Fourth (96)

NUOVA IDEA - Italy
A band with loads of great organ playing. You'll hear a Canterbury influence. Similar to the NEW TROLLS of the early seventies.

In the Beginning (71), Mr. E. Jones (72), Clowns (73)

NUVOLE DI PAGLIA - Italy
They produce a very seventies sound driven by the organ.

Live '73 ( ), And Then ( )

O TERCO - Brazil
Highly thought of band who produced a lot of material with Latin and ethnic influences. While their first two albums contained some run of the mill rock they also contained some classic symphonic material featuring Mellotron, organ etc. Their later work in the nineties took on more of a neo-prog tone.

O Terco (73), Criaturas da Noite (75), Casa Encantada (76), Mudanca de Tempo (78), Time Travelers (92), Live at the Palace (9?)

OBLIQUE - Holland
This is mostly instrumental with a New Age influence.

Oblique (85)

OCARINAH - France
A trio - organ, bass & drums - with a saturated organ sound in the same vein as the groups from Canterbury. Instrumental music in which the organ is particularly shown to advantage during long, complex and elaborate developments. Sound like- EGG, CARAVAN.

Premiere Vision de L'etrange (78)

OCTOBER - United States
Symphonic progressive rock.

October (72), After the Fall ( )

OCTOBRE - Canada
Band from Quebec, popular during the mid seventies, performed mainly in French. Strong cultural, folk-ish roots leaning to a more progressive folk sound.

OCTOPUS - Germany
They sound a bit like CURVED AIR at times, with some great progressive rock moments using the traditional line-up of instruments. Lots of good guitar, Hammond interplay, with Mellotron backing. While truly symphonic in nature, the band never forgot their more rock oriented roots.

The Boat of Thoughts (76), An Ocean of Rocks (78), Rubber Angels (79)

OCTOPUS - Norway
Bright symphonic progressive rock with a distinct Scandinavian attitude. The music is based around a solid wall-of-keyboards played with themes similar to Rick Wakeman's style.

Thaerie Wiighen (81)

ODEJA - Italy
Melodic progressive rock with nice female vocals.

Winds of May ( )

ODIN - Germany
Early style progressive rock with an ELP type organ sound and heavy guitar.

Odin (72)

ODISSEA - Italy
Overlooked band of the seventies that was one of the finest of the era. Symphonic structures based around organ and Mellotron. Influences are a little ELP, THE NICE and Nursery Cryme GENESIS.

Odissea (73)

ODYSSICE - Holland
Symphonic material in the same vein as CAMEL and some PINK FLOYD.

Moon Drive (96)

OHO - United States
Symphonic progressive rock in much the same style as the original CATHEDRAL, SURPRISE, LIFT or MIRTHRANDIR. Plenty of early GENESIS and YES references. Lots of great musicianship and instrumentation including Mellotron and analogue synths. If you like any of the groups mentioned, you'll enjoy this. Their album was originally recorded in 1975 but not released on vinyl until 1991.

Okinawa (73), Vitamin Oho (75/91), Ecce (97)

OLD MAN AND THE SEA - Denmark
This is a early progressive rock sound along the lines of WIND or very early NEKTAR. A mixture of long and short songs that are strong on melody and harmonies. Lots of Hammond organ and biting guitar which was very popular in the early seventies.

Old Man and the Sea (72)

OLDFIELD, MIKE - Great Britain
The first artist to single handedly give the concept of 'one-man-band' a good name. After an album recorded under the name SALLYANGIE in 1968 with his sister, his next four albums tend to reflect more a pastoral texture with the seminal Tubular Bells helping to launch Virgin records onto the international scene. Since that time there has been an ever more persistent movement to splitting his work up between shorter pop songs mixed in with longer more ambitious work. Oldfield has become similar to THE ALAN PARSONS PROJECT.

Tubular Bells (73), Hergest Ridge (74), Ommadawn (75), QE2 (80), Airborne (80), Five Miles Out (82), Crises (83), Discovery (84), Islands (87), Earthmoving (89), Amarok (90), Heaven's Open (91), Tubular Bells II (92), The Songs of Distant Earth (95), Voyager (96)

OMEGA - Hungary
The longest lived and best known Hungarian band. They've been in existence for over twenty years. Their history can be divided into three periods; the first three LPs-early psychedelic, the fourth to eleventh somewhat more progressive rock and eleventh on their more updated sound with synths and computers.

Trombitas Fredi [1] (68), 10,000 Lepes [2] (69), Ejszakai Orszagut [3] (70), ELO [4] (72), Omega [5] (73), Nem Tudom a Neved [6] (76), Idorablo [7] (77), Csillagok Utjan [8] (78), Gammapolis [9] (79), Az Arc [10] (81), Omega [11] (82), A Fold Arnyekos Oldalan [12] (8?), Babylon [13] (87), Trans and Dance [14] ( ), Nepstadion Koncert 1994 No. 1 (95), Nepstadion Koncert No. 2 (95) Omega Red Star From Hungary (68), Omega (73), 200 Years After the Last War (74), III (74), The Hall of the Floaters in the Sky (75), Time Robbers (76), Skyrover (78), Gammapolis (79), Live at the Kistadion (80), Working (81),

OMNI OPERA - Great Britain
OZRIC inspired material that is clearly in the spacey category.

ONIRIS - France
This group plays progressive rock that is like others based on the singers vocal delirium. They incorporate poetical, surrealistic lyrics with a dramatic, musical and vocal stress. Sound like - ANGE, MONA LISA.

L'Homme-Voilier (79)

ONZA - Spain
Spanish folk with a fusion influence composed in longish tracks.

Reino Rocoso (90)

OPALE - France
Progressive folk-rock with a bit of GENTLE GIANT. Nice melodies and polished instrumentation. If you are a fan of bands such as HARMONIUM or ET CETERA you'll enjoy this.

La Derniere Toile du Maitre (81)

OPEN AIR - France
Open Air plays a less complicated, less sophisticated, very melodic and accessible progressive rock. It abandons long instrumental development for more concise, direct, sober compositions which are based on the domination and elegance of the vocal parts and enhanced by the short flourishes on the guitar or the keyboard. Sound like - YES, GENESIS, IRRWISCH or MACHIAVEL.

Open Air (78)

OPUS 5 - Canada
A symphonic-fusion progressive in the CAMEL or HATFIELD AND THE NORTH style.

Contre-courant (76), Serieux ou Pas (89)

ORION - France
Orion create a symphonic prog based on a certain dramatic vocal pomposity and cleverly interpreted and constructed instrumental sequences with good interplay between guitars and keyboards. Sound Like - ANGE, MONA LISA, GENTLE GIANT, GRYPHON.

La Nature Vit, L'Homme Lui, Critique (79)

OSANNA - Italy
Many mourned the loss of this band as they represented some of the best Italy had to offer in the early phases of symphonic progressive rock. Their members went on to other bands and other production duties, so in some respect their legacy lives on. All their work can be considered high quality prog with classical and jazz influences.

L'uomo (71), Milano Calibro 9 (72), Palepoli (73), Landscape of Life (74), Uno (74), Suddance (78)

OSIRIS - Bahrain
Symphonic progressive rock group with a very European style. Six piece band with dual keyboards and the music loaded with their sound. Fans of the CAMEL or YES style will appreciate this.

Osiris (82), Myths and Legends (84)

OUTER LIMITS - Japan
Japanese band that plays a wonderful mixture of softer symphonic progressive rock with some great violin playing. Their music is very expressive, lots of dynamics and just a bit of humour. An eclectic blend of British and European prog styles.

Misty Moon (85), A Boy Playing With a Magical Bugle Horn (86), The Scene of Pale Blue (87), The Silver Apples on the Moon (89), Outer Mania (94)

OUT OF FOCUS - Germany
Heavy progressive material with nice organ and flute.

Wake Up (71), Out of Focus (72)

OVERDRIVE - Italy
Neo-progressive band with nice keyboard work. In the same vein as SAGA.

The Human Machine (90)

OVERFLOW - Mexico 1980's

OZONE - Canada
Nice melodic material with French vocals.

Premiere Couche ( )

OZONE QUARTET - United States
The material they create is distinctly fusion with progressive rock tendencies. The instrumental line-up includes drums, guitar, Chapman stick and violin. If you enjoy bands like DIXIE DREGS or BOUD DUEN you'll enjoy this.

Fresh Blood (97), Nocture (99)

OZRIC TENTACLES - Great Britain
Spacey progressive rock partly influenced by artists such as STEVE HILLAGE, GONG, HAWKWIND and others. Originally formed in 1984 they produce instrumental material featuring brilliant guitar, flute and synthesiser musicianship. Their later material even began incorporating elements of dance-electronica and even a little jazz-fusion.

Pungent Effulgent (89), Afterswisch (92), Live Underslunky (92), Sploosh EP ( ), Erpsongs (85), There is Nothing (86), Bits Between Bits (89), Tantric Obstacle (85), Sliding Gliding Worlds (88), Live Ethereal Cereal (86), Erpland (90), Strangeitude (91), Jurassic Shift (93), Arborescence (94), Become the Other (95), Curious Corn (97), Spice Doubt Streaming [Live] (98), Waterfall Cities (99)

P205 - Germany
Mixture of heavy psychedelic and progressive rock with PINK FLOYD and BLACK WIDOW influences.

P205 (75/93), Vivat Progressio Pereat Mundus (78)

P.F.M. - Italy
Formed in 1971 they became the Italian band in the first wave of progressive rock and definitely made an impression around the world. Incorporating flute and violin, PFM have created their unique blend of music that hangs close to the classics, yet imparts the aggressive emotionalism of rock. Influenced by early GENESIS and ELP. Still going in the nineties, PFM's style has morphed into more of a European counterpart to bands such as Mike and The Mechanics.

Storia Di Un Minuto (72), Per Un Amico (72), Photo's of Ghosts (73), The World Became the World (74), Live in the USA (74), Chocolate Kings (76), Jet Lag (77), PassPartu (78), ComeTi Va in Riva Alla Citta (81), Impressioni Vent'Anni Dopo (94), Bobo Club 2000 - 1972 (94), 10 Anni Live 1971 -1981 (96), Ulisse (97)

PFS - United States
Former keyboardist and percussionist with the band CARTOON go solo, with some fine progressive/jazz rock with distinct RIO overtones. The music sometimes reminds you of KING CRIMSON and at other times like HENRY COW.

Illustrative Problems (86), 279 (86)

PABLO EL ENTERRADOR - Argentina
Melodic symphonic prog-rock with dual keyboards. Very much in the same style as the Italian classics. They are the South American equivalent to LOCANDA DELLE FATE in that the emphasis is on instrumental interplay and the creation of an overall musical atmosphere. The band reformed to record a second album in 1998 which continued in the same musical style.

Pablo El Enterrador (79), Sentido De Lucha [2] (98)

PAESE DEI BALOCCHI - Italy

Italian symphonic in the classic style.

Paese Dei Balocchi (72)

PAGEANT - Japan

Symphonic progressive rock group, whose first album is very reminiscent of RENAISSANCE. Their later work took on a harder edge. The original line-up included MR. SIRIUS (Kazuhiro Miyatake) on acoustic guitar and flute.

La Mosaique De La Reverie (86), Kamen No Egao (87), Pay For Dreamers Sin (89)

PAIKAPPU - Japan

Instrumental progressive rock with a spacey element. Compositionally they are similar to CAMEL.

Paikappu (83)

PAINT BOX - Italy

Their overall approach hearkens back to the classic Italian symphonic prog era. Musically they are in the same league as MEN OF LAKE and other bands of that style. Lots of organ dominated songs in songs that are not overly complicated but still very enjoyable.

Monitor (98)

PALADIN - Great Britain

Early progressive rock band that fused some jazz and Afro-Cuban rhythms to create a very unique blend of music. Band member Keith Webb's complex drumming patterns merged very well with keyboardist Pete Solley who would later go on to perform with PROCOL HARUM. One of the most famous Roger Dean covers was created for Charge.

Paladin (71), Charge (72)

PALE ACUTE MOON - Japan

Led by MOTOI SEMBA (who later played keyboards in TERU'S SYMPHONIA), this album is half instrumental with a classically influenced symphonic style that's a cross between RENAISSANCE and THE ENID.

Newtopia (86)

PALLAS - Great Britain

Best known for creating dramatic symphonic musical epics like their Atlantis Suite. Melodic, arrangements full of lush keyboards, powerful guitar and huge endings. Pallas formed in Aberdeen, Scotland in 1976. The album The Sentinel was produced by Eddie Offord. The material that followed tended to become more mainstream. They reformed in 1998. The Sentinal re-release features the full Atlantis Suite, while the re-released Arrive Alive has roughly 20 minutes added. Will appeal to fans of RUSH and EVERON.

Arrive Alive (81), The Sentinel (84), The Knightmoves EP (85), The Wedge (86), Beat the Drum (99)

PANGAEA - United States

Symphonic progressive rock band whose first album is produced by ROBERT BERRY. Their material features long songs with solid instrumentation and above average arranging. Melodic and accessible.

The Rite of Passage (97), Welcome to the Theatre (98)

PANGEE - Canada

French Canadian band with a distinct late seventies sound and a jazzy feel. Longer symphonic instrumental tracks with Krautrockinfluences. Somewhat of a cross between ANGLAGARD and SHYLOCK in sound and style.

Hymnemonde (95)

PANNA FREDDA - Italy

A sound that is reminiscent of their contemporaries BANCO or SEMIRAMIS only a little spacier sounding.

Uno (71)

PANTANAL - Brazil
Symphonic flavoured music featuring MARCUS VIANA.

PARADISO A BASSO PREZZO - Italy
Classic Italian progressive rock sound with good dynamics, classical stylings and great vocals. In the same school as RDM and BANCO.

Live 1973 (9?)

PARAGONE - United States
Symphonic sound with the occasional Mellotron. Their style is mellow, melodic and slightly fusiony. In 1997 they changed their name to NIGHTALES.

Paragone (94)

PARALLEL OR 90 DEGREES - Great Britain
Influenced by such bands as VAN DER GRAAF and the NICE, this group creates a musical style that is every bit as dynamic as the prog bands of the seventies with long instrumental sections, recurring themes, and plenty of Hammond organ and guitar interplay. Their material is a mixture of both long and short songs with plenty of softer interludes.

Afterlifecycle (97), The Time Capsule (98), No More Travelling Chess (92/99)

PARALLEL SKIES - United States
Mostly the work of multi-instrumentalist Mike Donsi the music here is a fine blend of many different symphonic progressive rock motifs. You'll hear many tempo shifts, key changes, instrumental solos and all of it played quite well.

Parallel Skies (95), Paralle Skies II - Into the Vortex (99)

PARZIVAL - Germany
A little bit of folk and a little bit more rock. At times they sound like JETHRO TULL.

Legent (71), BaRock (73), A German Rock Legend (75)

PASTORAL - Argentina
A romantic, melodic, softer progressive rock sound.

De Michele ( ), Erausquin ( )

PATAPHONIE - France
An all instrumental band which inhabit the mid-period KING CRIMSON/HELDON realm, but with a heavy dose of HENRY COW and NATIONAL HEALTH. They are more experimental that KC but more accessible than their compatriots HELDON.

Pataphonie (75), Le Matin Blanc (79)

PATERNOSTER - Austria
Early seventies band with a dark and heavy prog sound including eerie vocals and lots of organ.

Paternoster (72)

PATTERSON, ROG - Great Britain
Former member of COLTSFOOT and TWICE BITTEN goes solo with an acoustic guitar only.

Flightless (89)

PAVLOV'S DOG - United States
Highly acclaimed progressive rock band whose sound revolved around the sometimes shrill voice of David Surkamp. Very inventive music with numerous guests including people like BILL BRUFORD.

Pampered Menial (75), At the Sound of the Bell (76)

PEEK, KEVIN - Great Britain
One of the two guitarists from the classical progressive rock band SKY. On his solo outings Australian Peek tends to do more work on the electric guitar in some great concept material. Melodic and rousing, Peek weaves a number of musical themes through his music to accomplish a very satisfying end. Will appeal to fans of HACKETT and GILTRAP.

Guitar Junction (80), Awakening (81), Life and Other Games (82)

PEGG, BOB - Great Britain
One album that might appeal to prog fans called Ancient Maps. The LP was produced and arranged by Graham Fields of FIELDS and RARE BIRD fame, it evokes a sort of classical folk fantasy feel.

Shipbuilder (74), Ancient Maps (75)

PELL MELL - Germany
This band is more classically oriented than most progressive rock bands. They would fit into THE NICE category quite well in their own way. They make good use of violin and keyboards. Some say their vocals could use some work.

Marburg (72), From the New World (73), Rhapsody (75), Only a Star (78), Moldau (81)

PELOSI, MAURO - Italy
La Stagione Per Morire ( )

PEMBROKE, JIM - Finland
Solo material from WIGWAM'S vocalist and leader that sounds very similar to WIGWAM.

Wicked Ivory (72), Pigworm (74), Flat Broke (80)

PENDRAGON - Great Britain
One of the successful bands to come out of the second wave of progressive rock in the eighties. Pendragon's musical direction came into focus in about 1981 and since that time they have gigged constantly. Their music, long songs with lots of instrumental excursions, is very majestic, full of pomp and ceremony and just a bit tentative to keep you wanting more. One of the more distinctive neo-progressive rock bands around today.

Sample Cassettes (83), Pendragon EP (84), The Jewel (85), 9:15 Live (86), Kowtow (89), The World (91), Window of Life (93), Live in Lille (9?), Fallen Dreams and Angels EP (9?), Utrecht...The Final Frontier (9?), The Masquerade Overture (96), Live in Krakow 1996 (97), Once Upon a Time in England-Vol. 1 & Vol. 2 (99)

PENTACLE - France
A symphonic style which is built around the nostalgic accents of the singers voice, the acoustic guitars refined chords and the delicate floating sounds of the keyboards, punctuated by the cymbals delicate twinklings and enhanced by the guitars quiet flourishes. Sophisticated and polished compositions tinged with gentle sadness. Sound like - KING CRIMSON, ANGE, ATOLL.

Pentacle ( ), La Clef des Songes (75)

PENTWATER - United States
A band with heavy Hammond organ work, sounding a bit like GENTLE GIANT, YES, and GENESIS. Each of the groups six members sang with four of them alternating on lead. Lot's of solos, harmonies, complex compositions, elaborate arrangements and tempo changes. Syn-Phonic released Out of the Abyss consisting of material not on their LP.

Pentwater (78), Out of the Abyss [76] (92)

PERRAUDIN, CLAUDE - France
He is well known as an author of sound illustration records. This multi instrumentalist has recorded an album which is not only destined for TV production or movie professionals but for a wider audience. He

creates an inventive, pleasant music full of imagery. Sounds like - SKY, GORDON GILTRAP.

Mutation 24 (77)

PERSEPHONE'S DREAM - United States

This highly melodic symphonic progressive rock outfit from Pittsburgh create music that is at times guitar-edge crisp and at other times spacey with new age moments. It all blends together in some well crafted songs that range in at 6 - 12 minutes in length.

Moonspell (99)

PETER & THE WOLF [VARIOUS ARTISTS] - Great Britain

This is a rock re-telling of the classic story used to acquaint children with the various sounds in the symphony orchestra. In this case the instruments are more contemporary in nature. The artist line-up is second to none...Eno, JACK LANCASTER, COZY POWELL, Phil Collins, Percy Jones, Gary Moore, Manfred Mann and others. An album conceived primarily by JACK LANCASTER and Robin Lumley.

Peter and the Wolf (75)

PHAESIS - France

PINK FLOYD inspired material, with elements of CAMEL and MIKE OLDFIELD.

Reminiscence (89), Labyrinthe (91)

PHILHARMONIE - France

Formed by ex-SHYLOCK guitarist, Fredric L'Epee, the style here is heavily influenced by nineties era KING CRIMSON. Lots of angular guitar and experimental style. The all instrumental material is inventive but not for everyone.

Beau Soleil (90), Les Elephants Carillonneurs (93), Nord (94), Rage (96), The Last Word (99)

PHILLIPS, ANTHONY - Great Britain

Former guitarist with GENESIS, Phillips disliked touring so much he quit and after a time, produced some very smooth and mellow works. Many times revolving around a sparsity of instruments, like a keyboard or a acoustic guitar, other times with many guests performing some great material. Mostly pastoral sounding there are times where the music takes on a symphonic nature.

The Geese and the Ghost (77), Wise After the Event (78), Private Parts and Pieces (78), Sides (79), Private Parts and Pieces II (80), 1984 (81), Private Parts and Pieces III (82), The Invisible Men (83), Private Parts and Pieces IV (84), Private Parts and Pieces V: Twelve (84), Private Parts and Pieces: New England (92), Sail the World (94), Dragonfly Dreams (96), The Meadows of Englewood (96)

PHILOSOPHY - United States

A mix of influences combining KANSAS and ELP. Keyboard driven arrangements with male-female vocals.

PH101 (9?), Hostage Heart (9?)

PHOLAS DACTYLUS - Italy

A heavy edged progressive rock that will remind you of NEW TROLLS.

Concerto Delle Menti (73)

PHREEWORLD - United States

Imagine a blend of YES and DREAM THEATRE, throw in a bit of odds and ends like FM and your can just barely begin to describe the musical influences of Phreeworld. It's safe to say their compositional style borrows from the best of symphonic progressive rock to create a unique sound all their own.

Crossing the Sound (98)

PHYLTER - Belgium
They are very influenced by mid-period GENESIS.

Phylter (79)

PICCHIO DAL POZZO - Italy
Complex progressive material more in the vein of Zappa's jazzier style. Jazz fans will enjoy.

Picchio Dal Pozzo (76), Abbiamo Yutti Suoi Problemi (80)

PICTURES - Italy
Symphonic progressive rock with a pop edge influence from the SI label. The compositions tend to be of a brighter more upbeat nature. Imagine a mixture of MARILLION, DREAM THEATRE, THRESHOLD etc.

Painting the Blue (97)

PIERPAOLO BIBBO - Italy
Keyboard dominated progressive rock with floating melodies.

PINEAPPLE THIEF - Great Britain
This is an off-shoot of VULGAR UNICORN and as such is the brainchild of guitarist Bruce Soord. The material is somewhat similar to VULGAR UNICORN but as you'd expect a little more guitar oriented. A mixture of seveties and nineties styles including a 25-minute epic song. You'll also hear elements of PORCUPINE TREE and even Radiohead.

Abducting the Unicorn (98)

PING PONG - Italy
Densely recorded material with good guitar interplay and swirling organ.

Ping Pong (70)

PINK FLOYD - Great Britain
Started out as the leaders in the London underground movement and then progressed musically as did the technology around them. After a couple of psychedelic albums they settled into some dreamy soundscapes and then created Dark Side of the Moon. What followed were a series of great concept albums that in many ways set the example for many bands. Great material, excellent production and fine musicianship.

Piper At the Gates of Dawn (67), A Saucerful of Secrets (68), More (69), Ummagumma (69), Atom Heart Mother (70), Meddle (71), Relics (71), Obscured by Clouds (72), Dark Side of the Moon (73), Wish You Were Here (75), Animals (77), The Wall (79), The Final Cut (83), Works (83), Momentary Lapse of Reason (87), Delicate Sound of Thunder (88), The Division Bell (94), Pulse (95),

PIRAMIS - Hungary
Inconsistent prog rock band. First couple albums qualify, they then lapsed into a simple straight ahead rock approach, until their seventh which saw the return of the old sax player and the singer departing.

I (77), Piramis II (78), III ( ), A Nagy Buli ( ), Piramis (81), Erotika ( ), Plusz (84),

PLACEBO - Great Britain
A band whose music bears a striking resemblance to the old RENAISSANCE, in particular because of the female vocalist.

Shells (83)

PLANETARIUM - Italy
Instrumental material with organ as the prime sound maker. Sounds like THE NICE, THE TRIP or LE ORME.

Infinity (71)

PLANET P - Germany
The brainchild of Tony Carey and Peter Hauke. Tony had replaced Mickey Lee Soule in Ritchie Blackmore's Rainbow in 1976 and found himself in Germany where he met up with Hauke who used to be in

NEKTAR. Carey for the most part does everything on these concept albums and they are spectacular aural-cinematic masterpieces. The second in particular sounds a bit like PINK FLOYD.

Planet P (83), Pink World (84)

PLJBAND - Greece

A unique sound with fuzz and twelve string guitar and mostly droning synths. The music tends to be dark and mysterious progressive, psych-rock similar in style to the German bands of the seventies.

Armageddon (82), Termites (8?)

POHJOLA, PEKKA - Finland

Formerly of the band WIGWAM. His guitar work incorporates jazz influences that build to symphonic proportions. B the Magpie is considered breathtaking and Air Display features MIKE OLDFIELD.

Pihkasilma Kaarnkorva (72), Harakka Bialoipokku [B the Magpie] (75), Keesojen Lehto [Skuggornas Tjuvstart or Mathematicians Air Display] (77), Visitation (79), Katkavaaran Lohikaarme (80), Urban Tango (82), Everyman (83), Space Waltz (85), Flight of the Angel (86), New Impressionist (87), Changing Waters (92), Live in Japan (95), Heavy Jazz - Live in Helsinki & Tokyo (95), Pewit (97)

POISONOUS MUSEUM - Great Britain

This is melodic, symphonic progressive rock that will appeal to a broad cross section of fans. Lots of Mellotron, with musical motifs from a variety of classic prog bands make this material seemingly recognizable and yet very enjoyable. This is a good blend of all the prog elements discussed in this this books definition.

Let It Go (99)

POLARSAGE - United States 1990s

Duo consisting of drums and guitars with the guitarist doing double duty on keyboards. They call their style thinking rock and it clearly shows musical elements of RUSH, KANSAS and MARILLION.

POLLEN - Canada

A French sounding YES or GENESIS. This quartet produced progressive rock in the Anglo style. Longer songs with lots of guitar and keyboard interplay.

Pollen (76)

POLYPHONY - United States

One of the first American progressive rock bands with much the same feel as the ealy seventies Anglo bands such as YES, GENESIS and ELP. Their compositions were long and complex featuring a strong Hammond sound much like ELP. A rare classic

Without Introduction (71)

POPOL ACE - Norway

Post POPOL VUH symphonic progressive rock.

Popol Ace (73), Stolen From Time (75), Curly Sounds (78)

POPOL VUH - Norway

PINK FLOYD inspired symphonic material. Their material incorporated lots of Mellotron and synths.

Popol Vuh (72), Quiche Maya (73)

PORCUPINE TREE - Great Britain

In the OZRIC vein these guys have taken up where PINK FLOYD left off in the psychedelic department. Lots of spacey electronic soundscapes punctuated by dissonant CRIMSON-esque angularity.

Tarquin's Seaweed Farm (89), The Nostrum Gallery (91), On the Sunday of Life (92), Voyage 34 EP (92), Radio Active EP (93), Up the Downstair (93), Spiral Circus (94), Yellow

Hedgerow Dreamscape (94), Live BBC (93), The Sky Moves Sideways (95), Waiting EP (96), Signify (96), Coma Divine (97), Staircase Infinities (97), Stupid Dream (99)

POWELL, COZY - Great Britain

Drummer extraordinaire, he has guested on many albums and been part of many groups, including the reformed Emerson Lake & Powell. His solo ventures are a mixture of powerful orchestra and over the top rock. Some great moments of both.

Over the Top (79), Tilt (81), Octopus (83)

PRAXIS - Mexico

Offshoot of ICONOCLASTA playing a similar high powered instrumental progressive rock with heavy guitar and keyboard.

La Eternidad De Lo Efimero (87)

PRE - United States

Originally recorded in 1973 their release has only recently seen the light of day. Primarily RUSH and YES influenced material.

Pre (73)

PRESENCE - Great Britain

One of the lessor known neo-progressive bands who surfaced during the early eighties resurgence. Presence were a three piece from Stratfordshire showing subtle influences from RUSH. They were known to have recorded a seven song cassette entitled Baby's First Words.

Baby's First Words (83 TAPE)

PRESENCE - Italy

Heavy and sinister symphonic, metalish-neo-progressive sound with female vocals vaguely reminiscent of Sonja Kristina of CURVED AIR. Rock rhythms criss-crossed with angular and frightening organ chords. In the same style as TALE CUE.

Makumba (9?), The Sleeper Awakes (95), Black Opera (96)

PRESENT - Belgium

Similar to UNIVERS ZERO, with a dark atmospheric sound and guitar style heavily influenced by Fripp. The music here is very angular with loads of dissonance. Even the Mellotron slides out on the dark side. If you enjoy challenging and adventurous prog, this is a good place to start.

Triskaidekaphobie (80), Le Poison Qui Rend Fou (85), C.O.D. Performance (94), Live (96), Certitudes (98), No 6 (99)

PRETTY THINGS - Great Britain

Claimed by some to have been ahead of their time by writing the first rock opera SF Sorrow. The following albums tended to be simply straight ahead rock.

S.F. Sorrow (68)

PRIAM - France

Instrumental progressive rock with plenty of symphonic overtones and a hint of fusion. The compositions are full of dynamic contrasts, plenty of variety, complexity, dense agrresive moments interspersed with many softer acoustic moments.

3 distances/irregular signs (98)

PRIMITIVE INSTINCT - Great Britain

Heavy neo-progressive rock borrowing elements of MARILLION and SAGA.

Floating Tangibility (94)

PRINCIPLE EDWARD'S MAGIC THEATRE - Great Britain

Part of the original psychedelic underground scene, they never really survived the transition to progressive rock, but got lost in their music, dance, lights and poetry. Unusual!

Soundtrack (69), The Asmoto Running Band (70), Round One (74)

PRISM - United States
see: HANDS

PROCESSION - Italy
Their material ranges from biting guitar oriented progressive rock to a more commercial sound. The earlier material is better. Fans of heavy Italian prog will probably really like this.

Frontiera (72), Fiaba (74)

PROCOL HARUM - Great Britain
Procol Harum carved out their style through the crafty combination of the individuals differences. They were certainly one of the first bands to create musical epics, long and winding stories that held your attention throughout. Keith Reid's lyrics and Gary Brooker's voice created some amazing aural images.

Procol Harum (67), Shine on Brightly (68), A Salty Dog (69), Home (70), Broken Barricades (71), Live In Concert (72), Grand Hotel (73), Exotic Birds and Fruit (74), Procol's Ninth (75), Something Magic (77), Prodigal Stranger (91)

PROGRES 2 - Czechoslovakia
Progressive rock band from behind the iron curtain, originally known as The Progress Organization, who've produced some interesting concept albums. At times they can be symphonic, at other times more electronic. Going from a dark and aggressive symphonic sound to jazz rock to spacious keyboard laden songs flowing into one another.

Barnodaj (71), Maugli (78), Dialog S Vesmirem (80), Third Jungle Book (82), Tretikniha Dzungli (81)

PROJETO - Brazil
The music here is a mix of pop, progressive and native Brazilian music. There is an overall symphonic prog feel to the material and the closest comparison might be to early RENAISSANCE.

Caleidoscopio (00)

PROVIDENCE - Japan
Progressive rock ala RENAISSANCE and VERMILLION SANDS. Scorching guitar solos, nice full keyboards, well crafted compositions and a fine rhythm section. Add to this multiple time changes and female vocalist and it turns out to be a very accomplished sound. Often regarded as one of the finest Japanese symphonic groups.

And I'll Recite an Old Myth From... (90), There Once Was a Night of Choko-Muro the Paradise (96)

PROWLERS - Italy
This five-piece band creates a symphonic progressive rock that hearkens back to the classic Italian style. Their music is full of many twists and turns, soft pastoral moments followed with dramatic keyboard excursions full of passion. A sound that is reminiscent of RENAISSANCE.

Mother and Fairy (9?), Morgana ( ), Sweet Metamorfosi (97)

PRUDENCE - Norway
Guitar dominated progressive material that falls into the folk-psychedelic mould.

Takk Te Dokk ( ), Drunk and Happy ( ), No. 3 ( ), 11 12 75 Live (75), Tomorrow Maybe Vanished ( ), The Ledgendary Tapes Vol. 1 ( )

PTS - Holland
Sounds like JADIS or MARILLION but perhaps more accessible.

Nightlines (92), Tides (94), Campaign (9?)

PUBLIC FOOT THE ROMAN - Great Britain
A progressive style reminiscent of the first CAMEL album.

Public Foot the Roman (73)

PULSAR - France

Forceful symphonic-progressive rock. Superb melodies built up around the continuous floating sounds of the Mellotron and punctuated by inspired passages from the flute or guitar. Gilbert Gandil's full, warm voice soars above these melodies. The musical developments are exquisite and grandiose and it's arrangements are sumptuous. Pulsar is a major progressive rock group in France and throughout the world. Their four albums are considered masterpieces and essential for any collection.

Pollen (75), The Strands of the Future (76), Halloween (77), Bienvenue au Conseil d'Administration (81), Gorlitz (89)

PUPPET SHOW - United States

A five-piece Bay area group with a refined and accessible symphonic progressive rock sound with plenty of good instrumental work. Longer compositions with plenty of tight tempo changes and displaying many moods. Very Dramatic vocals ala VAN DER GRAAF or DEUS EX MACHINA.

Traumatized (98)

PYE FYTE - United States

Music here is of the symphonic neo-progressive variety, with reference points being GLASS HAMMER and perhaps IQ. Lots of keyboards including Moogs and Mellotrons, but other instruments get their share of time. A combination of short and epic tracks.

The Gathering of the Krums (98)

QUANTUM - Brazil

They sound like CAMEL, HAPPY THE MAN, ELOY with a bit of fusion thrown in.

Quantum (82)

QUANTUM II - Brazil

The reformation of two of the members from QUANTUM has led to this version who are creating big, keyboard driven music in the style of ELP, KALABAN and a bit of ASIA.

Quantum II (94)

QUARKSPACE - United States

Space music specialists from Columbus, Ohio with vocals from the Meddle era PINK FLOYD. Their music is based around a loosely structured and rhythmic psychedelic style.

Quarkspace (96), Live orion (98), The Hidden Moon (99)

QUASAR - Great Britain

One of the early eighties progressive rock bands who maintain a fairly mellow sound choosing instead to develop power through lyrical repetition and strong chording, creating a grand symphonic sound that at times hints of THE ENID. They employed Tracy Hitching as vocalist for the second album.

Fire In the Sky (82), The Loreli (89)

QUASAR - Japan

Technical Japanese symphonic band featuring the guitarist formerly with AIN SOPH. Their musical style is heavily influenced by prog bands such as U.K.

Out From Quaser ( ), Remergence (99)

QUASAR LUX SYMPHONIAE - Italy

Their first recording is a classical symphonic concept based on the life of Biblical patriarch Abraham. Their progressive style is a mixture of well done neo-progressive, dense keyboards, and lots of powerful guitar. At times sounding very much like a staged musical with multiple voices, and musically very dynamic.

Abraham - One Act Rock Opera (94), The Enlightening (97), The Enlightening March of the Argonauts (97), MIT (99)

QUATERMASS - England
Aggressive organ dominated band who were at the forefront of the first wave of progressive rock bands. Ultimately they did not last long. The band included Peter Robinson and John Gustafson who go on to form BRAND X.

Quatermass (70)

QUATERNA REQUIEM - Brazil
CAMEL-esque sounding material from a band that works hard to sound like a seventies Italian band. Overall their style is similar to ICONOCLASTA.

Velha Gravura (90), Quasimodo (94)

QUATRO, MICHAEL - United States
His early works contain some very accomplished progressive rock keyboard work. Good Concepts, longer compositions with lots of drama and Mellotron. Even some great guitar thrown in.

Painting (72), Look Deeply Into the Mirror (73), In Collaboration With the Gods (75), Dancers, Romancers, Dreamers and Schemers (76)

QUEEN - Great Britain
Their first albums were slightly more progressive rock than their later ones, by virtue of their lyrical content. The musicianship tended to stretch out just that bit more as well.

Queen (73), II (74), Sheer Heart Attack (74), A Night At the Opera (75), A Day At the Races (76), Queen Live Killers (79), Flash Gordon (80), The Miracle (89)

QUELLA VECCHIA LOCANDA - Italy
According to Syn-Phonic this band has produced two symphonic progressive rock masterpieces. A little bit like CELESTE orPFM only with more violin. They impart a strong classical structure to their compositions.

Quella Vecchia Locanda (72), Tempo Della Goia (74), Live ( )

QUEST - United States
From Cleveland this five piece create neo-progressive rock music that is a mix of RUSH, YES and DREAM THEATRE. They opened for YES on the '94 tour.

Opposite Sides of the Picket Fence (94)

QUIDAM - Poland
Symphonic progressive rock that's a blend of seventies and eighties style featuring female vocals, flutes and violin. Hints of CARAVAN, MARILLION and later day PINK FLOYD along with a mixture of seventies Italian and eighties British prog styles.

Quidam (96), Angel's Dreams (98), Live in Mexico 1999 (00)

QUIET SUN - Great Britain
One of the first solo outings for Roxy Music guitarist PHIL MANZANERA. He along with a number of others created an album that bears more than a striking resemblance to something akin to SOFT MACHINE.

Mainstream (75)

QUIET WORLD - Great Britain
This band features the work of a pre-Genesis STEVE HACKETT on guitar.

The Road (70)

QUILL - United States
Progressive rock in the YES, ELP vein.

Sursum Corda (77)

QOPH - Sweden
A predominantly psychedelic band, Qoph still inject enough prog elements to keep the music interesting for prog fans.

Kalejdoskopiska Aktiviteter (99)

RABEIRO, FABIO [BLEZQI ZATSAZ] - Brazil
The former keyboardist with III MILENIO produces symphonic material with lush keyboards.

RACCOMANDATA RICEVUTA RITORNO - Italy
Six piece band who create a classical sound similar to OSANNA. They manage to incorporate a little jazz and some Arabic and just a little dissonance to create a very striking and unique sound.

Per...um Mondo di Cristallo (72)

RACHEL'S BIRTHDAY - Germany
Highly innovative neo-progressive rock band with influences that range from early MARILLION to IQ and even a little ECHOLYN.

An Invitation to Rachel's Birthday (97)

RADIO PIECE III - United States
From the Canterbury school, this band hails from Connecticut. Founded by keyboardist Tom Makucevich the groups material is firmly bedded in the NATIONAL HEALTH,or EGG style.

Tesseract & Monuments (9?)

RADIUS, ALBERTO - Italy
Former leader of FORMULA 3 and it shows in his music. Material is more progressive pop.

Radius ( ),Che Cosa Sei ( ),Carta Straccia ( )

RAEL - Argentina
This material sounds like it could have appeared on GENESIS' Lamb Lies Down on Broadway, but in a good way. They manage to infuse enought of their own ideas and ethnic elements to make it interesting.

Mascaras Urbanas (92)

RAGNAROK - New Zealand
Solid symphonic progressive rock style. Influences include some of the early British bands like the MOODY BLUES, YES and GENESIS. Their material also features a jazzier percussion and subtle acoustic moments, but still loaded with lots of Mellotron, analog synths and great dynamics.

Ragnarok (75), Nooks (76), Live in New Zealand (76)

RAGNAROK - Sweden
A rather simple, not overly complex jazzy progressive rock with symphonic touches similar to Finland's PEKKA POHJOLA.

Ragnarok (76), Fjarilarl Magen (79),3 Sings (83),

RAGSDALE, DAVID - United States
One time guitarist/violinist for KANSAS strikes out on his own and is joined by Jerry Peek and Tom Nordin formerly of The Steve Morse Band. The music here is more or less adventurous rock with a proggy flavour, helped in no small part by Ragsdale's classical training. Good solid musicianship.

David and Goliath (97)

RAINBOW THEATRE - Australia
Symphonic progressive rock with a classical influence incorporating the Mellotron. Some comparisons to AIRLORD and ALEPH. They had the distinction of incorporating lots of horns in the compositions.

The Armada (75),Fantasy of Horses (76)

RAISON DE PLUS - France
Five piece melodic-symphonic progressive rock band with influences from CAMEL and ROUSSEAU. Musically they also show elements of many French symphonic bands like ANGE or ATOLL.

Au Bout Du Couloir (96)

RAMASES - Great Britain
The first album Space Hymns, has 10cc as the back up band. Both albums have spacey-folk-ish overtones, with the second having a hint of early STRAWBS sound.

Space Hymns (71), Glass Top Coffin (75)

RAMSES - Germany
A band from the ELOY school of progressive rock. Fine material highlighted by organ and Mellotron. Their third release saw them move to a more commercial style.

La Leyla (75), Eternity Rise (78), Light Fantastic (81)

RAIPAILLE - France
Having been described as a combination of GRYPHON and GENTLE GIANT, you'll hear sound trademarks from both those bands here. The music has certain folkish overtones at times but can also be arranged in a very complicated manner. Add to this the use of older traditional instruments along side the more modern ones in compositions with lots of muted dynamics and starts-and-stops and you'll quickly see there's lots to like about this band.

La Vieille Our L'on Br La (77)

RARE BIRD - Great Britain
Formed in 1969 with a rather unique sound of no guitarist and two keyboard players. Had a hit with 'Sympathy' but then split with Graham Fields continuing in a more progressive rock vein with his new band. Rare Bird floundered. Their sound went from ELP to Crosby Stills Nash & Young.

Rare Bird (69), As Your Mind Flies By (70), Epic Forrest (72), Somebody's Watching (73), Born Again (74), Rare Bird (75), Sympathy (76)

RAVANA - Norway
A nineties era band with KING CRIMSON influences creating music similar to ANEKDOTEN only not as adventurous. A heavier prog that also incorporates cello and Mellotron, but at times drifts very close to an American grunge sound.

Common Daze (96)

RAW MATERIAL - Great Britain
Early prog material similar to GNIDROLOG and CRESSIDA.

Raw Material (70), Time Is Rare (71)

RAY - United States
This is Ray Roechner who makes no bones about being influenced by JETHRO TULL. His first CD, Somewhere In The Universe is peppered with references and dedications to JT. The covers and original tunes show a solid grasp of composition and musicianship and will definitely appeal to TULL fans.

Somewhere in the Universe (95)

R.D.M. - Italy
The next incarnation of the IL ROVESCIO DELLA MEDAGLIA, but more musically mature. One of the finest symphonic progressive rock projects.

Contaminazione (73), Contamination [English version] (75), Let's All Go Back/ Anglosaxon Woman (75)

REALE ACCADEMIA DI MUSICA - Italy
Early Italian art-progressive rock band.

Reale Accadaemia di Musica (72), Adriano Monteduro (74)

REALM - United States
If you like Going For the One, then you'll like this band because they really sound like YES. From the vocalist to the keyboards.

The Path (92)

REASON - United States
This band primarily creates standard arena rock, but includes some progressive elements to their compositions such as Mellotron, and inventive proggy arrangements.

Machine and Man (99)

REBEKKA - Germany
RENAISSANCE like symphonic material.

Phoenix (82), Labyrinth (84)

RECREATION - Belgium
A Belgian trio whose formation (organ/bass/drums) could evoke ELP or THE NICE but even if this influence shows through from time to time, Recreation moves away from it because of its less pronounced fondness for classical music and because of its determination to base its music on a search for sounds and for original, elaborate and carefully worked out compositions.

Don't Open (70), Music or Not Music (71)

RECORDANDO O VALE DAS MACAS - Brazil
Classic Brazilian progressive band using keyboards, guitar, flute and violin to great effect. The 1993 release is a reworking of some of the older tracks and some unreleased material.

As Criancas da Nova Floresta II (77), As Criancas da Nova Floresta II (93), Cycle of Life (97)

REDD - Argentina
Progressive rock in the same vein as PABLO and MIA

Tristes Noticias Del Imperio ( ), Cuentos Del Subsuelo ( )

RED JASPER - Great Britain
Influenced by JETHRO TULL in that there is a definite folky sound here. One of the primary instruments used is mandolin and that lends a unique sound to a band that creates a sound similar to STRAWBS Bursting at the Seams period. Sort of a neo-sympho sound in a folk format.

Action Replay (92), A Midsummer Nights Dream (93), The Winter's Tale (94), Anagramary (97)

REFUGEE - Great Britain
After THE NICE then what...well it turned out to be Refugee. Brian Davison, Lee Jackson and new keyboardist PATRICK MORAZ wanted to pick up where THE NICE had left off. Their only album is a great example of mid-seventies progressive rock keeping in mind the state of keyboards and recording at the time. It sounds nothing like THE NICE. This band is more on the Rock side of progressive.

Refugee (74)

REGENESIS - Great Britain
This is a first-class tribute band devoted to reproducing early GENESIS material. As such these discs take on an official bootleg charm. If you weren't there the first time around these discs may be as close as you can get.

ReGenesis Live (97), Here it Comes Again (98)

RELAYER - United States
A Chicago based group that as you might imagine is very much a YES influenced band. But while the influences are there they have managed to carve out their own original sound. It's not overly complicated music but well arranged and played.

A Grander Vision (95), The Teething Fashion (96), Last Man of Earth (98)

REJOICE - Germany
Keyboard led progressive rock with heavy emphasis on analog keys and Hammond organ. Lots of bombastic playing with plenty of time and tempo changes laced with

some spirited guitar solos. Its all well crafted in a style similar to TRIUMVIRAT and ELP.

Rejoice (97)

RELEASE MUSIC ORCHESTRA - Germany

Some call it jazz-rock some call it fusion, this is a good example of it.

Life (74), Garuda (75), Get the Ball (77), Beyond the Limit (78), News (79)

RENAISSANCE - Great Britain

The second incarnation of the band (the first was with Keith and Jane Relf), were billed as a breath of fresh air, and with ANNIE HASLAM on vocals set the tone for female vocalists in the progressive rock genre. Their sound was at once a mixture of earthy folk and lofty classical themes. A blend of beautiful dramatic and melodic music over the course of many albums. In the nineties they returned with two different groupings, one with ANNIE HASLAM and the other led by Michael Dunford.

Renaissance (69), Illusion (70), Prolog (72), Ashes Are Burning (73), Turn of the Cards (74), Scheherazade (75), Live at Carnegie Hall (76), Novella (77), A Song For All Seasons (78), Azure D'or (79), Camera Camera (81), Time Line (83), Blessing in Disguise [with Haslam] (96), The Other Woman [with Dunford] (96)

REVELATION - Great Britain

London based neo-progressive rock group easily comparable to MARILLION or IT BITES, perhaps not in sound so much as in composition. Some longer tracks featuring good guitar sound spiced up with some flute playing and bombastic musical sections to help create their own unique sound.

Addicted (95)

REVIVAL - Iran

Instrumental flute and guitar, free-form jazz influenced progressive rock sound originally recorded in '79 but only released in '93. As expected some of the tracks feature a strong middle-eastern flavour.

Revival (79)

RHAPSODY - Germany

Epic scale symphonic prog metal compositions with plenty of drama and dynamics. Their first release opted for real orchestral instrumentation instead of keyboards giving the recording a lush, full sound. Their material is squarely in the fantasy vein and the music becomes the soundtrack. If you like your prog bold and dynamic with a strong guitar edge, Rhapsody will certainly entertain.

Legendary Tales (98), Symphony of Enchanted Lands (99)

RIBA, PAU - Spain

The Spanish Daevid Allen. Very popular in Spain.

Diopria 1 (69), Dioptria 2 (70), Jo, La Donya I el Gripau (71), Electriccid Alquimistic Xoc (75), Licors (77), Dioptria [comp.] (78)

RICORDI D'INFANZIA - Italy

Beautiful Italian classical progressive rock.

Io Uomo (74)

RING OF MYTH - United States

Los Angeles trio compose and play in the YES Fragile style, with even a hint of Tangerine Dream. Their vocalist is in the same vocal range as JON ANDERSON but may take some getting used to. They have no permanent keyboardist, but keyboards do make the odd appearance ala RUSH.

Unbound (96),

RIPAILLE - France

On their only album the group plays an original music which is divided between progressive rock and folk music. Beautiful, exquisite, polished melodies are built up on a certain instrumental sophistication and clear, well played vocals. Sound like - GENTLE GIANT, MONA LISA, GRYPHON.

La Vieille que L'on Brula (77)

RITUAL - Sweden

Complex material incorporating many non-traditional instruments like bouzouki and mandolin. As a result there is a slight folk influence mixed with a slight Wind & Wuthering GENESIS feel. Progressive rock with an aspect of commerciality that doesn't detract. Sweden's answer to ECHOLYN, with hints of early YES, GENTLE GIANT, GRYPHON and 10cc.

Ritual (95)

RIVENDEL - Spain

Textured sound with emotional vocals in the classic Italian mould but with just a hint of neo-progressive sound. Nice flute & guitar backed up with some eighties style keyboards. The title track to their CD The Meaning runs nearly 29 minutes and covers many musical elements from metal to opera. Fans of LOCANDA DELLE FATE will enjoy this.

Manifesto (91), The Meaning (96)

RIVENDELL - Finland

Accomplished musicianship is the highlight of this symphonic prog outfit. Their material is melodic and well crafted with a strong focus on keyboards.

Rivendell EP (96)

ROAR - Germany

Semi symphonic progressive material with some folk and psychedelic influences..

The Roar of Silence (91)

ROCINANTE - Japan 1990's

This four piece took their name from the space ship appearing in Cygnus-X1 and started out performing cover tunes from the RUSH Permanent Waves era. They have since gone on to original material with a strong RUSH flavour.

ROCKET SCIENTISTS - United States

With each release the band becomes more and more adventurous. Their second CD proved to be much more progressive rock than the first, with multiple time signatures in music containing contrasting styles. Their fourth release took on a solid symphonic prog tone. Hints of KING CRIMSON and YES. The band uses both Mellotron and Stick and some great keyboard-guitar interplay.

Earthbound (93), Brutal Architecture (95), Earth Below Sky Above - Live in Europe and America (98), Oblivion Days (00)

ROMANTIC WARRIORS - Italy

ARTI'S keyboardist displaying ELP-ish symphonic playing in a modern neo-progressive style.

Battlefield (93)

RONGEY, KURT - United States

CAMEL influenced sound. Firmly in the tradition pioneered in the seventies by TONY BANKS and GENESIS. ZNR records says, Kurt is from Oklahoma but plays and sounds like he's from South London.

Book In Hand (92)

ROOM - Great Britain

Early seventies progressive sound with strings and horns.

Pre Flight ( ), Clear (83)

ROOTS OF CONSCIOUSNESS - United States

A heavy, quirky sound, that's unique. Influences include RUSH, MARILLION and a bit of Be Bop Deluxe.

Roots of Consciousness (93)

ROSALIA - Japan
All female progressive rock band whose sound is in the RUSH and DREAM THEATRE vein, although the massive keyboards provide a solid symphonic back drop. The use of Mellotron and many other keyboards keeps this out of the prog-metal category but is does have an edge.

Zillion Tears EP (90)

ROUSSEAU - Germany
Band from the middle eighties that creates some very pleasant melodies and strong musical passages using the traditional progressive rock formulas. They recognised they were moving against the flow and began to include some mainstream pop songs in their work. Sounds like CAMEL at times.

Flower In Asphalt (78), Retreat (80), Square the Circle (86)

ROVESCIO DELLA MEDAGALIA, IL - Italy see: RDM

ROXY MUSIC - Great Britain
More properly labelled an art rock band, they stood out of the glam-rock movement, from where they came, by virtue of their superior musicianship and compositional skills. The original line-up included Phil Manzanera on guitars and Brian Eno on keyboards. Manzanera would go on to many prog solo and band efforts, while Eno would delve into the ambient music world. While their early albums tended to be quirky-rockers their later work settled into a melodic art-rock style.

Roxy Music (72), For Your Pleasure (73), Stranded (73), Country Life (74), Siren (75), Viva (76), Manifesto (79), Flesh & Blood (80), Avalon (82), High Road (83)

ROYAL HUNT - United States
Like a number of the bands on the Magna Carta label Royal Hunt are primarily a hard rock band with plenty of progressive rock influences. Their style is a blend of DREAM THEATRE and ENCHANT but with more keyboard work. If you like your prog to be guitar oriented with a strong emphasis on songs this is a great place to start.

Paradox (97), Fear (99)

RUDESS MORGENSTEIN PROJECT - United States
Two man project from former Dixie Dregs drummer Rod Morgenstein and former Dregs, now DREAM THEATRE keyboardist Jordon Rudess. The compositions display solid musicianship and while not overy complex there is much to appreciate in terms of music.

Rudess Morgenstein Project (97)

RUMBLIN' ORCHESTRA - Hungary
This is an unusual mix of ELP-ish symphonic prog with a kind of Broadway musical score. The rock element comes and goes and in between is musical-ish theme.

Spartacus (99)

RUNAWAY TOTEM - Italy
This Italian five piece plays a heavy mixture of doomy chords tied to operatic vocals. This is predominantly prog-metal with a MAGMA influence.

Andromeda (99)

RUNDGREN, TODD - United States see: UTOPIA

RUNIC WAND - Germany
Symphonic progressive rock.

RUNNING MAN - Great Britain
Neo progressive rock.

The Running Man ( )

RUPHUS - Norway
In the same vein as RENAISSANCE with a bit of jazz influence. Lots of Hammond organ and flute passages fronted by both a female and male vocalists.

New Born Day (73), Ranshart (74), Let Your Light Shine (76), Inner Voice (77), Flying Colours (78), Hot Rhythms and High Notes (78), Hand Made (79)

RUSH - Canada
Formed in 1970 as primarily a hard rocking unit, they began to change direction by the second album and made the complete transition by the third into full fledged progressive rock with a guitar thrust. A real thinking man's band, Rush continue to create music with strength, dynamics, and emotion.

Rush (74), Fly By Night (75), Caress of Steel (75), 2112 (76), All the World's A Stage (77), A Farewell to Kings (77), Hemispheres (78), Permanent Waves (80), Moving Pictures (81), Exit Stage Left (81), Signals (82), Grace Under Pressure (84), Power Windows (85), Hold Your Fire (87), Presto (89), A Show of Hands (89), Roll the Bones (91), Counterparts (93), Test For Echo (96), Different Stages (98)

RUSTICHELLI E BORDINI - Italy
Keyboard driven progressive sound with great organ and Mellotron.

Opera Prima (73)

RUTHERFORD, MIKE - Great Britain
Before Mike and The Mechanics came into being, Rutherford created his first solo album that really picked up where GENESIS left off. His second however is where he really tried to make the change to pop and it was a sign of things to come.

Smallcreep's Day (80), Acting Very Strange (82)

RYAN, PAUL - Great Britain
Orchestrated masterworks from keyboardist Ryan and guests.

Scorpio Rising (76)

SADISTIC MIKA BAND - Japan
Formed in Tokyo in 1973 with the mission to challenge the MOR scene in Japan. They were discovered by Roxy Music, and their first album was produced by Chris Thomas. Influences include The Beatles through to KING CRIMSON. Only some of the material on their first album qualifies as progressive rock.

Sadistic Mika Band (74), Black Ship (75), Hot! Menu (75)

SAECVLA SAECVLORVM - Brazil
Music from MARCUS VIANA on violin before his days with SAGRADO.

Saecvla Saecvlorvm ( )

SAGA - Canada
Started out ambitiously with guitar/keyboard music that played progressive rock in shorter format, they eventually settled down to more mainstream rock with some progressive overtones. Still good but not the same sparkle. The first albums contained songs labelled chapters for a long involved concept. After a dry spell they returned in 1996 with Generation 13, a rock opera and have won high praise.

Saga (78), Images At Twilight (79), Silent Knight (80), Worlds Apart (81), In Transit (82), Head's or Tales (83), Behavior (85), Wildest Dreams (87), Beginners Guide to Throwing Shapes (89), Security of Illusion (93), Steel Umbrellas (94), Generation 13 (95), Pleasure and Pain (97), Detours Live (99), Full Circle (99)

SAGITARRIAN - Japan
A band with symphonic style similar to NOVALIS, CAMEL and PINK Floyd.

Sagitarrian (84)

SAGRADO CORACAO DA TERRA - Brazil
Brazil's number one symphonic rock band led by VIANA. A wide variety of influences from PELL MELL, Jean Luc Ponty, or even YES. With beautiful female vocals and VIANA'S violin work there are even bits of THE ENIDsound present.

Sagrado Coracao Da Terra (85), Flecha (87), Farol da Liberdade (91), Grande Espirito (93)

SAHARA - Germany
Classically oriented progressive rock. All the hallmarks of German symphonic prog, Mellotron, searing guitars, some light jazz parts and even the odd bit of saxophone. One of the more underrated bands deserving of more attention.

Sunrise (74), For All the Clowns (76)

SAILOR FREE - Italy
Accessible, not very complex progressive rock incorporating many other styles such aspsychedelic, grunge and ethnic. All songs are in the four-to-five minute range.

Sailor Free (92), The Fifth Door (94)

SAKRE - Spain
A legendary Basque symphonic progressive rockers that don't sound like any other Basque band. There is little folk influence and far more keyboard work rather than guitar. If you're a fan of BLOQUE or ASAFALTO you'll like this.

Bitzitako Gauzak (76)

SAKUBARU, MOTOI - Japan
Keyboardist from DEJA VU creates stunning fusion instrumental material with a slight symphonic touch. In the same vein as ARS NOVA and GERARD.

Gikyokuonsou (90), Force of Light (98)

SALAMANDER - Great Britain
Early seventies progressive concept work in the same symphonic style as early MOODY BLUES or DEEP PURPLE.

The Ten Commandments (71)

SALEM - Canada
From the Province of Quebec they sound a lot like JETHRO TULL. Their music has a strong medieval-acoustic quality with a distinct French feel.

Salem EP (96), Salem (98)

SALEM HILL - United States
Progressive rock band that brings to mind KANSAS, CRACK THE SKY and SAGA. They employ strong melodic composition and solid musicianship resulting from years of classical training.

Salem Hill (92), II (93), Catatonia (97), The Robbery of Murder (98), Not Everybody's Gold (00)

SAMADHI - Italy
Symphonic progressive rock featuring full orchestra.

Samadhi (74)

SAMLA MAMMAS MANNA - Sweden
This classic Swedish band specialised in a more progressive rock-fusion in the early seventies and then moved more into the world of RIO. A fascinating outfit that injected a lot of humour and weirdness into the music.

Samla Mammas Manna (71), Maltid (73), Klossa Knaitatet (74), Snorungamas Symfoni (76), For Aldre Nybegnnare/ Schlargerns Mystik [as Zamla Mannaz Manna] (78), Familjesprickor (80), Zamlaranamanna [as Zamla] (82), No Make Up! (84), Kaka (99)

SANCIOUS, DAVID - United States

Former keyboard player with Bruce Springsteen surprised everyone, with some fine music that started to sound a little like ELP, probably because it was produced by Eddie Offord. The Bridge tends to be a little more fusion oriented.

Forest of Feeling (75), Transformation (76), True Stories (78), Just As I Thought (79), Dance of the Age of Enlightenment ( ), The Bridge (81)

SANDROSE - France

Founded by Jean-Pierre Alarcen and former members of Eden Rose, Sandrose played a superb progressive rock based on Rose Podwojny's magnificent, beautiful, powerful, clear voice, the continuous floating sounds of the Mellotron and the furious incisive interventions by Jean-Pierre whose talented and original guitar playing explodes during a superbly constructed long instrumental passages. Sounds like a French EARTH AND FIRE.

Sandrose (72)

SANGIULIANO, ANTONIO - Italy

Keyboard dominated prog sound.

Take Off (78)

SAPPHIRE - Switzerland

The music is well done symphonic neo-progressive with many interesting musical motifs appearing throughout. A combination of short songs and epics, well played and influenced primarily by early GENESIS but not overtly so.

Triple (99)

SAQQARAH - France

Neo-progressive rock band with a lyrical focus, as the name implies on ancient Egypt, and other mystical issues. Their style borders closely to that of ASIA, but every so often they stretch out and when they do the material works very well.

Genese (96)

SARACEN - Great Britain

Once written about as a cross between Black Sabbath and STYX. A few good progressive moments on their first LP. Epic stories and music in the style of MAGNUM and NIGHTWING.

Heroes, Saints & Fools (81), Change of Heart (84)

SARCOFAGUS - Finland

Essentially hard rock with a slight progressive rock edge.

Sarcofagus (8?), Envoy of Death (8?)

SATIN WHALE - Germany

More classically oriented progressive rock with a bit of fusion thrown in from time to time. Interestingly, Barry Palmer and Jurgen Fritz from TRIUMVIRAT appeared on the last recording in 1980.

Desert Places (74), Lost Mankind (75), As A Keepsake (77), Whalecome Live (77), A Whale of a Time (78), Die Faust in Der Tasche (79), Don't Stop the Show (80)

SAVAGE ROSE - Denmark

Quirky material full of the psychedelic flavour of the times. The band featured three keyboard players, with female vocals and an assortment of other odd instruments.

Savage Rose (68), In the Plain (68), Travellin' (69), Your Daily Gift (71), Refugee (72), Babylon (73), Wild Child (73), I'm Satisfied (7?), En Vugge Af Stal ( ), Solen Var Ogsa Din (77), Oden's Triumph ( )

SBB - Poland

Poland's top symphonic progressive rock band. Their mid-seventies work tends to be the best. The bands leader Jozef Skrzek went on to record four solo efforts that wound up being somewhat jazzier than his work here.

SBB (74), Nowy Horizont (75), Pamiec (76), Ze Slowem Biegne Do Ciebie (77), SBB (77), Follow My Dream (78), Welcome (79), Memento Z Banalym Tryptikiem (80), Live 1992 (93), Live in America (94)

SCARAB - Finland
Pre-AGENESS symphonic material incorporating a blend of early GENESIS and CAMEL.

Scarab (83)

SCARAMOUCHE - Germany
Melodic progressive rock but not overly symphonic, and a little more commercial sounding. The band's influences include FLOYD, GENESIS, and mostly GROBSCHNITT.

Scaramouche (81)

SCHEHERAZADE - Japan
Nineties era Japanese supergroup featuring TOSHIO EGAWA and T. Hirayama of GERARD.

SCHERPENZEEL, TON - Holland
Former leader of KAYAK and then EUROPE, tries his hand at solo work.

Le Carnivaldes Animals (78), Heart Of the Universe (84)

SCHIFF, DON - United States
This member of The ROCKET SCIENTISTS goes solo with a Chapman Stick and creates some inventive, jazz influenced progressive rock.

Timeless (99)

SCHWARZARBEIT - Germany
Melodic instrumental material that is reminiscent of Dust and Dreams era CAMEL. They feature a good deal of acoustic guitar with a solid backdrop of synths.

James Gordon's Story (93)

SEA OF DREAMS - Norway
Symphonic progressive metal with loads of melody in epic compositions. Part of the new breed of prog-metal practitioners. If you enjoy the more progressive material from DREAM THEATRE you'll like this.

Dawn of Time (96), Land of Flames (98)

SEATE - Japan
This five-piece band features ex-CINDERELLA SEARCH violinist Junko Minobe creating folk-influenced symphonic music along the lines of SOLSTICE, first-era RENAISSANCE or country-mates AUGUST.

Kedarui Gogono EP (96)

SEBASTIAN HARDIE - Australian
Symphonic sound with lots of Mellotron. Originally formed in the seventies they reformed for a time in 1994. Their compositions are filled with powerful guitar work. Melodic, progressive rock in the classic style. In 1977 they changed their name to WINDCHASE.

Four Moments (76), Windchase (76)

SECOND MOVEMENT - Germany
Progressive rock in the same vein as ELOY, OCTOPUS and TIBET, but with the addition of sax and other woodwind instruments.

Blind Man's Mirror (78), Movement ( )

SECRET CINEMA - Italy
Heavy prog sound with massive synth chord accents. Very much in the style of seventies Italian prog. ARTI'S Keyboardist Beppe Corvello handled all the keyboard work in great style using everything from Mellotron to mini-Moog. Sounds like YES, and a better ASIA.

Dreamin' of My Past (94)

SECTA SONICA - Spain
Fusiony prog, similar to IMAN CALIFATO INDEPENDIENTE.

Fred Pedrables (76),Astroferia (77)

SEMIRAMIS - Italy
They performed a classic Italian symphonic sound on their only release Dedicato A Frazz. They were a five piece with two guitarists and managed to create a very large symphonic sound full of unique song structures, rich analog synths and great dynamics.

Dedicato A Frazz (73)

SENIOR, KEN - Great Britain
A multi-instrumentalists soloist from the same school as FONYA, who also goes by the name of Evolution. His influences include YES, GENESIS and others from the mainstream of progressive rock. He's produced quite a number of independent cassettes containing well crafted songs, with good arrangements that are never boring. His first CD was released in 1997.

The First Signs Of Life (97)

SENS - France
A symphonic progressive rock band from France but their musical style is very similar to the classic Italian sound. Lots of drama and plenty of prog dynamics. Lots of great keyboard sounds with some nice melodies.

Les Regrets d'Isidore (99)

SENSATIONAL ALEX HARVEY BAND - Great Britain
Started out as a basic blues outfit. Strong theatrical element to all their material not only musically expressed but conveyed physically by their live presence. Some good fun as well. Good guitar and keyboard interplay.

Next (73),The Impossible Dream (74),Tomorrow Belongs To Me (75),Live (75),The Penthouse Tapes (75),Stories (76),Fourplay (77),Rock Drill (78), BBC Live (96)

SENSATIONS FIX - Italy
Synthesiser guitar soundscapes made them one of the more interesting Italian bands of their day. Sometimes spacey, sometimes just good old rock...take your pick.

Portable Madness (74),Fragment of Light (74),Finest Finger (76),Boxes Paradise (77),Flying Tapes (78),Visions Fugitives ( )

SENSES - United States
Headed up by Joan Morbee, Senses is a quartet whose music is based on an arena rock sound with progressive rock elements sprinkled liberally through out.

FieldsUnsown (96)

SENSITIVA IMMAGINE - Italy
Rich symphonic progressive rock in the classic Italian tradition.

E Tutto Comincia Cosi [late '70s] (92)

SERU GIRAN - Argentina
Melodic, song oriented prog-Rock.

Seru Giran ( ),SR-II (78)

SEVENTH WAVE - Great Britain
Primarily a spacey keyboard oriented band, but they managed to hang on to a very orchestrated sound.

Things To Come (74),Psi-Fi (75)

SEZON DOZHDEI - Lithuania
Symphonic, synth-based progressive rock.

Vozvrasheniye (92)

SFF - Germany
Highly regarded, symphonic keyboard oriented trio. Lots of Mellotron, organ and classical influences in highly arranged and

long instrumental works.

Symphonic Pictures (76), Sunburst (77), Ticket To Everywhere (78), Collected Works (93)

SFINX - Romania
Romanian progressive rock band with their own unique sound. It's long songs that are very dramatic, melodic with prominent keyboards. If any comparison is to be made it's loosely with bands like PROGRES 2, MINIMUM VITAL or ELOY.

Zalmoxe (78)

SFUMATO - Germany
Symphonic prog with hints of PINK FLOYD and YES but clearing melded into their own style. Lots of interesting keyboard and guitar interplay with long songs and some solid instrumentals.

Sfumato (99)

SHAA KHAN - Germany
Symphonic prog with many similarities to PINK FLOYD, but you'll also hear elements of EELA CRAIG, GALAXY, NOVALIS and even ANYONE'S DAUGHTER. Five members who produce a very melodic style of music.

The World Will End on Friday (77), Anything Wrong? (79)

SHADOW GALLERY - United States
A neo-prog sound with traces of RUSH, MAGELLAN, KANSAS and DREAM THEATRE. Long compositions which include interesting orchestration and musical interludes. The music here is very dramatic and dynamic with tons of guitar, but it's also complex with plenty of melody.

Shadow Gallery (92), Carved In Stone (96), Tyranny (98)

SHADOWLAND - Great Britain
Neo-progressive rock sound like IQ and EGDON HEATH. CLIVE NOLAN produced this band and played keyboards on their release Ring of Roses so there's also a distinct PENDRAGON flavour here. Very song oriented, so don't expect overly long instrumental solos.

Ring of Roses (92), Through the Looking Glass (94), Dreams of the Ferryman EP ( ), Mad as a Hatter (96),

SHINGETSU - Japan
This legendary band creates symphonic progressive rock not unlike classic period GENESIS. Their music is full of passages featuring acoustic guitars, thick keyboards, heavy symphonics embellished with a liberal dose of Mellotron

Shingetsu (79), Night Collector (94), Akai Me No Kagami (95)

SHIRAKAWA, YOSHINOBU - Japan
A solo keyboardist who creates rich symphonic material that is in the same style as THE ENID or GANDALF. Lots of synthesisers, plenty of dynamics and some well placed rhythm provide some enjoyable and dramatic music.

Mellow Clouds II (92)

SHREEVE, MARK - Great Britain
The digital samplers run amok and it sound like a complete band and orchestra...great stuff. Big and grand with a touch mischief.

Embryo (80), Ursa Major (80), Phantom (80), Firemusic (81), Thoughts of War (81), Assasin (83), Legion (85)

SHYLOCK - France
A progressive rock group who play in a refined, elaborate, polished musical style. Exquisite symphonic compositions with long and complicated instrumental developments. Sound like - KING CRIMSON.

Gialorgues (77), Ile de Fievre (78)

SIDDHARTHA - Germany
Obscure band whose musical style crosses over from progressive rock to psychadelic with a dose of folk and jazz. Their line-up includes violin, keyboards, bass, drums and guitar. You'll hear hints of CURVED AIR, PINK FLOYD and a few other bands from that period.

Weltschmerz (/94)

SIDE STEPS - Japan
A Japanese four-piece that inhabit the same fusion world as KENSO. Lots of tight symphonic arrangements with furious playing

Out-and-Out (98), Alive (99)

SIGMA - Brazil
Their music is a blend of intense driving progressive rock with light mellow-jazz.

Implemental View (99)

SILOAH - Germany
Organ dominated progressive rock from early seventies band. Given the time period this was created you can also expect to hear a strong folk and psychedelic influence.

Saureadler (70), Surkram Gurk (72)

SIMMETRIE - Italy
Symphonic neo-prog sound.

Simmetrie (90)

SIMMONDS, MICKEY - Great Britain
Multi-instrumentalist solo artist whose material is in the same vein as CAMEL's Harbour of Tears.

The Shape of Rain (96)

SIMON SAYS - Sweden
Mellotron flavoured symphonic material with hints of UK, ELP and GENESIS. A modern sound where the keyboards don't dominate. They've been described as THE MOODY BLUES meets ANGLAGARD meets Devo, incorporating the dynamics, acoustic guitars and flutes to create their own sound.

Ceiwen (95)

SINCRONIA - Italy
Programmed synths abound here creating a style of classical symphonic prog that contains hints of VANGELIS and even a bit of GENESIS.

Odisea Del Tiempo Eterno (93)

SINFIELD, PETE - Great Britain
Best known for his work lyrically with KING CRIMSON and PFM. On his only solo LP he calls together GREG LAKE, Mel Collins and a host of others to translate his personal style.

Still (73)

SINISTER STREET - Great Britain
Neo-progressive rock band. Good song writing and some nice instrumental sections that will remind you of bands such as IQ, EGDON HEATH and SAGA.

The Eve of Innocence (92)

SINKADUS - Sweden
A very seventies symphonic sound produced in a very nineties way. Their first release Aurum Nostrum featured four Mellotron drenched, guitar spiced melodic epics. In many respects they're a lot like ANGLAGARD but slightly more accessible with songs that are somewhat more focused.

Aurum Nostrum (96), Live at Progfest (98), Cirkus (98)

SIRIUS - Germany
One known album that's mostly in the symphonic style of late seventies British prog band ENGLAND especially in the

vocal department. At other times he bears a resemblance to the vocalist from ANYONE'S DAUGHTER.

The Three Bushes (84)

SITHONIA - Italy
Lush arrangements with flute, guitar and keyboards, their sound is richly melodic. A soft symphonic prog that is similar to the classic Italian style. Music sounds a bit like CAMEL, LE ORME or PFM.

Lungo Il Sentiero Di Pietra (9?), Spettacolo Annulatto (92), Folla di Annullato ( ), Confine (95), Hotel Brun (98)

SIXTY NINE [69] - Germany
This duo created keyboard rock in the vein of ELP only not quite so flashy. Long songs dominated by the Hammond organ.

Circle of the Crayfish (72), 69 Live (74)

SKALDOWIE - Poland
Long lived Polish band who started out in the late sixties and went through to the mid seventies. The early work tends to be very sixties psychedelic pop, while the later work is very much progressive rock.

Skaldowie (68), Wsystka Mi Mowi Ze Ktos Mnie Pokochat ( ), Cata Jestes W Skowronkach ( ), Od Wschodu Do Zachodu Stonca ( ), Ty ( ), Wszystkim Zakochanym ( ), Krywan, Krywan (72), Szanujmy Wspomnienia ( ), Stworzenia Swiata Czesc Druga ( ), Rezerwat Milosci ( ), Droga Luzi ( ),

SKANTZE, PATRIK - Sweden
Solo artist whose musical style is similar to early MIKE OLDFIELD. The two long compositions build slowly and wind their way through many dramatic musical elements.

Music For My Ego's Sake (99)

SKIN ALLEY - Great Britain
Early blues based group with a style that was hot and cold, sometimes progressive, sometimes not.

Skin Alley (69), To Pagham and Beyond (70), Two Quid Deal (72), Skintight (73)

SKORPIO - Hungary
This is a spin-off band from Locomotive GT. Their prog-quotient is inconsistent. Sometimes it's just straight ahead rock.

A Rohanas (73), Unnepnap (74), Kelj Fel ! (75), Gyere Velem (76), Zene Tiz Hurra Es Egy Dobosra (77), Aranyalbum (78)

SKRYVANIA - France
A group which offers an excellently executed, constructed and very elaborate symphonic prog with complex instrumentation and developments. The musicians are remarkable especially the guitarist who displays the richness and finesse during superb solos. Sound like - ANGE, GENESIS.

Skryvania (78)

SKY - Great Britain
Formed in 1978 by classical guitarist John Williams and billed as 'the classic Classical rock band'. Their material comes at progressive rock from the classical side as you can well imagine, with lots of acoustic guitar. Great keyboards and electric guitar as well. FRANCIS MONKMAN plays on the first few LPs.

Sky (79), Sky 2 (80), Sky 3 (81), Sky 4 Fourthcoming (82), Sky 5 Live (83), Cadmium (83), The Great Balloon Race (85)

SLEEPY PEOPLE - Great Britain
An unusual mixture of symphonic prog with a goodly amount of pop and new wave.

Typhoid & Swans (97)

SLOCHE - Canada
Similar to MANEIGE, but with more GENTLE GIANT influence.

J'un Oeil (75), Stadacone (76)

SLOGANS - Italy
Mystical classical prog centred around the keyboards. A blending of GENESIS and PFM.

Photosynthesis (8?)

SMAK - Yugoslavia
A legendary progressive rock band from Yugoslavia. Listen for some fusion tinged spacey keyboard work.

Smak (75), Cma Dama (77), Black Lady (77), Smak Dab in the Middle (78), Rock Cirkus (80), Zasto Ne Volim Sneg (81),

SMALL FACES - Great Britain
Ogden's Nut Gone Flake is sort of a loose concept-come arty album that is the closest they ever got to progressive rock. Good fun.

Ogden's Nut Gone Flake (67)

SMELL OF INCENSE - Norway
As the name might imply there is a strong psychedelic influence in this folk oriented progressive rock. Instrumentation highlights include sitar, organ and Mellotron.

All Mimsy ( )

SNOPEK, SIGMUND - United States
Relatively unknown progressive artist who creates music that's a blend of contemporary classical and progressive rock. His compositions contain some very GENTLE GIANT-ish moments.

Who's Afraid of Virginia Woolf (94), Music for Pipe Organ (95), Thinking out Loud (96), Nobody to Dream (97), Charm School (98), Trinity Seaseizesees (00)

SNOWDONIA - Spain
The music here is a blend of prog-jazz and psychadelic influences.

Pallas (99)

SOCIAL TENSION - Japan
Keyboard dominated trio with a strong influence from ELP and MASTERMIND.

Macbethia (87), It Reminds Me of Those Days (90)

SOCRATES - Greece
Features VANGELIS on keyboards, but is more known for their twin guitar work. The music often uses an undercurrent of flamenco or middle eastern musical influences.

Socrates Drank the Conium ( ), On the Wings (76), Phos (76)

SOFT MACHINE - Great Britain
Coming out of the dissolution of Canterbury group THE WILDE FLOWERS the SOFT MACHINE have achieved lofty cult status in both the worlds of progressive rock and avant garde. Many consider them to be the very first jazz-rock group. The band were often found on the same bill as PINK FLOYD playing at such notable prog birthgrounds as the UFO club. They also played at the legendary 14 Hour Technicolor Dream concert at London's Alexandra Palace in April 1967. The band survived many personnel changes which included Robert Wyatt, Daevid Allen, Richard Sinclair, Kevin Ayers, Mike Ratledge and Andy Summers (later of the Police). Their album BUNDLES even featured Alan Holdsworth on guitar. Sinclair went on to found CARAVAN, Ayers pursued a successful solo career frequently accompanied by Mike Oldfield, Wyatt formed MATCHING MOLE, and Allen, who had often found himself in trouble with the British authorities, moved to France and founded GONG.

The Soft Machine (68), Volume 2 (69), Third (70), Fourth (71), Five (72), Six (72), Seven (73), Bundles (75), Softs (76), Rubber Riff (76), Triple Echo (77), Alive & Well in Paris (78), Land of Cockayne (81), Jet Propelled Photographs (89), Live at the Paradiso (95), Spaced (96), Virtually (98), Noisette (00)

SOHO ORANGE - Great Britain
A mix of heavy rock and early style progressive rock.

Soho Orange (71)The Final Solution ( ),World Games ( ),In Time (97)

SOLARIS - Hungary
They've been called the finest symphonic progressive rock group ever to come out from Eastern Europe. Tons of analog synthesisers, flute, fiery guitar and highly classical with rare compositional ability and masterful musicianship. The first LP The Martian Chronicles is all instrumental with a beautiful cover.

Marsbeli Kronikak [The Martian Chronicles] (83), 1990 (90), Live in Los Angeles (96), Nostradamus-Book of Prophecies (99)

SOLAR PROJECT - Germany
Dark prog rock from a MARILLION and late seventies PINK FLOYD influence. Lots of vintage keyboard sounds including Mellotron can be heard. Their compositions contain a good balance of vocals and instrumental sections where the music, while not overly complex is very enjoyable.

The Final Solution ( ),World Games ( ), House of S. Phernia ( ), ...In Time (97)

SOLID GROUND - Sweden
Hard edged prog rock.

Made in Rock ( )

SOLSTICE - Great Britain
Part of resurgence of progressive rock of the eighties. They sounded like RENAISSANCE meets YES. A little folk-rock with violin. Their first release was in 1984 and they simply toured and did session work until releasing a new album with a different female vocalist in 1993. Sounding just as good as ever.

The Peace Tape (83),Silent Dance (84),New Life (93),Circles (97)

SOLSTICE - France
Progressive rock in a typical French tradition. Sounds something like ATOLL or MONA LISA.

Miroir SP (79)

SOLUTION - Holland
This classically oriented keyboard group created music of great texture. Their later work tended more to a mellow jazz-rock in the SOFT MACHINE vein.

Solution (72), Divergence (73), Cordon Bleau (75), Fully Interlocking (77), It's Only Just Beginning (80), Runaway ( )

SOMA - Great Britain
Like OZRIC TENTACLES, only with vocals.

Epsilon (91),Dreamtime (9?)

SOMNAMBULIST - United States
A very dark and intense angular or gothic progressive rock with a prominent Hammond organ sound. Their promo material labels them as infusing progressive with a healthy dose of attitude. The music features long tracks filled with heavy guitar, heavenly Mellotron, thunderous organ and dark dramatic vocals. Good musicianship with elements of KING CRIMSON, GENESIS, ELP and Sweden's ANEKDOTEN.

Somnambulist (96), Paranormal Humidor (00)

SOM NOSSO DE CADA DIA - Brazil
A three piece with more to offer than an ELP-ish sound. Included in their sound is violin, sax and flute. They reformed in 1994 to perform material from the first LP, but their sound had changed more to a light jazz funky style.

Snegs (74),Live '94 (95)

SOPHISTREE - Germany
They create a neo-progressive rock style that betrays hints of a jazz influence.

Seed (98)

SORRENTI, ASLAN - Italy
Some say commercial...some say symphonic sound.

Aria (72), Come Un Vecchio Incensiere (73), Third (74)

SOUNDSCAPE - United States
Epic and dramatic progressive rock with just a hint of prog-metal, but more than enough punchy, complex instrumentals with a spotlight on keyboards. Their first CD contains two tracks both about 20 minutes long. They've been compared to Brazil's Angra.

Discovery (97)

SPEKTAKEL - Germany
Actually this is old material (1974) from two thirds of SFF. Ede Schicke and Heinz Frohling formed Spektakel in 1969 and by 1974 it was your typical four piece progressive rock band. The sound is like early GROBSCHNITT mixed with the mid seventies Anglo symphonic style.

Spektakel (96)

SPERMULL - Germany
Early progressive style that some said sounded like a weak Guru Guru. They were part of what came to be known more precisely as Krautrock.

Spermull (73)

SPINETTA JADE - Argentina
Song oriented progressive rock.

Bajo Belgrano ( ), Los Ninos ( ), Madre En ( )

SPIRIT CIRCLE - United States 1990s
Sacramento, California based five-piece with a dedicated lead singer. A strong folk and Celtic influence pervades a complex prog style. Their compositions have a strong seventies feel including the use of Mellotron. They changed their name to Maelstrom in 1997, the second U.S. band to use that name.

SPIRIT OF CHRISTMAS - Canada
Early style progressive rock with lots of keyboards and guitar. Sounds a little like JETHRO TULL without the flute at times. Long songs with busy guitar playing and some well placed Mellotron.

Lies To Live By (74)

SPIROSFERA - Italy
They create a quirky, theatrical sound that may remind some of DEUS EX MACHINA. This is primarily because of the vocalist's style. Musically they have lot's of irregular time signatures, starts and stops. Fans of AREA should appreciate what's going on here.

Umanamnesi (96)

SPITALERI, DAVID - Italy
Classic progressive rock from this singer/songwriter formerly with METAMORFOSI.

Uomo Irregolare (80)

SPLEEN - Italy
Spleen (9?)

SPLIT ENZ - New Zealand
Quirky art rock band with symphonic prog touches. Great playing and lyrics. If you enjoy bands like 10cc or CITY BOY, you'll like this.

Mental Notes (75), Second Thoughts (76), Dizrythmia (77), Frenzy (78), True Colours (80), Waiata (81), Time and Tide (82), Conflicting Emotions (84), See Ya 'Round (85), Living Enz (85)

SPOCK'S BEARD - United States
They've been hailed as the best U.S. prog band to emerge since the seventies! Material features piano, organ, Mellotron, guitar, bass and percussion sounding very nineties. Complex symphonic prog with great melodies and lots of time and tempo changes, never boring. In the same vein as ECHOLYN, CRACK THE SKY and GENTLE GIANT, but also betraying many YES and Beatle influences.

The Light (95), Beware of Darkness (96), Official Live Bootleg (96), The Kindness of Strangers (97), Day for Night (98), From The Vaults (98)

SPONSOR - Switzerland
Symphonic prog style.

What is Life (81)

SPRING - Great Britain
Melodic progressive rock featuring lots of Mellotron. They released one album in 1971 and had started work on a second but split up before it was completed. They featured as many as three Mellotron players for some of the songs. The material is a pleasant early progressive style with many songs in the six - seven minute range with the Mellotron firmly established as part of the song structure. Sort of like early KING CRIMSON meets STRAWBS Ghost period.

Spring (71)

SPYS - United States
For the most part hard rock oriented, but there are times where STYX like images creep out. A bit like STARCASTLE meets JOURNEY.

Spys (82), Behind Enemy Lines (83)

SQUIRE, CHRIS - Great Britain
YES bassist goes solo in a 1975 release with some great sounding YES-like material.

Fish Out Of Water (75)

STANDARTE - Italy
Organ and Mellotron soaked late sixties or early seventies sounding heavy psychedelic progressive rock in the style of DEEP PURPLE and some of the German bands like GROBSCHNITT or WALLENSTEIN. Not overly complex but good.

Standarte (94), Curses and Invocations (97), Stimmung (98)

STARCASTLE - United States
They borrowed from the YES school of progressive rock and as a result the similarities are obvious. The more they recorded, the more they seemed to bow to the pressure of the record company to streamline their music. Their later albums are pretty ordinary.

Starcastle (76), Fountains of Light (77), Citadel (77), Real to Reel (78)

STEALING THE FIRE - Great Britain
This hot new band seems to have everything in order as they create some sizzling symphonic prog that is full of great guitar and keyboard playing all topped with some excellent female vocals. The music is complex, full of time and tempo changes and features a combination of long and short songs including a 17 minute majestic finale.

Hot Ice and Wonderous Strange Snow (99)

STEENSLAND, SIMON - Sweden
If you enjoy the Zeuhl sub genre this is for you. Elements of MAGMA, UNIVERS ZERO and SAMLA MAMMAS MANNA abound

Led Circus (99)

STEIDL, BERND - Germany 1990's
Great acoustic guitar-driven prog. Similar to GORDON GILTRAP or PAUL BRETT.

STEP AHEAD - France
Superbly composed, constructed, recorded and mixed. Chris Robin, is the author of this albums music and lyrics is the leader of this formation. Formed by five musicians including the exceptional Irish singer, Danny Brown. Sound like - GENESIS, MARILLION, YES.

Step Ahead (81)

STERN MEISSEN - Germany
Originally known as Stern-Combo-Meissen, they are universally acclaimed as East Germany's greatest progressive rock band. A keyboard oriented sound with a grand orchestral sweep.

Weisses Gold (78), Weisses Gold (78), Der Werte Weg (79), Reise Zum Mittelpunkt des Menschen (81), Stundenschlag (82), Trufrisch (85),

STILL - United States
Former ECHOLYN members Brett Kull, Ray Weston and Paul Ramsey's new guitar oriented, harder edged outfit. There are still moments where the Echolyn sound surfaces but the guitars dominate.

Always Almost (97)

STILL LIFE - Great Britain
Organ drenched progressive rock.

Still Life (70)

STOLT, ROINE - Sweden
The solo work from KAIPA'S guitarist focuses on a symphonic prog sound with long tracks featuring Mellotron. Highly produced material on a grand scale in the style of the best seventies or eighties progressive rock. Sounds like STEVE HOWE, Robert Fripp, JON ANDERSON. See FLOWER KINGS

The Lonely Heartbeat (89), Fantasia ( ), The Flower King (94), Hydrophonia (98)

STORMKRO - United States
Vocal-oriented material that is reminiscent of STYX circa Man of Miracles and The Serpent is Rising. Good song writing and solid musicianship combine with an even stronger progressive rock emphasis to deliver the goods.

Some Odd Years (96)

STRANGE ADVANCE - Canada
They loved the Mellotron and it shows on their first two releases. The music is predominantly pop but has it's moments.

Worlds Away (82), 2wo (85), The Distance Between (88)

STRANGE DAYS - Great Britain
Their music encompassed elements of folk, rock, pop and classical. Their one album included some intelligent pop but also included a number of multi-part pieces that will bring to mind the Ghosts period of STRAWBS.

Nine Parts to the Wind (75)

STRANGERS ON A TRAIN - Great Britain
CLIVE NOLAN of PENDRAGON is involved in this group who released the concept work The Key. Part 1 features progressive rock with no drummer as the rhythmic drive here is provided by the interplay between keyboards and guitars. Vocalist Tracy Hitchings (QUASAR) is great. Part 2 not only includes a drummer but is musically fuller in every respect.

The Key Part 1: The Prophecy (90), The Key Part 2: The Labyrinth (93),

STRATOVARIUS - Finland
A heavier band with progressive touches in the same vein a DREAM THEATRE. Good arrangements with choir and orchestra on some tracks, however the rapid tempo of many of the songs may not appeal to all ears.

Fourth Dimension ( ),Episode (96),Visions (97)

STRAWBS - Great Britain

Strawbs came out of the folk circuit in Great Britain headed by David Cousins who with the addition of some others, notably RICK WAKEMAN, made the leap to a more progressive rock oriented sound. By the time of Grave New World they were creating masterpieces of Mellotron laced material. The shorter pieces were always there, but there were plenty of the longer epics.

Antiques and Curious (70),From the Witchwood (71),Grave New World (72),Bursting At the Seams (73),Hero and Heroine (74),Ghosts (75),Nomadness (75),Deep Cuts (76),Burning For You (77),Deadlines (78),Don't Say Goodbye (87), Heartbreak Hill (95)

STREETMARK - Germany

Part of the German progressive rock movement that incorporated a hint of jazz and lots of spacey music. Most of these influences were incorporated in some more refined songs. There isn't the same amount of musical meandering with STREETMARK.

Nordland (75),Eileen (78),Dry (79),Sky Racer (81)

STRICTLY INC. - Great Britain

New solo project from TONY BANKS. Musically it comes from the same style as The Fugitive and Still. The closing seventeen minute track is one of his best compositions.

Strictly Inc. (96)

STROMBOLI - Czechoslovakia

Guitarist Michael Pavlicek and company produced two highly regarded symphonic prog releases with a slight Zeuhl influence. Both releases focus on strong melodies and ambitious arrangements. If you like SYNKOPY or COLLEGIUM MUSICUM you'll enjoy this.

Stromboli (87),Shutdown (89)

ST. ELMO'S FIRE - United States

Long-lost band from the late seventies whose style is firmly in the symphonic prog category. Lots of keyboards including Moogs and Mellotron in compositions that were complex with elaborate arrangments.

Splitting Ions in The Ether (80/98)

ST. TROPEZ - Italy

Ex-CELESTE but more of a Canterbury influence. The music is space-rock but perhaps not as intense as GONG.

Icarus [77-78] (78)

STYX - United States

Most critics labelled Styx as America's response to the British progressive rock movement. While this may or may not be the case, they did create some fine music in their early days. The music was complicated, symphonic at times featuring lots of keyboard and guitar interplay. Their later material seemed to have run out of good ideas and it all started to sound the same.

Styx I (72), Styx II (73),The Serpent is Rising (73), Man of Miracles (74), Equinox (75), Crystal Ball (76),The Grand Illusion (77), Pieces of Eight (78), Cornerstone (79), Paradise Theatre (80), Kilroy Was Here (83), Caught in the Act (84),Turn of the Century (92), Return to Paradise (97), Brave New World (99)

SUB - Germany

Heavy prog sound with great organ work. Part of the early German underground music scene their style incorporated elements of progressive and psychedelic rock and a good dose of straight ahead blues rock.

In Concert (70)

SUBJECT ESQ. - Germany
Pre-SAHARA heavy progressive rock material.

Subject ESQ (72)

SUGARLOAF - United States
Early seventies pioneer US prog band that produced the hit Green Eyed Lady. Worth a listen.

Sugarloaf (70),I Got a Song (73),Space Ship Earth (74),Don't Call Us, We'll Call You (75)

SUI GENERIS - Argentina
They combine an Italian style symphonic, a dash of jazz and South American folk with great results. Excellent Spanish vocals and intelligent lyrics (if you understand Spanish). Their first recording comes highly recommended for fans of South American prog. Some of their other material leans more to a pop oriented sound.

Pequenas Anedotas Sobre Las Instituciones (74),Confesiones. ( ),Vida ( ),Institucion ( )

SUMMER INDOORS - Great Britain
Modern up-tempo symphonic like later YES or IT BITES. While they don't wear their influences out in the open you'll hear a bit of PINK FLOYD and RUSH. Mainstream but not overly commercial.

Summer Indoors (91 TAPE),There's Orangie ( ),Songs in the Key of H (95)

SUN, THE - Japan 1990's
A four piece producing Instrumental material very much in the same vein as COLISEUM II.

SUNDOME AND THE NIGHT - Germany
Heavy progressive rock. This material is not overly complicated and somewhat dated in sound. Other influences include a bit of 'grunge' and some psychedelic.

In Lean Hours (93)

SUNTOWER - United States
Ameri-prog that has a lot in common with bands such as KANSAS or CRUCIBLE. The music is well orchestrated with a fair amount of guitar and keyboard work.

Suntower (98)

SUPERNOVA - Argentina
This trio from Argentina create a symphonic prog with a strong classical base. The compositions are mostly up-tempo. The instrumentation is somewhat sparse resulting at times in a somewhat acoustic chamber music effect.

Uno Punto Infinito (99)

SUPERSISTER - Holland
At their best they sound like CARAVAN or early SOFT MACHINE. The difference is the injection of wit and mirth. They had some of the best progressive rock keyboards of any band.

Present From Nancy (70),To the Highest Bidder (71),Pudding and Gistern (72),Iskander (73), Super Starshine 3 ( ),Sweet Okay (74)

SUPERTRAMP - Great Britain
Supertramp are really not in the same league as a YES or ELP but what they do, they do very well and there are many times, with the way they have incorporated different styles, namely jazz, that they shine as a symphonic progressive rock band. Admittedly there are also many times where they are somewhat pop oriented, but at least it's very good pop music.

Supertramp (70),Indelibly Stamped (71),Crime of the Century (74),Crises, What Crises? (75),Even in the Quietest Moments (77),Breakfast In America (79),Famous Last Words (82),Brother Where You Bound (85),Free As a Bird (87), Some Things Never Change (97)

SURPRISE - United States
Symphonic progressive rock from the St.

Louis area. sounds like CAMEL - Moonmadness and STARCASTLE and URIAH HEEP's Magician's Birthday.

Assault on Merryland (77)

SVANFRIDUR - Iceland
What's Hidden There? (72)

SYLVAN -
Fans of symphonic neo-progressive bands such as IQ and PENDRAGON will enjoy the music created here. The keyboards are thick, the guitars are soaring and the compositions are long with plenty of starts-and-stops, tempo changes and dynamics.

Deliverance (99)

SYMPHONIC SLAM - Canada
Timo Lane was one of the first to demonstrate what the guitar synthesiser was capable of sounding like. Somewhat bombastic pomp-prog rock.

Symphonic Slam (76), S.S. II (78)

SYMPHONY X - United States
New Jersey based progressive Metal band featuring well constructed and intelligent songs. They also create moving and majestic epics providing lots of room for instrumental virtuosity. Fans of DREAM THEATRE style prog will enjoy this. Their first two albums tend to be less symphonic.

Symphony X ( ), The Damnation Game ( ), The Divine Wings of Tragedy (96)

SYNDONE - Italy
Multi-layered symphonic keyboard sound. Not your typical neo-progressive rock sound as they're more like a cross between COLISEUM and ELP.

Spleen (92), Inca (93)

SYNKOPY - Czechoslovakia
Headed by Oldrich Vesely, this band played some of the more innovative symphonic progressive rock around. Vesely is from M.EFEKT and this album is not unlike their later period sound. Their last release turned out to be a real pop effort.

Slunecni Hodiny (81), Kridleni (83), Zrcadla (85)

SYNOPSIS - France
Carefully worked out and constructed compositions during which the keyboards and guitars are shown to advantage. Synopsis's talent and personality are particularly evident on their second album which includes some forceful, elegant and refined melodies. Sound like - ATOLL, MONA LISA.

Minuit Ville (79), Gamme (81)

10cc - Great Britain
Art Rock band with symphonic prog elements. Originally called HOTLEGS, 10cc are noted for their witty, intelligent and thought provoking lyrics and brilliant use of studio wizardry. Comprised of Graham Gouldman, Eric Stewart, Lol Creme and Kevin Godley. Lots of very clever, melodic pop tunes shrouded in prog musicianship. Gouldman was responsible for numerous hits in the sixties with bands like Herman's Hermits and the Yardbirds. Godley and Creme on splitting from 10cc pursued a short-lived music career before moving into video production. Musically 10cc's albums have many moments with unusual instrumentation and tempo changes to appeal to symphonic fans.

10cc (73), Sheet Music (74), The Original Soundtrack (75), How Dare You (76), Deceptive Bends (77), Live and Let Live (77), Bloody Tourists (78), Look Hear (80), Windows in the Jungle (83), Meanwhile ( ), Mirror Mirror (95)

2112 - Argentina
As you would imagine this prog band is very RUSH influenced. These guys are definitely from the heavier school of bands such as DREAM THEATRE, ASGARD and VIENNA.

Alternado las Divisiones (90), Intro (94)

T2 - Great Britain
Trio of guitar, bass and drums who make unexpectedly complex music for their bare bones line-up. Emphasis is on the heavy side. Their first album, It'll All Work Out In Boomland, contains the original version of No More White Horses that LANDBERK covered in their debut album.

It'll All Work Out in Boomland (70)

TABULA RASA - Finland
Melodic progressive rock in the vein of CAMEL.

Tabula Rasa (75), Ekkedien Tanssi (76)

TAI PHONG - France
This band produced a well constructed, symphonic music developing around the background of continuous keyboards sounds and elaborate, polished vocal harmonies. Tai Phong managed to create a music both accessible and striking without falling into the trap of affectation. Sound Like - YES.

Tai Phong (75), Windows (76), Last Flight (79)

TAKO - Yugoslavia
Symphonic progressive rock material with a hint of jazz, fusion and Floydian influences.

Tako (78), U Vreci Za Spavanje (80)

TALAMASCA - United States
Post HARLEQUIN MASS symphonic rock with female vocals.

Rights of Passage ( )

TALE - Great Britain
The music here will appeal to fans of neo-progressive rock and symphonic prog. As a concept album the compositions mostly resemble the work of ALAN PARSONS. Nothing overly adventurous, but enjoyable if you are in the right mood.

Elysium Fields (97)

TALE - Italy
Senza Frontiere ( )

TALE CUE - Italy
Dynamic symphonic prog sound with aggressive female vocals. You'll hear elements of GENESIS, FLOYD, CAMEL mixed together for a more MARILLION sound.

Voices Beyond My Curtain (91)

TALIESYN - Germany
This is a prog-metal band where the keyboards not only are heard but get a chance at some solo work as well. They also feature Jennifer Holzschneider who is more from the EARTH AND FIRE school of vocals. While there are lots of loud parts, there are many softer parts for contrast.

When Silence Will Be Unbearable (96)

TALISMA - Canada
Folk tinged prog from Quebec featuring a female vocalist sounding a bit like GROWING DREAM. On some of the longer tracks you'll hear hints of YES.

TAMARISK - Great Britain
Formed in 1982, and by the end of the year had recorded some material on cassette. A couple of members had come from the band CHEMICAL ALICE which had been creating mostly space rock material. Consisting of the traditional line-up of instruments they were together such a short time, but did manage to forge their own sound in the world of progressive rock.

Ascension EP (82 TAPE), Lost Properties (83 TAPE)

TANGERINE DREAM - Germany
Formed in 1967 as a rock band, they remained virtually unknown until the advent of the Moog synthesiser, which changed their whole musical focus. They are without question one of the founding electronic rock bands to come out of the

space-rock genre. Mostly longer compositions consisting almost entirely of various synthesisers. The music exhibited the droning endless looping elements of space-rock, their mid period tends to incorporate more rhythmic sequencer pieces, while their later work includes shorter song based material. Much like Italy's GOBLIN, Tangerine Dream's music lends itself to film soundtracks, most notably Sorcerer, Thief and Risky Business.

Electronic Meditation (70), Aplpha Centauri (71), Zeit (72), Atem (72), Phaedra (74), Rubycon (75), Ricochet (76), Stratosfear (76), Sorcerer (77), Cyclone (78), Force Majeure (78), Tangram (80), Thief (81), Exit (81), White Eagle (82), Logos (83), Hyperborea (83), Le Parc (85), Canyon Dreams (87), Melrose (90)

TANTRA - Portugal
Premier Portuguese prog band. Very strong complex music combining Italian symphonic and KING CRIMSON, YES and GENESIS influences.

Misterios e Maravilhas (77), Holocausto (78)

TARANIS - Spain
One LP of Celtic inspired progressive rock.

TARANTULA - Spain
Five piece Spanish outfit with a keyboard driven sound. While not overly complex the material is well written and arranged. Some material is of a heavier progressive style.

Tarantula 1 (76), Tarantula 2 (78)

TASAVALLAN PRESIDENTTI - Finland
More on the jazz rock side of things.

Tasavallan Presidentti (69), Lambertland (72), Milky Way Moses (74)

TAURUS - Holland
A symphonic group made up of members of well known Dutch bands KAYAK and VITESSE. Their style is a very classical one and also somewhat romantic in nature. Somewhat more on the lush side.

Illusions of Light (81), Tapes Live (83), Works ( ), See You Again Live ( )

TAURUS V - France
They play an energetic, forceful and aggressive progressive hard rock, inflamed by the singers vocals and propelled along by an iron-like rhythmic section. Sound like - ATOLL or MONA LISA.

Taurus V (80)

TEA - Switzerland
They create a wall of sound that pivots around the keyboards...technically faultless. Adventurous arrangements provide a good backdrop for their English vocalist. Longer songs with solid keyboards from Phillipe Kienholz who won runner-up to PATRICK MORAZ in a Swiss music poll.

Tea (75), The Ship (75), Tax Exile (76)

TEA FOR TWO - Germany
Neo-progressive rock in the style of IQ.

Dream or Reality (9?)

TEA IN THE SAHARA - Germany
Neo progressive rock with fantastic piano work. There is a mellow jazzy undercurrent through much of the mostly instrumental music. Lots of guitar and keyboard interplay with a good blend of some popier material and more complicated compositions.

Behind the Door (94), Boomerang (96)

TELLAH - Brazil
This trio plays complex material similar to PULSAR and ELOY onlynot as spacey, but

with a hint of Latin style on the softer pieces.

Continente Perdido (80)

TEMPANO - Venezuela

Their sound is best described as a softer, melodic symphonic progressive rock which hearkens back to the classic Italian prog bands such as PFM. Longer compositions with many developments and recurring themes. Their compositions incorporate some local ethnic flavour mixed with some well played jazz-styled interludes.

Atabal Yemal (79), Pesadilla Sin Final (82), En Reclamation (83), Seduccion Sublimina (84), Tempano (87), El Tercer Lado (89), Atabal Yemal (79/98), Childhoods End/El fin de la infancia (00)

TEMPEST - Great Britain

The group featured John Hiseman and Alan Holdsworth playing an erratic mixture of rock and jazz.

Tempest (73), Living in Fear (74)

TEN JINN - United States

Progressive rock similar to Saga in it's simplicity. Strong songs with lots of melody, solid musicianship and good arrangements. Their second release began to move the band in a more complex direction but still attempting to balance symphonic prog with a more accessible sound.

Wildman (97), As On a Darkling Plain (99)

TEN TON TIDE - United States

Dynamic prog with metal and hard rock overtones. Great vocals, powerful keyboards, strong arrangements and featuring Al Pitreli on guitar. Highlights include the many well crafted instrumental segments. Hints of RUSH and DREAM THEATRE.

Ten Ton Tide (95), Deluge EP (96 TAPE), Til Tomorrow's TodayEP (97)

TEMPUS FUGIT - Brazil

This is symphonic progressive rock, rich with melody and lush orchestrations. If you enjoy other South American prog bands this will be a welcome addition to your library.

The Dawn After the Storm (00)

TERPANDRE - France

A warm, rich and melodic group featuring dual keyboards, violin, guitar and an extremely tight rhythm section which creates a soaring, symphonic sound that mixes classical and rock to perfection. Lots of Mellotron.

Terpandre (78)

TERRA MYSTICA - Slovacia

A cornucopia of Euro, dance, Techno and yes, seventies progressive rock. It's hard to imagine trying to inject more influences than heard here, but while there are some 'dance-able' moments there are many more prog moments with a very modern flavour.

Carsica (97)

TERRACED GARDEN - Canada

Their sound hearkens back to the sharp, edgy and staccato days of KING CRIMSON. Structured guitar and keyboard epics in shorter compositions overlaid with soaring violin and great lyrics. The first release even includes some nice, well placed Mellotron.

Melody and Menace (82), Braille (84), Within (89)

TERRENO BALDIO - Brazil

A Brazilian GENTLE GIANT. Complicated musical composition and vocal arrangement. Their original LP released in 1976, was re-recorded in 1992 and changed slightly by three of the bands original members when the masters were lost.

Terreno Baldio (76), Terreno Baldio (92)

TERU'S SYMPHONIA - Japan
Ex-NOVELLA guitarist Terutsugu Hirayama creates his own style of powerful, lush symphonic progressive rock in the same vein as GERARD. These epic compositions are grand and sweeping in style with lots of dynamics and drama.

Clockworked Earth ( ), Symphonia ( ), The Human Race Party (89), Egg the Universe (88), Fable on the Seven Pillows (91), Do Androids Dream of Electric Camels (97), The Gate (99)

TESKA INDUSTRIJA - Yugoslavia
Heavier sounding progressive rock.

Teska Industrija (76), Ho-Ruk (76)

TESSERACT - United States
A five piece band from California consisting of violin, twin keyboards, bass and drums who create a mostly instrumental music spanning jazz influenced pieces to straight ahead symphonic prog. Not overly complicated arrangements but solid musicianship. Their influences range from early GENESIS to the classical composers.

Tesseract (97)

TESTA, STEFANO - Italy
Symphonic style.

Una Vita Una Balena E Altre Cose ( )

TETRAGON - Germany
Progressive sounds with that underground organ drenched feel.

Tetragon ( ), Nature (71)

THALASSA - France
A four piece group whose compositions are superb with complex developments, refined arrangements, great vocals and practised instrumental work. Sound like - MARILLION, IQ, PENDRAGON, PFM.

Suffer and Misery (82)

THEATRE - Italy
With influences ranging from British neo-prog to the classic Italian seventies sound, Threatre craftmusic that is rich with melody and instrumentation against a backdrop of stunning atmosphere. Anyone who likes MARILLION or IQ will love this band.

No More Rhymes But Mr. Brainstorm (93)

THEATRE - United States
Seattle based band formed in early eighties playing a lushly orchestrated and complex style of seventiesprogressive rock. Their music was uncommercial and has been described as fiercely progressive. Their live show featured face make-up and costume changes as well. Vocalist Steve Collins left the band in 1983 to record a solo rock opera entitled The Diary of a Faceless Man.

THIEVES' KITCHEN - Great Britain
Symphonic progressive rock and more. The more is a strong fusion element swirling around these long and involved compositions. The playing is brilliant, the arrangements top-notch. Lots of musical starts and stops, twists and turns everything progressive rock should be. Similar to the work of NATHAN MAHL.

Head (00)

THIRD DEGREE - United States
Neo-progressive rock sound with hints of RUSH. Overall the material in vocal based without long meandering instrumental breaks.

Human Interest Story (96)

THIRD PERKINS - Canada
New sounding progressive rock from the Province of Quebec. Never blatantly commercial, this band shows influences from KING CRIMSON, and PINK FLOYD. A combination of both long and short songs.

Singularity (9?)

THIRD QUADRANT - Great Britain
Neo-progressive rock in IQ or ABEL GANZ vein.

Layered (9?)

THOMAS, DAVID & RONNIE GUNN - Great Britain
A musical style born out of the same ear as early GENESIS. The CD release of The Giants Dance even contains liner notes from friends TONY BANKS and PETER GABRIEL. The use of piano, 12-string guitar and harmonium and woodwinds creates a very chamber-music sound. Fans of Trespass and Nursery Cryme should enjoy this.

The Giants Dance (96)

THOMAS, RAY - Great Britain
Vocalist from THE MOODY BLUES. Perhaps the most romantic and full of melody. Deeper voice than either Lodge or Hayward. Lots of orchestration on his solo effort.

From Mighty Oaks (75), Hopes, Wishes and Dreams (76)

THREAD - Great Britain
Solo project of TULL drummer Doane Perry. This up-beat pop influenced prog is very reminiscent of the EMERSON and ROBERT BERRY project 3. Good playing with some longer material to play in.

Thread (96)

THREE - Great Britain
After the reincarnated Emerson Lake & Powell failed to excite the right people, LAKE left or was kicked out but ultimately replaced by one ROBERT BARRY. He managed to write a certain top 40 sound into the material. A few of the numbers stand out. Fortunately KEITH EMERSON'S arrangements lend a certain sense of importance to the whole album.

To the Power of Three (88)

III MILENIO - Brazil
Similar to PINK FLOYD or RUSH. They produced a great concept CD. Their vocalist is in the style of David Surkamp or David Cousins, you'll either love him or hate him. But the addition of FABIO RIBEIRO on keyboards lends a real EMERSON/WAKEMAN feel to some of the material.

Aliance Dos Tempos:Ato 1:Tawan (90), Alianca Dos Tempos (93)

THRESHOLD - Great Britain
Prog-metal band with a decided neo-progressive sound.

Wounded Land (93), Psychedelicatessen ( ), Extinct Instinct (96), Clone (99)

THULE - Norway
A bit on the heavy side for a symphonic sound, not really neo-prog, they tend to defy description. You'll hear hints of ROGER WATERS, PINK FLOYD, RUSH and even Midnight Oil.

Ultima Thule (87), Natt (90), Frostbrent (93)

TIBET - Germany
Symphonic prog with twin keyboards including Mellotron and a mid-period GENESIS sound.

Tibet (79)

TIBBETTS, STEVE - United States
Minnesota guitarist Tibbetts produced a couple of very accomplished progressive rock releases based around his acoustic guitar work, analog synths and percussion. In the style of GORDON GILTRAP.

Steve Tibbetts (77), Yr (80), Northern Song (82), Safe Journey (84), Exploded View (86), Big Man Idea (89), The Fall of Us All (94)

TIEMKO - France
Powerful symphonic prog trio. Material is very well arranged and performed. You'll hear hints of KING CRIMSON and CLEARLIGHT SYMPHONY.

Espace Fini (89), Ocean (90), Parade (90), Clone (95)

TIDELINE - Belgium
Melodic laid-back art-rock that barely borders on progressive material. If you like Roxy Music, GODLEY AND CREME or TODD RUNDGREN you may like this.

The Crowded Room ( ),Siren Song (95)

TILES - United States
Detroit based four piece that create music that falls into the LEGER DE MAIN, RUSH or DREAM THEATRE category. Their second release was even mixed by Terry Brown, well known for his longtime association with RUSH. Musically they create some longer material with some fine instrumental virtuosity.

Tiles (95), Fence The Clear (97), Presents of Mind (99)

TIME BEING - United States
Not overly progressive rock oriented, but with just enough hints of early KANSAS to sound interesting. Keyboards take a back seat to the acoustic or electric guitars. There are some tricky time signatures to keep it interesting. If you are a fan of streamlined melodic prog for the AOR crowd you'll enjoy this.

Time Being (94)

TIMELOCK - Holland
Like RUSH or SAGA with a certain harder edge than most Dutch progressive bands. They used to go by the name LAST DETAIL.

Louise Brooks ( ),Dawn ( )

TIMESCAPE - Sweden
Prog metal from Sweden. Lots of guitar crunch, melody and keyboards are kept quite high in the mix.

Two Worlds (98)

TIMOTHY PURE - United States
Based in Atlanta, these guys are squarely in the neo-progressive rock category, though not showing any direct references. Great vocals and guitar in what's been described as generally dark overtones. There are elements of PINK FLOYD or PORCUPINE TREE without being derivative.

The Fabric of Betrayal (95), Blood of the Berry (97), Island of the Misfit Toys (99)

TIPOGRAPHICA - Japan
They create a very complex progressive music in the style of Zappa and HENRY COW with Canterbury elements. Lot's of musical twists and turns to please the more adventurous.

Tipographica (94), The Man Who Does Not Nod (95), God Say's I Can't Dance (96), Floating Opera (97)

TIRELLI, ARMANDO - Uruguay
Very traditional sounding symphonic, progressive rock with a distinct seventies Italian influence. The compositions have the same romantic feel while not as fully arranged.

El Profeta (78)

TISARIS - Brazil
Neo-progressive material with beautiful piano, violin and guitar. With hints of RUSH and YES, the band tips it's hat to the 1975 era GENESIS and PINK FLOYD as well. They sing in English and craft long instrumental sections.

What's Beyond (92),Once Humanity (95),The Power of Myth (9?)

TITUS GROAN - Great Britain
Early prog style with a heavy blues influence.

Titus Groan (70)

TNR - Italy
VDGG influenced band, especially a vocalist who sounds a lot like PETER HAMMILL.

The Cheeseboard (9?), Samsara (9?)

TOKYO - Germany
For the most part pretty ordinary sounding styled rock. There are moments where they shine with hints of STYX or SAGA.

Tokyo (81), Fasten Seat Belts (82)

TOMORROW'S GIFT - Germany
Early German progressive with female vocals.

Tomorrow's Gift (70), Goodbye Future (73)

TOP LEFT CORNER - Italy
Sensitive guitar playing and massive keyboards create a musical style with hints of ASGARD and IQ. Uncomplicated melodic rock with symphonic embellishments.

Mystery Book (96)

TOPO - Spain
Heavy prog with Spanish vocals.

Topo (79)

TOPOS URANOS - Brazil
Dramatic, keyboard heavy prog similar to BLEZQI ZATSAZ.

Suite Mistica (8?)

TOUCH - United States
A band from Portland Oregon created a very early style with a hint of progressive rock in the way they incorporate some classics and a bit of jazz. Some nice Mellotron.

Touch (69)

TOWER - Italy
ARTI'S keyboardist Beppe Crovella plus a vocalist and drummer create music that is quite similar to ROMANTIC WARRIORS except a bit more GENESIS flavour mixed in with the neo-prog tone.

Tales From a Book of Yesterday (94)

TOWNSCREAM - Hungary
Townscream capture the essence of seventies style progressive rock and turn it out in their own unique nineties fashion. A trio line-up featuring bass, keyboards and drums, their sound is at once reminiscent of ELP and PFM without really sounding like either band.

Nagyvarosi Ikonok (97)

TRACE - Holland
Rick Vanderlinden of EKSEPTION creates his own band and does what he does best, play keyboards. Keyboard oriented with a blend of classical, electronic and rock. Symphonic progressive rock at it's finest. In a compositional structure style reminiscent of FOCUS' Eruption or Hamburger Concerto.

Trace (74), Birds (75), The White Ladies (76)

TRACTOR - Great Britain
One of the group of early British prog bands in the style of CRESSIDA, GRACIOUS and BEGGARS OPERA.

Tractor (72),

TRAMA - Italy
Their sound mixes the classic Italian symphonic prog style with a dash of arena rock. Lots of great playing with a strong guitar and keyboard presence. A superb female vocalist lends unique qualities to their overall style.

Prodromi Di Finzioni Sovrapposte (99)

TRANQUILITY - Great Britain
They toured with YES on one of the early tours. A sound similar to STARCASTLE, only less complicated compositions.

Tranquility (72), Silver (72)

TRANSATLANTIC - ?
The concept of symphonic progressive rock supergroup is taken up a notch with the combined talents of Roine Stolt (FLOWER KINGS), Neal Morse (SPOCK'S BEARD), Mike Portnoy (DREAM THEATRE) and Pete Trewavas (MARILLION) and the album works in every way. Long compositions with plenty of starts and stops, changing time signatures, hummable melodies, great musicianship, Mellotron and on, and on! If a friend asks what's happening in the world of progressive rock...give them this CD.

SMPTe (00)

TRANSIENCE - United States
LANDS END keyboardist Fred Hunter's solo project ended up incorporating not only his band mates but also a few guests. This is very much like LANDS END although it tends to sound a little more subdued and moody.

Sliding (99)

TREM DO FUTURO - Brazil
Although they're a new band their influences clearly lie in the seventies Italian prog era. A six piece group with a style rooted in the classical progressive rock era but with a big helping of folk elements. Solid melodies and good arrangements give their music a strong Italian influence.

Trem Do Futuro (95)

TREPONEM PAL - France
Another facet of French symphonic rock. The group shows a great fondness for rich vocal harmonies, beautiful, immediate melodies and complex instrumental passages.

Treponem Pal (77)

TRES DE UN PAR - Mexico
This trio produced a symphonic prog that is very much in the style of CAMEL.

En Vivo (96)

TRESPASS - Holland
Their music is in the same vein as GROBSCHNITT with elements of early GENESIS as well.

The Final Act (90)

TRETTIOARIGA KRIGET - Sweden
Heavy, complex, guitar dominated progressive material that puts you in the mind of RUSH in the eighties.

Krissang (75)

TRIANA - Spain
Symphonic progressive flamenco legends. The vocals are in Spanish with the music featuring a powerful synth/Mellotron sound.

Triana (75), El Patio (76), Hyos Del Agobio (77), Sombre Y Luz (79), Un Encuentro (80), Triana (81), Llego el Dia (82), En Directo [Live] (89)

TRIANGLE - France
One of the first French groups to have foretold the arrival of the rock movement in France in the early seventies. Initially formed by three old hands on the French musical scene, the group suffered the departure of their first guitarist, Alain Renaud, after they recorded their debut single. They did not find their bearings again until the renowned jazz musician Francois Jeanneau and the guitarist Mimi Lorenzini joined them. Triangle offered a rock drifting between slightly progressive rock and more commercial sound destined to appeal to the masses.

Triangle (70), Triangle (72), Homonymede (73)

TRIADE - Italy
Italian trio whose music is similar to LE ORME and ELP.

1998: La Storia Di Sabazio (73)

TRIBE OF CRO - Belgium
Hailed as one of the better practitioners of the current crop of space-rockers. Everything comes together with the right blend of influences from HAWKWIND to OZRICs.

Hydroculture (98)

TRIBUTE - Sweden
Definitive instrumental symphonic prog rock masters in Sweden. Fans of ISKANDER or ISILDUR'S BANE will like this band.

New Views (84), Breaking Barriers (86), Live: The Melody, The Beat, The Heart (87), Terra Incognita (90),

TRILLION - United States
Long instrumental passages give this band the distinction of falling into the progressive rock category. Sounds like STYX or STARCASTLE with a bit of JOURNEY thrown in.

Trillion (78), Clear Approach (80)

TRILOGY - Great Britain
Likened to RUSH and ELP, Trilogy came together in late 1982. A mixture a driving guitar and colourful keyboard textures give their sound a unique quality allowing them to rock hard and at other times explore the more pastoral side of progressive rock.

3 Cut EP (84 TAPE),

TRILOGY - Germany
Twin keyboard dominated instrumental symphonic progressive rock. Try to imagine FINCH with a second keyboard or an instrumental ANYONE'S DAUGHTER.

Here It Is (80),

TRINIDADE - Brazil
Obscure work from violinist MARCUS VIANA.

Trindade ( )

TRIP, THE - Italy
ELP-ish although not in terms of technique. The vocals are vaguely reminiscent of JON ANDERSON.

The Trip (70), Caronte (71), Atlantide (72), Time of Change (73)

TRIPOD - United States
This trio employs no guitars and no keyboards, but with their instrumentation of woodwinds, bass and drums they create a hard-edged progressive rock that is decidedly RIO in nature. Lots of angular moments.

Tripod (99)

TRISTAN, ALAIN - France
Former keyboardist with TAURUS V, Alain Tristan recorded a solo album on which he offers a slightly progressive rock, pleasantly sung in French with a certain vocal sophistication. The instrumentation is efficient and forceful. This music is in the same vein as TAURUS V, but with a lesser hard rock influence.

Alain Tristan (82)

TRISTAN PARK - United States
Neo-progressive rock that is not overly complex but is guitar driven similar to IT BITES or SAGA, however their later material, post 1997 tends to get much more involved incorporating complex concept pieces and stronger arrangements.

At the End of the Day (93), A Place Inside

(95), Looking Homeward (97), Leave To Enter (97)

TRITON – Japan 1990's
Keyboard trio with ton's of keyboards. One of the keyboardists doubles on violin as well. Influences include ELP and UK, only performed in a somewhat heavier style.

TRITONUS - Germany
A three piece band that borrows heavily from the EMERSON LAKE & PALMER school of progressive rock. Good keyboard work with lots of Mellotron.

Tritonus (75), Between the Universe (76)

TRIUMVIRAT - Germany
If you didn't know better you would think KEITH EMERSON guested here. Great band with wonderful albums. Soaring music with well placed crescendos. Their vocalist has a plaintive emotional quality, yet retains strength to deliver the more aggressive passages.

Mediterranean Tales (72), Illusions on a Double Dimple (73), Spartacus (75), Old Loves Die Hard (76), Pompeii (77), A La Carte (78), Russian Roulette (80)

TROYA - Germany
Their sound is like early NOVALIS.

Point of Eruption ( )

TRUE MYTH - Canada
Their first album is a classic that sounds similar to YES. One of the first digitally recorded LPs with longer songs featuring strong musicianship in the longer instrumental sections. Strong guitar work with lots of keyboards including Mellotron. Their second is a complete waste of talent.

True Myth (79), Telegram (81)

TRUTH IN ADVERTISEMENT - Unites States
Their musical style is very reminiscent of more recent CAMEL with it's long atmospheric elements overlaid with guitar soloing. Their first effort shows the rough edges of home production.

Balance (96)

TSS - Germany
High powered progressive rock with good arrangements and fine keyboard work.

TSUNAMI - Holland
Dutch five piece which sounds like MARILLION.

Anthem of the Great Wave (92)

TUNEFISH - Germany
Band fronted by former keyboardist and drummer from ANYONE'S DAUGHTER. This band picks up where they left off, with excellent keyboard/guitar interplay and beautiful female voice on some tracks.

Guitar Poetry (8?)

TWELFTH NIGHT - Great Britain
Described elsewhere in this work as 'punkfloyd'. Twelfth Night were one of the main bands involved in the eighties resurgence of progressive rock. Their style was always one that borrowed on the concept of what had gone before but solidly updated it to the present. Long songs...short songs it really made no difference they packed as much music as possible in the time they had.

Live At the Target (81), Fact and Fiction (82), Art and Illusion (84), Live and Let Live (84), Twelfth Night (86)

TWENTY SIXTY SIX AND THEN - Germany
Heavy early style prog with lots of guitar and organ. Similar to fellow countrymen SATIN WHALE and RAMSES. Their 1991 and 1994 releases feature remixes and unreleased tracks from the seventies.

Reflections on the Future (72), Reflections on the Past (91), Reflections [remix] (94)

TWICE BITTEN - Great Britain
Duo consisting of a variety of instruments but no drums or keyboards. They released a couple of cassettes in the mid eighties showing influences of early GENESIS and some of the acoustic side of ELP.

TWIN AGE - Sweden
A mixture of old and new influences featuring slower tempo material with lot's of Mellotron. Acoustic guitar like early GENESIS, keyboard work like KAYAK, electric guitar like IQ and a vocalist who sounds like IT BITES. If you're into early GENESIS, you'll probably like this.

Month of the Year (96), Lialim High (97)

TYBURN TALL -Germany
Organ drenched early styled heavy prog with great guitar. Some longer songs with simple arrangements. Similar at times to SATIN WHALE.

Tyburn Tall (72)

UBERFALL - Germany
German prog-Rock with touches of SBB and SFF.

So uferlos im Abendwind (9?)

UK - Great Britain
Much too short lived, featuring progressive rock notables, BILL BRUFORD, EDDIE JOBSON, JOHN WETTON and others. They challenged all the critics by bucking the trend and created imaginative, intelligent, boundary stretching progressive rock. Inventive rhythms, shifting textures and tempos and moving melodies. UK were one of the premier bands of the late seventies and helped form the bridge to the progressive bands of the eighties

UK (78), Danger Money (79), Night After Night (79)

ULYSSES - Germany
Neo-progressive rock like IQ, JADIS. Some of their material features TRACY HITCHINGS on vocals. Lots of atmosphere, good musicianship and solid arrangements.

Neronia (93)

UNDER THE BIG TREE - United States
Melodic progressive rock with a slight symphonic approach from former members of EPISODE and NOW. Their material also contains elements of out-right jamming with a bit of psychedalia thrown in. You'll hear slight influences from such bands as MOODY BLUES and It's A Beautiful Day.

Under The Big Tree (98)

UNDER THE SUN - United States
This is a four piece group strong on harmonies and texture that hearkens back to The Yes Album. It's described as powerful progressive music that will appeal to fans of YES, GENESIS, KANSAS and DREAM THEATRE. Of note is that their first album was mixed by Terry Brown

Under The Sun (99)

UNDERGROUND RAILROAD - United States
Their music is a mixture of the classic symphonic prog of the seventies combined with all the modern techniques, instruments and production. Long, epic scale compositions full of drama and musical gymnastics.

Through and Through (00)

UNDERGROUND ZERO - Great Britain
They come from the PINK FLOYD, Hawkwind/AMON DUUL II school, with a bit of spacey keyboards thrown in.

Complete with a female vocalist who sound at times Sonja Kristina and at other times sings like Ozzy Osbourne. The music is pretty aggressive most of the time, not overly complex but composed with some good riffs.

Never Reach the Stars (84)

UNDERWATER TRAFFIC - United States

An interesting mixture of progressive rock influences ranging from RUSH, YES, DIXIE DREGS, to CRACK THE SKY.

Return to the Deep (98)

UNICORN - Sweden

Melodic symphonic material with a definite YES influence and hints of KAYAK or ABEL GANZ.

Ever Since (93), Emotional Wasteland ( )

UNIFIED PAST - United States

The music here is heavy and features more than its share of prog-metal influences. However fans of symphonic prog with an aggressive edge may enjoy Unified Pst. There are a number of tracks with plenty of keyboards and melody rising to the surface.

From the Splintered Present Surfaces (99)

UNIVERS ZERO - Belgium

Elements of progressive rock along the lines of MAGMA and KING CRIMSON with a dark and gothic chamber music style. They started out with more of an acoustic sound (violin, viola, cello, bassoon, spinet etc.) but then moved quickly into a sinister style with traditional instrumentation.

1313 (77), Heresie (79), Ceux du Dehors (80), Crawling Wind (83), Uzed (84), Heatwave (87), The Hard Quest (99)

UNIVERSAL TOTEM ORCHESTRA - Italy

A mixture of all things RIO. You'll hear everything from symphonic sections to MAGMA inspired arrangements. Lots of aggressive guitar bits and more than enough twists and turns. If you like your music to be on the challenging side this Is for you.

Rituale Alieno (99)

UNIVERSE - United States

This symphonic prog band hails from California.

Universe (77)

UNO - Italy

Another great OSANNA progressive offshoot, with a mellow classical rock style.

Uno (74)

URIAH HEEP - Great Britain

Progressive rock with a metal touch to it. They perhaps more than most bands helped create the heavy metal sound whenever they weren't doing their glam-rock thing. But in amongst all that their early albums contained some interesting and for it's time, inventive material. Nice organ/keyboard work especially on the earlier releases like Salisbury and Demons and Wizards. Not overly challenging but enjoyable.

Salisbury (71), Demons and Wizards (72), Magicians Birthday (72),

UTOPIA, TODD RUNDGREN'S - United States

One of the finest pop musicians around proved when he wanted to, progressive rock was not above him. Some fine melodies woven together by scorching guitar and layers of keyboard work.

Todd Rundgren's Utopia (74), Another Live (76), Ra (77), Oops Wrong Planet

(77),Adventures in Utopia (80),Deface the music (81)

UTOPIAN FIELD - Norway
FLOYD/CAMEL inspired group.

Utopian Fields (89), White Pigeon, You Clean (90)

VAIL- United States
They used to go by the name System. Wall of sound, classical keyboard themes and splashy percussives.

Time Tales (88)

VALERIANA - France
After Introversion broke up in 1975 and before he joined ANGE, Claude Demet recorded a single. On this record, he only plays piano and sings the vocal parts with guitarist Robert Bertella. They present a rudimentary and less exquisite version of French progressive rock. Sound Like - ANGE or ATOLL.

Sans/Fin SP (76)

VALINOR'S TREE - Sweden
Fans of IQ, PENDRAGON and GALAHAD will appreciate the compositional style of Valinor's Tree. Lots of melody and interesting arrangements are packed into the symphonic neo-progressive sound.

Kingdom of Sadness (98)

VAN BOGAERT, FRANK - Belgium
A symphonic prog style that is light on rock and more heavy on softer ambient influences. Not overly complicated but full of pleasant sonic moods.

Colours (98)

VAN DER GRAAF GENERATOR - Great Britain
Troubled by shifting personnel they never really won the popular acclaim that YES or KING CRIMSON did. Yet in their own way they were just as creative. Good Guitar and keyboard work combined with PETER HAMMILL'S mythological or science fictiony lyrics. Easily recommended for fans of GENTLE GIANT, or even GENESIS.

Aerosol Grey Machine (68), The Least We Can Do is Wave (69), H to HE Who am the Only One (70), Pawn Hearts (71), Godbluff (75), Still Life (76), World Record (76), The Quiet Zone (77), Vital Live (78), Repeat Performance (80), Time Vaults (82),

VANDALOR - Holland
A progressive rock style that incorporates other contemporary influences such as alternative, spacerock and yes classical. The compositions are shorter but the arrangements lend themselves to the prog classification by virtue of their means in which they were put together.

Greetings From Europe [EP] (00)

VANGELIS - Greece
Vangelis is included here because of his wonderful concept albums that of course use synths, but more than that percussion and various other instruments. He was part of APHRODITE'S CHILD and was rumoured to be the replacement for WAKEMAN in YES. That never did happen but his soundscapes have been with us since.

Earth (73), Apocalypse des Animaux (73), Ignacio (75), Heaven and Hell (75), Albedo 0.39 (76), Spiral (77), Beaubourg (78), China (79), Opera Sauvage (79), See You Later (80), Chariots Of Fire (81), Antarctica (83), Soil Festivities (84), Mask (85),

VENT D'EST - France
Melodic rock with a touch of progressive rock and an inspiration coming from the Anglo-prog school. A unique album featuring elaborate themes, pleasant melodies, with carefully worked out instrumental pieces and a polished vocal style. Sound like - BJH, CAMEL.

Vent d'est (80)

VERDAGUER - Brazil
Their style is more jazz-rock with a small dose of symphonic and flamenco influences. The material features constant changes from melodic to more complex. Somewhat similar to CRUCIS at times.

Humahuaca (94)

VERMILLION SANDS - Japan
Beautiful RENAISSANCE influenced prog rock. A symphonic sound with a strong folk rock influence.

Water Blue (88)

VERSAILLES - France
A harder edged, powerful symphonic based rock with a very French feel, dramatic and emotional. Their sound is reminiscent of ANGE or ELIXIR. In fact they put their musical skills to the test in backing up vocalist Dominique Le Guennec on the 1998 MONA LISA release.

Le Cathedrale Du Temps (90), Don Giovanni (92), Le Tresor De Valliesres (94), Blaise Et Benjamin (98)

VERITAGE - France 1980's
Similar sound to the eighties English neo-prog bands.

VERSUS X - Germany
Heavy symphonic progressive rock with a gothic touch. The music is primarily instrumental with many quiet introspective sections opening up to grander flourishes, interlaced with intricate rhythms and instrumental interplay. Should appeal to fans of ELP and VDGG.

Versus X (94), Disturbance (97)

VESANIA - Brazil
This four piece create music that is complex, intense and full of dynamics. Solid musicianship creates a nice interplay between the scorching guitar, thundering bass and drumming all backed by a solid wall of keyboards.

Vesania (99)

VIA LUMINI - Brazil
From Sao Paulo, their sound is an original blend of accessible early progressive, neo-prog and light-jazz rock. Sound similar to III MILENIO or LOCH NESS.

Voos e Sonhos (91), What Have We Done About Us (95)

VIANA, MARCUS - Brazil
He was the violinist with the symphonic prog-pop band Coracao Da Terra and SAGRADO and his material is in the same style.

Pantanal [Suite Sinfonica] (92), Trilhas & Temas (92), Idade da Loba ( ), Fantasia de Natal ( ), Cancoes Do Eden ( )

VIDALES, ALPHONSO - Mexico
Keyboardist from CAST performing symphonic prog and what might be termed 'edgier' new age material. If you enjoy listening to CAST you'll certainly enjoy what hear here.

Entre Dos Paredes (95), Clavico (98)

VIENNA - Japan
Symphonic neo-progressive rock band who create music in a similar style to GERARD.

Overture (88), Step Into (88), progress Live (89)

VIGILANCE - Germany
Predominantly harder edged prog metal that is still very melodic with lots of changing time signatures.

Behind the Mask (96)

VINCENT, DAVID - Switzerland
Well excecuted RIO with a strong Zappa influence. If THINKING PLAGUE and

SAMLA MAMMAS MANNA is your cup of tea, listen to this.

No Entiendo (99)

VINCENT, JEAN-CLAUDE - France

Jean-Claude Vincent, alias Jean Claude Pognant, creator of Crypto Records, gave in to the temptation of recording an album accompanied by the best musicians of his label. He wrote the lyrics but the music and arrangements are the work of Christian Decamps which explains why a certain ANGE influence emanates from this album.

Lettre au Passe (77)

VIOLET DISTRICT - Germany

Neo prog sound similar to MARILLION, JADIS or PENDRAGON, but perhaps lighter in overall texture.

Terminal Breath (92)

VIOLETA DE OUTONO - Brazil

Traditional line-up of instruments is augmented with sitar and analog Mini-moog.

Violeta De Outono ( ),Em Toda Parte (89),Eclipse ( )

VIRUS - Germany

Their music perhaps bore more a resemblance to the earlier underground music from which it grew. A heavy sound with lots of organ, perhaps a little DEEP PURPLE-ish.

Thoughts (71),Revelation (71)

VISIBLE WIND - Canada

Music very much in the style of MARILLION. Four recorded releases with the third being a little more guitar oriented than the first two. They've carved out their own sound but if you listen carefully you'll hear bits of SAGA, RUSH and MARILLION. With the release of Narcissus Goes to the Moon, the band has created their most proggy release featuring lots of Mellotron, long-ish compositions full of brilliant guitar and atmosphere.

Catharsis (88), A Moment Beyond Time (91), Emergence (94), Narcissus Goes to the Moon (97)

VITALE, LITO - Argentina

Keyboardist from Argentina produces powerful symphonic progressive rock. Formerly of the band MIA his solo work embodies the best of their symphonic period.

Sobre Miedos, Creencias y Supersticiones (81),En Solitario (91), Pantallas ( )

VITA NOVA - Austria

Legendary progressive sound in the same vein as PATERNOSTER. The early style incorporates many of the analog keyboard sounds of the day with both rock and classical influences with a hint of the psychedelia of the times.

Vita Nova (72)

VOICE - Germany

Neo-prog band.

Welcome (8?)

VOLARE - United States

From Athens, Georgia this Canterburian influenced instrumental outfit features the keyboard work of Patrick Strawser which is a cross of TONY BANKS and Dave Stewart. Overall their sound is a mixture of NATIONAL HEALTH and HAPPY THE MAN.

Volare (96),The Uncertainty Principle (97), Memoirs… (99)

VON ZAMLA - Sweden

They arose out of the ashes of SAMLA MAMMAS MANNA and carried on the quirky musical fare to yet another level. This is distinctly in the Zeuhl school. If you enjoy your prog with an angular dissonant edge ala UNIVERSE ZERO this is for you.

1983 (99)

VOX DEI - Argentina
Heavy rock with progressive influence.

La Biblia (81), Cuero, Caliente ( )

VULGAR UNICORN - Great Britain
A British three-piece assisted by over a dozen session players who produce a spacey progressive rock showing influences of HAWKWIND and GENESIS etc.

Under the Umbrella (95), Sleep With the Fishes (97), Jet Set radio (99)

WAITE, MICHAEL - Canada
A strange mixture of progressive and psychedelic rock.

Cosmic Wave (83)

WAKEMAN, RICK - Great Britain
His work with THE STRAWBS, YES and as a solo artist is legendary. Taking the brunt of critics abuse Rick has forged ahead blending his classical training in a world of rock music, creating breathtaking epics. Along with KEITH EMERSON, Rick is probably the most well known keyboardist in the world of progressive rock music and together they created the prog keyboard ethic.

Six Wives of Henry the VIII (73), Journey to the Centre of the Earth (74), Myths and Legends of King Arthur and the Knights of the Round Table (75), Lisztomania (75), No Earthly Connection (76), White Rock (76), Criminal Record (77), Rhapsodies (79), 1984 (81), Rock n Roll Prophet (82), The Burning (82), G'ole (82), The Cost of Living (83), Silent Nights (85), Live at the Hammersmith (85), Beyond the Planets (85), Country Airs (86), Crimes of Passion (86), The Gospels (87), The Family Album (87), A Suite of Gods (87), Time Machine (88), Zodiaque (88), Sea Airs (89), In the Beginning (90), Night Airs (91), Black Knights at the Court of Ferdinand IV (91), Phantom Power (91), Aspirant Sunset (91), Aspirant Sunrise (91), Aspirant Shadows (91), Suntrilogy (91), Soft Sword (91), 2000 AD in the Future (91), African Bach (91), The Private Collection (91), The Classical Connection (93), The Heritage Suite (93), Wakeman with Wakeman (93), Prayers (93), No Expense Spared (93), Wakeman with Wakeman Live, The Official Bootleg (94), Live on the Test (94), Almost Live in Europe (95), The Seven Wonders of the World (96), Return to the Centre of the Earth (99)

WALKING ON ICE - Great Britain
Neo-progressive rock with a strong pop flavour. Some good instrumental sections and a slight TWELFTH NIGHT influence.

No Margin for Error (94)

WALLENSTEIN - Switzerland
Their early material is classic symphonic progressive rock. The right blend of keyboard antics with guitar theatrics. Changing tempos, moving melodies and soaring dynamics all add up to some fine work. Their later work took on more of a disco beat, but their originality continued to surface from time to time.

Lunatics (71), Blitzkrieg (71), Mother Universe (72), Cosmic Century (73), Songs, Stories and Symphonies (74), No More Love (77), Charlene (78), Blue Eyed Boys (79), Fraulines (80), Ssss...top (81)

WALLY - Great Britain
Keyboard band of the softer kind sounding a bit like BARCLAY JAMES HARVEST. Their first album had the aid of RICK WAKEMAN on production and string arrangements.

Wally (74), Wally Gardens (75)

WALPURGIS - Germany
Early prog featuring the keyboardist from WALLENSTEIN.

Queen of Saba (72)

WANKA - Canada
Obscure band in the same vein as NIEL MERRYWEATHER or early Max Webster. Offbeat with lots of theatrics and some great playing. One known LP with a couple of songs over 7 minutes one sounding a bit like Meddle PINK FLOYD and the other a bit like ANGE.

The Orange Album (77)

WAPASSOU - France
A different aspect of French symphonic progressive rock far removed from traditional trends and playing with an uncommon formation (keyboards/guitar/violin), Wapassou created a very lyrical, very beautiful progressive music with an ethereal and floating atmosphere. Their style was very classical, not spacey.

Wapassou (74), Messe en Re Mineur (76), Salammbo (77), Ludwig (78), Genuine (80)

WAPPA GAPPA - Japan
Symphonic progressive rock in a similar style to RENAISSANCE or PROVIDENCE. Their music features a very smooth female vocalist and some well integrated keyboard and guitar interplay.

Wappa Gappa (96), A Myth (98)

WATCH, THE - Italy
see: THE NIGHT WATCH

WATERLOO - Belgium
Early prog style incorporating Hammond and flute. Musically they incorporate many of the musical motifs of the day including blues and psychadelic although the keyboards give the band the distinct proggy feel. If you enjoy listening to early JETHRO TULL or BLODWYN PIG this is right up your alley.

First Battle (69)

WATERS, ROGER - Great Britain
Former lead vocalist, bassist and lyricist for PINK FLOYD out on his own adventures, creating some mind blowing progressive rock in the same mould as FLOYD. Concept albums full of great musicianship, sound effects and thought provoking lyrics.

Pros & Cons of Hitchhiking (84), When the Wind Blows (86), Radio Kaos (87),

WATKINS, KIT - United States
Formerly of HAPPY THE MAN, Watkins did time in CAMEL for a while and found the time to release his solo material. While the first one is more a departure from progressive rock, the second and particularly the third once again showcase his keyboard playing. He's since gone on to record many others, some more ambient experiments while others more electronic.

Labyrinth (81), Frames of Mind (82), In Time (85), Azure (89), Sunstruck (90), Early Solo Works (90), Thought Tones, Volume 1 (90), A Different View (91), Thought Tones Volume 2 (92), Wet Dark and Low (92), Kinetic Vapors (93), Circle (94), Holographic Tapestries (95), Beauty Drifting (96)

WATSON, KEN - United States
Guitarist, who is joined by other musicians on keyboards, bass and drums creating a style that is progressive rock with a fusion edge. Instrumental music that is a mixture of HAPPY THE MAN and BRUFORD. His later material became somewhat darker with elements of UNIVERS ZERO.

Assembly (85), The Twinkle Factor (99)

WAY, DARRYL [WOLF] - Great Britain
Darryl Way who used to be in CURVED AIR, packed up his violin and created a

number of rather adventurous albums on his own. Lots of sonic dynamics with some solid playing. A number of efforts include full orchestra.

Canis Lupis [Wolf] (73), Saturation Point (73), Night Music (74), Concerto For Electric Violin (78),

WAYBRIGHT, LEAH - United States
Keyboardist and orchestrator Waybright enlists the help of three members of HAPPY THE MAN to create a lush and panoramic concept revolving around flowers. The music is generally pastoral in nature with plenty of melodic symphonics. When the music opens up a bit you'll hear hints of HTM.

Beauty Gone Wild (99)

WAYNE, JEFF - Great Britain
One-off concept album based on the H.G. Wells classic. Stellar cast, including JUSTIN HAYWARD of the MOODY BLUES and narrated by Richard Burton.

War of the Worlds (78)

WEB - Great Britain
Heavy progressive sound.

Fully Interlocking (68), Theraphosa Blondi (70), I Spider (70)

WEBBER, ANDREW LLOYD - Great Britain
Before he got too busy and famous, Webber recorded an album based on a theme from Paganini with his brother Julian on Cello. The supporting band is basically Colosseum II including Don Airey, Gary Moore, Jon Hiseman with the additional talents of Rod Argent, Herbie Flowers and Phil Collins.

Variations (78)

WELCOME - Switzerland
Like many other bands who've been influenced by YES, it's not surprising to hear those influences. Captured here are some great musical moments inspired by early YES circa Fragile. Brilliant three-part harmony, delicate guitar work and multiple keyboards all very well done. If you liked DRUID this will appeal to you.

Welcome (76)

WEED - Germany
Early, heavy underground progressive sound with classical influences.

Weed (71)

WEJAH - Brazil
Instrumental prog-rock on their concept CD Senda. They've been described as sounding like PALLAS.

Senda ( )

WERWOLF - Germany
Symphonic material, they created a serene soundscape that echoes the golden years of progressive rock. Like a cross between GENESIS and EPIDAURUS.

Creation (84)

WEST, MICHAEL - United States
High intensity symphonic keyboard work in the WAKEMAN school. Produced by Mastermind's Bill Berends, this keyboard workout is dramatic, bombastic and richly dynamic.

God, Sex, Money (92)

WHERE ECHOS END - Australia
This trio of Australians create a symphonic progressive rock with a touch of techno-ish dance elements. Their lone CD is essentially one fifty-seven minute track divided into three parts with a number of subsections.

By the Pricking of My Thumb (98)

WHITE WILLOW - Norway

Symphonic prog sound with folk influences. The band's sound focuses on Mellotron-led keyboards with violin, flute, guitar, bass and drums weaving in and out of the sound tapestry. According to Expose' ANGLAGARD has met it's match. Their material is not overly complex, instead relying on recurring themes to build a compositions dynamics. The combination of male and female vocals adds to the appeal. As with many scandanavian bands there is an underlying melancholy tone.

Ignis Fatuus (95), Ex Tenebris (98), Sacrament (00)

WIGWAM - Finland

According I.T.C. they bridge the gap between YES and 10cc via HATFIELD AND THE NORTH.

Hard & Horney (69),Tombstone Valentine (70),Fairyport (71),Wigwam (72),Wicked Ivory (72),Being (74),Pigworm (74),Live From Twilight Zone (75),Dead at the Nuclear Nightclub (75),Lucky Golden Stripes (76),Dark Album (78)

WIND - Germany

They started out sounding like many early German underground bands with gritty vocals and fuzzy post psychedelic guitars but then incorporated elements of KING CRIMSON with hints of GENESIS. Lots of great Mellotron on their second release Morning.

Seasons (71),Morning (72)

WINDCHASE - Australia

Symphonic rock, ex - SEBASTIAN HARDIE people. Featured rolling organ and Mellotron.

Symphinity (77)

WINGS OF STEEL - Holland

Like RUSH or SAGA with a certain harder edge than most Dutch progressive bands, almost a straight ahead stadium styled rock.

Homesick (9?),Face of Truth (95)

WINTER - Ireland

Like SHADOWLAND, JADIS, IQ.

Across the Circles Edge (92)

WITHOUT WARNING - United States

Their style is aggressive symphonic progressive rock. The guitars are right up front and the crunchy organ isn't too far behind. It's in the intricate arrangements and compositional skills where the prog sensibilities shine. There's some great musicianship and even some well placed Mellotron.

Step Beyond (98)

WITSEND - United States

Mostly instrumental symphonic progressive rock, with great guitar and keyboard interplay. Adventurous arrangements with many shifts in tempo.

Cosmos and Chaos (93)

WITT, P. - France

Great vocals, guitar and keyboard parts from this mid-eighties artist. A very melodious form of progressive rock due to the involvement of ex - VENT D'EST keyboardist. Also sounds like CAMEL, BJH and TREPONEM PAL.

WLUD - France

A quartet with a classic instrument line-up which plays a purely instrumental progressive rock. Wlud presents a polished musical style, full of nuances. At times ethereal, soft, majestic and at other times violent. Sound like - CAMEL or SFF.

Carrycroach (78), Second (79)

WOLSTENHOLME, WOOLY - Great Britain
Keyboard player from BARCLAY JAMES HARVEST goes it alone. Not progressive, but still good.

Maestoso (80), Songs from the Black Box (81/93)

WOODENHEAD - United States
Fusion-prog, similar to the best of Dixie Dregs.

The Big Picture (92), Live (8?)

WORLD TRADE - Great Britain
This band is the on-going solo project of Billy Sherwood who has worked with CHRIS SQUIRE and YES since their 90125 days and the music here is pretty much in the same style. Mostly song oriented material with enough room for some strong keyboard and guitar interplay.

Euphoria (95)

WORLD OF SILENCE - Sweden
A unique mixture of hard edged rock, pop and symphonic prog all brought out on display at different times through complex compositions. Their material is rich with melody and strong with musicianship.

Mindscapes (98)

WOLVERINE - Holland
Another of the growing number of what's called epic/melodic/progressive metal. If you enjoy the work of DREAM THEATRE and Fates Warning this will be your cup-of-tea.

Fervent Dream [Mini CD] (00)

WURTEMBERG - France
Symphonic progressive rock that has a strong folk foundation and makes use of many unusual instruments. Lots of softer moments punctuated with flute in compositions that are briming with melody.

Rock Fantasia Opus 9 (80)

WUTHERING - Japan
Harder edged progressive rock similar to NOVELLA.

The Gate of Fate ( )

WYZARDS - United States
This offshoot of GLASS HAMMER is a mixture of prog rock and prog metal, but a good blending of the two. As Progression magazine said, Imagine Ted Nugent fronting YES. There's lots to appreciate here from the fantasy lyrics to the longer symphonic 19 minute compositions.

The Final Catastrophe (97)

XAAL - France
KING CRIMSON inspired trio with lots of MAGMA flavour thrown in. A progressive fusion band.

Xaal (90), On the Way/En Chemin (92), Seconde Ere (95)

XANG - France
Instrumental symphonic neo-progressive rock with a highly developed sense of musicianship. This five piece from France compose generally longish material which features any number of opportunities for each instrument to shine. They list their influences as YES, GENESIS, SPOCK'S BEARD, ANGE and many others so you get the idea. Great stuff with lots of drama and musical dynamics.

Destiny of a Dream (99)

XEN - United States
Keyboardists David Bagsby and Kurt Rongey create the music of Xen, a challenging progressive music coming from the RIO and 20th Century composition schools of dissonance and angular music.

Esotericity (95)

YAMASHTA, STOMU - Great Britain

Essentially a percussionist with loads of classical training. Stylistically his work is a melting pot of Western pop and jazz, classical timpani and Oriental forms. A mixture of progressive rock and fusion. His band Go has some of his best and most progressive rock music.

Contemporary (72), Red Budah (72), Come to the Edge (73), The Man From the East (73), Freedom is Frightening (73), One by One (74), Raindog (75), Go (76), Go Live From Paris (76), Go Too (77)

YATHA SIDRA - Germany

Classic electronic progressive unit. The music is FLOYD-ian space vein.

Meditation Mass (74)

YES - Great Britain

The band that helped start this whole thing. A mixture of musical styles, superb musicianship, adventurous song writing, the desire to stretch musically, everything a symphonic progressive rock band should be. Soaring keyboards, punctuated by intricate guitar, and a solid bottom end bass. The majesty of pomp and circumstance next to the delicacies of acoustic piano and classical guitar. A must!

Yes (69), Time and a Word (70), The Yes Album (71), Fragile (72), Close to the Edge (72), Yessongs (73), Tales from Topographic Oceans (74), Relayer (74), Yesterdays (75), Going For the One (77), Tormato (78), Yesshows (80), Drama (80), Classic Yes (82), 90125 (83), 90125 Live the Solos (85), Big Generator (87), Union (91), Yesyears (91), Yesstory (91), Highlights: The Very Best Of Yes (93), Talk (94), Keys To Ascension (96), Something's Coming (97), Keys To Ascension 2 (97), Open Your Eyes (97), Somethings Coming/Beyond and Before - The BBC Recordings 1969-1970 (98), The Ladder (99)

YEZDA URFA - United States

One of the more highly acclaimed American prog bands. Brilliant GENTLE GIANT style.

Sacred Baboon (76)

YOKE SHIRE - United States

This is an interesting mix of styles and instruments. The compositions mix parts of rock with prog embellishments set in some interesting arrangements. The use of Mellotron, flute, dulcimer and marimba keep the material just a little out of the normal rock category. Some solid playing, making some interesting atmospheres.

Masque of Shadows (99)

YOU AND I - Hungary

Symphonic prog-rock featuring female vocals in both English and Hungarian. Overall sound is a mix of RENAISSANCE, VERMILLION SANDS and MINIMUM VITAL. Listen for the STEVE HOWE influenced guitar work.

You and I (95), Go (98)

YPSILON - France

Loose concept album with wall of sound keyboards.

Metro Music Man (77)

YUN, JO - Korea

Multi-instrumentalist Jo Yun creates a cross between PINK FLOYD and Tangerine Dream. He draws on Western folk, Eastern traditional and progressive rock structures to create long and involved multi-movement suites.

Mobius Strip (96)

YWIS - Switzerland

Eurock says they take their inspiration from the first three YES LPs featuring dynamic interplay between the elaborate keyboard melodies and flashy guitar solos.

Polyrhythms abound and the instrumental work has notes bouncing in, out and around each other. Their later work has hints of SAGA and KANSAS.

Ywis (88), Leonardo's Dream (95)

ZAO - France

Jazz - fusion band from the seventies featuring members of MAGMA, who reformed to release an album in 1994. They've achieved legendary status and as you might expect show a strong Zeuhl influence.

Z=7L (73), Osiris (74), Shekina (75), Kawana (76), Typareth (77), Akhenaton (94)

ZAPPA, RICCARDO - Italy

Composer guitarist who produced about nine LPs, all with a strong classical leaning. Fans of ANTHONY PHILLIPS or PAUL BRETT should enjoy.

Celestion (77), Chatka (78)

ZARAGON - Denmark

Fans of IQ and GENESIS will enjoy their material. Zaragon's sound does hearken back to an even earlier sound dominated by the ever-present organ and some guitar solos reminiscent of DAVE GILMORE. KANSAS style vocalist with songs in the 5-12 minute range. Sounds similar to UTOPIAN FIELD.

No Return (84)

ZARATHUSTRA - Germany

Early seventies heavy prog style.

Zarathustra (71)

ZAUBER - Italy

Originally formed in the seventies and they've managed to stay together till the nineties. Classically inspired material worth investigating. A full sound that hearkens back to the Italian days of old. Tons of keyboards and guitar solos. Material in the GENESIS/CAMEL vein.

Phoenix (77), Il Sogno (78), Est (91), Aliens (9?)

ZAUNER, STEPHEN - Germany

Latter day keyboardist with AMON DUUL II on his own. Nothing spectacular but good solid material.

Prisms and Views (78)

ZAZEN - United States

Similar to SKY, Zazen's members come from a very musical background including classical orchestras, Jean-Luc Ponty and Dixie Dregs. As you might expect their music is a combination of classical-jazz-rock with a strong prog leaning.

Mystery School (91)

ZAZU - United States

One-shot band who released this heavy prog-rock gem on the Wooden Nickel label to general indifference. Their singer sounds like STYX's Dennis DeYoung. Their music however is nothing like STYX. Heavy prog guitar riffs, wild keyboard antics and complex arrangements abound. The standout track is the 10 minute-plus Ittsanottasonata, But it's close. If you like your prog with a heavy edge this is a must.

Zazu (75)

ZELLO - Sweden

A symphonic prog band, heavily influenced by bands such as KANSAS.

Zello (96), Quodlibet (99)

ZEN CARNIVAL - United States

Symphonic neo-progressive band with a lot to offer. Their sound is vaguely in line with more recent MARILLION but with more keyboard orchestrations. Their material is very melodic providing plenty of dynamic punctuation's.

Inheritance (99)

ZIFF - Germany

Neo-progressive sound similar to MARILLION, SAGA or ARENA. Catchy melodies, symphonic arrangements, changing rhythms and lots of keyboards.

Stories (95), Sanctuary (97)

ZINGALE - Israel

Obscure band with elements of a Canterbury sound. A cross between YES and GENTLE GIANT.

Peace (77)

ZNR - France

Avant-garde chamber rock of the Rock In Opposition variety. One of the better ones in that genre.

Barricades 3 (77), Traite de Mecanique Populaire (79)

ZON - Canada

Short lived band created a very pop oriented progressive rock. In interviews they paid homage to early prog bands, even to the point of using Gabriel-esqe masks on stage, but were attempting to create their music in a more mainstream manner. They come from the later STYX or SAGA sound department. Shorter songs with some interesting twists.

Astral Projector (78), Back Down to Earth (79), I'm Worried About the Boys (80)

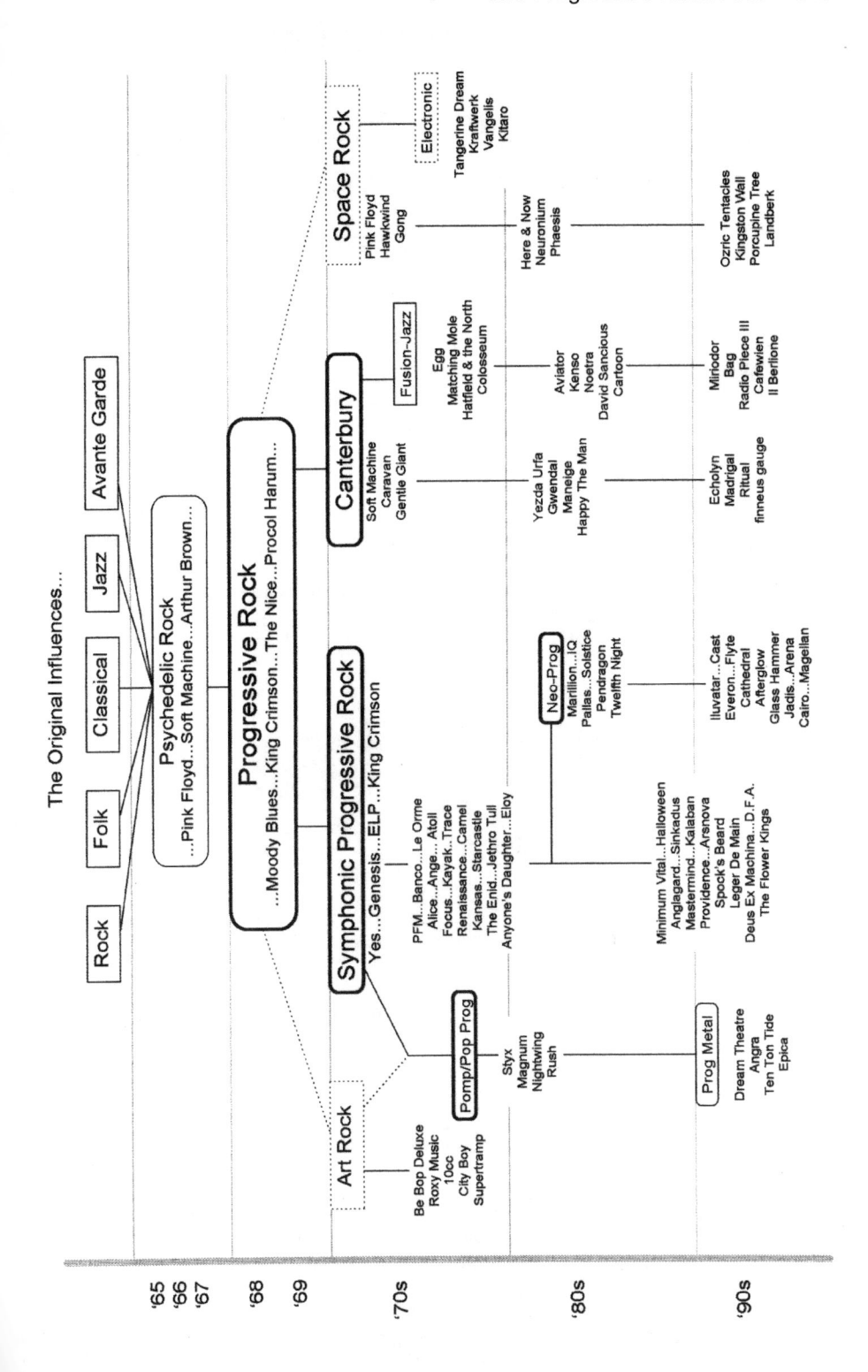

The Progressive Rock Files

The Original Influences...

Rock | Folk | Classical | Jazz | Avante Garde

Psychedelic Rock
...Pink Floyd...Soft Machine...Arthur Brown...

Progressive Rock
...Moody Blues...King Crimson...The Nice...Procol Harum...

Space Rock
Pink Floyd
Hawkwind
Gong

- Here & Now
- Neuronium
- Phaesis

- Ozric Tentacles
- Kingston Wall
- Porcupine Tree
- Landberk

Electronic
- Tangerine Dream
- Kraftwerk
- Vangelis
- Kitaro

Canterbury
Soft Machine
Caravan
Gentle Giant

- Yezda Urfa
- Gwendal
- Maneige
- Happy The Man

- Echolyn
- Madrigal
- Ritual
- finneus gauge

Fusion-Jazz
Egg
Matching Mole
Hatfield & the North
Colosseum

- Aviator
- Kenso
- Noetra
- David Sancious
- Cartoon

- Miriodor
- Bag
- Radio Piece III
- Cafewien
- Il Berlione

Symphonic Progressive Rock
Yes...Genesis...ELP...King Crimson

- PFM...Banco...Le Orme
- Alice...Ange...Atoll
- Focus...Kayak...Trace
- Renaissance...Camel
- Kansas...Starcastle
- The Enid...Jethro Tull
- Anyone's Daughter...Eloy

- Minimum Vital...Halloween
- Anglagard...Sinkadus
- Mastermind...Kalaban
- Providence...Arsnova
- Spock's Beard
- Leger De Main
- Deus Ex Machina...D.F.A.
- The Flower Kings

Neo-Prog
Marillion...IQ
Pallas...Solstice
Pendragon
Twelfth Night

- Iluvatar...Cast
- Everon...Flyte
- Cathedral
- Afterglow
- Glass Hammer
- Jadis...Arena
- Cairo...Magellan

Art Rock
- Be Bop Deluxe
- Roxy Music
- 10cc
- City Boy
- Supertramp

Pomp/Pop Prog
Styx
Magnum
Nightwing
Rush

Prog Metal
Dream Theatre
Angra
Ten Ton Tide
Epica

'65
'66
'67
'68
'69
'70s
'80s
'90s

Books to look for:

The Pink Floyd Reference Encyclopedia

by Vernon Fitch

The Pink Floyd Reference Encyclopedia is an in-depth reference work covering all the people, places, and history of the musical group Pink Floyd. From the earliest days of the band to the present, this book explains the band from The Abdabs to Zee. Written by **Vernon Fitch** author of the web's leading Floyd site "The Pink Floyd Archives", The book also features an appendix of unique reference works including Books, Concert Dates, Discographies, Session Work, and more. *The Pink Floyd Reference Encyclopedia* is a must for every Pink Floyd enthusiast, from the casual fan to the obsessive collector.

The Pink Floyd Archives
E-Mail: PFArchives@CompuServe.com
WWW: http://ourworld.compuserve.com/homepages/PFArchives

ISBN- 1896522-44-0
$24.95 US, $29.95 Can, £16.95 UK

Books to look for:

Which One's Pink?

by Phil Rose

An Analysis of the concept albums of Roger Waters and Pink Floyd

Anyone familiar with *The Wall* realises that the work of Roger Waters and Pink Floyd is characterised by an enigmatic quality that has lured fans for thirty years. For the first time a systematic and detailed discussion of these works is now available in Phil Rose's Which One's Pink?

Drawing on his extensive discussions with Roger Waters, Rose gives attention to lyrics, album covers, and the musical details of each album's conceptual translation. Among the recordings discussed are *The Dark Side Of The Moon, Wish You Were Here, Animals, The Wall and The Final Cut*.

This first time author's royalties will be donated to "The World memorial Fund For Disaster Releif". This charity's mandate is to provide medical care worldwide for those suffering as a result of war having devastated their area.

ISBN- 1896522-17-3
$9.95 US, $14.95 Can, £6.95 UK

Books to look for:

Progressive Rock

by Jerry Lucky

For Progressive Rock aficionados and all lovers of classical rock music, this book highlights the 50 most important progressive rock bands, past and present, from around the world. Exploring the artists and their music, from its origins to current prog music, the history and discography are presented in knowledgable detail.

Veteran author Jerry Lucky shares with us his vast experience in the Progressive Rock world detailing the development of Prog by looking closely at the players as well as their music.

Progressive rock music combines and transcends the various music genres to a greater extent than possibly any other type of music. This book will take you straight to the very best that Prog has to offer and make you comfortable with its roots and where it's going next.

This book is a must-have for lovers of Progressive Rock music everywhere.

ISBN- 1896522-20-3
$13.95 US, $17.95 Can, £9.95 UK